THE COMPLETE WHO'S WHO OF
ENGLAND
RUGBY UNION INTERNATIONALS

THE COMPLETE WHO'S WHO OF
ENGLAND
RUGBY UNION INTERNATIONALS

RAYMOND MAULE

BREEDON
BOOKS
SPORT

First published in Great Britain by
The Breedon Books Publishing Company Limited
44 Friar Gate, Derby DE1 1DA
1992

ISBN 1 873626 10 X

Printed and bound in Great Britain by The Bath Press Limited, Bath.
Jacket printed by BDC Printing Services Ltd of Derby.

Contents

Dedication

To my parents, Sheila and Raymond, for their love and encouragement over the years. Also to Dr J.Gore and Dr G.Overend, Bradford, whose interest, work and devotion helped provide a way of life which was not possible in the past.

Acknowledgements

This particular volume is the product of a hobby developed from an interest in Rugby Union first stimulated about four years ago through watching regular matches involving the University of Bradford and, more recently, my local club Phoenix Park RFC, and from spending many happy hours reading through books on the sport which my parents introduced into a curious man's attempts to digest ever more information about the game and the people involved in it. From that time, I have slowly built up a fine library which has been used as the basic means of research for this volume.

My special interest on individual players stems from an ever-increasing fascination for the game. Over those years since my taste buds were first given a taste of Rugby Union, I have painstakingly researched and indexed literally thousands of players' details from the Home Countries. I must, above all, state my thanks to such authors of Rugby Union literature as John Griffiths (whose books I not only enjoy, but who also provides a wealth of material for an inquisitive mind); J.B.G.Thomas, whose writings give accounts of the history of the game and in particular that of his beloved Wales; a list of titles I have consulted throughout is given in the bibliography section but I would like to say that Barry Bowker's *England Rugby* and *The Book of English International Rugby* by John Griffiths first gave me the idea of a more detailed Who's Who of England players and so I owe much to these two authors in particular.

I have corresponded with many people — families of former players, players themselves, universities, regimental historians — alas, far too many to list here. But I would like to express my thanks to all those who have freely given assistance and shown such an interest in this project. If I have missed anyone, then please forgive me. It is not intentional and your help is just as appreciated as those who have been acknowledged here.

Thanks, then, to the following: Mr D.T.Kemp (Hampshire RFU), Fred Ellison (Somerset RFU), Dr C.V.Phillips (Cornwall RFU), the Middlesex Regiment Association, Peter G.Yarranton (president, RFU), Ron Syrett, Michael Latham (Leigh), Malcolm and Ann Lorimer (Lancashire CCC), the University of Liverpool (A.R.Allan), Mrs M.Swayne, Dennis Shuttleworth OBE, *The Bulletin* (Australia), Mrs Peggy Radmore (daughter of F.W.Sanders), R.Cooke (Civil Service Sports Association, Plymouth), Mrs E.Kingdon (Plymouth Rowing Club), Devon Rugby Referees' Society, *The Financial Times*, the Devon and Dorset Regiment, Royal St George's Golf Club, Cambridge University and Oxford University (to their various sports clubs such as rugby, cricket, rowing, etc), the London Society of Referees, Angela Jelfs and Mrs B.C.Weeden (University of London Union), Albert Agar, S.J.Adkins, Warwickshire Bowls Association, the British Medical Association, Yorkshire, Lancashire and Northamptonshire CCCs, South African Defence Department, Indian High Commission, New Zealand High Commission, John Cranwell, T.G.Cooper (*Chronicle & Echo*, Northampton), Duke of Edinburgh's Regiment, various officers at Buckingham Palace, Major D.C.Murray (Army RFU), the Cheshire RFU, the Welch Regiment, the Royal Regiment of Wales, J.Firmini (Bromley AFC), J.Bailey (Hampshire Hockey Association), University of Bristol (J.H.M.Parry), Elizabeth Pook (English Golf Union), Middlesex RFU, Mr T.Gibson (Guy's Hospital RFC) and C.M.Barrington (son of T.J.M.Barrington). Garry Froggatt's help and assistance, particularly his knowledge of military matters, was most helpful. Peter Pickup also gave advice and details regarding many aspects of this book.

Regarding the entry 'Clubs' for each player, this is meant to include any appearances for county or divisional teams as well as recognised club sides.

AARVOLD
Sir Carl Douglas, OBE TD JP.

Centre-Wing. 1928-1933 (Blackheath, 15 caps).
Debut v NSW, 7 January 1928.
Born: 7 June 1907; Died: 17 March 1991.
Educated: Durham School, Cambridge University.
Clubs: Cambridge University (Blues 1925-8), Headingley, West Hartlepool, County Durham, Blackheath, Barbarians.

At Cambridge, Aarvold appeared in four successive winning Varsity teams and also won a fives Blue. A British Lion on tour of Argentina in 1927, he also toured New Zealand in 1930, playing in 19 matches. He scored ten tries and captained the Lions in three Tests. Captained England six times, scoring four tries. Played for Durham-Northumberland v South Africa in 1931.

After retiring from the game he became involved in lawn tennis and golf and was president of the Lawn Tennis Association 1963-1981. In 1982, the LTA instituted the Carl Aarvold Award for International Achievement.

Called to Bar 1932 (Inner Temple), he was later Recorder of London and a Circuit Judge, being knighted in 1968. During World War Two he served as a lieutenant-colonel in the Royal Artillery.

He died the day after England's 1991 Grand Slam. A tall, powerful player, he had sound positional abilities and was a much-loved and respected gentleman.

ACKFORD
Paul John

Lock. 1988-1991 (Harlequins, 22 caps).
Debut v Australia, 5 November 1988.
Born: 26 February 1958, Hanover, Germany.
Educated: Plymouth College (Devon), Cambridge University (Blue 1979), Kent University.
Clubs: Plymouth Albion, Rosslyn Park, Metropolitan Police, Harlequins, Barbarians, Devon, Surrey.
Played for British Universities v France (1977-8); English Students v Argentina (1973-4); England tour of Fiji and Australia (1991); British Lions tour of Australia (1989) when he was one of three policemen in the squad and played in three Tests; England 'B' v France (1979-80), whilst a post-graduate at Cambridge); represented South-West Division and, since 1981, London Division, for whom he had an outstanding game against the Australians on 7 November 1981.
Ackford, whose father played rugby for the Army, taught English Literature at Dulwich College before joining the police force. He studied at Bramshill Police College and is currently a

Paul Ackford

uniformed inspector at Clapham, London.

He was a latecomer to international rugby, his first cap coming at the age of 30. He played for the Barbarians v New Zealand in 1989 and was a member of the 1991 World Cup runners-up team. In November 1991 he announced that he was retiring from competitive rugby, the first England World Cup star to do so. In March 1992, Ackford became the Surrey representative on the RFU.

ADAMS
Alan Augustus

Centre. 1910 (London Hospital, 1 cap).
Debut v France, 3 March 1910.
Born: 8 May 1883, Greymouth, New Zealand; Died: 28 July 1963, Greymouth, New Zealand.
Educated: Auckland Grammar School (New Zealand), Otago University.
Clubs: Otago, South Island, London Hospital, London University, Barbarians.
Adams, who had a career in medicine,

was a New Zealand selector 1927-8 and 1934-7. He was also president of the New Zealand RFU in 1929.

ADAMS
Frank Reginald

Forward. 1875-1879 (Richmond, 7 caps).
Debut v Ireland, 15 February 1875.
Born: 1853; Died: 1932.
Educated: Wellington College.
Clubs: Richmond, Middlesex.
Adams worked in shipping as an insurer and also employed in the USA and in Australia. The son of Major-General F.Adams CB, Frank Adams was England's first captain in the Calcutta Cup, in 1879.

ADEY
Garry John

Forward 1976 (Leicester, 2 caps).
Debut v Ireland, 6 March 1976.
Born: 13 June 1947, Loughborough.
Club: Leicester.
Garry Adey worked as an engineer.

ADKINS
Stanley John ('Akker')

No 8/Lock. 1950-1953 (Coventry, 7 caps).
Debut v Ireland, 11 February 1950.
Born: 2 June 1922, Coventry.
Died: 2 January 1992, Coventry.
Educated: Stoke Council School and played rugby for Stoke Schoolboys.
Clubs: Stoke Old Boys, Army, Combined Services, Coventry 1946-1955 (later vice-president), Warwickshire (45 appearances), Barbarians.

Adkins worked as an aircraft factory machinist and was then a licensee for 27 years, serving as chairman of Coventry branch of the Licensed House Managers' Association. He was also president of Coventry LVA.

During World War Two he served as a lance-corporal in the Coldstream Guards and landed at Salerno before being injured and medically downgraded. He subsequently served in North Africa as an RASC staff-sergeant. Adkins played bowls for Warwickshire and for the Avenue BC, Coventry, the club of which he was vice-chairman until his death.

AGAR
Albert Eustace

Centre. 1952-1953 (Harlequins, 7 caps).
Debut v South Africa, 5 January 1952.
Born: 12 November 1923, Hartlepool.

Albert Ager

Educated: West Hartlepool Grammar School.
Clubs: Hartlepool Rovers, Lloyds Bank (two spells), Harlequins, Durham, Middlesex.

Agar played for Northumberland & Durham v Australia in 1948 and for London Counties v South Africa in 1951. In 1952 he had England trials. He retired to become an England selector from 1962 to 1971, although he still played occasionally for the Harlequins.

He was the Quins' chairman from 1969 to 1971; CB representative 1970-1984 and president 1979-1982; British Lions selector 1971; RFU representative; RFU president 1984-1985; RFU assistant treasurer 1975-1979; Home Unions tour committee secretary 1971-1978; International Board member; committee member of Home Unions; Five Nations committee member 1978-1985 and 1989 to date; International Board treasurer 1991 to date; RFU trustee 1986 to date; Middlesex RFU Memorial Fund trustee 1955 to date; RFU Charitable Trust trustee 1971 to date; Wavell Wakefield RU Youth Trust trustee 1984 to date.

ALCOCK
Arnold

Hooker. 1906 (Guy's Hospital, 1 cap).
Debut v South Africa, 8 December 1906.
Born: 18 August 1882; Died: 7 November 1973.
Educated: Newcastle under Lyme High School, Manchester University, Guy's Hospital (1905-06), University of London as an external student, graduated in 1906, awarded MBBS same year.
Clubs: Richmond, Blackheath, Surrey, Gloucester (president 1924).

Alcock, who worked as a GP in Gloucester, was a good, sound hospital player but almost everyone, including himself, was surprised when he received notice of his selection to play for England. Yet his only cap was awarded when a clerical error was made. The selectors had originally pencilled in 'Slocock' of Liverpool but notice of selection was misdirected to 'Alcock', and this resulted in him playing for England at Crystal Palace against the Springboks, while Slocock later went on to win eight caps.

ALDERSON
Frederick Hodgson Rudd, JP

Centre. 1891-1893 (Hartlepool Rovers, 6 caps).
Debut v Wales, 3 January 1891.
Born: 27 June 1867, Hartford, Northumberland; Died: 18 February 1925, Hartlepool.
Educated: Durham School,
Clubs: Cambridge University (Blues 1887-1888), Tyndale, Hartlepool Rovers, Blackheath (touring Germany with the club in 1895), Northumberland, Durham County, Barbarians.

Alderson was one of the original members of the Barbarians and played for Hartlepool Rovers against the Ba Ba's in the very first match played by the club on 27 December 1890.

Frederick Alderson

He captained England on his debut, scoring two conversions in a 7-3 win over the Welsh, and refereed the Scotland-Ireland match in 1903. He played lawn tennis for Durham County and was employed as an assistant master, then headmaster at Henry Smith School, Hartlepool in 1892.

ALEXANDER
Harry

Forward. 1900-1902 (Richmond, 7 caps).
Debut v Ireland, 3 February 1900.
Born: 6 January 1879, Oxton, Cheshire; Died: Hulluch, 17 October 1915 (killed in action).
Educated: Bromborough School, Uppingham School, Oxford University.
Clubs: Oxford University (Blues 1897, 1898), Birkenhead Park, Cheshire, Richmond, Middlesex, Barbarians.

Alexander also played county hockey, golf and was a keen ice-skater. He was known to have a good singing voice. Employed as a schoolmaster at Stanmore Park Preparatory School, during World War One he served as a second-lieutentant in the Grenadier Guards and was killed on his 13th day of active service.

ALEXANDER
William

Wing. 1927 (Northern, 1 cap).
Debut v France, 2 April 1927.
Born: 6 October 1905.

Clubs: Northern, Northumberland, Barbarians.

Alexander was employed as a chartered accountant and also worked in Canada for a short time. However, he lived mainly in France.

ALLISON
Dennis Fenwick

Full-back. 1956-1958 (Coventry, 7 caps).
Debut v Wales, 21 January 1956.
Born: 20 April 1931.

Educated: Dame Allan's School (Newcastle), Durham University.

Clubs: Northern, Coventry, Northumberland, Warwickshire, Barbarians.

Allison worked in the research department of chemical giants ICI, later becoming a director of the company. He scored a penalty-goal on his international debut.

ALLPORT
Alfred

Forward. 1892-1894 (Blackheath, 5 caps).
Debut v Wales, 2 January 1892.
Born: 12 September 1867, Brixton; Died: 2 May 1949, London.

Educated: London International College, Isleworth.

Clubs: Guy's Hospital, Blackheath, Surrey, Barbarians.

Allport was employed as a consultant surgeon at St Paul's Hospital and also served with the Royal Army Medical Corps. A remarkable athlete and great personality, he was renowned for his comic songs. He rowed for Thames in the Grand Challenge Cup at Henley.

ANDERSON
Stanley

Centre. 1899 (Rockcliff, 1 cap).
Debut v Ireland , 4 February 1899.
Clubs: Rockcliff, Northumberland.

Anderson, who was employed as a licensee, also played cricket for Northumberland.

ANDERSON
William Francis

Prop. 1972 (Orrell, 1 cap).
Debut v New Zealand, 6 January 1973.
Born: 1945, Ormskirk.

Clubs: Orrell, Barbarians, Lancashire (32 appearances).

Anderson was the first player to be capped from the Orrell club. He helped Lancashire win the 1972-3 County Championship, the same season he made his debut for the Barbarians, against Penarth. He also played for the Ba'Ba's against Newport that season.

ANDERTON
Charles

Forward, 1889 (Manchester FW, 1 caps).
Debut v Maoris, 16 February 1889.
Born: 1868; Died: 1959.

Clubs: Manchester Free Wanderers, Lancashire (34 appearances).

Anderton's only cap is currently displayed in the Manchester club house. He was also selected for the 1888 England XV that did not play.

ANDREW
Christopher Robert ('Rob')

Outside-half. 1985-1992 (Cambridge University, Nottingham, Wasps, 48 caps).
Debut v Romania, 5 January 1985.
Born: 18 January 1963, Richmond.

Educated: Barnard Castle School (Durham), Cambridge University.

Clubs: Middlesbrough, Cambridge University (Blues 1982-1984, captain each year), Nottingham, Gordon (Australia) summer 1986, Yorkshire (9 appearances, captain v Ulster in 1987 Ulster Centenary match), Wasps, Toulouse.

In 1989, Andrew became England's most capped outside-half, a record previously held by the late W.J.A.Davies. Against Wales in 1986 he equalled the world record of six penalty goals for an international match, until beaten recently by Mark Wyatt of Canada, and went on to score 21 points that day. Indeed, in his first six internationals he scored 71 points. After he

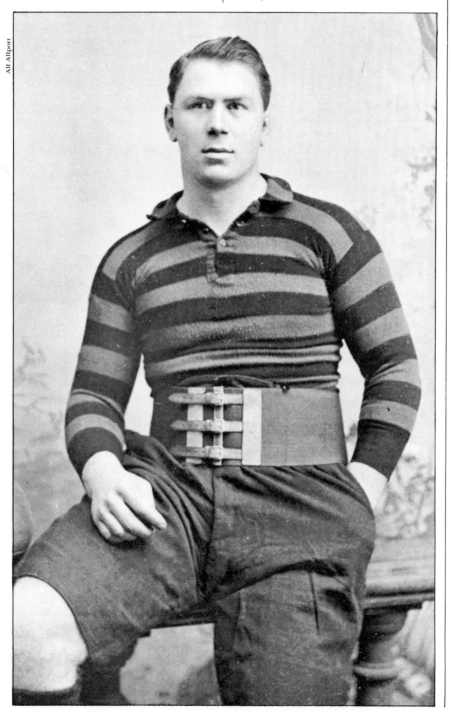

Alf Allport

Rob Andrew

arrived as replacement for the injured Paul Dean on the British Lions tour of Australia in 1989, he became the first English fly-half to play for the Lions in a Test for 27 years, when he appeared in the last two matches. He captained England in their 58-3 win over Romania in May 1989 and toured Australia and Fiji in 1991.

He first played divisional rugby for Northern Division and was in the London side which won the 1990 Toshiba Divisional Championship. His brother played for Yorkshire in 1990 Colts County Championship Final against Lancashire.

A chartered surveyor by profession, Rob Andrew also played cricket for Yorkshire 2nd XI and won a cricket Blue in his final summer at Cambridge. He scored 101 at Trent Bridge against Nottinghamshire in 1984.

He resigned as the Wasps' captain in 1991, due to international commitments, and after appearing in that year's World Cup Final he joined the Toulouse club in November. His face was still a familiar one to English rugby fans, however, as he helped his country to a second successive Grand Slam in 1992.

ARCHER
Herbert

Number 8. 1909 (Bridgwater Albion, 3 caps).
Debut v Wales, 16 January 1909.
Born: August 1884; Died: 26 December 1946, Nether Stowey, Bridgwater.

Educated: Blundell's School, Guy's Hospital.

Clubs: Bridgwater Albion, Somerset.

Archer, who was employed as a GP at Nether Stowey, served with the Royal Army Medical Corps. He went on the British Lions tour of Australia and New Zealand in 1908 and on the Anglo-Welsh tour to Australia in 1908.

ARMSTRONG
Reginald, ('Rex') OBE MB BS

Prop. 1925 (Northern, 1 cap).
Debut v Wales, 17 January 1925.
Born: 6 December 1897, Newcastle upon Tyne; Died: 17 February 1968, Morpeth.

Educated: Bootham (Yorkshire), Newcastle College of Medicine, Durham University.

Clubs: Northern, Barbarians, Northumberland.

Armstrong's education was interrupted by the outbreak of World War One and he joined the 18th Battalion of the Durham Light Infantry upon leaving school in 1916, fighting in France and Belgium. After demobilization he went up to Durham University on an entrance scholarship and captained the Durham Medicals and Durham University rugby teams, leading the Medicals to their first Northumberland Cup win.

Two years later he won his only England cap, against Wales at Twickenham in 1925, whilst with Northern RFC.

He graduated MB, BS in 1923 and entered a general practice partnership at Rothbury, Northumberland, where he remained until the end of 1967. During that time he became chairman of the Alnwick & Rothbury Hospital Management Committee and also a member of the local medical committee.

During World War Two he had a distinguished career with the RAMC when, as a lieutenant-colonel, he commanded a casualty clearing station; and he also served with the 8th Army at El Alamein, Salerno and Anzio. He was awarded the OBE in 1944 and upon demobilization returned to general practice.

In 1947-8 he was chairman of the North Northumberland division of the British Medical Association. A lifelong member of the BMA, with strong views on strike action by doctors to obtain satisfactory conditions, he was one of those who initiated an appointments system; and he reconstructed the practice premises in his village to be pleasing and friendly in a modern, efficient way. He remained in practice up to a few weeks before his death.

A noted actor and producer, in 1927 he gained the village of Coquetdale its first ambulance from proceeds of those entertainments. He had 44 years' continuous practice in the Rothbury Valley and in 1967 was the first doctor in the UK to identify foot and mouth disease in humans.

ARTHUR
Terence Gordon

Centre. 1966 (Wasps, 2 caps).
Debut v Wales, 15 January 1966.
Born: 5 September 1940, Hartlepool.
Educated: West Hartlepool Grammar School, Cambridge University.
Clubs: West Hartlepool, Manchester University, Cambridge University (Blue 1962), Wasps, Moseley, Waterloo, Barbarians, Durham County, Buckinghamshire, North Midlands.

Arthur was a partner in a company of actuarial consultants and author of *95 Per Cent Crap* (Libertarian Books, 1975), a book relating to the comical elements in politics.

ASHBY
Roland Clive

Scrum-half. 1966-1967 (Wasps, 3 caps).
Debut v Ireland, 12 February 1966.
Born: 24 January 1937, Mozambique.
Educated: Royal Grammar School (High Wycombe), Harper Adams Agricultural College.
Clubs: Wasps, High Wycombe (vice-president), Barbarians, Shropshire, Buckinghamshire, East Midlands.

Ashby was of South African parentage and he worked in the family business. Before RGS his early education came in South Africa. He lived for a short time in East Africa and when he was posted as a deserter by the Portugese, he abandoned his dual nationality and declared that he was a South African, thereby escaping National Service. Upon leaving school he spent some 18 months in Antarctica before returning to England to join Wasps.

ASHCROFT
Alan ('Ned')

Number 8. 1956-1959. (Waterloo, 16 caps).
Debut v Wales, 21 January 1956.
Born: 21 August 1930, St Helens, Lancashire.
Educated: Cowley Grammar School.
Clubs: RAF, St Helens, Waterloo, Barbarians, Lancashire 1953-1963 (52 appearances).

Ned Ashcroft went on the British Lions tour of Australia and New Zealand in 1959, playing in 17 matches but appearing in only two Test Matches.
A schoolmaster, he taught art at Liverpool College, where he also coached the rugby side. He was a popular member of any team at all levels of the game, he had a safe pair of hands — hardly anything was fumbled or dropped — and his tackling was said to be devastating. A skilful player, he learned the game mainly whilst with the St Helens club, itself a famous rugby nursery.

ASHCROFT
Alec Hutchinson, DSO

Fly-half. 1909 (Birkenhead Park, 1 cap).
Debut v Australia, 9 January 1909.
Born: 18 October 1887, Liverpool; Died: 18 April 1963, Bath.
Educated: Birkenhead School, Cambridge University.
Clubs: Cambridge University (Blues 1908-1909), Birkenhead Park, Blackheath, Edinburgh Wanderers, Cheshire.

Alec Ashcroft was one of ten new caps who played against the Australians in 1909, in the last international to be staged at Blackheath. He was employed as an assistant master at Fettes College (1910-1914) and was headmaster there (1919-1945). During World War One he served as a temporary major in the South Staffordshire Regiment and in 1916 was mentioned in despatches. He was awarded the DSO in 1919.

ASHFORD
William, OBE JP

Forward. 1897-1898. (Richmond, 4 caps).
Debut v Wales, 9 January 1897.
Born: 18 December 1871; Died: 1 January 1954, Topsham, Devon.
Clubs: St Thomas' Hospital, Richmond, Exeter, Barbarians, Surrey, Devon.

One of nine new caps awarded in the first match of the 1897-8 season, Ashford served as CO of the Topsham Volunteer Auxiliary Hospital during World War One and was awarded the OBE in 1918. He was a member of Devon County Cricket Club.

ASHWORTH
Abel

Forward. 1892. (Oldham, 1 cap).
Debut v Ireland, 6 February 1892.
Born: 1864, Moseley; Died: 10 January 1938, Oldham.
Clubs: Oldham, Rochdale Hornets.

Ashworth's only international appearance came in England's Triple Crown season of 1891-2, a season in which England did not concede a single point. He was employed as an engineer's labourer and turned to Rugby League when his club, Rochdale Hornets, helped form the Northern Union in 1895.

ASKEW
John Garbutt

Full-back. 1930 (Cambridge University, 3 caps).
Debut v Wales, 18 January 1930.
Born: 2 September 1908; Died: 31 August 1942, Stannington, Morpeth, Northumberland.
Educated: Durham School, Cambridge University.
Clubs: Durham City, Cambridge University (Blues 1929, 1930 and 1931), Durham County (7 appearances), Barbarians.

Askew played in the first three games of the Championship-winning side of 1929-30, when England's win at Cardiff Arms Park was their first since 1913 and only their second victory there since their first success in 1893.

He also played cricket for Cambridge University and Durham CCC 1926-1927. He worked for the Colonial Civil Service in Nyasaland in 1932, and from 1937 was a farmer in South Africa.

ASLETT
Alfred Rimbault, DSO

Centre. 1926-1929 (Richmond, 6 caps).
Debut v Wales (3-3) 16 January 1926.
Born: 14 January 1901; Died: May 1980, Cowfold.
Educated: Clifton College; RMC Sandhurst.

Alfred Aslett

Clubs: Blackheath, Lansdowne, Richmond, Army (20 caps v Royal Navy 1921, 1922, 1924, 1925, 1926, 1928 and 1929), Barbarians, Lancashire, Surrey.

Aslett, who was an England selector (1948-1959) and RFU vice-president (1958-1959), served in World War Two, reaching the rank of brigadier in the King's Own Royal Regiment. Twice mentioned in despatches, he was awarded the DSO in 1945. In 1946 he was appointed director of the Army Sports Control Board.

ASSINDER
Eric Walter

Centre. 1909 (Old Edwardians, 2 caps).
Debut v Australia, 9 January 1909.

Born: 29 August 1888; Died: 11 October 1974.

Educated: King Edward's School, Birmingham.

Club: Old Edwardians.

Assinder, who also represented the Midland Counties, was one of ten new caps in the England team that met Australia at Blackheath, the last international match to be staged at that ground. During World War One he served as a captain in the RAMC.

ASTON
Randolph Littleton

Centre. 1890 (Blackheath, 2 caps).
Debut v Scotland, 1 March 1890.
Born: 6 September 1869, Kensington; Died: 3 November 1930, Salisbury.
Educated: Cheltenham College, Westminster School, Berkhamstead School, Tonbridge School, Cambridge University.
Clubs: Cambridge University (Blues 1889-1890), Blackheath, Barbarians, Kent.

On the British Lions tour of South Africa in 1891, Aston played in all the tour matches, in which he scored 30 tries (tries in those days only counted as a single point). The brother of 'Ferdy', he was employed as a schoolmaster at Blair Lodge and Tonbridge.

AUTY
Joseph Richard

Fly-Half. 1935 (Headingley, 1 cap).
Debut v Scotland, 16 March 1935.

Joseph Auty

Born: 19 August 1910, Batley, Yorkshire.
Educated: Mill High School.
Clubs: Old Millhillians, Headingley, Leicester, Barbarians, Yorkshire (24 appearances).

Auty was employed in the woollen industry. His son, Tim Auty, is a noted rugby historian.

BAILEY
Mark David

Wing. 1984-1990 (Cambridge University, Wasps, 7 caps).
Debut v South Africa, 2 June 1984.
Born: 21 November 1960, Castleford.
Educated at Cambridge University.
Clubs: Cambridge University (Blues 1982-5), Ipswich, Bedford, Wasps, Barbarians.

Mark Bailey

Bailey played for Wasps in the 1986 John Player Cup Final against Bath and was vice-captain of Wasps 1986-7. He toured Italy with England 'B' in 1985-6 and played for London Division from 1981-8 (captain 1987) He works as a college lecturer. His father is a former secretary of Featherstone Rovers RLFC. An all-round sportsman, Mark captained Suffolk in the Minor Counties Cricket Championship 1988-1990. Author of *A Marginal Economy* (published in 1989).

BAINBRIDGE
Stephen

Lock. 1982-1987 (Gosforth, Flyde, 18 caps).
Debut v France, 20 February 1982.
Born: 7 October 1956, Newcastle upon Tyne.
Educated: John Marley School, Alsagar College.
Clubs: Gosforth, Fylde, Morley, Northumberland, Barbarians.

Bainbridge went on England's tour of Argentina in 1981 but although he played in four of the seven matches, he made no Test appearances. On the British Isles tour of New Zealand in 1983, he was the biggest player in the squad after being drafted in at the last minute to replace Donal Lenihan, who was ruled out due to a hernia on the eve of the Lions' departure. On England's trip to North America in 1982, he played in five of the eight games, including the matches against the USA and Canada.

In 1984, Bainbridge was refused

Steve Bainbridge

permission by the local education authority for whom he worked, to tour with England in South Africa in 1984. He was disqualified from international rugby after being sent off in a club match in 1985. In October 1990 his club, Newcastle Gosforth, gave him a life ban after the third sending off in his career. His third dismissal came in a League match against London Scottish, when his head-butting offence was seen on local television. In June 1991 he successfully applied for the ban to be lifted.

Bainbridge also appeared for England Students and England Under-23s and held the British Colleges high jump record as well as being British Students decathlon champion. In September 1990 he played in the Otley v President's XV match which celebrated Otley's 125th anniversary season.

BAKER
Douglas George Santley

Fly-half. 1955 (Old Merchant Taylor's, 4 caps).
Debut v Wales, 22 January 1955.
Born: 29 November 1929, Las Palmas.
Educated: Merchant Taylor's School, Oxford University.
Clubs: Oxford University (Blues 1951-2), Old Merchant Taylor's, Barbarians, Middlesex, London Counties, East Midlands.

Baker was one of six new caps in the side that began the 1954-5 season in Cardiff. He went on the British Lions tour of South Africa in 1955, appearing in both Tests, and made his Barbarians debut in Canada in 1957. He was employed as a master at Oundle School and went on a teaching exchange to Australia in 1962. Baker was a versatile, highly valued player at club and representative level. He played cricket for Oxford University Authentics.

BAKER
Edward Morgan

Centre. 1895-1897 (Moseley, 7 caps).
Debut v Wales, 5 January 1895.
Born: 12 August 1874; Died: 25 November 1940, Winchester.
Educated: Denstone College, Oxford University.
Clubs: Oxford University (Blues 1893-1896), Moseley, Blackheath, Wolverhampton, Burton, Barbarians, Midland Counties.

A clergyman, ordained in 1897, he held various curacies around the country until he became vicar of St Paul's in East Brisbane, Australia. He was headmaster of King's School in Parramatta, Australia, from 1919 until 1932, when he returned to Britain.

BAKER
Hiatt Cowles, JP

Forward. 1887 (Clifton, 1 cap).
Debut v Wales, 8 January 1887.

Born: 30 June 1863; Died: 19 September 1934, Almondsbury, Bristol.
Educated: Rugby School.
Clubs: Clifton, Gloucestershire.

He worked as managing director of his family clothing and drapery business. Pro-chancellor of Bristol University from 1929 to 1934, he was also a founding member of the university council in 1909 and remained a member until 1934. He received an honorary LLD degree from the university in 1931. His former house, The Holmes, has marvellous gardens which he created and now forms part of the university. Hiatt Baker Hall of Residence, opened in 1965, was named after him.

BANCE
John Forsyth

Lock. 1954 (Bedford, 1 cap).
Debut v Scotland, 20 March 1954.
Born: 15 January 1925.
Educated: Radley College, Cambridge University.
Clubs: Cambridge University (Blue 1945), Bedford, Barbarians, East Midlands.

England were Triple Crown winners in 1954 but Bance, a farmer by occupation, was resricted to the Calcutta Cup-winning side of that year. He played in three County Championship Finals for the East Midlands.

BARLEY
Bryan

Centre. 1984-1988 (Wakefield, 7 caps).
Debut v Ireland, 18 February 1984.
Born: 4 January 1960, Wakefield.
Educated: Normanton Grammar School, Leeds University.
Clubs: Wakefield, Yorkshire.

Barley was a member of Wakefield's successful Northern Merit and Yorkshire Challenge Cup sides of the early 1980s. He made his Yorkshire debut in 1979, against Lancashire, and appeared in the 1983 County Championship Final, making 29 appearances overall including a tour of France in 1980.

He represented Yorkshire Schools at 16 and 18 age groups and went on the England Senior Schools' tour of Australia in 1979. He played for England Under-23s in 1980 and 1982, for English Students in 1983, and, whilst at Normanton GS, played for England Under-19s against France at Otley in April 1979.

A management trainee, he broke his jaw in a club match in 1983 and this prevented him from playing against the All Blacks at Gateshead. He played in the Castleford XV v Russell Holmes XV game in 1991. In the final England trial of 1983, he replaced John Palmer in the 60th minute of the game. His hobbies include soccer, cricket and athletics.

BARNES
Stuart

Fly half/full-back. 1984-1988 (Bristol, Bath, 8 caps).
Debut v Australia, 3 November 1984.
Born: 22 November 1962, Grays, Essex.
Educated: Oxford University.
Clubs: Oxford University (Blues 1981-3), Newport, Bristol, Bath, Barbarians, Gloucestershire.

Barnes moved from Essex to Wales in 1972 and later captained the Welsh Senior Schools team. He was invited to the Welsh senior squad 1981 but decided to play for England instead. He went on the England Under-23 tour to Italy and Romania in 1983 but missed the

Stuart Barnes

full tour to South Africa in 1984 because of final exams at Oxford. He played in Bristol's 1983 JPS Cup-winning team and later captained Bath until Andy Robinson took over in June 1991. With Bath he appeared in the 1991 Courage League Championship side and in the 1986 JPS Cup-winning team which equalled Leicester's record of three successive Cup Final victories. He made his debut for the Barbarians at the Hong Kong Sevens in 1981-2.

BARR
Robert John, MC TD

Full-back. 1932 (Leicester, 3 caps).
Debut v South Africa, 2 January 1932.
Born: 26 May 1907, Blisworth, Northamptonshire; Died: 24 September 1975.
Educated: Stamford School.
Clubs: Leicester, Barbarians, Leicestershire.

Barr scored only one conversion in his

three appearances for England. Employed as an insurance broker, he later worked in the textile industry. During World War Two he served in the Army.

BARRETT
Edward Ivo Medhurst. CIE.

Centre. 1903 (Lennox, 1 cap).
Debut v Scotland, 21 March 1903.
Born: 22 June 1879, Winchester; Died: 10 July 1950, Bournemouth.
Educated: Cheltenham College, RMA Sandhurst.
Clubs: Lennox, Army, Surrey (12 appearances).

Barrett's career was spent mainly in the Army and then with the Ministry of Aircraft Production. He played cricket for Hampshire from 1895-1925, once scoring 215 against Gloucestershire. He also played hockey for Hampshire and the Trojans (Southampton) club. He was awarded Queen's and King's Medals in the South African War of 1899-1903 and served in the Shanghai Police (1907-1929). Awarded the CIE in 1916, during World War Two he was second-in-command of an internment camp in Norfolk. He was also an amateur golf champion in 1917.

BARRINGTON
Thomas James Mountsteven

Fly-half. 1931 (Bristol, 2 caps).
Debut v Wales, 17 January 1931.
Born: 8 July 1908; Died: 13 September 1973.
Educated: Dr Morgan Grammar School, Wrekin College.
Clubs: Bridgwater Albion, Harlequins, Richmond, Bath, Bristol, Somerset.

Barrington spent three years in the Wrekin College XV until 1925, latterly as vice-captain. His Richmond debut came at Rosslyn Park in February 1930 but his first game for Bristol had been in a charity match against Somerset in April 1927. He made one appearance for Bath, against Newport in March 1929.

His first appearance as a regular member of the Bristol side was in 1930-31 and he played regularly for that club until the end of 1934-5, captaining the side that season. In August 1935 he had an operation at Bristol Royal Infirmary for a cartilage injury, after damage first sustained in the England-Wales match in March 1931.

After consulting a knee surgeon, Mr J.K.Burrah, before his second and final international match (against Ireland) he was passed fit to play but went through the match wearing a knee bandage. He later presented Mr Burrah with his international jersey.

Further damage to his knee in July 1935, whilst playing in a tennis tournament at Curry Rivel in Somerset, meant that he could not play cricket that summer (he played for Bridgwater CC for over 20 years).

He appeared as a full-back for Somerset club North Petherton as a means of a trial period for his injured knee but decided to resign his Bristol captaincy in 1936, making only a handful of appearances the following year. He was reserve for England twice in 1933, first appeared for Somerset when he was 19 (29 appearances overall) and was president of Somerset RU in 1971-1972.

A member of Somerset Referees' Society, he refereed the Taunton School-Blundell's game in November 1936 and officiated during the seasons either side of World War Two as a member of London Referees' Society.

A solicitor in family practice, he was also a part-time clerk for the Somerset River Authority.

BARRINGTON-WARD
Sir Lancelot Edward, KCVO

Number 8. 1910 (Edinburgh University, 4 caps).
Debut v Wales, 15 January 1910.
Born: 4 July 1884, Worcester; Died: 17 November 1953, Bury St Edmunds.
Educated: Westminster School, Bromsgrove School, Oxford University, Edinburgh University.
Clubs: Oxford University, Edinburgh University.

He played in all four Championship-winning matches of 1910, the first season which saw the opening of Twickenham. Awarded the KCVO in 1935, he was surgeon to King George VI from 1936-1952 and extra-surgeon to Elizabeth II from June 1952 until his death. He was Huntarian Professor, Royal College of Surgeons, in 1952 and was also awarded the Grand Cross Order of St Olaf and the Order of St Sava.

BARRON
James Henry

Forward. 1896-1897 (Bingley, 3 caps).
Debut v Scotland, 14 March 1896.
Born: 28 August 1874, Micklethwaite, Yorkshire; Died: 2 December 1942, Bingley, Yorkshire.
Clubs: Bingley, Yorkshire.

Barron made 11 appearances for Yorkshire from 1895-1896, after his county debut against Lancashire, and was junior vice-president of Yorkshire in 1901-02 and 1902-03. He was a coal merchant and property owner.

BARTLETT
Jasper Twining

Lock. 1951 (Waterloo, 1 cap).
Debut v Wales, 20 January 1951.
Born: 17 October 1924; Died: 16 January 1969, Liverpool.
Educated: Birkenhead Institute, Liverpool University.
Clubs: Liverpool University, Northern

Universities, Combined Universities, Waterloo, Army, Combined Services, Barbarians, Cheshire (over 40 appearances).

Bartlett served in the Royal Engineers and made one appearance for the Army, against the Royal Navy in 1947. He was employed as a civil engineer at Mersey Docks.

BARTLETT
Richard Michael ('Ricky')

Fly-half. 1957-1958 (Harlequins, 7 caps).
Debut v Wales, 19 January 1957.
Born: 13 February 1929; Died: 5 March 1984, Liss, Hants.

Ricky Bartlett

Educated: Stowe School, KCS Wimbledon, Cambridge University.
Clubs: Cambridge University (Blue 1951), Harlequins, Barbarians, Surrey.

Bartlett first played for the Quins whilst still at school. A pig farmer and also a master at Millfield School, he played an important part in the 1957 Triple Crown and Grand Slam successes, England's first since 1928. It is said that he proved a constant danger to opposing defences and his running with the ball was 'quite brilliant'. A quiet, unobtrusive man on and off the rugby pitch, he was president of Surrey RFU and an England selector.

BARTON
John

Lock/Number 8. 1967-1972 (Coventry, 4 caps).
Debut v Ireland, 11 February 1967.
Born: 19 March 1943.
Educated: Caludon Castle School (Coventry).
Clubs: Caludon Castle Old Boys, Coventry, Nuneaton, Barbarians, Warwickshire (15 appearances).
Barton made his Coventry debut in 1962, against Guy's Hospital, but it was not until the 1963-4 season that he became a regular in the second-row at Coundon Road. In 1964-5 he played in one of the England trial matches but failed to make progress.

The 1966-7 season brought his first England cap, against Ireland, and further caps followed that season against France and Wales. Injuries prevented immediate further honours, despite a cartilage operation to put right the damage, although he toured Canada with an England squad in 1967. A final cap came five years later, in 1972 against France. He worked as an insurance broker in Coventry and also in farming. He married in 1972 and moved to Nuneaton. Nicknamed 'Bart', he toured South Africa with England in 1972 and was a member of the 1972-3 RFU Club KO Cup winners.

BATCHELOR
Tremlett Brewer MRCS 1914

Wing. 1907 (Oxford University, 1 cap).
Debut v France, 5 January 1907.
Born: 22 June 1884; Died: 21 December 1966, Liverpool
Educated: Rugby School, Oxford University.
Clubs: Oxford University (Blue 1906), London Hospital, Richmond, United Hospitals, Eastern Counties.
During World War One he served as an acting major in the RAMC and was mentioned in despatches in 1918.

BATES
Steven Michael

Scrum-half. 1989 (Wasps, 1 cap).
Debut v Romania, 13 May 1989.
Born: 4 March 1963, Merthyr Tydfil.
Educated: West London Institute.
Clubs: Welwyn, Wasps, Hertfordshire, London Division.

Bates' honours include playing for Wasps' 1987 JPS Cup Final team and their 1990 First Division Championship team. He also represented English Colleges, went on the England Students' tour of Japan in 1982 and appeared for England Under-23s against Spain in 1986. He was chosen as an England replacement for the first time against Australia in 1988, after being on the bench in England's last ten matches up to his debut. He suffered a broken jaw in 1983-4 and a broken arm in the 1986 JPS Cup Final. Employed as a sales executive, he also plays soccer for Hertfordshire and is a four-handicap golfer.

BATESON
Alfred Hardy

Prop. 1930 (Otley, 4 caps).
Debut v Wales, 18 January 1930.
Born: 10 August 1901, Otley; Died: 21 February 1982, Scarborough.
Clubs: Bramley Old Boys, Otley, Yorkshire.
Bateson played soccer until he was 23, but within a year of taking up rugby he made his Yorkshire debut against Derbyshire in 1927, the first of 20 appearances for the county, including playing in their 1928 County Championship-winning side against Cornwall. His first England cap was awarded along with fellow Otley player, F.W.S.Malir, when they became the first players to be capped from that club. He was employed as a heating engineer.

BATESON
Harold Dingwall, JP

Forward. 1879 (Liverpool, 1 cap).
Debut v Ireland, 24 March 1879.
Born: 2 May 1856; Died: 29 October 1927, Liverpool.
Educated: Rugby School, Oxford University.
Clubs: Oxford University (Blues 1874, 1875, 1877), Blackheath, Liverpool, Lancashire.
Bateson was a solicitor and the man who read the Riot Act as Liverpool JP during the police strike on August Bank Holiday weekend of 1919, when soldiers opened fire on the strikers, killing two.

BATSON
Thomas

Forward. 1872-1875 (Blackheath, 3 caps).
Debut v Scotland 5 February 1872.
Born: 1852; Died: 5 February 1933.
Educated: Oxford University.
Clubs: Bath, Oxford University (no rugby Blue but athletics Blue for hammer and shot putt), Blackheath.
Cousin of F. and L.Stokes. Employed as assistant master of Blackheath Prep School and later at the Rossall School.

BATTEN
John Maxwell

Full-back. 1874 (Cambridge University, 1 cap).
Debut v Scotland, 23 February 1874.
Born: 28 February 1853, Almora Kumaon; Died: 15 October 1917.
Educated: Haileybury and Imperial Service College, Cambridge University.
Club: Cambridge University (Blue 1871-4, captain 1873-4).
Employed as a schoolmaster at Kelly College, Newton Abbot School and Plymouth College, Batten was also a very good rackets player who represented Cambridge University.

BAUME
John Lea

Prop. 1950 (Northern, 1 cap).
Debut v Scotland, 18 March 1950.
Born: 18 July 1920.
Educated: Ashville College (Harrogate).
Clubs: Northern, Headingley, Harrogate; Army, Combined Services, Northumberland.
During World War Two, Baume served in the Northumberland Fusiliers and later made six appearances for the Army (v Royal Navy 1950, 1951 and 1953; RAF 1950-53; French Army 1950). He also served in the Korean War before retiring in 1961 to take up poultry farming.

BAXTER
James ('Bim')

Forward. 1900 (Birkenhead Park, 3 caps).
Debut v Wales, 6 January 1900.
Born: 8 June 1870; Died: 5 July 1940, Rock Ferry, Cheshire.
Educated: Liverpool Institute.
Clubs: Liverpool Institute, Birkenhead Park, Barbarians, Cheshire.
When his playing days were over, 'Bim' Baxter immediately became involved in the administration side of the game. He had a forceful, autocratic personality and demanded the highest standards on and off the field, exerting great influence at all levels of the game and holding numerous offices.

He refereed six international matches in the 1920s and was an RFU selector for 1922-3, vice-president in 1925-6, then president 1926-7. He was manager of the RFU tour to Argentina in 1927 and of the British Lions tour of Australia and New Zealand in 1930 (when the Lions won 20 of their 28 matches, including one Test against New Zealand, and scored 624 points against 318).

Baxter had captained Birkenhead Park when they lost only ten out of 85 games and he was club president from 1903-1940, captained Cheshire for several seasons and was their president from 1904-1940.

A member of the International Board from 1926 to 1939, he was, in 1905, a founding member of Liverpool District

Referees' Society and later its chairman. He was also captain of Mersey Rowing Club, won a yachting bronze medal at the 1908 Olympics as a crew member of 12-metre 'Mouchette'. His other posts included captain of the Royal Liverpool Golf Club in 1926 and president of the Cheshire Union of Golf Clubs 1929. During the early part of World War Two he served as a lieutenant-commander in the RNVR up to his death.

BAYFIELD
Martin Christopher Bayfield

Second-row forward. 1992 (Northampton, 6 caps).
Debut v Fiji, 20 July 1991.
Born: Bedford, 21 December 1966
Clubs: Bedford, Northampton, Metropolitan Police.

Bayfield joined Northampton in June 1991, at the age of 23, and was tipped to tour Australia and Fiji with England in the summer of that year after catching the eye with a series of impressive performances for Bedford in the Courage League Division Three during the 1990-91 season. His first international appearance was for England 'B' against Italy in March 1991 and he made an impressive full debut against Fiji when, at 6ft 10in tall, he equalled the record height for any international player. A member of the 1992 Grand Slam side, Bayfield works as a policeman in Luton.

BAZLEY
Reginald Charles

Wing. 1952-1955 (Waterloo, 10 caps).
Debut v Ireland, 29 March 1952.
Born: 15 December 1929, Barrow-in-Furness.
Educated: Barrow Grammar School, Liverpool University.
Clubs: Furness, Liverpool University, Waterloo, Universities Athletic Union, Army, Combined Services, Barbarians, Lancashire (58 appearances), North-West Counties.

Bazley, who played for North-West Counties against the New Zealanders in February 1954, was in the Royal Engineers whilst on National Service and made five appearances for the Army (v Royal Navy 1954-5; RAF 1954-5; French Army 1955). A fast and very dangerous attacking winger, he worked as a civil engineer.

BEAUMONT
William Blackledge, OBE

Lock. 1975-1982 (Fylde, 34 caps).
Debut v Ireland, 18 January 1975.
Born: 9 March 1952 Preston.
Educated: Council School, Cressbrook, Ellesmere College, Salford College of Technology.
Clubs: Fylde, Barbarians, Lancashire.

Bill Beaumont began playing rugby with his Under-10s school team. Originally he was a fly-half but later converted to full-back. At Salford College of Technology he took a diploma in business studies and textile technology and went into the family cotton business.

Beaumont joined Flyde in 1969 and stayed with that club until his retirement, through injury, in 1982. He began playing in the 6th XV, making his debut against Burnage. Soon afterwards he was switched from full-back to flank-forward, then to lock forward and then prop. He made his 1st XV debut against Waterloo in November 1970, when Fylde won 13-0, and made 60 appearances for Lancashire between 1971-1982, playing in three County Championship teams (1977, 1980 and 1982, captaining the latter side).

He played for the North of England against Tonga in 1974 and a few days later appeared for England Under-23s against the Tongans. Whilst playing for the North-West Counties he toured South Africa in 1979 and went to Argentina with England in 1981. He led the North of England to a 21-9 victory over the All Blacks at Otley on 17 November 1979, toured France with Lancashire in August 1981 and went with them to Rhodesia and South Africa in 1974.

A popular character, both on and off the rugby field, Beaumont was a very powerful figure in mauls and rucks and a clean catcher of the ball in the line-outs. He was appointed England captain in 1978 and led his country a record 21 times, 11 of which he was in a victorious England side. He is England's most capped lock and gained 33 consecutive caps. In 1980 he skippered the side to England's first Grand Slam title for 21 years. His only try at international level came against Scotland/Ireland when he played against them for England/Wales in Cardiff in 1980.

He was the first Englishman for 50

Martin Bayfield

Bill Beaumont

years to captain the British Lions, when they toured the Far East in the summer of 1979. For the Lions he appeared in nine matches on their tour of New Zealand in 1977 and ten matches on the South African tour of 1980. He was elected *Rugby World* Player of the Year in 1980.

His retirement from the game came after he sustained a head injury during the 1982 County Championship Final and doctors warned him not to play again. After retirement he joined the BBC as a commentator and is a resident team captain on the popular *A Question of Sport* programme. When he was forced to quit, Orrell made him an honorary member.

An uncle, Jim Blackledge, was captain of Lancashire CCC and Beaumont himself played for Chorley in the Northern Cricket League. His father was a rugby player with Flyde and Cambridge. In 1985, Bill established a school of rugby, sponsored by Wimpey Homes. His autobiography *Thanks to Rugby* was published in 1982.

BEDFORD
Harry

Forward. 1889-1890 (Morley, 3 caps).
Debut v Maoris, 16 February 1889.
Born: 1866, Gildersome; Died: January 1929, Leeds.
Clubs: Batley, Morley, Yorkshire (32 appearances).

Harry Bedford made his Yorkshire debut against Lancashire in 1886. He played in the first Yorkshire v Ulster match, in December 1887, the same year that the Yorkshire County RU was formed. He was a licensee.

BEDFORD
Lawrence Leslie

Full-back. 1931 (Headingley, 2 caps).
Debut v Wales, 17 January 1931.
Born: 11 February 1903, Leeds; Died: 25 November 1963, Hartlepool.
Clubs: Headingley, Barbarians, Yorkshire (32 appearances).

Lawrence Bedford made his Yorkshire debut against Cumberland in 1924 and was captain from 1931 to 1932. He has also captained Headingley and Yorkshire at cricket. He was employed as a director of a chemical company.

BEER
Ian David Stafford, JP

Number 8. 1955 (Harlequins, 2 caps).
Debut v France, 26 February 1955.
Born: 28 April 1931, Croydon.
Educated: Whitgift School, Cambridge University.
Clubs: Old Whitgiftians, Cambridge University (Blues 1952-4), Harlequins, Bath, Shropshire, Dorset, Wiltshire.

Ian Beer was recruited for Harlequins by John Worton, whilst serving as a subaltern in the Royal Fusiliers in

Ian Beer

BAOR. He captained the Oxford-Cambridge side which toured the USA in 1955 and was Cambridge University's CB representative on the RFU. He taught at Marlborough College, Ellesmere College and Lancing College and was headmaster at Ellesmere College during the mid-1960s. Currently he is headmaster at Harrow.

BEESE
Michael Christopher

Centre. 1972 (Liverpool, 3 caps).
Debut v Wales, 15 January 1972.
Born: 8 October 1948, Bristol.
Educated: Keynsham Grammar School, Liverpool Polytechnic.
Clubs: Bath, Liverpool, Somerset.

Until his late teens, Beese preferred soccer and during his last years at grammar school he captained the 1st XV from stand-off on Saturday mornings and played centre-forward for a local soccer club in the afternoons. Moving to Liverpool Polytechnic to study as a town planner, he still held a preference for the soccer code.

Indeed, rugby had to settle for second best until he returned to Bristol on a 12 months' course at the town-planning office in the city. He began playing club rugby at Bath after being persuaded to take up the game more seriously, and in 1968 he was made captain of the side. He played for Liverpool whilst studying at the polytechnic.

In 1970-71, Beese played for the combined Gloucestershire and Somerset side which beat the touring Fijians 25-13. His county rugby was played with Somerset, for whom he made 25 appearances. He also represented Somerset Schools at cricket and in the triple jump at athletics.

BELL
Fred J.

Forward. 1900 (Northern, 1 cap).
Debut v Wales, 6 January 1900.
Died: 1948.
Clubs: Northern, Hunslet, Northumberland..

Hunslet RLFC were said to have paid a fee of £30 and a weekly wage of 25s (£1.25) when they signed Bell from Northern. He retired from rugby to become a market gardener in Whitley Bay.

BELL
Henry

Forward. 1884 (New Brighton, 1 cap).
Debut v Ireland, 4 February 1884.
Born: 1860; Died: 20 September 1934, Marylebone.
Clubs: Liverpool Institute, New Brighton.

Employed as a banker, Bell was one of the founder members of Lloyds Bank RFC in 1913. He had a very extensive career in banking and was a member of many financial commissions.

BELL
John Lowthian

Half-back. 1878 (Darlington, 1 cap).
Debut v Scotland, 11 March 1878.
Born: 1853; Died: 16 December 1916.
Clubs: Darlington, Durham County.

BELL
Peter Joseph

Flanker. 1968 (Blackheath, 4 caps).
Debut v Wales, 20 January 1968.
Born: 28 April 1937.
Educated: Caterham School; Cirencester College.
Clubs: Caterham Old Boys, Cirencester College, Cranbrook, Ashford, Blackheath, Barbarians, Kent (over 16 appearances), Bay of Plenty (New Zealand).

Employed as a farmer in Kent, Peter Bell played his first international match at the age of 30, after appearing in six England trial matches.

BELL
Robert William

Forward. 1900 (Northern, 3 caps).
Debut v Wales, 6 January 1900.
Born: 19 December 1875, Newcastle upon Tyne; Died: 9 June 1940, Newcastle upon Tyne.
Educated: Durham School, Leeds Clergy School, Cambridge University.
Clubs: Cambridge University (Blues 1897-9), Northern, Blackheath, Barbarians, Northumberland.

Robert Bell was a clergyman, being ordained in 1901. He rowed for the Jesus College (Cambridge) VIII.

BENDON
Gordon John

Prop. 1959 (Wasps, 4 caps).
Debut v Wales, 17 January 1959.
Born: 9 April 1929.
Educated: King's College School (Wimbledon).
Clubs: King's College School Old Boys, RAF, Wasps, London Counties, Eastern Counties, Middlesex, Surrey.
Gordon Bendon, who spent over 20 seasons with Wasps, played for England-Scotland v Wales-Ireland in the 1960 Jubilee match at Twickenham. He worked as a sales representative and later as a marketing director.

BENNETT
Norman Osborn

Centre. 1947-1948 (St Mary's Hospital, Waterloo, 7 caps).
Debut v Wales, 18 January 1947.
Born: 21 September 1922.
Educated: Epsom College.
Clubs: St Mary's Hospital, Waterloo, US Portsmouth, Royal Navy, Barbarians, London Counties, Hampshire, Surrey, Lancashire.
Norman Bennett had an extensive career as a surgeon-lieutenant in the RNVR. He played cricket for Free Foresters, Royal Navy, Worcestershire and MCC.

BENNETT
William Neil

Fly-half. 1975-1979 (Bedford, London Welsh, 7 caps).
Debut v Scotland, 15 March 1975.
Born: 20 April 1951, Ramsey, Isle of Man.

Neil Bennett

Educated: Tiffin School.
Clubs: Bedford, Colwyn Bay, London Welsh, Surrey.
Bennett was a member of Bedford's 1974-5 RFU Club KO Cup-winning side. He scored a penalty-goal on his England debut and is the holder of England's most points record (48) on an overseas tour (Australia, 1975) and most points in any tour match (36 v Western Australia, 1975). He also toured South Africa with London Counties and was a keen cricketer.

BENNETTS
Barzillai Beckerleg ('Barrie'), MBE

Wing. 1909 (Penzance, 2 caps).
Debut v Australia, 9 January 1909.
Born: 14 July 1883; Died: 26 July 1958, Alverton, Penzance.
Educated: Bridgend College.
Clubs: Penzance, Davenport A, Redruth, Richmond, Barbarians, Cornwall (42 appearances).
Bennetts, who was a solicitor and county coroner, made nine appearances for the Barbarians between 1907 and 1908 and went on tour with the RFU to Argentina in 1910. He also represented Cornwall at cricket, golf and hockey and had a successful partnership with Bert Solomon for the Cornish rugby side. He received an RNLI award for services to Penlee Lifeboat Committee and was awarded the MBE in 1949. He was also a distinguished viola player and amateur dramatic actor.

BENTLEY
John

Forward 1988 (Sale, 2 caps).
Debut v Ireland, 23 April 1988.
Born: 5 September 1966, Dewsbury.
Clubs: Cleckheaton, Otley, Sale, Yorkshire, Leeds RL.
Bentley, a former England Colts player, made his first full international appearance came in the Dublin Millennium match at Lansdowne Road in 1988. He played the amateur Rugby League game for Dewsbury Moor before joining Cleckheaton RUFC. A police officer stationed at Headingley police station, he signed for Leeds RL in November 1988, for £80,000, and made his debut for them against Salford. Bentley scored a try for Great Britain against France in February 1992.

BENTLEY
John Edmund

Half-back. 1871-1872 (Gipsies, 2 caps).
Debut v Scotland, 27 March 1871.
Born: 1847; Died: 12 December 1913, Hampstead.
Educated: Tonbridge School.
Club: Gipsies.
John Bentley, who worked at the Royal Courts of Justice, played in the very first England-Scotland match in 1871.

BERRIDGE
Michael John

Prop. 1949 (Northampton, 2 caps).
Debut v Wales, 15 January 1949..
Born: 28 February 1923; Died: 2 October 1973.
Educated: King's School (Peterborough).
Clubs: Peterborough, Northampton, Leicester, Barbarians, East Midlands.
Berridge, a farmer, also played for the Combined Counties against Australia 1947 and against South Africa 1951.

BERRY
Henry

Forward. 1910 (Gloucester, 4 caps).
Debut v Wales, 15 January 1910.
Born: 8 January 1883, Gloucester; Died: 9 May 1915, Festubert, France (killed in action).
Educated: St Mark's School (Gloucester).
Clubs: Gloucester, Army, Gloucestershire.
Henry Berry served in the Gloucestershire Regiment during the South Africa War, during which he was awarded the Queen's Medal. He also served in St Helena and India and in the Army Reserve. Recalled for World War One, he was a corporal when he died in France.

BERRY
John

Half-back. 1891 (Tyldesley, 3 caps).
Debut v Wales, 3 January 1891..
Born: 25 September 1866; Died: 10 May 1930, Manchester.
Clubs: Kendal Harriers, Tyldesley, Tyldesley RL, Lancashire, (13 appearances).
Employed as a builder's labourer, John Berry later worked as a licensee. He turned to Rugby League when Tyldesley helped form the Northern Union in 1895.

BERRY
Joseph Thomas Wade

Flanker. 1939 (Leicester, 3 caps).
Debut v Wales, 21 January 1939.
Born: 17 July 1911, Slawston, Leicestershire.
Educated: Eastbourne College.
Clubs: Market Harborough, Leicester, Barbarians, Leicestershire.
Farmer Tom Berry has enjoyed high office in the rugby world. He was Leicestershire CB representative on the RFU from 1953-1968, an England selector from 1951-1966, president of the RFU from 1968-1969 and Leicester president from 1968-1969. Brother-in-law of J.McD.Hodgson, his wife, Margaret, was an England international golfer, who played for Gosforth Park, Northumberland and, after they moved to Market Harborough after World War

Two, for Leicestershire. Tom Berry broke his hip in 1991 but still managed to keep cheerful.

BESWICK
Edmund

Back. 1882 (Swinton, 2 caps).
Debut v Ireland, 6 February 1882.
Born: 1860, Penrith; Died: 22 January 1911, Salford.
Clubs: Swinton, Lancashire.

BIGGS
John Maundy

Forward. 1878-1879 (University College Hospital, 2 caps).
Debut v Scotland, 4 March 1878.
Born: 1855, Reading; Died: 3 June 1935, Barnstaple.
Clubs: University College Hospital, United Hospitals, Wasps.
Biggs was the first international player to join the Wasps club. Biggs was also captain of Wasps from 1877 to 1879.

BIRKETT
John Guy Giberne

Centre. 1906-1912 (Harlequins, 21 caps).
Debut v Scotland, 17 March 1906.
Born: 27 December 1884, Richmond, Surrey; Died: 16 October 1968.
Educated: Haileybury and Imperial Service College.
Clubs: Brighton, Harlequins, Barbarians, Surrey.
Birkett, who worked as a land agent, was the son of Reginald and nephew of Louis, both England internationals. He retired from rugby in 1912, having established a record 21 international appearances. He scored Harlequins' first-ever try at Twickenham in October 1909. The previous season he had suffered a broken collarbone against London Scottish. He played for Harlequins Past against Harlequins Present in April 1922, in a match to raise money for the King Edward VII Hospital Fund. He served in World War One as a captain in the Royal Field Artillery, was mentioned in despatches 1918 and awarded the Order of the Crown of Italy (5th Class). From 1943 to 1946 he was a captain in the Army Claims Commission for England.

BIRKETT
Louis H.

Full-back. 1875-1877 (Clapham Rovers, 3 caps).
Debut v Scotland, 8 March 1875.
Born: 1 January 1853; Died: 11 April 1943, Barnstaple.
Educated: Haileybury and Imperial Service College.
Clubs: Clapham Rovers, Middlesex.
He played alongside his brother, Reginald, against Scotland in 1875 and Ireland in 1877. He is the uncle of John.

One of England's longest-lived international players, he was 90 years old when he died.

BIRKETT
Reginald Halsey

Forward/Back. 1871-1877 (Clapham Rovers, 4 caps).
Debut v Scotland, 27 March 1871.
Born: 28 March 1849, London; Died: 30 June 1898.
Educated: Lancing College.
Clubs: Lancing Old Boys, Clapham Rovers, Surrey.
Reginald Birkett, who has a special place in rugby history as the man who scored England's first-ever try, was one of that rare breed who have been capped at both rugby and soccer. At Lancing College he was a member of the soccer XI and joined the Clapham Rovers club which played both soccer and rugger.
At rugby he appeared with his brother, Louis, against Scotland in 1875 and Ireland in 1877; and as a soccer goalkeeper he was capped against Scotland in 1879, although it was said that he could play just as well in any position.
A member of the original RFU committee in 1871, he was the father of John G.G., also an England international rugby player, who was with the Harlequins.
Employed as an hide and skin broker in the City of London, he met his death following an accident sustained whilst suffering from delirium during an attack of typhoid fever.

BISHOP
Colin Charles

Fly-half. 1927 (Blackheath, 1 cap).
Debut v France, 2 April 1927.
Born: 5 October 1903; Died: 4 March 1980.
Educated: University College School, Cambridge Univesity.
Clubs: Cambridge University (Blue 1925), Blackheath, Barbarians, Middlesex.

BLACK
Brian Henry

Lock. 1930-1933 (Blackheath, 10 caps).
Debut v Wales, 18 January 1930.
Born: 27 May 1907, South Africa; Died: 29 July 1940, Chilwark, Wiltshire (killed in action).
Educated: Oxford University.
Clubs: Oxford University (Blue 1929), Blackheath, Barbarians.
South African Rhodes Scholar Brian Black was invited to play for the Probables in the second England trial in December 1929 and went on to score a penalty-goal and a conversion on his international debut against Wales the following year, as a member of the team that won the Championship. He went

with the British Lions to New Zealand and Australia in 1930 and headed the tourists' scorers with 82 points (3 tries, 26 conversions and 7 penalty-goals). He was also in the 1931-2 Calcutta Cup winning side, when he scored a try.
A solicitor and company director, Black was a member of two Great Britain teams which won world championship bobsleigh titles (two-man with F.McEvoy in 1937; and four man with F.McEvoy, D.Looker and C.Green in 1939). He also won a squash rackets championship in the South of France. He was on active service in the RAF when he was killed in World War Two.

BLACKLOCK
Joseph

Forward. 1898-1899 (Aspatria, 2 caps).
Debut v Ireland, 5 February 1898.
Born: 20 October 1878; Died 28 June 1945.
Clubs: Aspatria, Cumberland.
Joe Blacklock was employed as a deputy foreman in a coal mine.

BLAKEWAY
Philip John

Prop. 1980-1985 (Gloucester, 19 caps).
Debut v Ireland, 19 January 1980.
Born: 31 December 1950, Cheltenham.
Educated: Wells House School (Malvern) King's School (Sherborne).

Phil Blakeway

Clubs: Cheltenham, Gloucester, Barbarians, Gloucestershire.

Blakeway left school at 15 to work in the family fruit and vegetable firm and joined Cheltenham to play in the colts XV. He moved to Gloucester in 1972 and in a game against South Wales Police in 1978 suffered a broken neck. A member of England's 1980 Grand Slam team, against France that year he suffered a broken rib which curtailed his appearances with the British Lions on their tour of South Africa to one match. The same year he made his debut for the Barbarians against Leicester.

He retired from the game in 1981 and again in 1982 but changed his mind each time to regain an England place. His other tours were with England to Australia in 1975, but he did not play in either of the internationals, and with England to USA and Canada in 1982. In October 1973 he played for England Under-23s against Japan.

Blacklock was the British Under-21 modern pentathlon champion in 1968 and reserve for that year's world junior championships. His sister, Gill, was a member of the Great Britain show pony team against the USA in 1959 and his mother, Joyce, was a county lawn tennis player who qualified for Junior Wimbledon in 1939.

BLAKISTON
Sir Arthur Frederick, Bt MC

Forward. 1920-1925 (Northampton, 17 caps).
Debut v Scotland, 20 March 1920.
Born: 16 June 1892; Died: February 1974.
Educated: Bedford School, Trent College, Cambridge University.
Clubs: Cambridge University, Northampton, Liverpool, Blackheath, Barbarians, East Midlands, Lancashire, Surrey.

A farmer, Blakiston served as a trooper in King Edward's Horse during World War One and was later a captain in the Royal Field Artillery, when he was wounded. In 1924 he celebrated his 32nd birthday on tour with the British Lions in South Africa, making two Test appearances and appearing in 14 other tour matches, scoring two tries. He was in the England side which won four International Championships, including three Grand Slams. He inherited his father's baronetcy in 1941.

BLATHERWICK
Thomas

Forward. 1878 (Manchester, 1 cap).
Debut v Ireland, 11 March 1878.
Born: 25 December 1855; Died: 29 January 1940.
Educated: Epsom College.
Clubs: Manchester, Lancashire.

BODY
James Alfred

Forward. 1872-1873 (Gipsies, 2 caps).
Debut v Scotland, 5 February 1872.
Born: 1846; Died: 9 September 1929, Manitoba, Canada.
Educated: Tonbridge School.
Club: Gipsies.

A founder member of the Gipsies club, Body was employed in the brewery industry and later owned a flax-crushing company. He emigrated to Canada, where he died.

BOLTON
Charles Arthur, CBE

Flanker. 1909 (United Services, 1 cap).
Debut v France, 30 January 1909.
Born: 3 January 1882; Died: 23 November 1963, Eastbourne.
Educated: Marlborough College, Oxford University.
Clubs: Oxford University, United Services College (Portsmouth), Barbarians, Surrey.

Bolton had a long army career, serving in World War One in the Manchester Regiment as a lieutenant-colonel and being mentioned in despatches three times. Awarded the CBE in 1919, he joined the Royal Tank Corps in 1923 and was made a brigadier in 1931. In 1939 he went to France with the British Expeditionary Force and in 1940 was with the Middle East Forces. He was twice mentioned in despatches. He was awarded Order of the Nile, and the Order of the Redeemer (Greece) 3rd Class.

BOLTON
Reginald MBE

Flanker. 1933-1938 (Harlequins, 5 caps).
Debut v Wales, 21 January 1933.
Born: 20 November 1909.
Educated at Queen Elizabeth Grammar School (Wakefield), University College Hospital.
Clubs: Wakefield, University College Hospital, Harlequins, Barbarians, Yorkshire.

Reginald Bolton went to grammar school at the age of seven and played rugby three times a week until he left at 18. He made his Yorkshire debut against Cheshire in 1928 and was captain in 1931-2. His England debut was made in difficult circumstances, originally being chosen as a wing-forward, he was put on the wing when R.A.Gerrard was injured during the game. There were no replacements in those days and England, a man short, went down 7-3, the first time Wales had won at Twickenham. He scored a try against Scotland on 21 March 1936, playing in the side for the first time since his debut game in 1933, and it was the first time that he had appeared on the winning side. He also represented the University of London at swimming.

Bolton served in the RAMC during World War Two and was injured during an air-raid on Naples harbour, but returned to take up a social membership at the Harlequins. He was awarded the MBE in 1944.

BOLTON
Wilfrid Nash, OBE

Back. 1882-1887 (Blackheath, 11 caps).
Debut v Ireland, 6 February 1882.
Born: 14 September 1862, Ireland; Died: 12 August 1930, Contrexeville Vosges, France.
Educated: Royal Military College Sandhurst, Royal Naval Academy.
Clubs: Gosport, Blackheath, Kent.

Wilfred Bolton scored a try on his debut, against Ireland. An army athletic champion and noted gymnast, during the Boer War he was wounded three times, mentioned in despatches twice and was awarded the Queen's Medal (three clasps) and King's Medal (two clasps). He stayed on in South Africa after the war and became a resident magistrate in Transvaal. Later he was provost marshall and food controller of Cyprus.

BONAVENTURA
Maurice Sydney

Prop. 1931 (Blackheath, 1 cap).
Debut v Wales, 17 Janaury 1931.
Born: 28 April 1902.
Educated: Cranleigh School.
Clubs: Honourable Artillery Company, Lensbury, Blackheath, Barbarians, Surrey.

Employed by a petroleum company, he also played rugby for Singapore Cricket & Sports Club and was captain of the Royal Bangkok Sports Club from 1926 to 1927.

BOND
Anthony Matthew

Centre. 1978-1982 (Sale, 6 caps).
Debut v New Zealand, 25 November 1978.
Born: 3 August 1954, Urmston, Manchester.
Educated: Wellacre County Secondary School.
Clubs: Sedgeley Park, Broughton Park, Sale, Lancashire.

Bond was introduced to rugby at school and after joining Sedgeley Park moved from prop to full-back and then to centre, graduating from the colts to the 1st XV. He joined Broughton Park after playing against them in a preliminary round of the Manchester Sevens. Again he played for the colts side, for two seasons, before graduating to the 1st XV. He moved to Sale in December 1977. He made 34 appearances for Lancashire, including the 1976 defeat of Middlesex in the County Championship Final.

He toured Canada with England Under-23s and broke his leg in the

Tony Bond

England-Ireland match in 1980, Paul Dodge taking his place in the Grand Slam season. Bond, who is employed as an advertising representative, turned down an offer of £15,000, plus numerous other benefits, to join a major Rugby League club.

BONHAM-CARTER
Sir Edgar, KCMG CIE

Forward. 1891 (Oxford University, 1 cap).
Debut v Scotland, 7 March 1891.
Born: 2 April 1870; Died: 24 April 1956, Alton, Hants.
Educated: Clifton College; Oxford University.
Clubs: Oxford University (Blues 1890-1891), Blackheath, Barbarians.

Bonham-Carter won his only cap when Ernest Bromet withdrew through injury. He enjoyed a career in law and was called to the Bar in 1895, later holding several overseas posts including one with the Sudan Civil Service. He was awarded the CIE in 1919 and the KCMG (Knight Commander of St Michael and St George) in 1920. He also held the Order of the Nile (1st Class).

BONSOR
Frederick, DCM

Half-back. 1886-1889 (Bradford, 6 caps).
Debut v Wales, 2 January 1886.
Born: 1865 (some biographies state 1861); Died: February 1932.

Clubs: Bradford, Yorkshire (33 appearances).

Selected for the 1888 England side that did not play, Bonsor was the first Yorkshire player to captain England (v New Zealand in 1889). In 1890 he chose to play for his club in a Yorkshire Cup game rather than play for England against Scotland. He was never selected for his country again.

He made his Yorkshire debut against Midlands in 1881 and was captain from 1888 to 1890. Bonsor, who worked in farming, was awarded the DCM in the Boer War.

BOOBBYER
Brian

Centre. 1950 (Rosslyn Park, 9 caps).
Debut v Wales, 21 January 1950.
Born: 25 February 1928, Ealing, London.
Educated: Uppingham School, Oxford University.
Clubs: Oxford University (Blues 1949-1951, plus four cricket Blues), Rosslyn Park, Barbarians, Middlesex.

The son of a doctor, Boobbyer gave up all sporting activities in 1952 and dedicated his life to Moral Rearmament, mainly living in Asia and the USA, then at Oxford in 1962. He toured France (1949) and Japan (1952) with Oxford University RU and made 40 appearances for Oxford University CC (1949-1952).

His grandfather, E.C.Shaw, who was later to become Archdeacon of Oxford and Bishop of Buckingham, scored 78 not out for Oxford University against the Australians in 1882. His father was also a fine cricketer, who played for St Mary's Hospital, and so was his mother. Two of his mother's sisters represented England at lacrosse. His wife (neé Rodd) is related to Tremayne Rodd (later Lord Rennell). He has two sons, Brian and Mark, both rugby players.

He remained in Japan after the Oxford University tour in 1952, with a view to trying to dispel some of the hatred lingering from the war, and worked abroad for ten years before returning to the UK.

BOOTH
Lewis Alfred

Wing Threequarter. 1933-1935 (Headingley, 7 caps).
Debut v Wales, 21 January 1933.
Born: 26 September 1909, Horsforth; Died: 25 June 1942 (killed in action).
Educated: Giggleswick School
Clubs: Bohemians, Headingley, RAF, Barbarians, Yorkshire (56 appearances, captain 1934-5.

Booth had a useful turn of speed and a clever side-step which often caught out opposing players. A very accomplished winger, it was often said of him that in this position he was of a very high standard. He was employed in the

Lewis Booth

woollen industry before serving as an RAF pilot officer during World War Two.

BOTTING
Ian James

Wing. 1950 (Oxford University, 2 caps).
Debut v Wales, 21 January 1950.
Born: 18 May 1922, Dunedin, New Zealand; Died: 9 July 1980, Christchurch, New Zealand.
Educated: John McGlashan College, Christ's College (New Zealand), Ashburton College, Otago University, Oxford University.
Clubs: Otago, New Zealand Universities, Oxford University, (Blues 1949-50), RAF, Blackheath, Leicester, Barbarians, New Zealand (9 appearances, no internationals), Notts, Lincs & Derbys.

Botting, a school master and chaplain, served in World War Two as a lieutenant in the New Zealand Army and as a flying officer in the Royal New Zealand Air Force. On his return to New Zealand, he won Blues for athletics, cricket and rugby whilst studying at Otago University. In 1949 he toured South Africa with the All Blacks.

He was an undergraduate at Oxford when originally selected by England. After graduating he returned to New Zealand, where he took Holy Orders (Church of England) and became chaplain at Christ's College and St Margaret's College. He was later precentor at Christ's College and St Margaret's College and precentor at

Christchurch Cathedral. He died from injuries sustained in a road traffic accident.

BOUGHTON
Harold J.

Full-back 1935 (Gloucester, 3 caps).
Debut v Wales, 19 January 1935.
Born: 7 September 1910, Gloucester.
Clubs: Gloucester; Gloucestershire.

Boughton was a very accurate place-kicker and he saved England from the wooden spoon in 1935, when he kicked four penalty-goals and a conversion, including a penalty-goal on his debut. He was employed as a bus driver.

BOYLE
Cecil William

Half-back. 1873 (Oxford University, 1 cap).
Debut v Scotland, 3 March 1873.
Born: 16 March 1853, London; Died: 5 April 1900, South Africa (killed in action).
Educated: Clifton College, Oxford University.
Club: Oxford University (cricket Blue 1873).
A stockbroker, Boyle was serving in the Queen's Own Oxfordshire Hussars and Imperial Yeomanry when he died in the Boer War.

BOYLE
Stephen Brent

Lock. 1983 (Gloucester, 3 caps).
Debut v Wales, 5 February 1983.
Born: 9 August 1953, Warrington.
Educated: Sir Thomas Rich's Grammar School.

Clubs: Sir Thomas Rich's Old Boys, Gloucester, Moseley, Barbarians.
Boyle, who played soccer for Herefordshire Schoolboys, was in the England Under-23 rugby teams against Canada and Japan and went on the tour of Romania in 1978. He played in Gloucester's JPS Cup-winning side of 1978 and made his Barbarians debut against East Midlands in March 1983.

BOYLEN
Francis

Forward. 1908 (Hartlepool Rovers, 4 caps).
Debut v France, 1 January 1908.
Born: 1879; Died: 3 February 1938, Kingston upon Hull.
Clubs: Hartlepool Excelsior, Hartlepool Rovers, Durham County, Hull RL.
Boylen played for Hull RL from 1908 to 1923, making 141 appearances, scoring 14 tries and kicking two goals. He was in the Great Britain side against Australia in 1908, played for a Hartlepool XV against New Zealand in 1909 and went on the Northern Union tour to New Zealand and Australia in 1910. He was employed at BOC in Hull.

BRADBY
Matthew Seymour, MBE

Centre. 1922 (United Services, 2 caps).
Debut v Ireland, 11 February 1922.
Born: 25 March 1899, Rugby.
Educated: Rugby School, Royal Naval Engineering College (Keyham), Cambridge University.
Clubs: Cambridge University, United Services (Portsmouth), Royal Navy, Barbarians, Hampshire.
Bradby served as a Royal Naval lieutenant-commander during World War Two. He was later captain of the Nautical School at Heswall and of the TS *Mercury* on the Hamble River.

BRADLEY
Robert

Forward. 1903 (West Hartlepool, 1 cap).
Debut v Wales, 10 January 1903.
West Hartlepool, Durham County.

BRADSHAW
Harry

Forward. 1892-1894 (Bramley, 7 caps).
Debut v Scotland, 5 March 1892.
Born: 17 April 1868, Bramley; Died: 31 December 1910, Halifax.
Clubs: Bramley, Yorkshire (28 appearances), Leeds RL.
Bradshaw, a licensee, was in England's Triple Crown side of 1891-2. He scored two tries for England on 4 February 1893, against Ireland, and on 6 January 1894, against Wales.

BRAIN
Stephen Edward

Hooker. 1984-1986 (Coventry, 13 caps).
Debut v South Africa, 9 June 1984.
Born: 11 November 1954, Moseley.
Educated: Harold Malley Grammar School (Solihull).
Clubs: Moseley, Coventry, Rugby.

Steve Brain, a builder by trade, was the inspiring captain who helped Rugby RFC up the League ladder in recent years. He played for England Secondary Schools, England Colts, England Under-23s and went on the tour of South Africa in 1984, playing in the Second Test. He also played for the Five Nations XV v Overseas XV at Twickenham in 1986.

BRAITHWAITE-EXLEY
Bryan JP

Number 8. 1949 (Headingley, 1 cap).
Debut v Wales, 15 January 1949.
Born: 30 November 1927, Wetherby.
Educated: Sedburgh School.
Clubs: RAF, Headingley, North Ribblesdale, Yorkshire (31 appearances, captain 1948-9).
A director in the family quarrying business, he had 18 seasons with the Headingley club and a short spell with South Malaya.

BRETTARGH
A.T.

Centre. 1900 (Liverpool Old Boys, 8 caps).
Debut v Wales, 6 January, 1900.
Clubs: Liverpool Old Boys, Barbarians, Lancashire (42 appearances).

Brettargh scored one try for England, on 9 January 1904 against Wales.

BREWER
J.

Forward. 1875 (Gipsies, 1 cap).
Debut v Ireland 13 December 1875.
Club: Gipsies.

BRIGGS
Arthur

Half-back. 1892-1893 (Bradford, 3 caps).
Debut v Wales, 2 January 1892.
Born: 1871; Died: 18 August 1943.

Clubs: Otley, Bradford, Yorkshire (9 appearances).

Briggs' only caps came in England's Triple Crown success of 1892. A notable breeder of Sealyham Terriers, he was an iron moulder by trade.

BRINN
Alan

Lock. 1972 (Gloucester, 3 caps).
Debut v Wales, 15 January 1972.
Born: 21 July 1942, Ystrad, Rhondda, Wales.

Educated: Annandale Grammar School (Belfast), Aylesbury Grammar School, Royal Grammar School (High Wycombe).

Clubs: Hereford, Gloucester.

Brinn was born whilst his father was stationed in Wales during RAF service. Service life took the family to many parts of Britain and abroad and from an early age, Alan moved from Wales to the Isle of Man, then to Yorkshire and on to Southern Rhodesia, where he captained his school soccer team as a centre-half. When his family returned to Britain they moved to Belfast where he went to the Annadale Grammer School and had his first taste of rugby. At that time Robin Thompson, the captain of the 1955 British Lions, was coach and Brinn received excellent tuition. When his family finally settled in Hereford he joined the local club and in 1962 moved up in the ranks to Gloucester. Originally he wanted to become a veterinary surgeon but went into banking before going into partnership with the former Gloucester centre, Ron Pitt, in a sports outfitting business. He was a member of the Gloucester side which won the very first RFU KO Championship in 1971-2.

BROADLEY
Thomas

Forward. 1893-1896 (Bingley, 6 caps).
Debut v Wales, 7 January 1893.

Born: 18 August 1871, Bingley; Died: 26 November 1950, Bradford.
Clubs: Bingley (until 1892), West Riding, Bingley again (until 1896), Yorkshire (38 appearances, captain 1895-6), Bradford RL.
Broadley was a licensee.

BROMET
William Ernest

Forward. 1891-1896 (Richmond, 12 caps).
Debut v Wales, 3 January 1891.
Born: 17 May 1868, Tadcaster; Died: 23 January 1949.

Educated: Richmond School (Yorkshire), Oxford University.
Clubs: Oxford University (Blue 1889), Richmond (Yorkshire), Tadcaster, Yorkshire (17 appearances, captain 1891-2), Middlesex.

When Bromet appeared with his brother, Edward, in two Tests on the British Lions tour of South Africa in 1891 they became the first brothers to play for the Lions. He scored one try for England, against Scotland on 5 March 1892. It was a vital one, though, for it was the only try of the match and settled the Triple Crown victory for his country. He worked as a solicitor.

William Bromet

BROOK
Peter Watts Pitt

Flanker/number 8. 1930-1936 (Harlequins, 3 caps).
Debut v Scotland, 15 March 1930.
Born: 21 September 1906, Thornton Heath.
Educated: Whitgift School, Cambridge University.
Clubs: Westminster Bank, United Banks, Cambridge University (Blues 1928-1931), Harlequins, Bristol, Barbarians, Wiltshire, Eastern Counties, Sussex.
Brook was a clergyman, being ordained in 1935 and later becoming chaplain at Clifton College. A large, genial man, he served in World War Two as chaplain of the XIV Army in Burma. He represented Surrey at the pole vault and hurdles and was a member of the Quins team that won the 1935 Middlesex Sevens, beating London Welsh 10-3.

BROOKE
Terence John

Right/Centre Threequarter. 1968 (Richmond, 2 caps).
Debut v France, 24 February 1968.
Born: 8 November 1940.
Educated: Purley County Grammar School, Battersea College of Advanced Technology.
Clubs: Warlingham (Surrey), Richmond, Warlingham again (1971-2), Surrey.
A member of the 1968 Calcutta Cup team. He broke his nose in a game at the end of September 1971. Employed as a structural engineer.

BROOKS
Frederick G.

Wing. 1906 (Bedford, 1 cap).
Debut v South Africa, 8 December, 1906.
Born: 1 May 1883; Died: September 1947.
Educated: Bedford Grammer School.
Clubs: Bedford, East Midlands, Rhodesia.
Brooks played for Rhodesia in the Currie Cup in 1906. In his England appearance he scored the only English try of the game to earn them a 3-3 draw against the first Springboks at Crystal Palace.

BROOKS
Hon Marshall Jones

Full-back. 1874 (Oxford University, 1 cap).
Debut v Scotland, 23 February 1874.
Born: 30 May 1855; Died: 5 January 1944, Tarporley, Cheshire.
Edcuated: Rugby School, Oxford University.
Club: Oxford University (Blue 1873).
Son of the 1st Baron Crawshaw, he also won athletics Blues (1874-6) and broke the world high-jump record (6ft 2in) at Lillie Bridge, London, on 4 April 1876.

BROPHY
Thomas John

Fly-half. 1964-1966 (Liverpool, 8 caps).
Debut v Ireland, 8 February 1964.
Born: 8 July 1942, Liverpool.
Educated: Westpark Grammar School, Liverpool University.
Clubs: Liverpool, Loughborough Colleges, Barbarians, Lancashire (32 appearances), Barrow RL.
Brophy, who stood only 5ft 6ins tall, was a master at Rossall School and then Barrow Grammar School.

BROUGH
James Wasdale ('Jim')

Full-back. 1925 (Silloth, 2 caps).
Debut v New Zealand, 3 January 1925.
Born: 5 November 1903, Silloth; Died: 16 September 1986, Workington.
Clubs: Silloth, Cumberland.
Jim Brough, who once signed for Liverpool AFC as a trialist goalkeeper and full-back, was chosen to represent Cumberland before his 20th birthday. He played in all nine Championship matches of 1923-4 and scored a match-winning 50-yard drop-goal in the semi-final against Leicestershire as Cumberland went on to beat Kent in the Final at Carlisle.
In June 1925, however, he was tempted by Rugby League and signed for Leeds for a fee of £600. By 1944, he had made 442 appearances for the Leeds club, scoring 34 tries and 82 goals. His total points for the club was 266. He played for Cumberland and England after a few months with the RL club and gained six Yorkshire League Championship medals, five Yorkshire Challenge Cup winners' medals and two triumphs in the Rugby League Challenge Cup Final in 1932 and as captain in 1936. He was again on the winning side as a 38-year-old in a wartime Final in 1942. He toured Australia twice as a player, appearing in four Test matches, in 1928 and 1936 (captain in the latter year). He skippered Cumberland to a hat-trick of Championships between 1932 and 1935, and to victory over the 1933 Australian tourists. He retired from the game in 1938 to accept a business appointment in South Africa with Waddington's, the playing card manufacturers, but soon returned at the outbreak of war to play 12 more matches in the 'Emergency Competitions' organised throughout that period. He became coach in 1948-9 and was also coach at Whitehaven for a short spell. In 1958 he became the manager of Workington Town and then was appointed the Great Britain coach for a tour to Australia, the first time Great Britain had appointed a coach for such a tour.

BROUGHAM
Henry

Wing. 1912 (Harlequins, 4 caps).
Debut v Wales, 20 Janaury 1912.
Born: 8 July 1888, Wellington College;
Died: 18 February 1923, La Criox.
Educated: Wellington College, Oxford University.
Clubs: Oxford University (Blues at rackets and cricket), Harlequins.
Brougham scored a try on his international debut and a try in three out of four England appearances altogether. An all-round sportsman, he scored 84 in the 1911 Varsity match and also represented Berkshire from 1905 to 1914, playing for Minor Counties against the South Africans in 1912. He was all-comers singles rackets champion and won doubles championships with B.S.Foster. His career was spent mainly in the Army and during World War One he was badly gassed whilst serving as a major in the Royal Field Artillery. He died from phthisis contracted whilst serving in Ireland in 1918.

BROWN
Alan Arthur

Flanker. 1938 (Exeter, 1 cap).
Debut v Scotland, 19 March, 1938.
Born: 28 August 1911, St Helens.
Educated: Cowley School (St Helens), Carnegie College, St Luke's College (Exeter).
Clubs: Exeter, Aldershot Services, Barbarians, Lancashire, Devon.
Alan Brown served in the 4th Devonshire Regiment during World War Two. He was employed as a PE advisor.

BROWN
Leonard Graham, ('Bruno') MC

Prop. 1911-1922 (Oxford University, Blackheath, 18 caps).
Debut v Wales, 21 January 1911.
Born: 6 September 1888, Brisbane, Australia; Died: 23 May 1950, Charing Cross Hospital, London.
Educated: Brisbane Grammar School (Australia), Oxford University.
Clubs: Oxford University (Blues 1910-12, captain latter), London Hospital, Blackheath, Barbarians, Surrey, Queensland (Australia).
An ear, nose and throat specialist, Brown was a Rhodes Scholar who captained England against Wales in 1922. He played in the 1911 Calcutta Cup side, in the 1913 Grand Slam team (scoring a try in the Calcutta Cup match) and in the Triple Crown, Championship and Grand Slam side of 1914 (scoring a try against Wales in the opening match). He was also in the Triple Crown, Championship and Grand Slam XV of 1921 (with tries against Ireland and Scotland).
He represented New South Wales on the RFU Committee from 1922-1949

and was president from 1948-1949. His other posts included chairman of the Dominions Conference in 1947 and as an International Board representative he was chiefly responsible for obtaining International Board status for Australia, New Zealand and South Africa. He assisted in the founding of the Australian RFU in 1926.

During World War One he served as a captain in the RAMC and was later promoted to lieutenant-colonel. Awarded the Military Cross in 1917, he was mentioned in despatches in 1918.

BROWN
Thomas W.

Full-back. 1928-1933 (Bristol, 9 caps).
Debut v Scotland, 17 March 1928.
Born: 1907; Died: 14 May 1961.
Educated: Colston School, Bristol University.
Clubs: Bristol, Barbarians, Gloucestershire, Broughton Rangers RL.

Thomas Brown, who played in the Calcutta Cup wins of 1928 and 1932, made 171 appearances for Bristol before joining the Broughton Rangers RL club in 1933, later regretting his decision to change codes after the RFU refused him reinstatement. He worked as a licensee.

BRUNTON
Joseph, MC DSO

Lock. 1914 (North Durham, 3 caps).
Debut v Wales, 17 Janaury 1914.
Born: 21 August 1888; Died: 18 September 1971.
Clubs: North Durham, Rockcliffe, Army, Northumberland, North Midlands.

Brunton was a member of the 1914 Triple Crown, Championship and Grand Slam side. He was awarded the Military Cross in 1916, and bar in 1917, the DSO in 1918 and was mentioned in despatches three times. He served in World War Two with the Seaforth Highlanders and the Northumberland Fusiliers, the latter as a lieutenant-colonel commanding. He refereed Wales-New Zealand in 1925 and represented Northumberland on the RFU from 1945 to 1954, serving as RFU president from 1953 to 1954. He was a director of an engineering company.

BRUTTON
Ernest Batholomew (Rev)

Back. 1886 (Cambridge University, 1 cap).
Debut v Scotland, 13 March 1886.
Born: 1863, Newcastle upon Tyne; Died: 26 February 1942, Botleigh, Glastonbury.
Educated: Durham School, Cambridge University, Lichfield Theological College.
Clubs: Cambridge University (Blues 1883, 1884, 1886, the latter as captain), Northumberland, Durham County.

Brutton, who also won an athletics Blue in 1884, was a clergyman, ordained in 1888. He was assistant master at Lancing College and later vicar of Aylesbeare. He played cricket for Northumberland in 1891 and for Devon from 1901 to 1904.

BRYDEN
Charles Cowper

Forward. 1875-1877 (Clapham Rovers, 2 caps).
Debut v Ireland, 13 December 1875.
Born: 16 June 1852; Died: 20 February 1941.
Educated: Cheltenham College.
Club: Clapham Rovers.

He was the brother of Henry Bryden.

BRYDEN
Henry Anderson

Forward. 1874 (Clapham Rovers, 1 cap).
Debut v Scotland, 23 February 1874.
Born: 3 May 1854; Died: 23 September 1937, Park Stone, Dorset.
Educated: Cheltenham College.
Club: Clapham Rovers.

Brother of Charles Bryden, he was a good all-round sportsman who ran second to Walter Slade (RFU treasurer 1875-76), when he set the world mile record of 4min 24.5sec at Stamford Bridge on 19 June 1865. Between 1889 and 1936, Henry Bryden wrote numerous books specializing in African sport and natural history subjects.

BUCKINGHAM
Ralph Arthur, BEM

Centre. 1927 (Leicester, 1 cap).
Debut v France, 2 April 1927.
Born: 15 January 1907, Leicester.
Educated: Stoneygate Prep School, Rossall School.
Clubs: Leicester, Stoneygate, Barbarians, Leicestershire.

He served in World War Two with the Civil Defence Force and later as an RAF flight-lieutenant. He was awarded the British Empire Medal for gallantry in 1942.

BUCKNALL
Anthony Launce ('Tony')

Flanker 1969-1971 (Richmond, 10 caps).
Debut v South Africa, 20 December 1969.

Tony Bucknall

Born: 7 June 1945, Torquay.

Educated: Ampleforth College, Oxford University.

Clubs: Oxford University (Blues 1965-6; also boxing Blue), Chelmsford, Richmond, Middlesex, London Counties, Eastern Counties 1968-1978, Honourable Artillery Company (as member and coach).

A stockbroker, Tony Bucknall captained England against Wales on 16 January 1971. He is the brother-in-law of Allan Lamb, the Northamptonshire and England cricketer.

BUCKTON
John Richard

Centre. 1988-1990 (Saracens, 3 caps).
Debut v Australia, 12 June 1988.
Born: Hull, 22 December 1961.

Clubs: Hull & East Riding, Marist Old Boys, Saracens (Second Division champions 1988-9), Barbarians, Yorkshire (1987 champions).

Buckton was on the England tour to Australia and Fiji in 1988, playing in matches against Queensland Country and Queensland. He played for England 'B' against USSR and France in 1989-90.

BUDD
Arthur James

Forward. 1878-1881 (Blackheath, 6 caps).
Debut v Ireland, 11 March 1878.
Born: 14 October 1853, Bristol; Died: 27 August 1899, South Africa.

Educated: Clifton College, Cambridge University.

Clubs: Cambridge University, Bart's Hospital, Blackheath, Kent.

Budd emigrated to South Africa in 1893, where he died six years later. He was a touch-judge in the Scotland-England match of 1892. President of the RFU (1888-9) and member of the International Board (1890-95), he was one of the people mainly responsible for the formation of the London Society of Rugby Football Union Referees; as president of the RFU at that time he was voted to the chair at the inaugural meeting of the Society on 30 September 1889, which was held at the Anderton Hotel in Fleet Street, London. As chairman, he formally proposed the formation of the society and the motion was seconded by Sir G.Rowland-Hill. Budd was elected as the founder secretary of the Society and served in this position from 1889 to 1890. Budd also served as a referee during the Society's early days.

BUDWORTH
Richard Thomas Dutton

Forward. 1890-1891 (Blackheath, 3 caps).
Debut v Wales, 15 February, 1890.
Born: 17 October 1867; Died: 7 December 1937, London.

Educated: Christ's College (Brecon), Oxford University.

Clubs: Oxford University (Blues 1887-9), Blackheath, London Welsh, Barbarians, Kent, Sussex.

One of the original members of the Barbarians club, Budworth was a clergyman, being ordained in 1902. He taught at Lancing College, Clifton College and Durham School and served in World War One.

BULL
Arthur Gilbert

Prop. 1914 (Northampton, 1 cap).
Debut v Wales, 17 January 1914.
Clubs: Old Bedford Modernians, Northampton, Barbarians.

BULLOUGH
E.

Forward. 1892 (Wigan, 3 caps).
Debut: Wales, 2 January 1892.
Clubs: Wigan, Lancashire.

Bullough played for Wigan in their Union days but did not move over to the new code when they helped form the Northern Union in 1895. A strong, speedy player, known for his workmanlike displays, he was always to be found in the front-row forward positions. He was capped in England's Triple Crown season of 1892.

BULPITT
Michael Philip

Wing. 1970 (Blackheath, 1 cap).
Debut v Scotland, 21 March, 1970.
Born: 12 April 1944, Richmond, Yorkshire.

Educated: Berkhamsted School.

Clubs: Chelmsford, Osterley, Blackheath, Barbarians, London Counties, Eastern Counties.

Bulpitt is employed in advertising.

BULTEEL
A.J.

Forward. 1876 (Manchester, 1 cap).
Debut v Ireland, 13 December 1875.
Club: Manchester.

BUNTING
William Louis

Centre. 1897-1901 (Moseley, 9 caps).
Debut v Ireland, 6 February 1897.
Born: 9 August 1873; Died: 15 October 1947, Oldham, Hants.

Educated: Bromsgrove School, Cambridge Univesity.

Clubs: Cambridge University (Blues 1894-5), Bromsgrove, Richmond, Moseley, Kent, Barbarians, Midlands.

Bunting captained England twice in 1901, against Ireland on 9 February and against Scotland on 9 March. A member of Kent's County Championship side of 1897, he worked at Bromsgrove School whilst a member of the Moseley club.

BURLAND
Donald William

Centre. 1931-1933 (Bristol, 8 caps).
Debut v Wales, 17 January 1931.
Born: 22 January 1908; Died: 26 January 1976.

Clubs: Bristol, Barbarians, Gloucestershire.

Burland scored a try and a conversion on his England debut, against Wales at Twickenham in 1931, and a try against France the same year. In 1932 he was on the score-sheet again: in February, against Ireland at Lansdowne Road, he scored a try, a conversion and two penalty goals in England's 11-8 victory; the following month he kicked two conversions to help England to a Calcutta Cup victory against Scotland. He worked as a licensee and during World War Two served as a major in the Royal Army Service Corps.

BURNS
Benjamin Henry

Forward. 1871 (Blackheath, 1 cap).
Debut v Scotland, 27 March 1871.
Born: 28 May 1848, Scotland; Died: 3 June 1932.

Educated: Smerston's Private School (St Andrew's), Edinburgh Academy.

Clubs: Blackheath, Calcutta.

Burns played in the very first international between Scotland and England in 1871 at Raeburn Place. He was employed in banking, working mainly overseas.

BURTON
George William

Forward. 1879-1881 (Blackheath, 6 caps).
Debut v Scotland, 10 March 1879.
Born: 29 August, 1855; Died: 17 September 1890, Hampstead West, London.

Educated: Winchester College

Club: Blackheath.

A solicitor who scored the first try in the inaugural Calcutta Cup match in 1879, on his debut for England. In 1881 he scored four tries in the first England-Wales international.

BURTON
Hyde Clark

Wing. 1926 (Richmond, 1 cap).
Debut v Wales, 16 January 1926.
Born: 10 June 1898.

Educated: Royal Naval Engineering College (Keyham).

Clubs: Bishops Stortford, Richmond, Royal Navy, Barbarians, Eastern Counties.

He was employed as a chartered accountant and served in World War One with the Grand Fleet and in World War Two with Royal Naval Control in West Africa. He was later with the Trade and Naval Intelligence bodies at the Admiralty.

BURTON
Michael Alan

Prop. 1972-1978 (Gloucester, 17 caps).
Debut v Wales, 15 January 1972.
Born: 18 December 1945, Maidenhead.
Educated: Longlevens School.
Clubs: Longlevens, Gloucester, Barbarians, Berkshire, Gloucestershire.

Mike Burton's early sporting life was spent playing soccer but he joined the Longlevens club upon leaving school and qualified to play for Berkshire by birth, appearing for them in the Southern Group. In 1965 he joined Gloucester and played eight games for the United side before making his senior debut against Moseley. In 1972 he helped Gloucester win the very first RU KO Championship. He represented Gloucestershire at county level and appeared in the area England trial at Exeter in 1971 and in two full England trials. He was a member of the victorious Calcutta Cup team of 1975.

Mike Burton

Burton has the unenviable record of having been sent off in both hemisphere's of the rugby world. Whilst on tour with England to Australia in 1975 he was given his marching orders in the Second Test by referee R.T.Burnett in Brisbane, making him the first Englishman to be dismissed in an international match; the same year he was given the chance of an early bath when playing for Gloucestershire against Hertfordshire.
A director of a property company. His autobiography *Never Stay Down* was published in 1982.

BUSH
James Arthur

Forward. 1872-1876 (Clifton, 5 caps).
Debut v Scotland, 5 February 1872.
Born: 28 July 1850, Cawnpore, India; Died: 21 September 1924, Clevedon.
Educated: Clifton College.
Clubs: Clifton, Gloucestershire.

Jim Bush was also a fine cricketer. He appeared for England and Gloucestershire as a wicketkeeper, toured Australia with W.G.Grace's England side of 1873-74, and for the Gentleman v Players in 1874 and 1875.

BUTCHER
Christopher John Simon

Number 8. 1984 (Harlequins, 3 caps).
Debut v South Africa, 2 June 1984.
Born: 19 August 1960, Karachi.
Educated: St Peter's (Bournemouth).
Clubs: Harlequins, Middlesex, London Division.

Chris Butcher

Butcher played for England Schoolboys against Australia in 1978 and for the England Under-23s v the Netherlands in 1980. He went on the England senior tour to South Africa 1984 and remained there after the tour was over. He now works as a fisherman. He played alongside his brother, John, whilst with Harlequins. Another brother, David, played prop for London Scottish.

BUTCHER
Walter Vincent

Half-back. 1903-1905 (Streatham, 7 caps).
Debut v Scotland, 21 March 1903.
Born: 2 February 1878; Died: 26 August 1957, Bexhill.
Educated: Carlisle School.
Clubs: Bristol, Streatham, Barbarians, Gloucestershire.

Butcher, who played in the winning Calcutta Cup team of 1903, is still Streatham's most capped player. Later employed on the Indian Railways, he served in World War One as a captain in the Royal Engineers. He played cricket for Surrey 2nd XI.

BUTLER
Arthur Geoffrey

Wing. 1937 (Harlequins, 2 caps).
Debut v Wales, 16 January 1937.
Born: 30 September 1914, Oxford.
Educated: Royal Henley Grammar School.
Clubs: Henley, Harlequins, Barbarians, Oxfordshire, East Midlands.

Butler joined the Quins as a schoolboy in 1932 and played in their winning Middlesex Sevens team of 1935. Two of his three caps were awarded in England's Triple Crown success of 1927, when he scored a try in the 9-8 win against Ireland, his only international score. He had an electrifying burst of speed and was in the Great Britain athletic squad which went to Antwerp in 1937. He also won the Southern Countes 'double' of 100 and 220 yards. Butler, who was a farmer, was Oxfordshire representative on the RFU from 1950 and RFU president in 1963-4.

BUTLER
Peter Edward

Full-back. 1975-1976 (Gloucester, 2 caps).
Debut v Australia, 24 May 1975.

Peter Butler

Born: 23 June 1951, Gloucester.

Educated; Crypt Grammar School (Gloucester).

Clubs: Gloucester, Gloucestershire.

Peter Butler was a prolific goal-kicker, who in 1972-3 scored 324 points for Gloucester and the same season scored 102 points for Gloucestershire when they were County Championship runners-up. In 1973-4 his points total amounted to 574.

He was on the England tour of Australia in 1975, his debut coming in the First Test when he kicked one penalty-goal and a conversion. Despite being such a prolific kicker, he appeared in only two internationals, scoring in both. On his last appearance, against France in March 1976, he again kicked a conversion and a penalty-goal in a 30-9 defeat by the French.

BUTTERFIELD
Jeffrey

Centre. 1953-1959 (Northampton, 8 caps).
Debut v France, 28 February 1953.
Born: 9 August 1929, Heckmondwike, Yorkshire.

Jeff Butterfield

Educated: Cleckheaton Grammar School, Loughborough College.

Clubs: Cleckheaton, Northampton, Barbarians, Yorkshire (54 appearances, captain 1951-8).

Butterfield was on the British Lions tour of South Africa in 1955 and the trip to Australia and New Zealand in 1959, although he did not play in any of the Tests because of a thigh injury. When he retired from representative rugby at the end of that series he was England's most capped centre with 28 consecutive appearances.

He is one of only two Englishman to have scored tries on their debuts for both country and the Lions. He was in England's Five Nations Championship team of 1953, in the Calcutta Cup teams of 1954, 1955, 1956 and 1957 and in the Triple Crown and Grand Slam side of 1957. He played for the International XV which met Wales in April 1957, in a match organised to raise funds for the staging of the 1958 Empire Games in Cardiff.

He was the proprietor of the Rugby Club in London and also a PT master at Worksop College.

BYRNE
Francis A.

Centre. 1897 (Moseley, 1 cap).
Debut v Wales, 9 January 1897.
Born: 1873, Birmingham.

Clubs: Moseley, Midland Counties.

He played alongside his brother, Fred, in the England-Wales match in 1897, his only cap.

BYRNE
James Frederick

Full-back. 1894-1899 (Moseley, 13 caps).
Debut v Wales, 6 January 1894.
Born: 19 June 1871, Penns, Birmingham; Died: 10 May 1954, Birmingham.

Clubs: Moseley, Barbarians, Midland Counties (18 appearances).

A renowned tackler and drop-kicker, James Byrne played with his brother, Francis, in the 1897 England-Wales match. The following year he captained England three times (v Ireland, Scotland and Wales). Altogether he scored five penalty-goals and one conversion for England and on the British Lions tour of South Africa in 1896 he played in all 21 matches (including four Tests), scoring 127 points to become the only player to reach 100 points on a tour of that country until 1960.

Byrne also played cricket for Warwickshire from 1897 to 1907, captaining the county from 1903 to 1907, and appeared for the Gentleman v Players

in 1905. He served in the Boer War and when his playing days were over, he went on to become a leading industrialist in the Midlands.

CANDLER
Peter Lawrence

Fly half. 1935-1938 (St Bart's Hospital, 10 caps).
Debut v Wales, 19 January 1935.
Born: 28 January, 1914.
Died: 27 November 1991, Natal.

Educated: Sherborn School, Cambridge University.

Clubs: Cambridge University (Blue 1934), Bart's Hospital, Richmond, Barbarians, Middlesex.

Candler scored a try in the 1936 Calcutta Cup game and was in the Triple Crown team of 1937. His only other try was scored against Wales in 1938. He served in World War Two as a lieutenant-colonel in the Royal Army Medical Corps.

CANNELL
Lewis Bernard

Centre. 1948-1957 (Oxford University, St Mary's Hospital, 19 caps).
Debut v France, 29 March 1948.
Born: 10 June 1926, Coventry.

Educated: St Richard's College (Droitwich), Northampton Grammar School, Oxford University.

Clubs: Oxford University (Blues 1948-50), St Mary's Hospital, Northampton, RAF, Combined Services, Barbarians, London Counties, East Midlands, Middlesex.

Cannell was in the 1949 Calcutta Cup-winning side. His only try was scored in the 8-3 win over France in February 1949. Employed at Addington Hospital, Durban, South Africa.

CAPLAN
David William Nigel

Full-back. 1978 (Headingley, 2 caps).
Debut v Scotland, 4 March 1978.
Born: 5 April 1954, Leeds.

Educated: Leeds Grammar School, Newcastle University, Oxford University.

Clubs: Oxford University, Headingley, Yorkshire (26 appearances).

A dentist by profession, Caplan was in the 1978 Calcutta Cup-winning side.

CARDUS
Richard Michael

Centre. 1979 (Roundhay, 3 caps).
Debut v France, 3 March 1979.
Born: 23 May 1956, Leeds.
Educated: Foxwood School.

Richard Cardus

John Carleton

Clubs: Roundhay, Wasps, Cardiff.

Cardus captained both Rounday and Wasps, leading the latter club to the 1986 JPS Cup Final.

CAREY
Godfrey Mohun

Forward. 1895-1896 (Blackheath, 5 caps).
Debut v Wales, 5 January 1895.
Born: 17 August 1872, Guernsey; Died: 18 December 1927.
Educated: Sherborne School, Oxford University.
Clubs: Oxford University (Blues 1891, 1892 and 1894), Barbarians, Blackheath, Somerset (captain).

Carey, who scored a try on his international debut, was a member of the Barbarians committee and a master at Sherborne School from 1897 to 1927. He was the son of Sir Godfrey Carey.

CARLETON
John

Wing. 1979-1984 (Orrell, 26 caps).
Debut v New Zealand, 24 November 1979.
Born: 24 November 1955, Orrell.
Educated: Upholland Grammar School, Chester College.
Clubs: Orrell, Cheshire, Lancashire, North & Midlands, North.

In the Grand Slam win of 1980, John Carleton scored three tries against Scotland to become the first Englishman to score a hat-trick in an international match since H.P.Jacob in 1924.

Carleton's rugby career had taken shape as he qualified as a schoolteacher at Chester College. He played for British Colleges and England Students (against Japan) in 1976, for England Under-23s against France and against Canada

(under the managership of Budge Rogers) in 1977 and for an England XV against the United States in 1979, the year that he went on the full England trip to the Far East.

He was a member of the historic North of England team which beat the All Blacks in November 1979 and the following year resigned his job as a PE and maths master so that he could tour South Africa with the Lions. In ten matches on that tour he scored three tries.

He went with England to Argentina in 1981 and to the USA and Canada in 1982. And he was on the British Lions tour of New Zealand in 1983, heading the list of try scorers with nine. Work, though, prevented him from touring with England to South Africa in 1984. In all he scored seven tries in his 26 internationals.

He also made 20 appearances for Lancashire including the 1980 County Championship-winning side for whom he scored a try in the Final.

CARLING
William David Charles

Centre. 1988-1992 (Durham University, Harlequins 36 caps).
Debut v France, 16 January 1988.

Born: 12 December 1965, Bradford-on-Avon, Wiltshire.
Educated: Sedbergh School, Durham University, Royal Military Academy (Sandhurst).
Clubs: Durham University, Army, Harlequins, Barbarians.

Will Carling, skipper of England's 1991 World Cup Final team, is one of the most high-profile rugby players of recent times, a man said by many to be England's best captain for over 50 years.

The son of an Army brigadier, who played rugby for Cardiff, Carling read psychology at Durham and played for the Army whilst on a scholarship at Sandhurst, helping them win the Inter-Services Tournament. He resigned his

Will Carling

commission upon returning from England's tour of Fiji and Australia in 1988 and formed his own business, *Inspirational Horizons,* a company which uses top sportsmen to teach executives how to succeed.

He played for England Schools for two seasons, finishing as captain in 1984 and his first game in charge of the senior team was against Australia in November 1988. He recovered from a fractured leg in 1989 to continue in the job in great style, leading England to consecutive Grand Slams in 1991 and 1992 and to a successful World Cup campaign. Just before the World Cup he turned down a million-pound offer to switch to Rugby League.

He toured Argentina with England in 1990, appeared in that year's London Division Toshiba Championship-winning team and helped Quins win the 1991 Pilkington Cup.

Carling, who survived a serious traffic accident in December 1990, is a keen artist who enjoys painting and sketching. When he skippered England to a second Grand Slam he became the second former Sedburgh School pupil to do so, the other being the great Wavell Wakefield.

CARPENTER
Alfred Denzel

Prop. 1932 (Gloucester, 1 cap).
Debut v South Africa, 2 January 1932.
Born: 23 July 1900, Mitcheldean; Died: 18 April 1974.
Clubs: Littledean, Cinderford, Gloucester, RAF, Barbarians, Gloucestershire.

Carpenter served with the RAF in World War Two. His early education was spent in Swansea and was employed as a collier upon leaving school.

CARR
Robert Stanley Leonard, MC

Wing. 1939 (Manchester, 3 caps).
Debut v Wales, 21 January 1939.
Born: 11 July 1917; Died: 1977.
Educated: Cranleigh School.
Clubs: Old Cranleighans, Manchester, Moseley.

Carr was in the Calcutta Cup-winning side of 1939. He served with the Manchester Regiment and later the King's African Rifle Brigade in World War Two and was awarded the Military Cross in 1941.

CARTWRIGHT
Vincent Henry, DSO

Forward. 1903-1906 (Nottingham, 14 caps).
Debut v Wales, 10 January 1903.
Born: 10 September 1882, Nottingham; Died: 25 November 1965, Loughborough.
Educated: Rugby School, Oxford University.
Clubs: Nottingham, Oxford University

(Blues 1901-1904), Harlequins, Barbarians, Midlands.

A fast and devastating tackler, Cartwright captained Nottingham to their Midland Counties Cup win of 1906 and is that club's most capped player. He captained England on five occasions, against New Zealand, Wales, Ireland, Scotland (a Calcutta Cup-winning game) and France in 1906 but despite playing in 14 internationals, his only score for his country were four conversions against France in 1906. He played for Midland Counties against New Zealand in 1905 and captained the Harlequins from 1905 to 1907.

An England selector, he represented South Africa on the RFU from 1921 to 1929 and on the International Board from 1929 to 1931. An RFU committeeman, he was president from 1928 to 1929.

As a referee he took charge of Ireland-Scotland in 1906, Scotland-Ireland in 1909, Ireland-Scotland and France-Ireland in 1910, Scotland-Ireland in 1911 and the centenary match at Rugby School on 1 November 1923. He also played cricket for Nottinghamshire from 1901 to 1904.

During World War Two, Cartwright, who was a solicitor by profession, served as a major in the Royal Marines, twice being mentioned in despatches and awarded the DSO in 1918 and the Croix de Guerre.

CATCHESIDE
Howard Carston, OBE

Wing. 1924-1927 (Percy Park, 8 caps).
Debut v Wales, 19 January 1924.
Born: 18 August 1899.
Educated: Oundle School.
Clubs: Percy Park, Northumberland.

Catcheside scored six tries in his first four England games and tries in every match of the 1924 Grand Slam season — a record for an England player. He served as a second-lieutenant in the Royal Field Artillery during World War One and in World War Two reaching the rank of lieutenant-colonel. He was awarded the OBE (Mil) 1945 and was an England selector from 1936 to 1962, being chairman from 1951 to 1962.

CATTELL
Richard Henry Burdon

Half-back. 1895-1900 (Blackheath, 7 caps).

Richard Cattell

Debut v Wales, 5 January 1895.
Born: 23 March 1871, Birmingham; Died: 19 July 1948.
Educated: Trinity College (Stratford upon Avon), Oxford University.
Clubs: Oxford University (Blue 1893), Blackheath, Moseley, Barbarians, Midland Counties.
Cattell was England's skipper against Wales in 1900. A clergyman who was ordained in 1897, he served in World War One as Chaplain to the Forces. He changed from playing rugby to soccer in 1898, when he joined Welwyn AFC until 1903 and then Tring Town until 1906.

CAVE
John Atkins
Forward. 1889 (Richmond, 1 cap).
Debut v Maoris, 16 February 1889.
Born: 5 February 1867, Surbiton; Died: 4 December 1949, Wokingham.
Educated: Wellington School, Cambridge University.
Clubs: Cambridge University (Blues 1887-8), Richmond, Surrey.
Cave was a master at Wellington College from 1893 to 1923. He was the son of the Honourable Justice Cave.

CAVE
William Thomas Charles.
Forward. 1905 (Blackheath, 1 cap).
Debut v Wales, 14 January 1905.
Born: 24 November 1882.
Educated: Tonbridge School, Cambridge University.
Clubs: Cambridge University (Blues 1902-04), Blackheath, Barbarians, Kent.
He went on the British Lions tour of South Africa in 1903. A solicitor by profession, he was a PoW in World War One.

CHALLIS
Robert
Full-back. 1957 (Bristol, 3 caps).
Debut v Ireland, 9 February 1957.
Born: 9 March 1932.
Educated: Cathedral School (Bristol).
Clubs: Old Chaedralians, Bristol, Somerset (20 appearances).
Challis scored a penalty-goal on his international debut but played only three games for England, all in the 1957 Grand Slam season when he scored a penalty-goal and two conversions against Scotland in the Calcutta Cup match. Challis has been credited as the first player to place-kick penalties into touch, the first occasion coming on his debut against Ireland in 1957. He played cricket for Somerset 2nd XI.

CHAMBERS
Ernest Leonard MC
Forward. 1908-1909 (Bedford, 3 caps).
Debut v France, 1 January 1908.

Born: 24 July 1882, London; Died: 23 November 1946, Cheam.
Educated: Bedford School, Cambridge University.
Clubs: Cambridge University (Blue 1904), Blackheath, Bedford, Kent, East Midlands.
Besides winning Blues at Rugger, Chambers also gained a Blue at athletics, in the hammer throw in 1904. A teacher at Bedford Grammar School, he served in World War One with the Bedfordshire Regiment and the Northumberland Fusiliers, and later with the Yorkshire Light Infantry. Mentioned in despatches, he was awarded the Military Cross in 1917.

CHANTRILL
Bevan Stanislaus
Full-back. 1924 (Bristol, 4 caps).
Debut v Wales, 19 January 1924.
Born: 11 February 1897.
Educated: Bristol Grammar School.
Clubs: Clifton, RAF, Durban R (South Africa), Natal, Weston-super-Mare, Bristol, Richmond, Manchester, Rosslyn Park, Gloucestershire, Somerset.
All Chantrill's caps were won during the 1924 Grand Slam, Calcutta Cup and Triple Crown season. He served in both world wars, in World War One in the Queen's Own Hussars and in the Gloucestershire Regiment, joining up at the age of 17; and in World War Two in the South African Air Force and Royal Air Force. In 1920 he went to South Africa to prospect for gold until the early 1960s.

CHAPMAN
Charles Edward
Back. 1884 (Cambridge University, 1 cap).
Debut v Wales, 5 January 1884.
Born: 26 August 1860, Swinsted; Died; 23 August 1901.
Educated: Horncastle Grammar School, Trent College, St Paul's School (Stoney Stratford), Oxford University, Cambridge Univesity.
Clubs: Oxford University, Cambridge University (Blues 1881 and 1884), Eden Wanderers, Trojans, Hampshire.
Besides a rugger Blue, Chapman also won an athletics Blue in 1894 for throwing the hammer. A clergyman, ordained in 1894, he played cricket for Cambridge University. He committed suicide.

CHAPMAN
Frederick Ernest
Wing or Centre. 1910 (Hartlepool, 7 caps).
Debut v Wales, 15 January 1910.
Born: South Shields in 1888; Died: 8 May 1938.
Educated: South Shields High School, Durham University.

Clubs: Westoe, Hartlepool Rovers, Durham Counties.
In the first ever international match at Twickenham, Chapman scored a try, a penalty-goal and a conversion in England's first victory over the Welsh since 1898. In total he scored one try, one penalty-goal and six conversions for England and was in the Calcutta Cup-winning side of 1910, the Championship-winning side of 1910 and played in the first game of the 1914 Triple Crown, Championship and Grand Slam triumph. He toured New Zealand with the British Lions in 1908. During World War One he served with the Royal Army Medical Corps and was twice wounded.

CHEESMAN
William Inkersole
Scrum-half. 1913 (Old Merchant Taylor's, 4 caps).
Debut v South Africa, 4 January 1913.
Born: 20 June 1889; Died: 20 November 1969.
Educated: Merchant Taylor's School, Oxford University.
Clubs: Oxford University (Blues 1910-11), Old Merchant Taylor's.
An accomplished all-round sportsman, who played soccer, hockey, cricket and lawn tennis, his caps came in what was to be England's golden era from 1913 when they won the Championship, Triple Crown and Grand Slam titles. Employed as a teacher at Marlborough College, he later worked in Kenya and the Sudan.

CHESTON
Ernest Constantine
Forward. 1873-1876 (Richmond, 5 caps).
Debut v Scotland, 3 March 1873.
Born: 24 October 1848; Died: 9 July 1913.
Education: Haileybury and Imperial Service College, Oxford University.
Clubs: Oxford University, Richmond.

CHILCOTT
Gareth James ('Coochie')
Prop. 1984-1989 (Bath, 14 caps).
Debut v Australia, 3 November, 1984.
Born: 20 November 1956, Bristol.
Educated: Aditon School (Bristol).
Clubs: Old Redcliffians, Bath, Somerset, South West.
Gareth Chilcott was one of the most recognisable figures in British rugby in the 1980s. He played for Bath from 1975, latterly as vice-captain, and appeared in five winning JPS/Pilkington Cup Final teams and in the side which won the Courage League Championship in 1989, 1991 and again in 1992. He went on the British Lions tour of Australia in 1989, playing in five matches but no Tests, and captained a Bath XV which took part in the 1991 centenary tournament in Toulouse.

Gareth Chilcott

CLARKE
Allan James

Lock. 1935-1936 (Coventry, 6 caps).
Debut v Wales, 19 January 1935.
Born: 21 February 1913; Died: 25 September 1975, Coventry.
Clubs: Coventry, Warwickshire.

Allan Clarke

A giant of a man who weighed 17st, Clarke was definitely an asset to any scrum and could easily hold his own in the roughest of situations. He was a farmer, then a hotelier.

CLARKE
Simon John Scott

Scrum-half. 1963-1965 (Cambridge University, Blackheath, 13 caps).
Debut v Wales, 19 January 1963.
Born: 2 April, 1938, Westcliff.
Educated: Wellington College, Cambridge University.
Clubs: Cambridge University (Blues 1962-3), Hove, Davenport Services, Royal Navy, Bath, Yokohama (Japan), Blackheath, Rosslyn Park, Barbarians, Kent, Devon, Sussex.

Chilcott suffered many injuires during his career, including a broken nose and dislocation of both knees. He was omitted from the England squad in 1987 because of disciplinary reasons after an incident during the game in Cardiff that year. He was in the England team which competed in the Great North Race (half-marathon).

Employed in various jobs from lumberjack, managing director of a car-hire company and security officer, he worked for ITV during the 1991 World Cup. His autobiography *Cooch: Mr Chilcott to You* was published in November 1990.

CHRISTOPHERSON
Percy, JP

Back. 1891 (Blackheath, 2 caps).
Debut v Wales, 3 January 1891.
Born: 31 March 1866, Blackheath; Died: 4 May 1921, Folkestone.
Educated: Marlborough College, Bedford School, Oxford University.

Clubs: Oxford University (1886-8, latter as captain), Blackheath, Barbarians, Kent.

Christopherson scored a try on his international debut for England. He captained Blackheath and Kent and also played cricket for Oxford University, Berkshire and, briefly, for Kent. He was employed as a teacher at Wellington College.

CLARK
Charles William Henry

Half-back. 1876 (Liverpool, 1 cap).
Debut v Ireland, 13 December.
Born: 19 March 1857; Died: 11 May 1943, Battersea.
Educated: Rugby School.
Clubs: Liverpool, Lancashire, Ormskirk GS.
Clark was captain of Ormskirk in 1914.

Clarke played in the Championship and Calcutta Cup-winning sides of 1963. His only score came against Australia in January 1963, when he scored a try in the 18-9 defeat by the Aussies. He had an outstanding game in the 1963 Varsity match, served as a second lieutenant in the Royal Marines and played for the Royal Navy in the Inter-services tournament. He played cricket for Cambridge University (1961-1962) as well as for the Combined Services and Kent 2nd XI.

CLAYTON
John Henry

Forward. 1871 (Liverpool, 1 cap).
Debut v Scotland, 27 March 1871.
Born: 24 August 1849; Died: 21 March 1924.
Educated: Rugby School.
Clubs: Liverpool, Lancashire.

His only cap came in the very first international, Scotland v England in 1871. He played golf for the Royal Liverpool Golf Club, captaining the side. He lost his life in a London taxi cab, unfortunately the details are unclear.

CLEMENTS
Jeffrey Woodward

Flanker. 1959 (Old Cranleighans, 3 caps).
Debut v Ireland, 14 February 1959.
Born: 18 August 1932.
Educated: Cranleigh School, Cambridge University.
Clubs: Old Cranleighans, Cambridge University (Blues 1953-1955), Royal Navy, Devonport Service, US Portsmouth, Barbarians, Hampshire (9 appearances).

Clements was a master at his old school, Cranleigh. He played cricket for Singapore and Malaysia.

CLEVELAND
Sir Charles Raitt, KCIB KBE

Forward. 1887 (Blackheath, 2 caps).
Debut v Wales, 8 January 1887.
Born: 2 November 1866, Bombay, India; Died: 18 January 1929.
Educated: Christ's College (Finchley), Oxford University.
Clubs: Oxford University (Blues 1885-6), Blackheath, Kent.

Whilst at Oxford he also won an athletic Blue for the hammer throw. He held a post in the Indian Civil Service.

CLIBBORN
W.G.

Forward. 1886-1887 (Richmond, 6 caps).
Debut v Wales, 2 January 1886.
Club: Richmond.

He was selected for the 1888 England side that did not play.

CLOUGH
Francis John

Centre. 1986-1987 (Cambridge University, Orrell, 4 caps).
Debut v Ireland, 1 March 1986.
Born: 1 November 1962, Wigan.
Educated: St John Rigby Roman Catholic VI College, Durham University, Cambridge University.
Clubs: Cambridge University (Blues and captain 1986-7), Orrell.

He also played for England Under-23s and for England 'B' against France 'B'.

COATES
Charles Hutton

Forward. 1880-1882 (Yorkshire West, 3 caps).
Debut v Scotland, 28 February 1880.
Born: 4 May 1857; Died: 14 February 1922, Boscombe, Hampshire.
Educated: Christ's College (Finchley), Cambridge University.
Clubs: Cambridge University (Blues 1877-9), Leeds and Yorkshire West, Bishop Auckland, Surrey, Yorkshire (3 appearances, 1880-81).

Coates also won Blues at archery and rowing. A clergyman, he was ordained in 1881 and was Chaplain to the Royal Navy from 1885 to 1891.

COATES
Vincent Middleton Hope, MC

Wing. 1913 (Bath, 5 caps).
Debut v South Africa, 4 January 1913.
Born: 18 May 1889; Died: 14 November 1934, Maidenhead.
Educated: Monkton Combe School, Haileybury Imperial Service College, Cambridge University.
Clubs: Cambridge University (Blue 1907), Bridgwater, Bath, Leicester, Richmond, Barbarians, Somerset (20 appearances, later as captain).

In his only season as an internationalist, Coates scored six tries in the Championship to create a record which was surpassed by C.N.Lowe the following year. Coates scored one try against Wales, three against France and two against Ireland. He also played cricket for Somerset. He served in World War One with the Royal Army Medical Corps. Mentioned in despatches, he was awarded the Military Cross on the Somme battlefield in 1916. He died after falling from a moving train.

COBBY
William

Forward. 1900 (Hull, 1 cap).
Debut v Wales, 6 January 1900.
Born: 5 July 1877, Kingston upon Hull; Died: 15 January 1957.
Educated: Uppingham School, Cambridge University.
Clubs: Cambridge University (Blue

1900), Hull, Castleford, Hull & East Riding, Barbarians, Yorkshire (17 appearances, captain 1901-02).

COCKERHAM
Arthur

Forward. 1900 (Bradford Olicana, 1 cap).
Debut v Wales, 6 January 1900.
Clubs: Bradford Olicana, Manningham RL, Yorkshire (6 appearances).

COLCLOUGH
Maurice John

Lock. 1978-1986 (Angouleme, Wasps, Swansea, 25 caps).
Debut v Scotland, 4 March 1978.
Born: 2 September 1953, Oxford.

Maurice Colclough

Educated: Duke of York's Royal Military School, Liverpool University.
Clubs: East Grinstead, Liverpool, Rosslyn Park, Wasps, Sussex, Liverpool University, Lancashire, Queensland 'B', Angouleme (France), Swansea.

In November 1983, red-haired Maurice Colclough scored the decisive try early in the second half of England's first home win over the All Blacks for 47 years.

In 1980, the year he was a member of England's Grand Slam side, he played in all 11 matches on the British Lions tour to South Africa and went to New Zealand in 1983 only after a late fitness test. His other representative games include London v Argentina and New Zealand in 1978, London v Australia in 1981 and London v New Zealand in 1983. He also toured the Far East with England in 1979 and the USA and Canada in 1982 as well as going with Lancashire to Rhodesia and South Africa in 1974 and starring for Queensland 'B' against New Zealand in 1979. He is an honorary member of the Fiji RFU.

COLEY
Eric, OBE TD

Number 8. 1929-1932 (Northampton, 2 caps).
Debut v France, 1 April, 1929.
Born: 23 July 1903, Northampton; Died: 3 May 1957, Northampton.
Educated: Northampton Town & County School.
Clubs: Northampton, East Midlands, Army, Barbarians.
Coley was an England selector from 1937 to 1948 and Northamptonshire CCC secretary from 1933 to 1937. He served in World War Two as a brigadier in the Royal Artillery and was awarded the OBE (Military) in 1952. His son, David, played for Northampton and East Midlands. Eric Coley was a hotel owner.

COLLINS
Philip John

Full-back. 1952 (Camborne, 3 caps).
Debut v Scotland, 15 March 1952.
Born: 4 November 1928.
Clubs: Camborne, Cornwall (25 appearances).
Collins made his debut in the Calcutta Cup victory of 1952.

COLLINS
William Edward, CMG

Half-back. 1874-1876 (Old Cheltonians, 5 caps).
Debut v Scotland, 23 February 1874.
Born: 14 October 1853, Monghyr, India; Died: 11 August 1934, Wellington, New Zealand.
Educated: Cheltenham College, Oxford University.
Clubs: Old Cheltonians, St George's Hospital, Oxford University (no Blue).
He was a member of the Legislative Council for New Zealand in 1907, after emigrating to that country in 1878. He served in World War One in the New Zealand Medical Corps and was awarded the CMG in 1917. He played in the first Hospital Cup Final between St George's and Guy's Hospitals in 1875.

CONSIDINE
Stanley George Ulick

Wing. 1925 (Bath, 1 cap).
Debut v France, 13 April 1925.
Born: 11 August 1901, India; Died: 31 August 1950, Bath.
Educated: Blundell's School.
Clubs: Bath, Somerset (23 appearances).
As well as playing rugger, he also had a successful cricket career, scoring over 3,000 runs for Somerset. He played in the 1920 Irish trials. He was a solicitor.

CONWAY
Geoffrey Seymour, MC TD.

Lock/Number 8. 1920-1927 (Cambridge University, Rugby, Manchester, 18 caps).
Debut v France, 31 January 1920.
Born: 15 November 1897.
Educated: Fettes College, Cambridge University.
Clubs: Cambridge University (Blues 1919-1921), Rugby, Harlequins, Hartlepool Rovers, Manchester, Blackheath, Barbarians, Lancashire, Durham.

Geoff Conway

Conway scored England's most conversions in a Championship when he kicked seven in four games. He was a very reliable all-round forward, a member of the 1920 Calcutta Cup team and of the Grand Slam sides of 1923 (scoring a try against France and two conversions against Ireland) and 1924 (scoring seven conversions in four games). A teacher at Rugby School, he later became a schools inspector and worked as an archaeologist in the Greek islands from 1961 to 1969 before settling in France. He served in World War One, being awarded the Military Cross in 1917. In World War Two he gained promotion to lieutenant-colonel.

COOK
John Gilbert

Flanker. 1937 (Bedford, 1 cap).
Debut v Scotland, 20 March 1937).
Born: 16 May 1911, Hougton Regis, Bedford; Died: 1979, Overstrand, Norfolk.
Educated: Bedford School.
Clubs: Bedford, Barbarians, East Midlands (14 appearances).
Cook was in the 1937 Calcutta Cup side and played cricket for the Gentlemen of Ireland and Bedfordshire.

COOK
Peter William

Wing. 1965 (Richmond, 2 caps).
Debut v Ireland, 13 February 1965.
Born: 8 January 1943, Eycombe.
Educated: Dulwich College.
Clubs: Richmond, Barbarians, Surrey, London Counties.
Peter Cook was an engineering student.

COOKE
David Alexander

Centre. 1976 (Harlequins, 4 caps).
Debut v Wales, 17 January 1976.
Born: 10 February 1949, Malta.
Educated: Gravesend Grammar School.
Club: Harlequins.
A school teacher by profession, David Cooke went on England's Under-23 three-match tour of France and Italy in 1979.

COOKE
David Howard

Flanker. 1981-1985 (Harlequins, 12 caps).

Dave Cooke

Debut v Wales, 17 January 1981.
Born: 19 November 1955, Brisbane, Australia.
Educated: Haileybury Imperial Service College, North-East London Polytechnic.
Clubs: Harlequins, London Division, Middlesex, Barbarians.

An estate agent, this David Cooke played in the 1985 Calcutta Cup team and for England Under-23 v France in 1977 and went on the Under-23 tour to Canada, France, Italy and the Netherlands in 1977. He also went on the England tour to the USA and Canada in 1982.

COOKE
Paul

Scrum-half. 1939 (Richmond, 2 caps).
Debut v Wales, 21 January 1939.
Born: 18 December 1916; Died: 1 May 1940, Calais (killed in action).
Educated: Oxford University.
Clubs: Oxford Univesity (Blues 1936-7), Richmond, Barbarians.

Paul Cooke toured with the British Lions to Argentina in 1936. A bank offcial by profession, he served in World War Two as a second lieutenant in the Oxfordshire & Buckinghamshire Light Infantry.

COOP
Thomas

Full-back. 1892 (Leigh, 1 cap).
Debut v Scotland, 5 March 1869.
Born: 10 February 1863, Tottington, Lancashire.
Clubs: Tottington, Broughton, Leigh, Lancashire (20 appearances).

Tom Coop turned to Rugby League when Leigh helped form the Northern Union in 1895, three years before he retired. He was said to be one of the finest players ever to appear in Leigh's colours and a player who had the largest single influence on the early development of the club. A regular in the Lancashire side, he was selected for England's Triple Crown decider against Scotland in March 1892, his only cap. He was a regular in the Leigh side, even at a veteran age, and proved himself a capable tactician and place-kicker. A fine left-footed kicker, a serious shoulder injury ended his career in 1898.

COOPER
John Graham

Forward. 1909 (Moseley, 2 caps).
Debut v Australia, 9 January 1909.
Born: 3 June 1881; Died: 26 October 1965.
Educated: Aston Grammar School.
Clubs: Moseley, Midlands.

John Cooper was a solicitor who later emigrated to Canada. He served in World War One with the Royal Warwickshire Regiment and was mentioned in despatches in 1917.

COOPER
Martin John

Fly-half. 1973-1977 (Moseley, 11 caps).
Debut v France, 24 February 1973.
Born: 23 April 1948, Burton upon Trent.

Martin Cooper

Educated: Burton upon Trent Grammar School, Wednesfield Grammar School.
Clubs: Wolverhampton, Moseley, Barbarians, Staffordshire.

Employed by a building society, he played for the Midlands side in the England regional trial in December 1971.

COOPPER
Sidney Frank

Wing. 1900-1907 (Blackheath, 7 caps).
Debut v Wales, 6 January 1900.
Born: 1878, October; Died: 16 January 1961.
Educated: Royal Naval Engineering College (Keyham).
Clubs: Blackheath, Barbarians, Devon.

Coopper served in World War One as a Royal Naval engineering officer on destroyers and once his ship was sunk. He was mentioned in despatches. From 1924 to 1947 he was secretary of the RFU. He was the RFU secretary in 1924-5, 1932-3, 1933-4 and 1946-7.

CORBETT
Leonard James

Centre. 1921-1927 (Bristol, 16 caps).
Debut v France, 28 March 1921.
Born: 12 May 1897, Bristol; Died: 26 January 1983, Taunton.
Educated: Fairfield School.

Clubs: Bristol Saracens, Bristol, Gloucestershire.

Leonard Corbett, who captained England four times, was known as the 'd'Artagnan' of centre-threequarters. He was said to have been an immaculate dresser and a very quick-witted gentleman. He made his debut in the last match of the Grand Slam season of 1921 and his first score for his country came in February 1924, when England beat Ireland 14-3, in what was also a Grand Slam-winning season. He made 222 appearances for the Bristol club.

Corbett was superintendant of the Royal Ordnance Factory at Bridgend, serving with the Royal Army Service Corps during World War One. Later he was the rugby and cricket correspondent of the *Sunday Times*.

CORLESS
Barrie James

Centre. 1976-1978 (Coventry, Moseley, 10 caps).
Debut v Australia, 3 January 1976.
Born: 7 November 1945, Booton, Norfolk.

Barrie Corless

Educated: Wymondham College.
Clubs: Coventry, Moseley, Barbarians.

Corless scored a try on his debut for England and was in the 1978 Calcutta Cup team. He is a schoolmaster.

Fran Cotton

COTTON
Francis Edward

Prop. 1971-1981 (Loughborough College, Coventry, Sale, 30 caps).
Debut v Scotland, 20 March 1971.
Born: 3 January 1948, Wigan.
Educated: Newton-le-Willows Grammar School, Loughborough College.
Clubs: Liverpool, Loughborough Colleges, Coventry, Sale, Barbarians, Lancashire (74 appearances).

Fran Cotton took up rugby at grammar school. He helped Loughborough Colleges, where he was studying to become a teacher, win the UAU Championship in 1972-3 and the same season was in the Lancashire side which won the County Championship.

In 1970 he had appeared for England Under-25s against Fiji and had a long international career. He won his first full cap whilst still at college and was 33 when he played in the 1981 Grand Slam side. In 1972 he captained the North-West Counties to victory over the All Blacks, the first occasion they had

lost to an English provincial side. Once England's most capped prop, he went on the British Lions tours of South Africa in 1974 and New Zealand in 1977. Recurring leg infections compelled him to retire from the game in 1981 and he is joint owner and founder of rugby merchandising company *Cotton Traders* with former England stars Steve Smith and Tony Neary. His father was a Rugby League player. Cotton's book *Fran — an autobiography* was published in 1981.

COULMAN
Michael John

Prop. 1967-1968 (Moseley, 9 caps).
Debut v Australia, 7 January 1967.
Born: 6 May 1944, Stafford.
Educated: Rising Brook Secondary Modern School (Stafford).
Clubs: Stafford, North Midlands, Staffordshire, Staffordshire Police, Knowsley, Moseley, British Police (captain), Salford RL.

Coulman, whose first taste of interna-

tional rugby was for England Under-19s, played in the Calcutta Cup teams of 1967 and 1968 and went on the British Lions tour of South Africa in 1968.

As a policeman at Stone, he was Midlands Police heavyweight boxing champion in 1964-5 and Staffordshire Police 100 yards and 220 yards champion in 1967.

He joined Salford RL club in September 1968, making his debut for them against Rochdale Hornets the following month. He helped Salford to the 1968-9 RL Challenge Cup Final, was the 'Man of the Match' in the 1973-4 Lancashire Cup Final (which Salford lost) and was in their 1973-4 and 1975-6 First Division Championship teams. He scored five tries on three occasions during his RL career, including one try for Great Britain. He represented Lancashire RL and shared a joint-testimonial with Colin Dixon in 1978-9.

Coulman, one of the few Rugby Union forwards to succeed in the League game, last played for Salford at Bramley in April 1983 and then became the club's coach but was sacked in May 1984. His 135 tries are a record for a Salford player and he amassed 408 points altogether with one goal and one drop-goal. He played 441 times for the club and was substitute on 22 occasions. He appeared for both the Great Britain and England RL teams and played in the 1975 World Championships in Australia. He later worked as a restaurant manager.

COULSON
Thomas John

Prop or number 8. 1927-1928 (Coventry, 3 caps).
Debut v Wales, 15 January 1927.
Born: 31 December 1896; Died: 26 March 1948.
Clubs: Gloucester, Coventry, Warwickshire, Midlands Counties.

Coulson was employed in the aircraft industry. He served in World War One with the 4th Hussars.

COURT
Edward Darlington

Forward. 1865 (Blackheath, 1 cap).
Debut v Wales, 3 January 1885.
Born: 22 June 1862; Died: 2 April 1935.
Educated: Rugby School, Oxford University.
Clubs: Oxford University (Blues 1882-3), Blackheath, Kent.

He was employed in the Civil Service.

COVERDALE
Harry

Fly-half. 1910-1920 (Blackheath, 4 caps).
Debut v France, 3 March 1910.
Born: 22 March 1889, Hartlepool; Died: 29 October 1965, South Africa.
Educated: Rossall School.
Clubs: Hartlepool Rovers, Blackheath, Barbarians, Durham County, Surrey.

Coverdale, who played soccer at Rossall School, was an England selector from 1931 to 1948. In 1949 he emigrated to South Africa, where he lived until his death. He served in World War One in the Army and the Royal Flying Corps, and in World War Two in the RAF.

COVE-SMITH
Ronald ('Cove')

Lock. 1921-1929 (Old Merchant Taylor's, 29 caps).
Debut v Scotland, 19 March 1921.
Born: 26 November 1899.
Educated: Merchant Taylor's School, Cambridge University.
Clubs: Old Merchant Taylor's, Cambridge University (Blues 1919-21), King's College Hospital, London University, United Hospitals, Middlesex (captain in 1922-3).
Cove-Smith, who captained a strong Merchant Taylor's School XV in his last year before going up to Cambridge, skippered Cambridge in the first Varsity match to be played at Twickenham. He captained Old Merchant Taylor's from 1922 to 1929 and also proved to be a fine leader at international level.

In his first season with England he led them to five wins and the Grand Slam, and they won the International Championship four times between 1921 and 1928, when Cove-Smith, a skilful all-round scrummager and expert lock forward, was an automatic choice on each occasion. He played on six winning sides against the Welsh and went on the British Lions tour to South Africa in 1924, leading the team in 13 matches.

At Cambridge he also gained a half-Blue at swimming and water polo. A doctor, he held many medical posts between 1919 and 1956.

COWLING
Robin James

Prop. 1977-1979 (Leicester, 8 caps).

Robin Cowling

Debut v Scotland, 15 January 1977.
Born: 24 March 1944, Ipswich.
Educated: Sidcot School.
Clubs: Leicester, Barbarians, Gloucestershire.
Cowling was in England's 1977 Calcutta Cup team. He helped Gloucestershire to the 1973 County Championship runners-up position. Employed on the management side of the farming industry.

COWMAN
Alan Richard (Dick)

Fly-half. 1971-1973 (Loughborough Colleges, Coventry, 6 caps).
Debut v Scotland, 20 March 1971.
Born: 18 March 1949, Workington.
Educated: Workington Grammar School, Newcastle University, Loughborough Colleges.
Clubs: Newcastle University, UAU, Loughborough Colleges, Coventry, Cumberland and Westmorland.
Cowman made his debut for Coventry in the 2nd XV during the 1971-2 season. He helped them win the RFU Club KO Cup in 1973. A school teacher by profession.

COX
Norman Simpson

Centre. 1901 (Sunderland, 1 cap).
Debut v Scotland, 9 March 1901.
Born: 3 September 1877; Died: 29 March 1930, Sunderland.
Educated: Repton School.
Clubs: Sunderland, Barbarians, Durham County.

CRANMER
Peter

Centre. 1934-1938 (Richmond, Moseley, 16 caps).

Peter Cranmer

Debut v Wales, 20 January 1934.
Born: 10 September 1914, Acock's Green, Birmingham.
Educated: St Edward's (Oxford), Oxford University.
Clubs: Oxford University (Blues 1933-4), Richmond, Moseley, Barbarians, North Midlands.
England won the Triple Crown in Cranmer's first season as an international rugby player and in 1938 he captained his country twice, in Dublin and in Cardiff. He played for the British Army against French Army in Paris in 1940 and later saw active service in Egypt and Burma. He won his first cap in his first season from school and likewise gained his first Blue in 1933. An excellent cricketer, he made 166 first-class appearances for Warwickshire from 1934 to 1954 and was captain from 1938 to 1947. He played in Indian domestic cricket in 1944-5 and for Cheshire in 1948. He worked as a journalist with the BBC and *Sunday Times.*

CREED
Roger Norman
Flanker. 1971 (Coventry, 1 cap).
Debut v President's Overseas XV, 17 April 1971.
Born: 19 November 1945, Solihull.
Educated: Solihull Grammar School.
Clubs: Old Sillhillians, Moseley, Coventry, Warwickshire.
Creed also played for England Under-25s against Fiji in 1970 and helped Coventry to the 1973 RFU Club KO Cup. He is employed in a family business.

CRIDLAN
Arthur Gordon
Flanker. 1935 (Blackheath, 3 caps).
Debut v Wales, 19 January 1935.
Born: 9 July 1909, Ealing.
Educated: Uppingham School, Oxford University.
Clubs: Oxford University (Blues 1928-30), Blackheath, Barbarians, Middlesex.
Cridlan served in World War Two with the Royal Engineers and was awarded the Order of the Crown of Belgium in 1946. He was a member of the Alpine Skiing Club.

CROMPTON
Charles Arthur
Forward. 1871 (Blackheath, 1 cap).
Debut v Scotland, 27 March 1871.
Born: 21 October 1848; Died: 6 July 1875, Bengal, India.
Educated: Cheltenham College, Royal Military Academy (Woolwich).
Clubs: Royal Engineers, Blackheath.
He played in the very first international between Scotland and England at Raeburn Place in 1871 and, with C.W.Sherrard, has the distinction of being one of the first soldiers to win international honours. He died in India whilst on active service with the Royal Engineers in which he reached the rank of lieutenant. He played soccer for England in an unofficial international.

CROSSE
Charles William
Forward. 1874-1875 (Oxford University, 2 caps).
Debut v Scotland, 23 February 1874.
Born: 13 June 1854; Died 28 May 1905, Paris, France.
Educated: Rugby School, Oxford University, Royal Military Academy (Sandhurst).
Club: Oxford University (Blue 1874).
One of many England internationals who had a career in the armed forces, he served as a major in the Dragoon Guards and saw action in the Transvaal Campaign of 1881. He was also selected to play for England against Scotland in 1875 but was refused permission by Oxford University. He played cricket for that university.

CUMBERLEGE
Barry Stephenson, OBE
Full-back. 1920-1922 (Blackheath, 8 caps).
Debut v Wales, 17 January 1920.
Born: 5 June 1891, Newcastle upon Tyne; Died: 22 September 1970, Folkestone.
Educated: Durham School, Cambridge University.
Clubs: Cambridge University (Blues 1910-13), Blackheath, Barbarians, Northumberland.
Cumberlege was issued with an invitation to tour with the British Lions in South Africa in 1910 but decided to remain at school. Employed by Lloyds Bank as an underwriter, he served in World War One with the RASC and then with the New Zealand forces, twice being mentioned in despatches. He was awarded the OBE (Military) in 1918 and served in World War Two with the Royal Observer Corps. Between 1926 and 1934, he refereed 16 international matches. An all-round sportsman, he also played cricket for Durham, Northumberland, Kent and Oxford University.

CUMMING
Sir Duncan Cameron, KBE CB
Number 8. 1925 (Blackheath, 2 caps).
Debut v Scotland, 21 March 1925.
Born: 10 August 1903; Died: 10 December 1979.
Educated: Giggleswick School (Yorkshire), Cambridge University.
Clubs: Cambridge University (Blues 1922-4), Blackheath, Barbarians.
Cumming was awarded the CB in 1948 and the KBE in 1953. He spent most of his working life in the Sudan.

CUNLIFFE
Foster Lionel
Forward. 1874 (Royal Military Academy (Woolwich), 1 cap).
Debut v Scotland, 23 February 1874.
Born: 20 April 1854; Died: 15 April 1927.
Educated: Rugby School, Royal Military Academy (Woolwich).
Clubs: Royal Military Academy (Woolwich), Royal Artillery.
One of many English internationals who enjoyed a successful career in the army, he served in the Afghan War of 1878-9 and on the North-West Frontier from 1897 to 1898. In 1899 he was a lieutenant-colonel with the Royal Horse Artillery.

CURREY
Frederick Innes
Forward. 1872 (Marlborough Nomads, 1 cap).
Debut v Scotland, 5 February 1872.
Born: 3 May 1849; Died: 18 December 1896, London.
Educated: Marlborough College.
Club: Marlborough Nomads.
Currey, who was a founder member of Marlborough Nomads in 1868, shared the distinction of serving in all RFU chief offices: secretary & treasurer 1873-4, after A.Guillemard went on a world tour, resuming the post upon his return in 1874; president 1884-6; vice-president 1881-4. He was a member of the committee appointed to draft the laws and bye-laws of the game in 1871 and was an International Board member from 1891 to 1892. He refereed the Scotland-Wales match in 1887. He was a solicitor.

CURRIE
John David (Muscles)
Lock. 1956-1962 (Oxford University, Harlequins, Bristol, 25 caps).

John Currie

Debut v Wales, 21 January 1956.
Born: 3 May 1932, Clifton, Bristol; Died: 8 December 1990.
Educated: Bristol Grammar School, Oxford University.
Clubs: Oxford University (Blues 1954-7), Clifton, Harlequins, Northern, Bristol, Barbarians, Somerset (32 appearances, captain 1960-61 to 1962-3.)
Currie partnered David Marques in 22 consecutive internationals from 1956 to 1961, in which England were beaten only four times. He was in the 1957 Grand Slam team and in the side which shared the Championship after taking the Triple Crown in 1960. Later an England selector, he was Quins' chairman from 1980 to 1988. A noted cricketer, he played nine times for Oxford University (1956 and 1957) without winning a Blue, and made one appearance for Somerset, scoring 4 and 13 against Leicestershire in 1953.

CUSANI
David Anthony

Lock or Number 8. 1987 (Orrell, 1 cap).
Debut v Ireland, 7 February 1987.
Born: 16 July 1959, Wigan.
Clubs: Wigan, Liverpool St Helens, Orrell, Lancashire.
Cusani enjoyed over ten years with Orrell before stunning the club in June 1991, when he announced that he was to retire from rugby for personal reasons, just a month before his 31st birthday. During his days with Orrell, he enjoyed a remarkable second-row partnership with Bob Kimmins which was one of the most feared in English club rugger.
   Cusani toured Italy with England Under-23s in 1982, made his England 'B' debut in Belfast in 1983, went on the England tour to South Africa in 1984 and played for an England XV against Italy in 1989-90.
   At county level he represented Lancashire Colts and has made over 12 appearances for the full Lancashire side, appearing in the 1990 Championship Final against Middlesex. His brother, Charles, players for Orrell, and an uncle also played for Lancashire. Dave was out of the game for two years when he had a cartilage problem. He is employed as a travel agent.

CUSWORTH
Leslie

Fly-half. 1979-1988 (Leicester, 12 caps).
Debut v New Zealand, 24 November 1979.
Born: 3 July 1954, Wakefield.
Educated: Normanton Grammar School, West Midlands Teacher Training College.
Clubs: British Colleges, UAU, Wakefield, Moseley, Leicester, Yorkshire, North-East Counties, North Midlands, Barbarians.
In 1974-5, Les Cusworth scored 204

Les Cusworth

points in 21 games for Wakefield (25 penalty-goals, 21 conversions, 3 tries and 25 drop-goals) to beat the record set by Keith James of Newport in 1971-2. His first taste of international rugby was with the England Colts team and he went on the 'B' tour of Romania in 1978-9 and the full tour to the USA and Canada in 1982. He appeared in three successful JPS Cup Final teams for Leicester, from 1979 to 1981, and made his Barbarians debut in the team that won the 1987 Hong Kong Sevens.

D'AGUILAR
Francis Burton Grant

Forward. 1872 (Royal Engineers, 1 cap).
Debut v Scotland, 5 February 1872.
Born: 11 December 1849; Died: 24 July 1896, Bath.
Educated: Cheltenham College, Royal Military Academy (Woolwich).
Clubs: Royal Engineers, Army, Somerset.
A major in the Royal Engineers, he served in the Afghan War of 1878 to 1880. Scored a try on his international debut.

DALTON
Timothy J.

Wing. 1969 (Coventry, 1 cap).
Debut v Scotland, 15 March 1969.
Educated: Warwick School.

Clubs: Kenilworth, Coventry, Rugby, Warwickshire.
He was the first player to be used as a replacement by England in an international match, when he replaced K.J.Fielding.

DANBY
Thomas

Wing. 1949 (Harlequins, 1 cap).
Debut v Wales, 15 January 1949.
Born: 10 August 1926, Trimdon, Durham.
Educated: Barnard Castle School, St John's College (York).
Clubs: Durham City, Gosport, Harlequins, Army, British Army, Combined Services, Barbarians, Durham County, Hampshire, Salford RL.
Employed as a master at Sherborne College, Devon, he gained only one cap for England despite being on the bench on three previous occasions. He made his Rugby League debut for Salford against Liverpool Stanley in August 1949, when he scored a try. Selected for England RL in March 1950 against Wales, he went on to win three caps. He toured Australia with the Great Britain team in 1950 and was their leading try scorer with 34 tries in 18 appearances. He played for Great Britain in Tests on three occasions. His final game for Salford was at Workington Town in April 1954 and altogether he made 174 appearances, scoring 61 tries, 2 goals — a total of 187 points.

DANIELL
John

Forward. 1899-1904 (Richmond, 7 caps).
Debut v Wales, 7 January 1899.
Born: 12 December 1878, Bath; Died: 24 January 1963, Somerset.
Educated: Clifton College, Cambridge University.
Clubs: Cambridge University (Blues 1898-1900), Taunton, Richmond, Barbarians, Middlesex, Somerset.
An injury ended Daniell's rugby career after he had captained England six times. He was an England selector from 1913 to 1939 (chairman 1932-1939), RFU president for 1945-1947 and a member of the International Board for 1947-8. A cricket blue, he also played cricket for Somerset from 1904 to 1912, later as captain, and was an England cricket selector in 1921 and 1924. He served in World War One with the Sportsmen's Battalion as a private, then as an RASC captain.

DARBY
Arthur John Lovett

Forward 1899 (Birkenhead Park, 1 cap).
Debut v Ireland, 4 February 1899.
Born: 9 January 1876; Died: 16 January 1960, Dartmouth.
Educated: Cheltenham College, Cambridge University, Sorbonne (Paris).

Clubs: Cambridge University (Blues 1896-8), Sorbonne, Birkenhead Park, Richmond, Barbarians, Surrey.

He served in World War One as a lieutenant in the RNVR and fought in the Battle of Jutland. Later he was employed at the Royal Naval College (Dartmouth) as a languages teacher.

DAVENPORT
Alfred

Forward. 1871 (Ravenscourt Park, 1 cap).
Debut v Scotland, 27 March 1871.
Born: 5 May 1849; Died: 2 April 1932.
Educated: Rugby School, Oxford University.
Clubs: Oxford University, Ravenscourt Park (captain in 1869).

Davenport played in the Oxford University XV in 1869 and in the first international match between Scotland and England in 1871. He was a solicitor.

DAVEY
James

Fly-half. 1908-1909 (Redruth, 2 caps).
Debut v Scotland, 21 March 1908.
Born: 25 December 1880, Redruth; Died: 21 October, 1951.
Educated: Trewirgie School.
Clubs: Redruth, Cornwall (35 appearances), Coventry, Mines RFC (Transvaal), Transvaal (later as captain).

Employed as a gold miner in South Africa, to which country he emigrated 1901, Davey returned to the United Kingdom in 1907. He appeared in the Cornwall side that represented Great Britain in the 1908 Olympics, winning a silver medal in the Final against Australia. He was on the British Lions tour of New Zealand and Australia in 1908 and he also represented Cornwall at bowls.

DAVEY
Richard Frank

Flanker. 1931 (Teignmouth, 1 cap).
Debut v Wales, 17 January, 1931.
Born: 22 September 1905.
Educated: Wellington School.
Clubs: Wellington, Teignmouth, Wanstead, Leytonstone, Exeter, London Counties, Devon, Eastern Counties.

Davey was an Inland Revenue employee.

DAVIDSON
James

Forward. 1897-1899 (Aspatria, 5 caps).
Debut v Scotland, 13 March 1897.
Born: 28 December 1868; Died: 23 December 1945.
Clubs: Aspatria, Cumberland.

A builder by trade, he played alongside his brother, Joseph, against Scotland in 1899. Later he had a seat on the RFU committee.

DAVIDSON
Joseph

Forward. 1899 (Aspatria, 2 caps).
Debut v Wales, 7 January 1899.
Born: 5 October 1878; Died: 8 October 1910.
Clubs: Aspatria, Cumberland.

Employed in the building industry, he lost his life in a quarry accident in 1910. He appeared with his brother, James, in the England-Scotland match in 1899. A keen sportsman, he also enjoyed boxing and athletics.

DAVIES
Geoffrey Huw

Fly-half or full-back. 1981-1986 (Cambridge University, Coventry, Wasps, 21 caps).
Debut v Scotland, 21 February 1981.
Born: 18 February 1959, Eastbourne.
Educated: King Edward VI Grammar School (Stourbridge) UWIST, Cambridge University.

Huw Davies

Clubs: Cambridge University (Blues 1980-81), Coventry, Cardiff, Wasps, Barbarians.

He scored a try in the 100th Varsity match in 1981 and also scored a try on his international debut. His parents were Welsh, his father working as a lecturer. He played for UWIST against Exeter in the 1980 UAU Final, for England Students, England Under-23s and went on the England tours to Fiji and Japan in 1980, Argentina in 1981, South Africa in 1984 and New Zealand in 1985. He captained England 'B' against France. He is employed as a chartered surveyor.

DAVIES
Patrick Harry

Flanker. 1927 (Sale, 1 cap).
Debut v Ireland, 12 February 1927.
Born: 17 March 1903; Died: 21 February 1979, Ware, Hertfordshire.
Educated: Denstone College.
Clubs: Manchester, Sale, Cheshire (48 appearances).

He became Sale's president in their centenary year of 1961 and his appearances for Cheshire included games against the New Zealanders in 1924-5 and the County Championship semifinal of 1926-7. He was president of the county from 1958 to 1960. During World War Two, he served in the RAF

DAVIES
Vivian Gordon

Fly-half. 1922-1925 (Harlequins, 2 caps).
Debut v Wales, 21 January 1922.
Born: 22 January 1899, Durham; Died: 23 December 1941 (killed in action).
Educated: Marlborough College.
Clubs: Harlequins, Barbarians, Surrey.

He lost his life during World War Two, killed by a bomb whilst serving as a captain in the Royal Artillery. During World War One he served in the Duke of Cornwall's Light Infantry. He played for Harlequins Past against Harlequins Present on 22 April 1922, in a match organised to raise money for the King Edward VII Hospital Fund.

DAVIES
William John Abbott, OBE

Fly-half. 1913-1923 (United Services, Royal Navy, 22 caps).
Debut v South Africa, 4 January 1913.
Born: 21 June 1890, Pembroke; Died: 26 April 1967.
Educated: Royal Naval Engineering College (Keyham), Royal Naval College (Greenwich).
Clubs: US Portsmouth, Royal Navy, Harlequins, Hampshire.

It was whilst playing for the Fleet against the Rest of the Navy in March 1919 that William Davies began his famous England half-back partnership with Cyril Kershaw that was to run up a record 14 appearances by 1923.

In 1919-20, Davies cracked a small bone in his leg but the following season took over as captain of England, a post he held for three years. England won the Championship in 1921 and 1923 and were never beaten with Davies as their leader, their worst experience being a draw with France in 1922. Indeed, in his 22 international matches, Davies appeared on the losing side only once, on his debut.

He retired from representative rugger after the French match in 1923 but returned for the Rugby School centenary match on 1 November 1923, playing for England/Wales against Scotland/Ireland.

He was England's most capped outside-left until Rob Andrew overtook his total, and was arguably the country's finest rugby player of all time.

A star pupil at both his naval colleges — he was awarded the 1910 Champions' Cup as the best athlete at Greenwich — he served in World War One with HMS Iron Duke in the Grand Fleet, later being transferred to HMS Queen Elizabeth. He captained the Royal Navy from 1919 to 1923 and was later a selector. In 1924 he played for the Harlequins side which beat the United States 21-11, prior to the Americans becoming Olympic Champions.

Author of *Rugby Football* (published in 1923) and *Rugby Football and How To Play It* (1933).

DAVIES
William Philip Cathcart

Centre. 1953-1958 (Harlequins, 11 caps).
Debut v Scotland, 21 March 1953.
Born: 6 August 1928, Abberley, Worcestershire.
Educated: Denstone College, Cambridge University.
Clubs: RAF, Cambridge University (no Blue), Cheltenham, Harlequins, Barbarians, Sussex, North Midlands.

On the British Lions visit to South Africa in 1955 — the most successful Lions tour of that country — William Davies celebrated his birthday by playing in the side that beat the Springboks 23-22 in First Test. On that tour, with Jeff Butterfield, he had the distinction of being one of the best centres to have played in the country. Davies was a fair-haired, very large gentleman, a devastating tackler and runner who also represented Cambridge University at athletics.

He played in the International XV which met Wales in April 1957, in a game in aid of the following year's Empire Games at Cardiff, and continued to play rugby until he was 49. Indeed, he won a local junior club medal as a 44-year-old.

He taught at Christ's Hospital and Denstone Preparatory School and was headmaster at Cheltenham College Junior School, where he was in charge of the school side for 22 years. President of the Cheltenham club, he also played hockey, soccer and cricket. Today he is involved with the Conservative Party and builds kit cars and classic motorcycles as well as doing much charity work for the disabled and the Leonard Cheshire Homes.

DAVIS
Alec Michael

Lock. 1963-1970 (Harlequins, 16 caps).
Debut v Wales, 19 January 1963.
Born: 23 January 1942, Lichfield.
Educated: Tor School (Torquay), Tor-

quay Grammar School, St Luke's College (Exeter).
Clubs: Torquay Colts, St Luke's College, Royal Navy, Devonport Services, Harlequins, Barbarians, Staffordshire, Devon, Aberavon (guest), Rosslyn Park (guest).

A schoolteacher and former England coach (1979), whose father, A.Davis, was a wing-forward with Cheltenham and Gloucestershire, Alec Davis also coached England Schoolboys at 16 and 19 age groups. Co-author, with Donald Ireland, of *Science of Rugby Football* (1985). He went on the England tour to New Zealand in 1963 and was a regular for Devon from 1961 to 1966.

DAWE
Richard Graham Reed

Hooker. 1987 (Bath, 4 caps).
Debut v Ireland, 7 February 1987.

Born: 4 September 1959, Plymouth.
Clubs: Launceston, Bath, Cornwall (31 appearances), South-West Division 1988-91, Barbarians.

Dawes, who was in the 1987 World Cup party, played against Australia in 1988 and against Spain and Ireland 'B' in 1990-1991. He played in the 1986 JPS Cup Final for Bath's winning team. He also appeared for Cornwall v USSR in 1989 and was a member of the Cornish ADT County Championship team in 1991. He is a farmer at Milton Abbot and his hobbies include bell-ringing, cycling and sheep-shearing. After the 1987 Wales game he was suspended by England.

DAWSON
Ernest Frederick

Forward. 1878 (RIE College, 1 cap).
Debut v Ireland, 11 March 1878.
Born: 10 May 1858; Died: 7 April 1904, Hampstead.
Clubs: RIE College, Richmond, Surrey.

DAY
Harold Lindsay Vernon

Wing. 1920-1926 (Leicester, 4 caps).
Debut v Wales, 17 January 1920.
Born: 12 August 1898, Darjeeling; Died: 15 June 1972, Hadley Wood.
Educated: Bedford Modern School.
Clubs: Leicester, Army, Royal Artillery, Midlands, Hampshire, Leicestershire.

Day gained his first England cap in quite unusual circumstances. The original choice had been W.M.Lowry but after the pre-match team photographs had been taken (which included Lowry) it was decided that Day would be better suited for the conditions and he went on to score all the points (one try and a conversion) in the 19-5 defeat by Wales.

He played the Army against the Royal Navy in 1920, 1922 and 1923 and against the RAF and the French Army 1922, and captained the Army side once. He served in World War One with the Royal Artillery and later taught at Felstead School, also writing for numerous newspapers on rugby. He refereed the Scotland-Wales match in 1934 and played cricket for the Army, Hampshire and Bedfordshire.

DEAN
Geoffrey John (Tinny), MC

Scrum half. 1931 (Harlequins, 1 cap).
Debut v Ireland, 14 February 1931.
Born: 12 November 1909.
Educated: Rugby School, Cambridge University.
Clubs: Cambridge University (no Blue), Army, Harlequins, Barbarians, Sussex.

He had a career in the Royal Tank Corps and represented the Army against the Royal Navy (five times) and the RAF (six times). He was also in the Harlequins team which won the 1935 Middlesex Sevens. A good hockey and lawn tennis player, he served in World War Two and was awarded the Military Cross in 1940. He lost a leg in North Africa and was later held as a POW.

DEE
John MacKenzie
Centre/Wing. 1962-1963 (Hartlepool Rovers, 2 caps).
Debut v Scotland, 17 March 1962.
Born: 22 October 1938, Hartlepool.
Educated: Henry Smith School (Hartlepool).
Clubs: Hartlepool Rovers, Barbarians, Durham County.
A schoolteacher, he was on the British Lions tour to South Africa in 1962.

DEVITT
Thomas Gordon, (Sir), Bt
Wing. 1926-1928 (Blackheath, 4 caps).
Debut v Ireland, 13 February 1926.
Born: 27 December 1902, Bishopsgate, Surrey.
Educated: Sherborne School, Cambridge University.
Clubs: Cambridge University (Blues 1923-5) Blackheath, Army, Barbarians, Middlesex.
Devitt, who also won an athletics Blue in the long jump, played for the Army against the Royal Navy from 1928 to 1930 and against the RAF and the French Army in 1928. He served in the Seaforth Highlanders during World War Two and rose to the rank of lieutenant-colonel.

DEWHURST
John Henry, MBE
Forward. 1887-1890 (Richmond, 4 caps).
Debut v Wales, 8 January 1887.
Born: 27 December 1863, Skipton, Yorkshire; Died: 22 April 1947.
Educated: Mill Hill School, Cambridge University.
Clubs: Cambridge University (Blues 1885-6), Richmond, St Thomas's Hospital, Surrey.
Dewhurst was also selected for the 1888 England team that did not play.

DE WINTON
Robert Francis Chippini.
Half-back. 1893 (Marlborough Nomads, 1 cap).
Debut v Wales, 7 January 1893.
Born: 9 September 1868, Newport; Died: 14 March 1923, Porterville, California, USA.
Educated: Summer Fields School, Marlborough College, Oxford University.
Clubs: Marlborough Nomads, Oxford University (Blues 1888-90), Blackheath.
De Winton fought with the Lancashire Fusiliers during World War One. He lost his life after falling from an hotel window in California.

Robert De Winton

John Dicks

DIBBLE
Robert

Forward. 1906-1912 (Bridgwater Albion, 19 caps).
Debut v Scotland, 17 March 1906.
Born: Bridgwater.
Clubs: Bridgwater Albion, Newport, Somerset.
Dibble is Bridgwater Albion's most capped player. A farmer, and later a licensee, he served in the Boer War. He captained England in 1909 and 1912 and appeared in the Calcutta Cup teams of 1906 and 1911.

DICKS
John

Lock/Prop. 1934-1937 (Northampton, 8 caps).
Debut v Wales, 20 January 1934.
Born: 12 September 1912, Ecton, Northamptonshire.
Educated: Northampton Grammar School.
Clubs: Old Northamptonians, Wellingborough, Northampton, Barbarians, East Midlands.
In his debut season, England won the Triple Crown for the first time since 1928. He also played in the 1936 Calcutta Cup team. He worked as a farmer.

DILLON
Edward Wentworth

Centre. 1904-1905 (Blackheath, 4 caps).
Debut v Wales, 9 January 1904.
Born: 15 February 1881, Surrey; Died: 20 April 1941.
Educated: Rugby School, Oxford University.
Clubs: Oxford University (no Blue), Blackheath, Harlequins, Barbarians, Kent.
Dillon, who was employed in the insurance business, served in World War One as a captain in the Royal West Kent Regiment and was mentioned in despatches and wounded. Although he failed to gain a rugger Blue, he won Blues at cricket in 1901 and 1902. He scored 110 not out on his first-class debut, for London Counties against Worcestershire in 1900, and played for Kent from 1900 to 1904 and as captain from 1909 to 1914.

DINGLE
Arthur James

Centre. 1913-1914 (Hartlepool Rovers, 3 caps).
Debut v Ireland, 8 February 1913.
Born: 1891 Hetton-le-Hole, Durham; Died: 22 August 1915, Gallipoli (killed in action).
Educated: Bow School, Durham School, Oxford University.
Clubs: Hartlepool Rovers (captain, 1914) Oxford University (Blue 1911), Hartlepool Rovers, Richmond, Barbarians, Durham County, Surrey.
The date of his death is given as above, but he was originally posted as 'missing presumed killed' at Suvla Bay in Gallipoli.

DIXON
Peter John

Flanker. (Harlequins, Gosforth, 1971-1978, 22 caps).
Debut v President's Overseas XV, 17 April 1971.
Born: 30 April 1944, Keighley, Yorkshire.
Educated: St Bees College, Durham University. Oxford University.
Clubs: Workington, Oxford University (Blues 1967-70), Harlequins, Gosforth, Barbarians, Cumberland & Westmorland.
Dixon, who captained England twice in 1972, was selected for the 1971 British

Peter Dixon

Lions before gaining his first full England cap, touring Australia and New Zealand with the Lions that year.

His first international rugby was played for England Schools and he also represented the UAU. A very versatile player, appearing either as flanker or number 8, upon his return from the 1971 tour he was put into the England back row where he partnered Andy Ripley and Tony Neary. They had a run of a dozen matches which remains a record combination for the trio. He went with England to South Africa in 1972 and succeeded Bob Hiller as captain. Dixon was Oxford University's representative on the RFU.

DOBBS
George Eric Burroughs

Flanker. 1906 (Devonport Albion, 2 caps).
Debut v Wales, 13 January 1906.

Born: 21 July 1884; Died: 17 June 1917, Poperinghe.
Educated: St Stephen's Green School (Dublin), Shrewsbury School, Royal Military Academy (Woolwich).
Clubs: Royal Military Academy (Woolwich), Plymouth Albion, Devonport Albion, Llanelli, Army, Barbarians, Devon.

Dobbs, who captained his school's soccer XI, played for the Army against the Royal Navy in 1907. He served in World War One as a lieutenant colonel in the Royal Engineers. Awarded the Legion d'Honneur at Mons in 1914, he was mentioned in despatches three times. Died of wounds incurred in battle.

DOBLE
Samuel Arthur

Full-back. 1972-1973 (Moseley, 3 caps).
Debut v South Africa, 3 June 1972.

Born: 9 March 1944, Wolverhampton; Died: September 1977.
Educated: Regis School (Wolverhampton), St Paul's College (Cheltenham).
Clubs: Moseley, Staffordshire.

Sam Doble was a prolific scorer, who in 1971-2 set a world club record of 450 points in a season (11 tries, 77 penalties, 83 conversions and 3 dropped goals) for Moseley, the club for whom he was leading scorer for six consecutive seasons. He scored on his England debut, in South Africa in 1972, and ended the tour with 47 points in five appearances.

For Staffordshire he scored a record 64 points in 1969-70, when they won the County Championship, and held the overall record of 3,651 points until Dusty Hare overtook him on the same Moseley ground that Doble had established his record.

He was leading points scorer in the South of England, the Midlands and

South Wales for five successive seasons. Doble, a school teacher by profession, was a member of Moseley's 1971-2 RU KO Cup runners-up side in the first season the competition was played.

DOBSON
Denys Douglas

Forward. 1902-1903 (Newton Abbot, 6 caps).
Debut v Wales, 11 January 1902.
Born: 28 October 1880; Died: 10 July 1916, Ngama, Nyasaland.
Educated: Newton College, Cheltenham College, Oxford University.
Clubs: Oxford University (Blues 1899-1901), Newton Abbot, Barbarians, London Welsh, Devon.

Dobson, who scored a try on his international debut, went on the British Lions tour of Australia and New Zealand in 1904 and was sent off during one of the matches for using obscene language. He later worked in the Colonial Civil Service and was killed by a rhinoceros, one of the strangest examples of an international player losing his life.

DOBSON
Thomas Hyde

Centre. 1895 (Bradford, 1 cap).
Debut v Scotland, 9 March 1895.
Born: February 1872; Died: 12 November 1902, Bradford.
Clubs: Bowling, Bradford, Yorkshire.

Employed as a master tailor, besides rugger he enjoyed attending any kind of athletic meeting held in the county. He turned to Rugby League in 1895, when Bradford helped in the formation of the Northern Union, and stayed in the League game until 1900. His father, Harry, trained the Bradford side which won the Yorkshire Challenge Cup against Hull in 1884.

DODGE
Paul William

Centre. 1978-1985 (Leicester, 32 caps).
Debut v Wales, 4 February 1978.
Born: 22 February 1958, Leicester.
Educated: Wreake School (Leicester).
Club: Leicester.

Paul Dodge began his representative career with the Leicester Secondary Schools XV and England Colts. He first played senior rugby whilst still at school, when he appeared for the Midland Counties East side which beat an Australian touring side in 1975 at Leicester. In 1976 he played for the Midlands and North of England side which beat the Argentinians, also at Leicester.

Dodge played for the England Under-23 team that beat Japan, and in 1977, appeared in the England XV which beat the American Eagles. That same year he toured Canada with England Under-23s.

He came into the 1980 Grand Slam side, replacing Tony Bond who broke his leg against Ireland, and the same year he scored a try in his first tour game with the British Lions in South Africa. Although he was not included in the original squad, he was flown out when the Lions suffered a spate of injuries and played in five of the last seven matches, including two Tests. Dodge ended his England career as the country's most-capped centre.

Paul Dodge

A quiet, strong running centre, renowned for his sledgehammer tackling, he helped Leicester to six JPS Cup Finals, captaining the side in 1989, and led the team which won the first Courage Clubs' Championship in 1988. He retired from playing at the end of 1990-91, after scoring 90 tries in 437 games for Leicester. He remains with the club, assisting with the Under-21 side, and works as a bookbinder and dealer in the family business.

DONNELLY
Martin Paterson ('Squib')

Centre. 1947 (Oxford University, 1 cap).
Debut v Ireland, 8 February 1947.
Born: 17 October 1917, Ngaruawahia, New Zealand.
Educated: Plymouth Boys' High School (New Zealand), Canterbury University, Oxford University.
Clubs: Canterbury University, Canterbury, New Zealand Universities, Oxford University (Blue 1946), Blackheath, Barbarians.

Martin Donnelly was much better known as one of New Zealand's finest cricketers. A left-handed batsman, who played in Plunkett Shield cricket for Wellington and Canterbury, he won an Oxford Blue and made 23 appearances for the university in 1946 and 1947. He made one appearance for Middlesex in 1946 and played 20 times for Warwickshire between 1948 and 1950.

Donnelly toured England with New Zealand in 1937 and 1949 and played against Australia in 1937-38 and 1938-39. He totalled 59 matches for New Zealand, playing in seven Tests, and scored 3,745 runs with a highest score of 206 against England at Lord's in 1949. His highest-ever score was 208 not out for MCC against Yorkshire at Scarborough in 1948 and he had the distinction of scoring centuries at Lord's in Varsity matches.

He served in World War Two as a major in the 4th Armoured Brigade. On a bursary at Oxford, he was employed in the sales and marketing business.

DOOLEY
Wade Anthony

Lock. 1985-1992 (Preston Grasshoppers, Fylde, 50 caps).
Debut v Romania, 5 January, 1985.
Born: 2 October 1957, Warrington.
Educated: Beaumont Secondary Technical School.
Clubs: Fylde, Preston Grasshoppers, British Police, Lancashire (over 12 appearances).

A Blackpool community policeman (who is married to a woman police officer), Dooley is one of the tallest players to appear for England. He played Rugby League at school, switching to Union in 1975, when he was a police cadet and became the first Lancashire policeman to be capped. Not surprisingly, he was voted Lancashire Constabulary Sportsman of the Year in 1985. He also appeared for Blackpool Police Division at volleyball.

His representative rugby career is impressive: North of England against Romania in 1984; British Police v New Zealand Combined Services in 1986; British Lions tour of Australia in 1989, appearing in the 2nd and 3rd Tests and in a further six matches, scoring two tries; England tour of Argentina in 1990.

A big, powerful line-out specialist, he equalled Bill Beaumont's record of

Wade Dooley

appearances as lock when he played against Scotland in the 1990 Calcutta Cup match. He was banned for one match for his part in the violent Wales-England game in 1987.

Dooley, a member of the 1991 Grand Slam side, went on the England tour of Fiji and Australia that year but sustained a broken bone in his hand against Queensland. He recovered to play in the 1991 World Cup Finals and the 1992 Grand Slam.

His father played Rugby League and a brother also plays for Preston.

David Duckham

DOVEY
Beverley Alfred
Prop. 1963 (Rosslyn Park, 2 caps).
Debut v Wales, 19 January 1963.
Born: 24 October 1938.
Educated: Lydney Grammar School, Leeds University, Cambridge University.
Clubs: Cambridge University (Blue 1960), Rosslyn Park, Roundhay, Barbarians, Gloucestershire, Hertfordshire, Yorkshire (11 appearances).
A master at Merchant Taylor's School, Northwood, Middlesex, he once played for England Schools Over-15s.

DOWN
Percy John
Prop. 1909 (Bristol, 1 cap).
Debut v Australia, 9 Janaury 1909.
Born: 14 October 1883, Clifton; Died: 22 July 1954.
Educated: Dr Kempe's School (Long Ashton).
Clubs: Redland, Bristol, Somerset.
Down captained Bristol and was the club's chairman from 1945 until his death in 1954. He was a farmer.

DOWSON
Aubrey Osler, MC
Forward. 1899 (Moseley, 1 cap).
Debut v Scotland, 11 March 1899.
Born: 10 November 1875; Died: 5 October 1940.
Educated: Rugby School, Oxford University.
Clubs: Oxford University (Blue 1896), Moseley, Manchester, Midlands.
Dowson, a farmer, served in World War One with the 12th. Rifle Brigade, was mentioned in despatches in 1917 and awarded the Military Cross in 1918. Besides rugger he won athletics Blues for the hammer and shot in 1895-7 and was a member of the New College VIII which won the Grand Challenge Cup at Henley in 1897.

DRAKE-LEE
Nicholas James
Prop. 1963-1965 (Cambridge University, Leicester, 8 caps).
Debut v Wales, 19 January 1963.
Born: 7 April 1942.
Educated: Stonyhurst College, Cambridge University.
Clubs: Cambridge University (Blues 1961-3), Kettering, Leicester, Rosslyn Park, Manchester, Waterloo, East Midlands, Lancashire.
Drake-Lee came to prominence in 1961, when, as a freshman, he played as a forward and gained his first Blue for Cambridge University. When he made his England debut he was the youngest player in the match against Wales in Cardiff.
He comes from a well-known rugby-playing family. His elder brother, J.W., plays for St Thomas' Hospital, and another brother, T.D.P., is also a member of Rosslyn Park. Nicholas Drake-Lee also plays for Kettering Cricket Club. Employed in the construction industry, he was also a schoolmaster.

DUCKHAM
David John
Wing. 1969-1976 (Coventry, 36 caps).
Debut v Ireland, 8 February 1969.
Born: 28 June 1946, Coventry.
Educated: King Henry VIII Grammar School (Coventry).
Clubs: Coventry, Warwickshire, Barbarians.
Duckham, who scored a try on his international debut, was on the British Lions tour to South Africa in 1969 and to New Zealand in 1971. He scored 11 tries on tour, his greatest achievement being six tries against West Coast-Buller Combined.
Originally a centre who switched to the wing later in his career, he was a strongly-built player, speedy, yet graceful, and had the ability to beat opponents with deft little side-steps and swerves which often frustrated opposing players. He captained Coventry's 1972 RFU Club KO Cup-winning side. Employed in banking, his autobiography *Dai for England* was published in 1980.

DUDGEON
Herbert William
Forward. 1897-1899 (Richmond, 7 caps).
Debut v Scotland, 13 March 1897.
Died: 4 October 1935.
Educated: Guy's Hospital, Durham University.
Clubs: Association Geneva, Guy's Hospital, Durham University, Richmond, Northern, Barbarians, Surrey.
Dudgeon captained the Association Geneva side for about two years, most of his education being gained whilst living in Switzerland. He was a fast, strong and skilful wing-forward.

DUGDALE
John Marshall, JP
Forward. 1871 (Ravenscourt Park 1 cap).
Debut v Scotland 27 March 1871.
Born: 15 October 1852; Died: 30 October 1918.
Educated: Rugby School, Oxford University.
Clubs: Oxford University, Ravenscourt Park.
A barrister and later JP for Montgomeryshire, he played in the first international between Scotland and England.

DUN
Andrew Frederick
Flanker. 1984 (Wasps, 1 cap).
Debut v Wales, 17 March 1984.
Born: 26 November 1960, Bristol.
Educated: Bristol Grammar School, Bartholomew's Hospital.
Clubs: Bartholomew's Hospital, Bristol, Gloucestershire, London Scottish, Wasps, Middlesex.
Dun played for England Senior Schools on their tour of Australia and New Zealand in 1979 and captained England Students on their tour of Japan in 1983. He played for London Division against Australia in 1981 and was captain of England Under-23s on their tour of Italy and France the same year and against Romania in 1983.

DUNCAN
Robert Francis Hugh
Prop. 1922 (Guy's Hospital, 3 caps).
Debut v Ireland, 11 February 1922.
Born: 10 June 1896, Glamorgan.
Educated: Cardiff University, Guy's Hospital.
Clubs: Guy's Hospital, Barbarians, Middlesex.
Employed as a sales representative, he was the son of R.T.Duncan, who also played for Cardiff. He served in World War One as a temporary second lieutenant in the Welch Regiment and as a captain in the Royal Welch Fusiliers, being mentioned in despatches. In World War Two, he was a lieutenant, temporary captain, captain and temporary major in the Royal Welch Fusiliers, serving in the Far East.

DUNKLEY
Philip Edward ('Pop')
Number 8. 1931-1936 (Harlequins, 6 caps).
Debut v Ireland, 14 February 1931.
Born: 9 August 1904; Died: 17 June 1985.
Clubs: Old Laurentians, Leicester, Harlequins, Barbarians, Warwickshire.
A bank manager, who was a teetaller and a very religious man, he was a strong supporter of the Toc H charity organisation. He captained the Quins from 1933 to 1935 and was a member of their Middlesex Sevens winning side in the latter year.

DUTHIE
James
Forward. 1903 (West Hartlepool, 1 cap).
Debut v Wales, 10 January 1903.
Born: 1878; Died: 29 May 1946, Hartlepool.
Clubs: West Hartlepool, Winlaton Vulcans, Durham County.
Duthie worked in a Hartlepool shipyard.

DYSON
John William

Wing. 1890-1893 (Huddersfield, 4 caps).
Debut v Scotland, 1 March 1890.
Born: 6 September 1866, Skelman-
thorpe; Died: 3 January 1909,
Huddersfield.
Clubs: Skelmanthorpe, Huddersfield,
Yorkshire (27 appearances).
Dyson, who scored a try on his inter-
national debut, was an all-round
sportsman who also enjoyed athletics.
He made his Yorkshire debut against
the Maoris in 1888 and scored over 30
tries and six drop-goals for the county.
He turned to Rugby League when
Huddersfield helped form the Northern
Union in 1895.

EAGLES
Harry L.

Forward.
Clubs: Salford, Lancashire (1 cap).
Harry Eagles was awarded an England
cap in the 1888 side that did not play
due to a dispute when the International
Board was formed. He therefore failed
to make a full international appearance,
although he toured Australia and New
Zealand with the British Lions in 1888,
playing in every tour match between 28
April and 3 October, a record which has
not been equalled.

EBDON
Percy John

Forward. 1897 (Wellington, 2 caps).
Debut v Wales, 9 January 1897.
Born: 16 March 1874, Milverton,
Somerset; Died: 16 February 1943,
Wellington.
Clubs: Wellington, Somerset (23
appearances, later as captain).
Percy Ebdon also played for Somerset
in 1894.

EDDISON
John Horncastle, MC

Forward. 1912 (Headingley, 4 caps).
Debut v Wales, 20 January 1912.
Born: 25 August 1888, Edinburgh; Died:
18 November 1982, Edinburgh.
Educated: Ilkley Grammar School,
Bromsgrove School.
Clubs: Headingley, Barbarians, Yorkshire (36 appearances).
Employed in the insurance trade, he
later became of the game's leading
referees as well as one of the longest
'lived' England internationals. He
served during World War One as
lieutenant in the Royal Field Artillery,
was mentioned in despatches and
awarded the Military Cross in 1916.

EDGAR
Charles Stuart

Forward. 1901 (Birkenhead Park, 1 cap).
Debut v Scotland, 9 March 1901.

Born: 1876; Died: 26 May 1949, Chester.
Clubs: Birkenhead Park, Barbarians,
Cheshire.

EDWARDS
Reginald

Prop. 1921-1925 (Newport, 11 caps).
Debut v Wales, 15 January 1921.
Born: 11 December 1887; Died: August
1951.
Educated: Preswell School (Newport).
Clubs: Newport, Somerset.
He was employed as a butcher but was
soon to emigrate to Canada.

EGERTON
David William

Number 8. 1988-1990 (Bath, 7 caps).
Debut v Ireland, 23 April 1988.
Born: 19 October 1961, Pinner,
Middlesex.
Educated: Bishop Wordsworth's
School, Loughborough Colleges.
Clubs: Salisbury, Loughborough Stu-
dents, Wasps (3rd XV), Bath.

David Egerton

Egerton, who made his debut in Dublin
Millenium match, represented Dorset
and Wiltshire at schools and Under-21
levels. A player with a good sense of
humour, his house is called 'Scrummage'. His most serious injuries have
been the fracture of the lower back and
a dislocated knee cap. He enjoys
Country and Western music and can
play the guitar. He represented Dorset
and Wiltshire at the shot putt and won
the UAU title whilst at Loughborough.
He helped Bath to win the Pilkington
Cup in 1990. He is a broker/consultant.
His brother, Andrew, plays for the
Saracens and his father also played for
Wasps 3rd XV.

ELLIOT
Charles Henry

Forward. 1886 (Sunderland, 1 cap).
Debut v Wales, 2 January 1886.
Born: 31 May 1861; Died: 1 April 1934,
Bristol.
Educated: Repton School.
Clubs: Sunderland, Blackheath, Dur-
ham Counties.
He was the uncle of Edgar William
Elliott.

ELLIOT
Edgar William

Wing. 1901-1904 (Sunderland, 4 caps).
Debut v Wales, 5 January 1901.
Born: 9 July 1879; Died: 1931.
Educated: Wellington College.
Clubs: Sunderland, Barbarians, Dur-
ham County.
The Sunderland club's most capped
player, he left the UK for a short time
to work in the USA. He was the nephew
of Charles Henry Elliot.

ELLIOT
Walter, DSC MP

Fly-half 1932-1934 (United Services
(Portsmouth), Royal Navy, 7 caps).
Debut v Ireland, 13 February 1932.
Born: 17 February 1910.
Educated: HMS Conway, Royal Naval
Engineering College (Keyham).
Clubs: United Services (Portsmouth),
Royal Navy.
He became a Conservative MP for
Carshalton and Banstead in 1960, after
retiring from the Royal Navy in 1958.
He was re-elected in 1964, 1966 and 1970.
Served in World War Two and was
mentioned in despatches. Awarded the
DSC in 1944.

ELLIOTT
Albert Ernest

Forward. 1894 (St Thomas' Hospital,
1 cap).
Debut v Scotland, 17 March 1894.
Born: 5 March 1869, Southampton;
Died: 1 December 1900, Middelburg,
South Africa.
Educated: Cheltenham College, Cam-
bridge University.
Clubs: Cambridge University (Blue
1891), St Thomas' Hospital, Barbarians,
Middlesex.
He died on active service whilst a civil
surgeon with the Royal Artillery during
the Boer War, after contracting a fever.

ELLIS
Jack

Scrum half. 1939 (Wakefield, 1 cap).
Debut v Scotland, 18 March 1939.
Born: 28 October 1912, Leeds.
Clubs: Wakefield, Yorkshire 1938.
Jack Ellis, a schoolteacher, was known
as 'a lively player'.

ELLIS
Sidney S., JP
Forward. 1880 (Queen's House, 1 cap).
Debut v Ireland, 30 January 1880.
Born: 13 March 1859; Died: 1 December 1937.
Educated: Dulwich College.
Clubs: Faversham, Queen's House, Blackheath, Kent.
Ellis was a member of the Stock Exchange from 1882 to 1937 and a Justice of the Peace for Croydon.

EMMOTT
Charles
Half-back. 1892 (Bradford, 1 cap).
Debut v Wales, 2 Janary 1892.
Born: 1868; Died: 10 March 1927, Saltaire.
Clubs: Bradford, Saltaire, Yorkshire, (7 appearances).
Emmott made his Yorkshire debut against Cheshire in 1890.

ENTHOVEN
H.J.
Back. 1878 (Richmond, 1 cap).
Debut v Ireland, 11 March 1878.
Club: Richmond.

ESTCOURT
Noel Sidney Dudley
Full-back. 1955 (Blackheath, 1 cap).
Debut v Scotland, 19 March 1955.
Born: 7 January 1929, Rhodesia.
Educated: Plumtree School (Rhodesia), Rhodes University, Cambridge University.
Clubs: Eastern Province, Cambridge University (no Blue), Blackheath, Barbarians, Kent.
Estcourt played in the Cambridge XV without gaining a Blue but did win cricket Blues in 1953 and 1954, making 21 appearances. He became the first Blackheath player to gain international honours when he played against Scotland. He returned to Rhodesia in 1955.

EVANS
Barry J.
Winger. 1988 (Leicester, 2 caps).
Debut v Australia, 12 June 1988.
Clubs: Leicester, Midlands.
Evans stunned Leicester in 1991 by announcing a move to Coventry, then changed his mind and stayed with the Welford Road club. In 1990-91 he was plagued by injury.

EVANS
Eric
Hooker. 1948-1958 (Sale, 30 caps).
Debut v Australia, 3 January 1948.
Born: 1 February 1925, Droylsden; Died: 12 January 1991.
Educated: Audenshaw Grammar School, Loughborough College.

Clubs: Old Aldwinians, Loughborough College, Sale, Barbarians, Lancashire (85 appearances).
Eric Evans captained England 13 times, scoring tries in 1953 and 1957. No other hooker since World War Two has scored tries in the Home series. He captained England to the International Championship and Triple Crown in 1957, and to the Championship in 1958. He is Sale RFC's record cap holder. He set a unique record when he captained England against Australia ten years after he had played against that same country in his first international.

Eric Evans

He captained the International XV which met Wales on 6 April 1957, in a match arranged to raise funds to enable the Empire Games to be played in Cardiff in 1958. He also skippered the Barbarians on their tour of Canada in 1957 and was Lancashire's chairman of selectors. A great leader he had a passion for physical fitness and was employed as Director of PE at Openshaw Technical College.

EVANS
Geoffrey William
Centre. 1972-1974 (Coventry, 9 caps).
Debut v Scotland, 18 March 1972.
Born: 10 December 1950, Coventry.
Educated: Bablake School (Coventry), Manchester University.
Clubs: Manchester University, Sale (as a 'loan' player), Coventry, Barbarians, Warickshire.
Geoff Evans played in an England Schools 15 group final trial as a fly-half, going

on to win a 19-group place in 1968-9 as a centre. He made his debut for Coventry in 1969-70, playing seven games as a replacement, and helped the club to win the RFU KO Cup in 1972-3. His debut for England was made in the Calcutta Cup match at Murrayfield, when he was only 21. He went on the England tour of the Far East in 1970-71. He is a former All-England Schools long jump champion.

EVANS
Nevill Lloyd ('Barney')
Prop. 1932-1944 (Royal Naval Engineering College, 4 caps).
Debut v Wales, 16 January 1932.
Born: 16 December 1908.
Educated: Eltham College, Royal Naval Engineering College (Keyham).
Clubs: Royal Naval Engineering College (Keyham), Devonport Services, United Services (Portsmouth), Combined Services, Royal Navy, Barbarians, Hampshire, Devon.
Nevill Evans served during World War Two as an engineering officer and was later promoted to lieutenant-commander. He was secretary of St Enodoc Golf Club from 1965 to 1966.

EVANSON
Arthur Macdonnell, JP
Back. 1883-1884 (Richmond, 4 caps).
Debut v Wales, 16 December 1883.
Born: 15 September 1859; Died: 31 December 1934.
Educated: Oundle School, Oxford University.
Clubs: Oxford University (Blue 1880-1881, captain 1882 but did not play), Richmond, Middlesex.
He scored two conversions on his international debut. Brother of Wyndham Evanson. Besides his rugger Blues he also won Blues at athletics for putting the shot in 1880-2.

EVANSON
Wyndham Alleyn Daubney
Back. 1875-1879 (Richmond, 5 caps).
Debut v Scotland, 8 March 1875.
Born: 1851; Died: 30 October 1934.
Educated: St John's School (Leatherhead).
Clubs: Owls, Civil Service, Richmond.
Brother of Arthur Wyndham, he played golf at 60 years of age and became a scratch player as a member of the Crowborough Golf Club. An all-round sportsman, he also became a known sculler and oarsman. He was employed in the Civil Service.

EVERSHED
Frank
Forward. 1889-1893 (Blackheath, 10 caps).
Debut v Maoris, 16 February 1889.
Born: 6 September 1866, Winshill, Staffordshire; Died: 29 June 1954, Winshill.

Frank Evershed

tals, Richmond, Tiverton, Devon, Middlesex.

Fagan was 'capped' in the England side of 1888 that did not play.

FAIRBROTHER
Keith Eli ('Batman')

Prop. 1969-1971 (Coventry, 12 caps).
Debut v Ireland, 8 February 1969.
Born: 8 May 1944, Coventry.
Educated: Caludon Castle School (Coventry).
Clubs: Stoke Old Boys, Nuneaton, Coventry, Warwickshire (39), Leigh RLFC.

Keith Fairbrother

Fairbrother made 229 appearances for Coventry and helped them to win the 1972 RFU KO Cup. He went on the British Lions tour of South Africa 1969. His debut for Leigh RLFC was made in a home match against Workington Town on 12 January 1975. His last appearance for that club was a home match against Blackpool Borough on 6 April 1975, after which he left the club by mutual consent with only eight appearances to his name.

FAITHFULL
Charles Kirke Tindale ('Bull' or 'Chubby')

Prop. 1924-1926 (Harlequins, 3 caps).
Debut v Ireland, 9 February 1924.
Born: 6 January 1903; Died: 8 August 1979.
Educated: Wellington College.

Educated: Burton upon Trent Grammar School, Amersham Hall School (Reading), Oxford University.

Clubs: Oxford University, Burton, East Sheen, Blackheath, Barbarians, Midland Counties.

Frank Evershed scored a try on his international debut. Employed as a solicitor, he was the son of S.Evershed MP, and father of the Rt Hon Lord Evershed. He played hockey for Derbyshire in 1906, at the age of 40, and cricket for Derbyshire from 1889 to 1894. He was the first player from the Midland Counties to be capped for England.

EYRES
Wallace C.T.

Number 8. 1927 (Richmond, 1 cap).
Debut v Ireland, 12 February 1927.

Educated: Royal Naval College (Greenwich).

Clubs: United Services (Portsmouth), Richmond, Royal Navy, Barbarians, Kent, Hampshire.

Eyres was employed at the White City Stadium, London. He served in World War Two as aide to Admiral Bonham-Carter. He helped Kent become the first south-east county to win the County Championship since 1904.

FAGAN
Arthur Robert St Leger

Full-back. 1887 (Richmond, 1 cap).
Debut v Ireland, 5 February 1887.
Born: 24 November 1862; Died: 15 March 1930.
Clubs: Guy's Hospital, United Hospi-

Clubs: Devonport Services, United Services (Portsmouth), Halifax, Harlequins, Combined Services, Army, Barbarians, Surrey, Hampshire, Yorkshire (15 appearances).

Charles Faithfull

A noted amateur boxer, he served in World War Two with the Duke of Wellington's Regiment reaching the rank of lieutenant-colonel after joining the regiment's second battalion in 1923. He played for the Army from 1924 to 1928, making several appearances against the Royal Navy, Royal Air Force and French Army. A good front-row forward and a very fast player, he would have gained more caps had a knee injury early in his playing career not hindered his play. He refereed from 1929 to 1936.

FALLAS
Herbert

Back. 1884 (Wakefield Trinity, 1 cap).
Debut v Ireland 4 February 1884.
Clubs: Wakefield Trinity, Yorkshire (14 appearances).
Fallas made his Yorkshire debut against Lancashire in 1882. He was one of the mainstays of the Wakefield club in the 1880s, a period when Trinity played in nine Yorkshire RU Finals in 13 years, winning four of them. A centre-threequarter, he was in the Wakefield team that toured Wales in 1884, winning all their games, against Cardiff, Newport and Swansea. He also played for Trinity in an exhibition game against Dewsbury at Blackburn in 1883.

John Fegan

FEGAN
John Herbert Craugle

Wing. 1895 (Blackheath, 3 caps).
Debut v Wales, 5 January 1895.
Born: 20 January 1872, Old Charlton, Kent; Died: 26 July 1949.
Educated: Blackheath Proprietary School, Cambridge Univesity.
Clubs: Cambridge University, Blackheath, Barbarians, Kent.

FERNANDES
Charles Walker Luis

Forward. 1881 (Leeds, 3 caps).
Debut v Ireland, 5 February 1881.
Born: 3 April 1857, Wakefield; Died: 12 August 1944, Thirsk, Yorkshire.
Educated: Rossall School.
Clubs: Wakefield, Leeds, Yorkshire West, Yorkshire (11 appearances).
Leeds were one of the founding members of the Northern Union in 1895.

FIDLER
John Howard

Lock. 1981-1984 (Gloucester, 4 caps).
Debut v Argentina, 30 May 1931.
Born: 16 September 1948, Cheltenham.
Clubs: Cheltenham, Gloucester, Gloucestershire (9 appearances in County Championship).
Fidler was on the England 'B' tour to Romania in 1978 and the full England tours to Argentina in 1981 and to South Africa in 1984. He is a policeman.

FIELD
Edwin

Full-back. 1893 (Middlesex Wanderers, 2 caps).
Debut v Wales, 7 January 1893.
Born: 16 December 1871, Hampstead; Died: 9 January 1947, Bromley.
Educated: Clifton College, Cambridge University.
Clubs: Cambridge University, (Blues

Edwin Field

Keith Fielding

1892-4), Middlesex Wanderers, Richmond, Barbarians, Middlesex.

Besides his rugger Blues he also won a Blue at cricket in 1894 and played for Berkshire in 1895 and for Middlesex from 1904 to 1906. He was a solicitor.

FIELDING
Keith John

Wing. 1969-1972 (Moseley, Loughborough Colleges, 10 caps).
Debut v Ireland, 8 February 1969.
Born: 8 August 1949, Birmingham.
Educated: King Edward School (Birmingham), Loughborough College.
Clubs: Loughborough Colleges, Moseley, North Midlands, Salford RL.

Keith Fielding, who was 19 when he was capped on the right wing, had an explosive acceleration and swerve technique which proved particularly effective in sevens competitions. He scored 11 tries for Loughborough Colleges on Middlesex Finals day in 1970 and was the top try scorer (with 39) in England in 1972-3, when he was with Moseley. His fame, though, was firmly established in Rugby League after he joined Salford in May 1973 for a reported fee of £8,000. He scored a club record 46 tries in his first season with Salford and captained the club in 1979.

He scored a hat-trick of tries for the Great Britain RL team against France in 1974 and was in the England RL World Cup squads in 1975 and 1977. With Salford he appeared in three successive losing Lancashire Cup Final sides but won First Division Championship medals in 1973-4 and 1975-6. He appeared in BBC TV's *Super Stars* competition, winning his European heat but failed to get into the Final. His last appearance for Salford was against Keighley on 20 April 1983, after which he retired from the game. He made 316 appearances (four as substitute). He scored 253 tries, 133 goals, a total of 1,025 points. He is a schoolteacher.

FINCH
Richard Tanner

Half-back. 1880 (Cambridge University, 1 cap).
Debut v Scotland, 28 February 1880.
Born: 1857, Kensington; Died: 12 January 1921, Seaton.
Educated: Sherborne School, Cambridge University.

Clubs: Cambridge University (Blues 1876-80, captain 1879-80), St George's Hospital, Richmond, Surrey, Kent.

Finch was a GP in Salisbury. His only England cap is displayed at the RFU museum.

FINLAN
John Frank

Fly-half. 1967-1973 (Moseley, 13 caps).
Debut v Ireland, 11 February 1967.
Born: 9 September 1941.
Educated: Saltley Grammar School.
Clubs: Old Saltleians, Moseley, Barbarians, North Midlands.

He was on the England tour of Canada in 1967 and was later an England selector. A swift mover with the ball, his quick passing brought the best out of his threequarter players. He partnered R.D.A.Pickering (Bradford).

FINLINSON
Horace William
Forward. 1895 (Blackheath, 3 caps).
Debut v Wales, 5 January 1895.
Born: 9 June 1871, Bedford; Died: 31 October 1956.
Educated: Bedford Modern School, Blair Lodge.
Clubs: Blackheath, Barbarians, Kent, Eastern Counties.

FINNEY
Stephen (Sir), CIE KB
Half-back. 1872-1873 (Royal Indian Engineering College, 2 caps).
Debut v Scotland, 5 February 1872.
Born: 8 September 1852; Died: 1 March 1924.
Educated: Clifton College, Royal Indian Engineering College.
Clubs: Royal Indian Engineering College, Crewe Britannia, Calcutta.

Finney scored a try on his international debut and England's first try as a back. The Royal Indian Engineering College at Cooper's Hill then boasted one of the strongest teams in England and Stephen Finney was one of the great half-backs of the era. It was said that 'the harder the game and the more wounds he received, the better he seemed to play'. Employed on the railways, he played for Calcutta whilst working in India and continued until the club disbanded. He worked for the East Bengal State Railway (1891-99), for Indian Public Works (1874) and Indian North-West Railway (1899-1907). Awarded the CIE in 1904 and the KB in 1913.

FIRTH
Frederick
Wing. 1894 (Halifax, 3 caps).
Debut v Wales, 6 January 1894.
Born: 1870 or 1871, Cleckheaton, Yorkshire; Died: February 1936, Olneyville, USA.
Clubs: Brighouse Rangers, Halifax, Wakefield Trinity, Halifax, Manningham, Yorkshire (20 appearances).

After the split to the Northern Union in 1895, Firth made 119 first-team appearances, scoring 32 tries and 43 goals with a total of 184 points. A member of England's first four-three quarter line against Wales in 1894, he turned to RL when Halifax did so in 1895. His spell with Wakefield Trinity was only short before he returned to Halfiax, and he retired after only a handful of games for Manningham. Employed as a foreman in a machine workshop, he later worked as a landlord in Halifax for a number of years before emigrating to the USA around 1908.

FLETCHER
Nigel Corbet, OBE
Forward. 1901-1903 (Old Merchant Taylor's, 4 caps).

Debut v Wales, 5 January 1901.
Born: 3 August 1877, London; Died: 21 December 1951, Hampstead.
Educated: Merchant Taylor's School, Cambridge University.
Clubs: Old Merchant Taylor's, Cambridge University, University College Hospital, Barbarians, Middlesex.

FLETCHER
Thomas
Wing. 1897 (Seaton, 1 cap).
Debut v Wales, 9 January 1897.
Born: 1874, Seaton, Cumberland; Died: 28 August 1950, High Harrington.
Educated: Northside Council School (Seaton).
Clubs: Seaton, Seaton RL, Oldham RL.
Tom Fletcher was the first Cumbrian back to play for England.

FLETCHER
William Robert Badger
Forward. 1873-1875 (Marlborough Nomads, 2 caps).
Debut v Scotland, 3 March 1873.
Born: 10 December 1851; Died: 20 April 1895, London.
Educated: Marlborough College, Oxford University.
Clubs: Oxford University (Blues 1871, 1872 and 1874), Blackheath, Marlborough Nomads.

FOOKES
Ernest Faber
Wing. 1896-1899 (Sowerby Bridge, 10 caps).
Debut v Wales, 4 January 1896.
Born: 31 May 1874, Wairoa, New Zealand; Died: 3 March 1948, New Plymouth, New Zealand.
Educated: New Plymouth Boys' High School (New Zealand), Heath Grammar School, Owen's College (Manchester), Manchester University.
Clubs: Halifax, Sowerby Bridge, Yorkshire (captain 1896-8), Taranaki, Tukapa, Taranaki-Wanganui-Manawatu.

Ernie Fookes, who came to England to continue his education, scored two tries on his international debut and altogether scored five tries in his ten appearances. A winger who took a lot of stopping and who had an excellent defence, he played for Halifax until they turned to the Rugby League code in 1895. He then left to join Sowerby Bridge, with whom he won his England caps. He returned home in 1900 and was chosen by New Zealand to tour the British Isles with them in 1905 but had to decline. He became president of Taranaki RFU in 1933. He had three sons, all of whom also played first-class rugby, one of them, Kenneth, appearing in the New Zealand trials of 1934.

FORD
Peter John
Flanker. 1964 (Gloucester, 4 caps).
Debut v Wales, 18 January 1964.
Born: 2 May 1953.
Educated: Central Modern School (Gloucester).
Clubs: RAF, Barbarians, Gloucestershire.
Ford won his first cap as a 31-year-old and after his playing days ended he became an RFU selector. Employed in the wholesale fruit trade.

FORREST
J.W.
Lock. 1930-1934 (United Services (Portsmouth), Royal Navy, 10 caps).
Debut v Wales, 18 January 1930.
Clubs: United Services (Portsmouth), Royal Navy (captain 1932-5), Combined Services, Hampshire 1924.

FORREST
Reginald
Wing. 1899-1903 (Wellington, 6 caps).
Debut v Wales, 7 January 1899.
Born: 12 May 1878, Bristol; Died: 11 April 1903, Minehead.
Educated: Christ's College.
Clubs: Blackheath, Wellington, Taunton, Barbarians, Somerset (25 appearances, later as captain).

An electrical engineer, he died two months after contracting typhoid fever when on duty for England in Dublin on 14 February 1903.

FOULDS
Robert Thompson
Number 8. 1929 (Waterloo, 2 caps).
Debut v Wales, 19 January 1929.
Born: 27 April 1906.
Educated: King William's College (Isle of Man).
Clubs: Birmingham, Furness, Moseley, Waterloo, Barbarians, North Midlands, Lancashire (44 appearances).
Foulds was employed in the wholesale meat trade.

FOWLER
Frank Dashwood
Forward. 1878-1879 (Manchester, 2 caps).
Debut v Scotland, 4 March 1878.
Born: 16 August 1855.
Educated: Cheltenham College, Royal Indian Engineering College.
Clubs: Manchester, Lancashire.

An engineer, he worked for the Indian Public Works Department in 1879 and was Secretary for Railways to the Government of India in Madras in 1908. Besides rugger he was a reknowned oarsman at RIE College.

FOWLER
Howard
Forward. 1878-1881 (Oxford University, 3 caps).
Debut v Scotland, 4 March 1878.
Born: 20 October 1857, Tottenham, London; Died: 6 May 1934, Burnham-on-Sea.
Educated: Clifton College, Oxford University.
Clubs: Oxford University (Blues 1877-8), Walthamstow, Blackheath, Middlesex.
Fowler was an all-round sportsman, gaining cricket Blues (1877-80), appearing for Essex CCC and playing golf and billiards. A barrister, he was called to the Bar in 1883.

FOWLER
R. Henry
Forward. 1877 (Leeds, 1 cap).
Debut v Ireland, 5 February 1877.
Clubs: Leeds, Yorkshire.
He stayed with Leeds when they helped form the Northern Union in 1895.

FOX
Francis Hugh, JP
Half-back. 1890 (Wellington, 2 caps).
Debut v Wales, 15 February 1890.
Born: 12 June 1863, Wellington; Died: 28 May 1952.
Educated: Marlborough College.
Clubs: Marlborough Nomads, Wellington, Somerset (45 appearances, captain 1888-93), Barbarians.
Fox was an International Board member in 1909 and RFU president from 1900 to 1902. He was capped in the 1888 England side that did not play. He was secretary of Somerset from 1884 to 1891, treasurer from 1885 to 1891 and president from 1901 to 1902.

FRANCIS
Thomas Egerton Seymour, OBE
Centre. 1926 (Cambridge University, 3 caps).
Debut v Wales, 16 January 1926.
Born: 21 November 1902, South Africa; Died: 24 February 1969, Bulawayo, South Africa.
Educated: Tonbridge School, Cambridge University.
Clubs: Cambridge University (Blues 1922-5), Bridgwater, Blackheath, Somerset, Transvaal, Barbarians.
Francis was a member of the 1925 Cambridge XV that beat Oxford 33-3, which is still Oxford's heaviest defeat in the Varsity match. He gained a cricket Blue in 1925 and also played cricket for Somerset and Eastern Province (South

Thomas Francis

Africa). In World War Two he reached the rank of lieutenant-colonel. Awarded the OBE in 1965.

FRANKCOM
Geoffrey Peter
Centre. 1965 (Cambridge University, Bedford, 4 caps).
Debut v Wales, 16 January 1965.
Born: 5 April 1942, Bath.
Educated: King Edward's School (Bath), Cambridge University.
Clubs: Cambridge University (Blues 1961-4), Bedford, Headingley, Bath, RAF, Barbarians, Somerset.
He made over 100 appearnces for Bath. Employed at Bedford School as a teacher from 1965-7, he served in the RAF as a flight-lieutenant in Strike Command in 1967.

FRASER
Edward Cleather (Sir), CMB
Forward. 1875 (Blackheath, 1 cap).
Debut v Ireland, 15 February 1875.
Born: 1853; Died: 15 October 1927.
Educated: Blackheath Proprietary School, Oxford University.
Clubs: Oxford University (Blues 1872-5), Blackheath.
He was a council member of the Government of Mauritius. Awarded the CMB in 1912.

FRASER
George
Forward. 1902-1903 (Richmond, 5 caps).
Debut v Wales, 11 January 1902.

Born: September 1878; Died: 20 August 1950.
Educated: Godolphin School (Hammersmith).
Clubs: Richmond, Barbarians, Surrey, Middlesex.
Fraser was a Stock Exchange member from 1904 to 1949.

FREAKES
Hubert Dainton
Full-back. 1938-1939 (Oxford University, 3 caps).
Debut v Wales, 15 January 1938.
Born: 2 February 1914; Died: March 1942, in England (killed in action).
Educated: Maritzburg College (South Africa), Rhodes University, Oxford University.
Clubs: Oxford University (Blues 1936-8, captain 1938), Harlequins, Barbarians.

Hubert Freakes

He scored a conversion on his international debut and was also an athletics Blue. Served in World War Two as an RAF flying officer. Employed in business in Johannesburg from 1939 to 1940.

FREEMAN
Harold

Back. 1872-1874 (Marlborough Nomads, 3 caps).
Debut v Scotland, 5 February 1872.
Born: 15 January 1850; Died: 15 July 1916, London.
Educated: Marlborough College, Oxford University.
Clubs: Oxford University, Marlborough Nomads, Wells, Somerset.

He scored England's first drop-goal on his international debut against Scotland. Indeed, it was said that he was one of the finest drop-kickers of his era, although he won only three caps. He was a member of the very first Oxford University RU committee

FRENCH
Raymond James

Lock. 1961 (St Helens, 4 caps).
Debut v Wales, 21 January 1961.
Born: 23 December 1939, St Helens.
Educated: Cowley School, Leeds University.
Clubs: St Helens RUFC, Barbarians, Lancashire, St Helens RL.

Ray French, who played for the North-West Counties against South Africa in November 1960, coached at Cowley School (Union code), one of the great nurseries of rugby football in the North of England. After moving to Rugby League, he was vice-captain of the Great Britain team for the 1968 World Cup. Originally employed as a schoolmaster, he later worked as chief commentator on television, covering Rugby League matches. He is the author of *My Kind of Rugby — Union and League* which was published by Faber in 1979.

FRY
Henry Arthur, TD

Flanker. 1934 (Liverpool, 3 caps).
Debut, Wales, 20 January 1934.
Born: 22 December 1910; Died: 3 November 1977, Formby Lancashire.
Educated: Liverpool College,
Clubs: Liverpool, Fylde, Waterloo, Rosslyn Park, Army, Barbarians, Lancashire (44 caps).

He served during World War Two, reaching the rank of lieutenant-colonel. Awarded the TD in 1946, he was a solicitor.

FRY
Thomas William

Full-back. 1880-1881 (Queen's House, 3 caps).
Debut v Ireland, 30 January 1880.
Club: Queen's House.

He played for Queen's House, part of the Royal Palace at Greenwich, until the club was dissolved in 1883 and was said to be England's first 'sole' full-back player. He later emigrated to Canada.

FULLER
Herbert George

Forward. 1882-1884 (Bath, 6 caps).
Debut v Ireland, 6 February 1882.
Born: 4 October 1856, Finchley; Died: 2 January 1896, Streatham, London.
Educated: Christ's College (Finchley), Cambridge University.
Clubs: Cambridge University (Blues 1878-1883), Bath, Somerset.

Fuller was Bath's first international player and captain of Somerset from 1882 to 1884. His record of six Blues was achieved before the University changed their rules to stop fifth-year students from playing in a Varsity match. He moved overseas in 1884 until 1886, when he returned to be elected president of Cambridge University RFC in 1885. His bald pate was so conspicuous in the scrums and rucks that he is said to have invented the scrum cap.

GADNEY
Bernard C.

Scrum-half. 1932-1938 (Leicester, Headingley, 14 caps).
Debut v Ireland, 13 February 1932.
Born: 16 July 1909, Oxford.
Educated at Dragon School (Oxford), Stowe School.
Clubs: Richmond, Leicester, Headingley, Barbarians, Leicestershire, East Midlands, Oxfordshire, Yorkshire.

In 1933-4 Gadney captained England to their first Triple Crown since 1928. He captained the British Lions tour of Argentina in 1936, when the Lions won all ten fixtures. He played for Leicestershire and East Midlands against New Zealand in 1936. Served in World War Two with the Royal Naval Volunteer Reserve. He is the brother of Cyril (who was president of the RFU from 1962 to 1966).

Bernard Gadney

GAMLIN
Herbert Tremlett

Full-back. 1899-1904 (Blackheath, 15 caps).
Debut v Wales, 7 January 1899.
Born: 12 February 1878, Wellington Somerset; Died: 12 July 1937, London.
Educated: Wellington School.
Clubs: Wellington, Devonport Albion, Blackheath, Somerset (50 appearances, captain 1901-1904).

Gamlin won his first cap as a 20-year-old. A 14st full-back, it was said that he did not simply tackle an opponent, he 'crushed him with an octupus-like grip'. He represented Somerset at rugger and cricket, first appearing at the age of 16. He was employed in the Civil Service.

GARDINER
Ernest Robert

Hooker. 1921-1923 (Devonport Services, 10 caps).
Debut v Wales, 15 January 1921.
Born: 6 October 1866; Died: 26 January 1954.
Clubs: Devonport Services, Devon, Cornwall (14 appearances).

Gardiner had a career in the Royal Navy and was selected to play for England in 1921 (when England won the Grand Slam) whilst a private in the RMLI.

GARDNER
Herbert Prescott, JP

Forward. (Richmond, 1878, 1 cap).
Debut v Ireland 11 March 1878.
Born: 1855; Died: 1938.
Educated: Wellington College.
Clubs: Richmond, Middlesex.

A dairy farmer, he later emigrated to Australia and became Justice of the Peace in Queensland. He scored a try on his international debut for England.

GARNETT
Harry Wharfedale Tennant

Forward. 1877 (Bradford, 1 cap).
Debut v Scotland 5 March 1877.
Born: 16 September 1851, Otley, Yorkshire; Died: 27 April 1928.
Educated: Blackheath Proprietary School.
Clubs: Bradford, Yorkshire (22 appearances, captain 1873-9).

He was the first President of Yorkshire, from 1876 to 1883, and was president of the RFU in 1889-1890. Bradford turned to Rugby League when they helped form the Northern Union in 1895.

Garnett had an unusual habit of turning out for matches without wearing stockings.

GAVINS
Michael Neil

Full-back. 1961 (Leicester, 1 cap).
Debut v Wales, 21 January 1961.

Born: 14 October 1934, Leeds.
Educated: Roundhay School, Loughborough Colleges, Leeds University,
Clubs: Leeds, Middlesbrough, Moseley, Leicester, Leicestershire, Midland Counties, North Midlands.
Gavins was one of the more travelled players in Rugby Union.

GAY
David John

Number 8. 1968 (Bath, 4 caps).
Debut v Wales, 20 January 1968.
Born: 10 March 1948.
Educated: Oldfield Boys' School, City of Bath Technical School.
Clubs: Bath, Harlequins, Barbarians, Somerset.

He won two caps playing for the England Under-19 group against Wales and France in 1966. Employed as solicitor's clerk.

GENT
David Robert (Dai)

Half-back/Full-back. 1905-1910 (Gloucester, 5 caps).
Debut v New Zealand, 2 December 1905.
Born: 9 January 1883, Llandovey; Died: 16 January 1964, Hellingly, Sussex.
Educated: St Paul's College (Cheltenham).
Clubs: Plymouth, Gloucester, Gloucestershire, Cornwall.

Gent played in the Welsh trials of 1905 and chosen as Welsh reserve. He once tried to displace the 35-times capped R.M.Owen as the Welsh scrum-half but failed to do so and joined Gloucester, becoming, in due course, England's regular choice in that position. He played cricket for Cornwall and worked for the *Sunday Times* as rugger correspondent.

GENTH
J.S.M.

Forward. 1874-1975 (Manchester, 2 caps).
Debut v Scotland, 23 February 1874.
Club: Manchester.

GEORGE
James Thomas

Lock. 1947-1949 (Falmouth, 3 caps).
Debut v Scotland, 15 March 1947.
Born: 24 August 1918.
Clubs: Falmouth, Barbarians, Cornwall (20 appearances).

George won only three caps, against Scotland in the Calcutta Cup triumph of 1947, against France also in 1947 and two years later against Ireland.

GERRARD
Ronald Anderson, DSO

Centre. 1932-1936 (Bath, 14 caps).
Debut v South Africa, 2 January 1932.
Born: 26 January 1912, Hong Kong;

Died: 22 January 1943, Libya (killed in action).
Educated: Taunton School.
Clubs: Bath, Barbarians, Somerset.

Gerrard is Bath's most capped player and possibly their most distinguished of all England internationals. A powerful centre-threequarter player, he captained Gloucestershire and Somerset against New Zealand in 1934 and also played cricket for Somerset. He served in World War Two, being awarded the DSO in 1942. Taunton School have a Gerrard Memorial Fund which was set up in his memory after he lost his life in Libya. After the war his wife, Molly, became the president of Bath and is the only women to have given a commentary on a rugger match on radio.

GIBBS
George Anthony, TD

Prop. 1947-1948 (Bristol, 2 caps).
Debut v France, 19 April 1947.
Born: 31 March 1920.
Educated: Clifton College.
Clubs: Bristol, Northern, Barbarians, Gloucestershire, Northumberland.

He was employed in the tobacco industry, working as manager. He is the brother of Nigel and served during World War Two.

GIBBS
John Clifford, JP

Wing. 1925-1927 (Harlequins, 7 caps).
Debut v New Zealand, 3 January 1925.
Born: 10 March 1902.
Educated: Queen's College (Taunton), Cambridge University.
Clubs: Cambridge University (no Blue), Harlequins, Kent.

John Gibbs is certainly one of the game's longest-lived servants, for he was the Harlequins' subscriptions treasurer at the age of 89. However, he was originally a soccer player, turning out for Morgan Athletic (later Morgan Tower) on Wednesdays and playing rugby on Saturdays. He was known as the 'Human Torpedo' when he played for Athenian League club Bromley AFC from 1932 to 1934.

A rather unorthodox winger, albeit one of the fastest of his day, he played on the right wing at soccer and on the left wing at rugby. Apparently, when playing soccer he sometimes forgot which game he was involved in and would occasionally pick the ball up and run with it.

Gibbs, who broke an ankle in his very first trial game in 1920, first played for the Harlequins 'A' XV and was selected for Kent a few months later. He scored five tries, then appeared for Quins' 1st XV against Richmond, playing until 1930. In April 1922, he played for Harlequins Present against Harlequins Past in a match in aid of Kind Edward VII's Hospital Fund.

During World War Two he served in

the RAF and it was Gibbs' squadron which dropped new artificial legs for Douglas Bader (a fellow Harlequin), after his original artificial legs had been damaged when he was shot down over France.

Gibbs became honorary superintendent of Bromley Central Hall Methodist Mission from 1933 to 1955 and was later a Diocesan lay reader at Birchington-on-Sea. He was the youngest son of W.J.Gibbs (founder of the Farwig Wesleyan Mission, later known as Bromley Central Hall Methodist Mission) and brother of W.D.Gibbs (RFU president 1955-6, Lord Mayor of Bromley 1932-4 and an Old Millhillians player).

GIBBS
Nigel

Full-back. 1954 (Harlequins, 2 caps).
Debut v Scotland, 20 March 1954.
Born: 24 September 1922.
Educated: Clifton College, Oxford University.
Clubs: Oxford University (no Blue), Guildford & Godalming, Bristol, Harlequins, London Counties, Gloucestershire, Surrey.

Nigel Gibbs scored two conversions on his international debut and although he did not win a rugby Blue at Oxford, he did gain one at cricket. He served during World War Two as a lieutenant in submarines in the RNVR and was mentioned in despatches. Employed as a schoolmaster, he held a number of posts including one at Charterhouse from 1950 to 1962 and was head teacher at Colston's in 1965. He is the brother of George.

GIBLIN
Lyndhurst Falkiner, DSO MC

Forward. 1896-1897 (Blackheath, 3 caps).
Debut v Wales, 4 January 1896.
Born: 29 November 1872, Tasmania; Died: 2 March 1951.
Educated: Hutchins School (Hobart), London University, Cambridge University.
Clubs: Cambridge University (Blues 1894-6), Blackheath, Barbarians, Middlesex.

Giblin returned to Tasmania to become a fruit grower and once tried his hand at gold mining in the Klondyke. He was also employed at Melbourne University as a professor of economics from 1929 to 1940 and served in World War One, being awarded the MC and DSO in 1918.

GIBSON
Arthur Sumner

Forward. 1871 (Manchester, 1 cap).
Debut v Scotland, 27 March 1871.
Born: 14 July 1844, Hampshire; Died: 23 January 1927, Berkshire.
Educated: Marlborough College,

Oxford University.
Clubs: Oxford University (no Blue), Manchester, Lancashire.
Employed as a civil engineer, he played in the very first international between Scotland and England in 1871 whilst with the Manchester club.

GIBSON
Charles Osborne Provis, MC DL

Forward. 1901 (Northern, 1 cap).
Debut v Wales, 5 January 1901.
Born: October 1876; Died: 9 November 1931, Stocksfield, Northumberland.
Educated: Uppingham School, Oxford University.
Clubs: Oxford University (no Blue), Northern, Barbarians, Northumberland.
Employed as a solicitor, Charles Gibson was the brother of G.R. and T.A.Gibson. He served during World War One as a colonel in the Northumberland Fusiliers (TA), was awarded the MC in 1916 and was mentioned in despatches twice, in 1915 and 1918.

GIBSON
George Ralph

Forward. 1899-1901 (Northern, 2 caps).
Debut v Wales, 7 January 1899.
Born: March 1878; Died: October 1939.
Educated: Uppingham School.
Clubs: Northern, Barbarians, Northumberland (1895 County Champions).
George Gibson was employed in the timber trade and was the brother of Charles and Thomas Alexander. He went on the British Lions tour of Australia in 1899.

GIBSON
Thomas Alexander

Forward. 1905 (Northern, 2 caps).
Debut v Wales, 14 January 1905.
Born: 30 January 1880, Gateshead; Died: 27 April 1937.
Educated: Uppingham School, Cambridge University.
Clubs: Cambridge University (Blues 1901-02), Northern, Barbarians, Northumberland.
Employed in the timber industry, like his brother George, he was also brother of Charles and was the only one of the three to win a Blue.

GILBERT
F.G.

Full-back. 1923 (Devonport Services, 2 caps).
Debut v Wales, 20 January 1923.
Born: 1885.
Clubs: Devonport Services, Royal Navy, Cornwall (22 appearances).
Gilbert won two caps as a 39-year-old, against Wales and Ireland, in 1923. He was elected to a position on the Naval Rugby Union Committee in 1922 and worked as a chief shipwright.

GILBERT
R.

Forward. 1908 (Devonport Albion, 3 caps).
Debut v Wales, 18 January 1908.
Clubs: Devonport Albion, Royal Navy.
Gilbert played his first international on the Bristol City AFC ground. He had a career in the Royal Navy and reached the rank of petty officer. He was the first non-commissioned officer in the regular Navy to be capped by England.

GILES
James Leonard

Scrum-half. 1935-1938 (Coventry, 6 caps).
Debut v Wales, 19 January 1935.
Born: 5 January 1912; Died: 28 March 1967, Coventry.

James Giles

Clubs: Coventry, Warwickshire.
Giles was on the 1938 British Lions tour of South Africa, with Sam Walker as manager, and set a precedent when he played centre in the Third Test. In the provincial matches he scored five conversions and a drop-goal. He captained Warwickshire to the County Championship.

GITTINGS
William John

Scrum-half. 1967 (Coventry, 1 cap).
Debut v New Zealand, 4 November 1967.
Born: 5 October 1939, Coventry.

Educated: Barker Butts School (Coventry).

Clubs: Coventry, Warwickshire, Midland Counties.

Gittings was in the Coventry team which won the RFU Club KO Cup in 1972-3.

GLOVER
Peter Bernard

Wing. 1967-1971 (Bath, 3 caps).
Debut v Australia, 7 January 1967.
Born: 25 September 1945.

Educated: De Aston School, RAF Cranwell.

Clubs: RAF, Selby, Bedford, Bath, Combined Services, Barbarians, Yorkshire.

An RAF instructor-pilot, he also represented the RAF at athletics in 1966. He went on England's tour to the Far East in 1971.

GODFRAY
Reginald Edmund

Centre. 1905 (Richmond, 1 cap).
Debut v New Zealand, 2 December 1905.
Born: 10 May 1880; Died: 4 February 1967.

Educated: Victoria College (Jersey).

Clubs: Park House, Richmond, Middlesex.

A member of the Stock Exchange from 1914 to 1968. He was president of Chiswick Park Lawn Tennis Club.

GODWIN
Herbert O.

Hooker. 1959-1967 (Coventry, 11 caps).
Debut v France, 28 February 1959.
Born: 21 December 1935.

Educated: Broadway Secondary Modern School (Coventry).

Clubs: Coventry, Army, Combined Services, Barbarians, Warwickshire.

His England cap in 1959 was the fourth international cap to be awarded to a serving member of the Royal Leicestershire Regiment and only two infantry regiments had more international players. Whilst on National Service he played for the Army against the Royal Navy in 1960 and against the RAF in 1959 and 1960. He was employed as a machine-fitter at the Standard works in Coventry.

GORDON-SMITH
Gerald W.

Centre. 1900 (Blackheath, 3 caps).
Debut v Wales, 6 January 1900.
Died: 23 January 1911, Carbis Bay.
Educated: Camborne School of Mines.

Clubs: Redruth, Cornwall (15 appearances), Blackheath, Barbarians, Kent.
Gordon-Smith was the first Cornishman to be capped by England when he was selected in 1900.

GRAHAM
David

Forward. 1901 (Aspatria, 1 cap).
Debut v Wales, 5 January 1901.
Born: June 1875; Died: January 1962, Carlisle.

Clubs: Aspatria H, Aspatria, Keswick, Rochdale, New Brighton, Cumberland.

David Graham was employed as a headmaster.

GRAHAM
H.J.

Forward. 1875-1876 (Wimbledon H, 4 caps).
Debut v Ireland. 15 February 1875.

Clubs: Wimbledon H, Surrey.

He played alongside his brother, J.D.G.Graham, against Ireland in 1875, the only time they appeared together in an international. He was elected treasurer of the RFU in 1876, a post he kept until 1878.

GRAHAM
John Duncan George

Forward. 1875 (Wimbledon H, 1 cap).
Debut v Ireland, 13 December 1875.
Born: 1856.

Educated: Wellington College.

Clubs: Wimbledon H, Surrey.

He appeared with his brother, H.J.Graham, against Ireland in 1875, the only occasion they played together in an international.

GRAY
Arthur

Full-back. 1947 (Otley, 3 caps).
Debut v Wales, 18 January 1947.
Born: 4 September 1917, Leeds.

Clubs: Otley, Wakefield Trinity RL.

Gray scored a conversion on his international debut and made six appearances for Yorkshire. After joining Wakefield Trinity, he made only 15 appearances from 1947-1950, scoring one try and nine goals, with a total of 21 points. He was employed as a fruit merchant. He served in World War Two. His son, Martin, is a former captain of Yorkshire Colts and an Otley full-back.

GREEN
John

Forward. 1905-1907 (Skipton, 8 caps).
Debut v Ireland, 11 February 1905.
Born: 17 September 1881, Skipton; Died: 27 December 1968.

Educated: Giggleswick School.

Clubs: Skipton, Yorkshire (28 appearances, captain from 1906 to 1907).

GREEN
Joseph Fletcher

Half-back. 1871 (West Kent, 1 cap).
Debut v Scotland, 27 March 1871.
Born: 28 April 1847; Died: 28 August 1923, Leeds.

Educated: Rugby School.

Club: West Kent.

He played in the first international between Scotland and England but his career ended tragically when he sustained an injury in the match which forced his early retirement from the game at all levels. He was the brother-in-law of Fred Stokes.

GREENWELL
John Henry

Forward. 1893 (Rockcliff, 2 caps).
Debut v Wales, 7 January 1893.
Born: 1864; Died: 1942.

Clubs: Rockcliff, Tynemouth, Northumberland (over 100 appearances), Barbarians.

Greenwell was a special constable who received a long-service medal.

GREENWOOD
John Eric, JP

Forward. 1912-1920 (Cambridge University, Leicester, 13 caps).
Debut v France, 8 April 1912.
Born: 23 July 1891; Died: 23 July 1975.

Educated: Dulwich College, Cambridge University.

Clubs: Old Alleynians, Cambridge University (Blues 1910-1919), Leicester, Harlequins, Surrey, Barbarians.

Greenwood scored most conversions in an international match when he converted six kicks against France in 1914, a record he held with G.W.Parker. England's first post-war captain, he returned to Cambridge in 1919 to resume the captaincy of the University XV, going on to win five Blues in ten years. He retired from international rugby in 1920. He became president of the Hawks club and represented Cambridge University on the RFU from 1919 to 1937. An International Board member in 1937, he was president of the RFU from 1935 to 1937 and later a trustee (1948).

During World War One he served with the Artists' Rifles, later joining the East Surrey Regiment and then the Grenadier Guards (as a captain). He was mentioned in despatches and in 1918 was wounded at the Battle of Nieppe. After World War Two he became a Justice of the Peace in Nottingham (1947-1953). He was a director of Boots the Chemists.

GREENWOOD
John Richard Heaton

Flanker. 1966-1969 (Waterloo, 5 caps).
Debut v Ireland, 12 February 1966.
Born: 11 September 1941.

Educated: Merchant Taylor's School (Crosby), Cambridge University.

Clubs: Cambridge University (Blues 1962-3), Waterloo, Coventry, Lancashire (26 appearances), Barbarians.

He scored a try on his international debut and was later England's captain and coach. He was employed as a school teacher, then as burser at Stonyhurst College. He had a spell coaching in Italy, returning in late-1979 to take over as coach to Preston Grasshoppers. A hard-tackling player and an excellent reader of the game, he was an inspiring captain who led Lancashire to the 1969 County Championship. His son, Will, plays for Waterloo.

GREG
Walter

Forward. 1875-1876 (Manchester, 2 caps).
Debut v Ireland, 13 December 1875.
Born: 14 February 1851, Cheshire; Died: 6 February 1906.
Educated: Marlborough College.
Clubs: Marlborough Nomads, Manchester, Lancashire.

GREGORY
Gordon George

Hooker. 1931-1934 (Bristol, 13 caps).
Debut v Ireland, 14 February 1931.
Born: 8 December 1908, Taunton; Died: 4 December 1963, Newton Abbot.
Educated: Huish School (Taunton), Reading University.
Clubs: Taunton, Reading University, Bath, Bristol, Somerset (33 appearances, captain 1932-1933).
Gordon Gregory was a farmer.

GREGORY
John Arthur

Wing. 1949 (Blackheath, 1 cap).
Debut v Wales, 15 January 1949.
Born: 22 June 1923.
Educated: St Andrew's College (Dublin), Rydal School.
Clubs: Dublin Wanderers, Clifton, Blackheath, Bristol, Barbarians, Gloucestershire, Huddersfield RL.

John Gregory's international cap was unusual in that it came following his suspension from the Union game after he had played for Huddersfield Rugby League Club. He had been banned by the RFU in 1946, for assisting Huddersfield whilst he was stationed near the town as a soldier. He was reinstated in April 1948 and gained his only cap a year later.

Whilst serving in the RAMC, he played for the Army against the Royal Navy and the RAF. An excellent athlete, he was All-Ireland 100 yards and 220 yards champion from 1947 to 1949 and represented Great Britain at the 1948 Olympics in London, winning a silver medal in the 4 x 100 yards relay race. In 1950 he took a European champion-

ship and again represented Great Britain at the 1952 Olympics in Melbourne. He is the president of Bristol Athletic Club.

GRYLLS
William Michell

Lock. 1905 (Redruth, 1 cap).
Debut v Ireland, 11 February 1905.
Born: 9 January 1855.
Educated: Haileybury and Imperial Service College, Royal Military Academy (Sandhurst).
Clubs: Redruth, Army, Cornwall.
A regular soldier, Grylls served with the Indian Army and reached the rank of lieutenant-colonel. His father was a founder member of the Redruth club in 1875.

GUEST
Richard Heaton ('Dickie').

Wing. 1939-1949 (Waterloo, 13 caps).
Debut v Wales, 21 January 1939.
Born: 12 March 1918.
Educated: Cowley School, Liverpool University.
Clubs: St Helens, Barbarians, Lancashire (49 appearances).

Dickie Guest first played for England

Dickie Guest

whilst still an undergraduate at Liverpool University and altogether scored five tries in his 13 internationals. He became an England selector in 1963, a post he held until 1966. He played in the same England team as his cousin, J.Heaton, in six internationals. He served in World War Two as a captain in the Royal Artillery.

GUILLEMARD
Arthur George

Full-back. 1871-1872 (West Kent, 2 caps).
Debut v Scotland, 27 March 1871.
Born: 18 December 1846; Died: 7 August 1909.
Educated: Rugby School.
Club: West Kent.

A solicitor by profession, Arthur Guillemard was born of French refugee parents. He played in the first international between Scotland and England in 1871 and, as the fifth president of the RFU, was the man who decided that the Calcutta Cup would be used as 'an international challenge cup to be played for annually by England and Scotland'. His England cap was presented to the RFU and is now in the museum at Twickenham. He refereed several international games in the late-1870s and early-1880s and also umpired in the Scotland-England match of 1873. One of the original members of the Rugby Football Union in 1871, he went on to hold all five main RFU offices.

GUMMER
Charles Henry Alexander

Number 8. 1929 (Plymouth Albion, 1 cap).
Debut v France, 1 April 1929.
Born: 20 November 1905; Died: 4 February 1974, Bishop's Waltham.
Clubs: Plymouth Albion, Moseley, British Police, Devon.

Gummer scored a try on his international debut. A policeman from 1927 to 1944, he represented the British Police at rugby. He served in World War Two as an army major and was later in the RAF from (1952 to 1957) and also held a position in the Ministry of Defence.

GUNNER
Charles Richard

Back. 1875 (Marlborough Nomads, 1 cap).
Debut v Ireland, 13 December 1875.
Born: 7 January 1853; Died: 4 February 1924.
Educated: Marlborough College.
Club: Marlborough Nomads.
Gunner was a solicitor.

GURDON
Charles

Forward. 1880-1886 (Richmond, 4 caps).
Debut v Ireland, 30 January 1880.

Charles Gurdon

skippered his country in Dublin in 1882. A county court judge, he was called to the Bar in 1881 and is the co-author of the centenary book on the Oxford and Cambridge Boat Race, published in 1927.

GURDON
Edward Temple

Forward. 1878-1886 (Richmond, 16 caps).
Debut v Scotland, 4 March 1878.
Born: 25 January 1854, Barnham Broom, Norfolk; Died: 12 June 1929, London.
Educated: Haileybury and Imperial Service College, Cambridge University.
Clubs: Cambridge University (Blues 1874-6), Richmond.

The eldest son of the Reverend Edward Gurdon and brother of Charles (with whom he appeared in ten international matches), Temple Gurdon played in the last 20-a-side team to represent Cambridge University. Elected to the RFU Committee in 1877, before he gained his first England cap, he retired as holder of a record 16 England appearances. He captained the side from December 1882 and remained for nine matches (eight wins and a draw). He led the first Championship side and the first Triple Crown winners in 1883. He also skippered Richmond for ten years and later returned as president.

He refereed two matches (Ireland-Scotland in 1898 and Scotland-Ireland in 1899) and was one of the touch-judges for the 1891 England-Scotland match. He became an RFU selector and International Board representative from 1890 to 1928 and was RFU president from 1890 to 1892. He was a solicitor.

GUSCOTT
Jeremy Clayton

Centre. 1989-1992 (Bath, 22 caps).
Debut v Romania, 13 May 1989.
Born: 7 July 1965, Bath.
Educated: Ralph Allen CS (Bath).
Clubs: Bath, Barbarians.

Jeremy Guscott began with Bath by playing mini-rugger as a seven-year-old and progressed through the ranks to the 1st XV and then into England's full side. He became the first Englishman since Jeff Butterfield to score tries for both England and the Lions on his debut.

He won two England 'B' caps, celebrated his international debut with a hat-trick of tries and went on the 1989 British Lions tour of Australia, playing in the Second and Third Tests after coming into the squad when Will Carling had to stay behind because of injury.

Guscott, who appeared for the Barbarians against New Zealand in 1989, played in the 1991 Grand Slam team, toured Fiji and Australia that year and was also a member of the World Cup runners-up team, after which he was

Born: 3 December 1855, Norfolk; Died: 26 June 1931, Middlesex.
Educated: Haileybury and Imperial Service College, Cambridge University.
Clubs: Cambridge University (Blue 1877), Richmond, Middlesex (captain 1879-83).

Gurdon, also gained three rowing Blues, played alongside his brother, Edward, ten times for England and

Edward Gurdon

Jeremy Guscott

linked both with a move to Rugby League and a 'transfer' to Harlequins. He stayed with Bath, however, the club he helped to the Courage League Championship in 1989, 1991 and 1992 and to victory in the 1989 and 1992 Pilkington Cup Finals. In 1992 he helped England to a second successive Grand Slam.

He works as a public relations officer for British Gas.

HAIGH
Leonard

Prop. 1910-1911 (Manchester, 7 caps).
Debut v Wales, 15 January 1910.
Born: 19 October 1880, Prestwich; Died: 6 August 1916, Woolwich.

Clubs: Sandringham House (Southport), Manchester, Lancashire (18 appearances), Barbarians.

Haigh made his international debut in the 1910 Championship season. He died whilst on a training exercise for active service during World War One.

HALE
Peter Martin

Wing. 1969-1970 (Moseley, 3 caps).
Debut v South Africa, 20 December 1969.
Born: 12 August 1943, Birmingham.

Educated: Solihull School.

Clubs: Solihull, Moseley, Midland Counties, North Midlands.

Hale scored 44 tries for Moseley in 1967-8 and also represented Warwickshire at lawn tennis.

HALL
C.

Forward. 1901 (Gloucester, 2 caps).
Debut v Ireland, 9 February 1901.
Club: Gloucester.

Hall appeared in the last two games of the 1901 season, in which England used 28 players in three games, all lost.

HALL
John

Forward. 1894 (North Durham, 3 caps).
Debut v Wales, 6 January 1894.

Clubs: Gateshead Institute, North Durham, Hartlepool Rovers, Blackheath, Durham County.

HALL
John Peter

Flanker. 1984-1990 (Bath, 20 caps).
Debut v Scotland, 4 February 1984.
Born: 15 March 1962, Bath.

Educated: Beechen Cliff School.

Clubs: Oldfield Old Boys, Bath.

A former England Colts player, Hall made his full international debut as a replacement for the injured Peter Winterbottom. Hall was also to suffer injury, however, breaking a thumb in the England-Scotland game in 1986, a

John Hall

blow which ruled him out for the rest of that season. A member of the England squad which toured South Africa in 1984, his club honours include an appearance in the JPS Cup-winning side of 1986, when Bath won the title for the third successive time, beating Wasps 25-17 to equal record set by Leicester in 1981.

HALL
Norman MacLeod ('Nim').

Centre. 1947-1955 (Richmond, 17 caps).
Debut v Wales, 18 January 1947.
Born: 2 August 1925, Huddersfield; Died: 26 June 1972, London.

Educated: Worksop College.

Clubs: St Mary's Hospital, Army, Huddersfield, Combined Services, Richmond, Barbarians, Yorkshire (8 appearances, captain 1947-8), Middlesex.

Nim Hall, who scored a drop-goal on his international debut in the same year that England won the Calcutta Cup, captained England 13 times and was regarded as a *nonpareil* of drop-kickers. He played three times for the Army, against the Royal Navy, RAF and French Army. He died in St Mary's Hospital, London, and there were many distinguished figures from the rugby world at his funeral. They included the RFU president, past presidents and the presidents of the Barbarians and Richmond. A telegram from Dr Danie Craven (South Africa RFU) was one of many messages of sympathy received.

HALLIDAY
Simon John

Centre. 1986-1992 (Bath, Harlequins, 23 caps).
Debut v Wales, 18 January 1986.
Born: 13 July 1960, Haverfordwest, Pembrokeshire.

Educated: Downside School, Oxford University.

Simon Halliday

Clubs: Oxford University (Blues 1979-81), Harlequins, Bath.

Simon Halliday, who played in five winning Cup Final teams for Bath, had his first taste of representative rugby with Dorset and Wiltshire Under-19s. He went on the England Under-23 tour to the Far East in 1982, played against Romania in 1983 and for the England XV against Canada the same year. He captained the South-West to victory over the USA and Australia in 1988, went on the full tour of Fiji and Australia in 1991 and was a member of that year's World Cup runners-up team.

A fracture and dislocation of his left foot, sustained whilst playing for Somerset against Middlesex in the 1983 County Championship, probably delayed his full international debut and he was also out for a year when he broke a leg in the England 'B' game against Ireland in 1985. He gained a Pilkington Cup winners' medal with the Quins in 1991 and a runners-up medal in 1992 and was the Whitebread/*Rugby World and Post* Player of the Month for February 1992. Soon afterwards he was helping to celebrate a second successive Grand Slam.

Halliday, a stockbroker, won a cricket Blue at Oxford and also played for the Free Foresters, Dorset and the Minor Counties. His father played rugby for the Royal Navy.

HAMETT
Ernest Dyer Galbraith

Centre. 1920-1922 (Newport, 8 caps).
Debut v Wales, 17 January 1920.
Born: 15 October 1891, Radstock; Died: 23 June 1947.
Educated: Newport Intermediate School, Newport High School.
Clubs: Newport, Radstock, Cardiff, Blackheath, Barbarians, Surrey, Somerset (champions 1923).

Hamett, a schoolteacher, was offered a trial by the Welsh Rugby Union in 1919 but preferred to play for England. He won a rugby cap for England and an amateur soccer cap for Wales. He helped Somerset win their only County Championship and also represented Wales against England at lawn tennis. Despite a lack of pace, he had good positional sense on the rugby field.

HAMILTON-HILL
Edward A. ('Ham'), OBE

Flanker. 1936 (Harlequins, 3 caps).
Debut v New Zealand, 4 January 1936.
Born: 22 November 1908; Died: 23 October 1979.
Clubs: HMS Conway, Royal Navy, Harlequins, Surrey.

He became a resident of Malta in 1946 after serving in the Royal Navy during World War Two. He was in the Harlequins' 1935 Middlesex Sevens winning team. Awarded the OBE in 1961.

HAMILTON-WICKES
Richard Henry

Wing. 1924-1927 (Cambridge University, 10 caps).
Debut v Ireland, 9 February 1924.
Educated: Bilton Grange School, Wellington College, Cambridge University.
Clubs: Cambridge University (Blues 1920-23, captain 1922-3), Harlequins.

Richard Hamilton-Wickes

His England debut in 1924, when he was chosen to replace the injured Locke, brought about the fact that all the Cambridge captains from 1920 to 1924 (Conway, Cove-Smith, Wakefield, Young and Hamilton-Wickes) were in the same England team. Hamilton-Wickes scored a try on his international debut and his first England season of 1924 saw him as one of the few successes in the national team. Played in the Harlequins Past-Harlequins Present match on 22 April 1922, a game organised in aid of the King Edward VII Hospital Fund.

HAMMERSLEY
Alfred St George

Forward. 1871-1874 (Marlborough Nomads, 4 caps).
Debut v Scotland, 27 March 1871.
Born: 8 October 1848, Great Haseley, Oxfordshire; Died: 25 February 1929, Bournemouth.
Educated: Marlborough College.
Clubs: Marlborough Nomads, Canterbury (New Zealand).

Hammersley, who played in the first international match between England and Scotland, was a lawyer, called to the Bar in 1873. He was Conservative MP for Woodstock from 1910 to 1918 and later became legal advisor to the city of Vancouver and to Canadian Pacific Railways.

During World War One he served as a recruiting and training officer with the artillery and in 1917 went to France as CO of a heavy artillery battery. He was then 68 and completed the war as a lieutenant-colonel.

It is said that he was mainly responsible for introducing rugby to British Columbia during the 1880s and he is given credit throughout the rest of Canada for introducing the game to that country.

HAMMOND
Charles Edward Lucas ('Curly')

Forward. 1905-1908 (Harlequins, 8 caps).
Debut v Scotland, 18 March 1905.
Born: 3 October 1887; Died: 15 April 1963.
Educated: Bedford Grammar School, Oxford University.
Clubs: Oxford University (Blues 1899-1900), Harlequins, Barbarians, Middlesex.

Curly Hammond, who played for Middlesex against the New Zealanders in 1905, was elected unofficial 'Beer King of All Germany' in 1908-09 when, as a Harlequins player, it is said that he drank ten glasses of beer when challenged by their German hosts.

It came about after a game against the German national XV, when the Harlequins were over 40 minutes late in arriving for the after-match social supper. The German president jokingly ordered that a Harlequins player should be penalised by drinking ten glasses of beer. Hammond had no hesitation in taking up the challenge, then promptly requested more. This so impressed the Germans that they bestowed upon him that title.

A teacher, he held posts at various schools and colleges including Wellington College (1906-07) and Felstead School (1940-1943). His sister married Ernest Prescott, who was an RFU administrator during the early-1900s. He was the uncle of Robin Prescott, the RFU secretary from 1963 to 1971.

HANCOCK
Andrew William

Wing. 1965-1966 (Northampton, 3 caps).
Debut v France, 27 February 1965.
Born: 19 June 1939.
Educated: Framlingham College, London University, Cambridge University.
Clubs: Sidcup, Cambridge University (no Blue), Northampton, Stafford, Wasps, London Counties, Barbarians, Staffordshire, Eastern Counties

His first cap came at 25 years of age, when he was chosen as a last-minute replacement for Ted Rudd. He scored a memorable try against Scotland at Twickenham on 20 March 1965, running the ball from 85 yards out, going around two Scots, well inside his own 25-yard line and reaching the line to score in the corner. The match ended 3-3 with Hancock saving England from defeat.

HANCOCK
George Edward

Centre. 1939 (Birkenhead Park, 3 caps).
Debut v Wales, 21 January 1939.
Born: 21 March 1912.
Educated: Rock Ferry High School.
Clubs: Old Rockferrians, Birkenhead Park, RAF, Mount Hope (Canada), Cheshire.

Hancock went on the British Lions' tour of Argentina in 1936 and played in Cheshire's 1938-9 County Championship semi-final against Warwickshire. A solicitor, he served during World War Two as a flight-lieutenant in the RAF.

HANCOCK
Philip Froude

Forward. 1886-1890 (Blackheath, 3 caps).
Debut v Wales 2 January 1886.
Born: 29 August 1865, Wellington, Somerset; Died: 16 October 1933, Clifton.
Educated: Cavendish College, Cambridge University.
Clubs: Cambridge University (no Blue), Wiveliscombe, Blackheath, Barbarians, Somerset (47 appearances, captain 1893-6).

He was one of five brothers who played rugger for Wiveliscombe and Somerset. Brother Frank played for Cardiff and was captain of Wales. Philip went on the British Lions tours of South Africa in 1891 and 1896, and was the only international player to make both tours. He was also capped in the 1888 side that did not play.

HANCOCK
Patrick Sortain

Fly-half. 1904 (Richmond, 3 caps).
Debut v Wales, 9 January 1904.
Born: 1883.
Educated: Dulwich College.
Clubs: Leytonstone, Streatham, Richmond, Eastern Counties, Surrey.

A farmer, he went on the British Lions tour of South Africa in 1903 and during World War One lost a leg whilst serving with the Canadian forces. He emigrated to Canada and, alas, nothing further is known of him after that.

HANCOCK
William Jack Henry

Lock. 1955 (Newport, 2 caps).
Debut v Wales, 22 January 1955.
Born: 26 September 1932.
Clubs: Army, Cross Keys, Newport, Salford RL.

He enjoyed a career in the Royal Signals and played for the Army six times, against the Royal Navy, RAF and French Army. He made his Rugby

League debut for Salford against Doncaster in August 1955 and soon became a regular member of the side, making his last appearance at Oldham on 19 November 1960 after clocking up 104 games, scoring two tries, 15 goals and 36 points. After the Army he worked for the chemical giants ICI.

HANDFORD
Frank Gordon

Flanker. 1909 (Manchester, 4 caps).
Debut v Wales, 16 January 1909.
Educated: Leys School.
Clubs: Kersal, Manchester, Barbarians, Lancashire (21 appearances).

An all-round scrummager and very square-shouldered, he went on the British Lions tour of South Africa in 1910, playing in 18 matches. He scored one of eight tries in the win against Border, played in all three Tests. He later emigrated to South Africa.

HANDS
Reginald Harold Myburgh

Forward. 1910 (Blackheath, 2 caps).
Debut v France, 3 March 1910.
Born: 26 July 1888, Cape Town, South Africa; Died: 20 April 1918, France (died of wounds).
Educated: Diocesan College (Rondebosch, South Africa), Oxford University.
Clubs: Oxford University (Blues 1908-09), Manchester, Blackheath, Middlesex, Barbarians.

A lawyer, called to the Bar in 1911, he had two brothers, K.C.M. and P.A.M. Hands, both of whom were also Oxford Blues. All three played Test cricket for South Africa against England in 1913.

During World War One, Reginald served in the Imperial Light Horse and later in the South African Heavy Artillery, in German South-West Africa and in France. When he was fatally wounded he was an acting major and second-in-command of a battery. He was awarded the 1914-1915 Star, British War Medal and Victory Medal.

HANLEY
Joseph

Flanker. 1917-1928 (Plymouth Albion, 7 caps).
Debut v Wales, 15 January 1927.
Born: 14 September 1901.
Clubs: Plymouth Albion, Civil Service, Devon.

A fine wing forward, he replaced Periton to make his debut.

HANNAFORD
Ronald Charles

Number 8. 1971 (Bristol, 3 caps).
Debut v Wales, 16 January 1971.
Born: 19 October 1944, Gloucester.
Educated: Crypt School, Durham University, Cambridge University.
Clubs: Gloucester, Durham University,

Cambridge University (Blue 1967), Rosslyn Park, Bristol, Durham County, Gloucestershire.

Hannaford, who scored a try on his international debut, played for Bath in the 1972-3 RFU Club KO Cup Final and for Gloucestershire in the County Championship Final the same season. A teacher at Clifton College, he emigrated to New Zealand early in 1975 and became player-coach to Naenae Old Boys, who play in the Wellington League.

HANVEY
Robert Jackson ('Bob')

Prop. 1926 (Aspatria, 4 caps).
Debut v Wales, 16 January 1926.
Born: 16 August 1899; Died: 17 October 1989.

Bob Hanvey

Clubs: Aspatria, Blennerhasset, Cumberland & Westmorland.

Served during World War One, he served Cumbrian rugger for over 50 years. A cobbler by trade, he was a stalwart forward in the county's packs of the 1920s, helping Cumberland and Westmorland win the Championship in 1924. He later served as a referee, selector and county president. In 1926 he won four England caps in a side led by Sir Wavell Wakefield.

HARDING
Ernest Harold

Number 8. 1931 (Devonport Services, 1 cap).

Debut v Ireland, 14 February 1931.
Born: 22 May 1899; Died: 25 January 1980, Liskeard, Cornwall.
Clubs: Devonport Services, Royal Navy.
Harding was a regular Royal Navy listing.

HARDING
Richard Mark

Scrum-half. 1985-1988 (Bristol, 12 caps).
Debut v Romania, 5 January 1985.
Born: 29 August 1953.
Club: Bristol.

Richard Harding

Harding played in the 1985 Calcutta Cup-winning team and captained the South and South West Divisions in 1987. With Bristol he played in the JPS Cup Final 1987-8.

HARDING
Victor Sydney James.

Lock. 1961-1962 (Saracens, 6 caps).
Debut v France, 25 February 1961.
Born: 18 June 1932.
Educated: St Marylebone Grammar School, Cambridge University.
Clubs: Army, Cambridge University (Blues 1958-1960), Sale, Saracens, Harlequins, Edinburgh Wanderers, Barbarians, London Counties, Middlesex (captain 1962-64).
Vic Harding scored a try on his international debut and was a member of the 1961 Calcutta Cup-winning side. He is Saracens' most capped player.

HARDWICK
Peter F.

Forward. 1902-1904 (Percy Park, 8 caps).
Debut v Ireland, 8 February 1902.
Born: 1877; Died: February 1925, North Shields.
Clubs: Percy Park, Northumberland.
Hardwick, who was in the 1902 Calcutta Cup-winning team, appeared on the winning England side three times out of eight international matches. Employed as a marine engineer, he served in World War One as superintendant of a repair yard for damaged warships.

HARDY
Evan Michael Pearce, OBE

Half-back/Fly-half. 1951 (Blackheath, 3 caps).
Debut v Ireland, 10 February 1951.
Born: 3 November 1927, Bareilly, India.
Educated: Ampleforth College.
Clubs: Blackheath, Army, Combined Services, Headingley, Barbarians, Yorkshire (29 appearances).

Evan Hardy played in the 1951 Calcutta Cup-winning team, alongside Shuttleworth in what was an army first with the half-backs in an international coming from the same regiment, The Duke of Wellington's. Hardy, who served during the Korean War, reached the rank of colonel. He represented the Army 11 times, against the Royal Navy, RAF and French Army, and later on the RFU. He also played for the Combined Services and the Army at cricket.

HARE
William Henry ('Dusty')

Full-back. 1974-1984 (Nottingham, Leicester, 25 caps).
Debut v Wales, 16 March 1974.
Born: 29 November 1952, Newark.
Educated: Magnus Grammar School (Newark).
Clubs: Newark, Nottingham, Leicester, Barbarians.
Farmer Dusty Hare, was England's most capped full-back, scored most points in internationals (424), most points in any

Dusty Hare

one season for England (44 in 1983-84) and most penalties in a Championship (14 in 1983) — yet he failed to score in his first two internationals (albeit the only England games in which he did not score). For Leicester he scored 4,507 points in 257 appearances, sending him way past Sam Doble's world record.

His representative honours include: Midland Counties East v Fiji in 1970 at the age of 17, as a fly-half; England Under-23s v Japan in 1973 and v Tonga in 1974; Midland Counties East v Australia in 1975; North and Midlands v Argentina in 1976; England XV v USA in 1977; Midlands v New Zealand in 1978, v New Zealand in 1979, v Fiji in 1982, v New Zealand in 1983, v Australia in 1984. His tours include England to Japan in 1979, to Argentina in 1981, to Canada and the USA in 1982, to South Africa in 1984; British Lions to New Zealand in 1983.

Besides his points for England and Leicester, he scored 88 for the Lions and a further 598 points for others, taking him to the remarkable grand total of 7,118.

He made ten appearances for Nottinghamshire CCC between 1971 and 1977. His autobiography *Dusty* (co-written with David Norrie) was published in 1985. In April 1990 he was appointed Nottingham's director of rugby.

HARPER
Charles Henry (later Sir), KBE CMB OBE

Forward. 1899 (Exeter, 1 cap).
Debut v Wales, 7 January 1899.
Born: 24 February 1876; Died: 14 May 1950, Heswall.
Educated: Blundell's School, Oxford University.
Clubs: Oxford University (Blues 1897-8), Blackheath, Exeter, Devon.
A lawyer, called to the Bar in 1909, he was awarded the OBE in 1919, the CMB in 1921 and was made Knight of the British Empire in 1930.

HARRIMAN
Andrew Tuoyo

Right-wing. 1988 (Harlequins, 1 cap).
Debut v Australia, 5 November 1988.
Born: 13 July 1964, Lagos, Nigeria.
Educated: Cambridge University.
Clubs: Cambridge University (Blue 1985), Harlequins, Barbarians.
Harriman, who played for Quins in their 1988 JPS Cup-winning team, is one of the fastest men in rugby and it is perhaps surprsing that he has been capped only once to date. Since joining the Quins he has played in more than 15 sevens tournaments, including the Estoril Sevens, and is unbeaten in any sevens game. He has played in three Middlesex Sevens winning sides and was in the Quins' 1991 Pilkington Cup winning side. He played for London against Australia. A Great Britain

Under-16 tennis doubles champion, he won an athletics Blue as well as rugger Blue at Cambridge and also plays squash.

HARRIS
Stanley Wakefield, CBE

Left-wing. 1920 (Blackheath, 2 caps).
Debut v Ireland, 14 February 1920.
Born: 13 December 1893; Died: 1973.
Educated: Bedford Grammar School.
Clubs: Blackheath, Pirates (Johannesburg), Kenya, Transvaal, East Midlands.
Harris, who set Blackheath's try-scoring record, joined the Pirates in Johannesburg when chosen to play as a winger on the British Lions' South African tour in 1924. He later took over the full-back position due to injuries amongst the squad and on that tour played in 15 matches, heading the list of appearances and scoring one try in the 3rd Test.

He spent the majority of his life in South Africa, emigrating in the 1920s, and was eventually awarded his Springbok colours at tennis and boxing, winning the South African amateur light-heavyweight title in 1921. He represented South Africa in the Davis Cup and won All-England mixed doubles title. He also represented England at polo.

During World War One he served as a gunnery officer at the Somme, in which he was seriously wounded. Whilst recuperating he showed an interest in dancing and made progress to the World Ballroom Championships. Offered a chance to represent Britain in the modern pentathlon at the 1920 Olympic Games, he decided to decline in favour of rugger. In World War Two

he was a prisoner of the Japanese, working on the famous 'railway of death' in Siam. He was awarded the CBE in 1946.

HARRIS
Thomas William

Number 8. 1929-1932 (Northampton, 2 caps).
Debut v Scotland, 16 March 1929.
Born: 1906, Northampton; Died: November 1958, Northampton.
Educated: Barry Road School (Northampton).
Club: Northampton.

HARRISON
Arthur Clifford, TD

Wing. 1931 (Hartlepool Rovers, 2 caps).
Debut v Ireland, 14 February 1931.
Born: 10 May 1911.
Clubs: Hartlepool Rovers, Durham County, Barbarians, Mombasa Sports Club, Selangor Sports Club.
Arthur Harrison made his debut as one of six new caps in the England side. A small, auburn-haired winger, he served during World War Two.

HARRISON
Arthur Leyland, VC

Forward. 1914 (United Services (Portsmouth), Royal Navy, 2 caps).
Debut v Ireland, 14 February 1914.
Born: 3 February 1886, Torquay; Died: 23 April 1918, Zeebrugge (killed in action).
Educated: Dulwich College, Royal Naval College (Dartmouth).
Clubs: United Services (Portsmouth), Royal Navy, Hampshire.
English Rugby Union's only Victoria Cross award, he fought at the Battle of Jutland and was mentioned in despatches in 1916. He lost his life in the famous action at the blockading of Zeebrugge in 1918, when he was killed on the second day of the action which cost the lives of 588 soldiers and sailors. Awarded the VC posthumously. He managed to play in only two international matches, both on the winning side, and no doubt would have added many more caps had the war not intervened.

HARRISON
Gilbert

Forward. 1877-1885 (Hull, 7 caps).
Debut v Ireland, 5 February 1877.
Born: 13 June 1858, Cottingham; Died: 9 November 1894.
Educated: Cheltenham College.
Clubs: Hull, Yorkshire (48 appearances, captain 1885-8).
Harrison's Hull helped form the Northern Union after the split in 1895.

HARRISON
Harold Cecil, ('Dreadnought'),
CB DSO

Forward. 1909-1914 (United Services (Portsmouth), Royal Navy 4 caps).
Debut v Scotland, 20 March 1909.
Born: 26 February 1889; Died: 26 March 1940, Maryleybone, London.
Educated: King Edward's School (Birmingham).
Clubs: Royal Marine Artillery (Woolwich), Army, United Services (Portsmouth), Royal Navy, Barbarians, Kent.
He represented both the Royal Navy and the Army and holds the unique record of never having played on a losing side in service matches. He refereed the France-Scotland match in 1922. and served during World War One as commander of a South African siege battery. He was awarded the DSO in 1916 and the CB in 1939. He earned his nickname whilst serving with the Royal Marines.

HARRISON
Michael Edward

Wing. 1985-1988 (Wakefield, 15 caps).
Debut v New Zealand, 1 June 1985.
Born: 9 April 1956, Barnsley.
Educated: Queen Elizabeth's Grammar School (Wakefield), Loughborough Colleges.

Mike Harrison

Clubs: Loughborough Colleges, Wakefield, Yorkshire (44 appearances, captain 1986-91).
Mike Harrison scored a try in each of his first two internationals, the First and Second Tests against the All Blacks, and

is particularly adept at 'poaching' tries from almost anywhere on the pitch. Indeed, he is extremely fast and for Yorkshire Schools he once clocked 10.7 seconds for the 100 metres.
He played on the left wing for England, although he turned out on the right wing for his county, and he captained England to their Calcutta Cup triumph of 1987, scoring a try in the 21-12 win. He also captained the North of England to Divisional Championships and Yorkshire to the County Championship in 1987 and to the Final again in 1991. He also played in the Japanese President's XV against New Zealand.
An injury sustained in a car accident kept him out of rugger for two years. He works as an assistant bank manager.

HARTLEY
Bernard Charles, CBE OBE

Forward. 1901-1902 (Blackheath, 2 caps).
Debut v Scotland, 9 March 1901.
Born: 16 March 1877, Woodford; Died: 24 April 1960.
Educated: Dulwich College, Cambridge University.
Clubs: Cambridge University (Blue 1900), Blackheath, Barbarians, Sussex, Kent.
Hartley was a stockbroker and represented Cambridge University on the RFU from 1907 to 1908 and the Army in 1921-2 and from 1928 to 1948. He was an England selector in 1923-4 and managed the British Lions tour of South Africa in 1938 (23 games, of which 17 were won and six lost). He was an International Board representative from 1945 to 1954 and was elected president of the RFU from 1947 to 1948. From 1918 to 1941 he was secretary of the Army Sports Council and on the National Playing Fields Association Committee from 1926 to 1946. He was awarded the OBE in 1925 and the CB in 1946. In World War One he served with the Hertfordshire Regiment and was gassed and wounded.
He also gained athletics Blues (1899-1901) and rowed for Jesus College, rowing at either sixth or fifth position in the Cambridge VIII (1898-1901). He rowed at Henley in 1899 and 1901 and appeared in the Thames Cup semi-final in the former year.

HASLETT
Leslie Woods

Lock. 1926 (Birkenhead Park, 2 caps).
Debut v Ireland, 13 February 1926.
Born: 5 June 1900.
Educated: Cheltenham College, Royal Military Academy (Woolwich).
Clubs: Blackheath, Birkenhead Park, Eastern Counties.
Haslett scored a try on his international debut but won only two caps before he emigrated to Canada.

HASTINGS
George William D.

Prop. 1955-1958 (Gloucester, 13 caps).
Debut v Wales, 22 January 1955.
Born: 7 November 1924, Dursley.
Clubs: Old Patesians, Gloucester, Barbarians, Gloucestershire.
In his 13 appearances he scored one try, two penalty-goals and one conversion. He went on the Barbarians' tour of Canada in 1957 and to South Africa in 1958. Hastings had an acute sense of positioning and was recalled to the England side in 1957 (not being selected in 1956) after D.L.Saunders was injured in a road accident.

HAVELOCK
Harold

Flanker. 1908 (Hartlepool Rovers, 3 caps).
Debut v France, 1 January 1908.
Clubs: Hartlepool Rovers, West Hartlepool, Durham County, Hull RL.
Havelock played for both major Hartlepool clubs before switching codes.

HAWCRIDGE
John Joseph ('Artful Dodger')

Back. 1885 (Bradford, 2 caps).
Debut v Wales, January 1885.
Born: 1863, Macclesfield; Died: 1 January 1905, San Francisco, USA.
Clubs: Manningham Athletic, Manningham, Bradford, Yorkshire (5 appearances).
Hawcridge scored a try in each of his two international matches. He was a prolific try scorer for his clubs, too, and totalled 38 for Bradford. He emigrated to the United States in 1892. His nickname came from his wonderful swerve.

HAYWARD
Leslie William

Centre. 1910 (Cheltenham, 1 cap).
Debut v Ireland, 12 February 1910.
Born: 17 May 1886, Cheltenham.
Educated: Cheltenham Grammar School.
Clubs: Cheltenham, Gloucestershire.
Hayward's cap came in the Championship season of 1910, the same season that Twickenham was opened. It was his only appearance on that ground.

HAZELL
David St George

Prop. 1955 (Leicester, 4 caps).
Debut v Wales, 22 January 1955.
Born: 23 April 1931.
Educated: Taunton School, Loughborough College.
Clubs: Loughborough Colleges, Leicester, Bristol, Barbarians, Leicestershire, Somerset (captain 1963-4).
He was a teacher at his local Taunton School when he appeared for England,

scoring three penalty-goals. One particularly vital penalty-goal came against Scotland to enable England to win the Calcutta Cup, 9-6.

HEARN
Robert Daniel

Centre. 1966-1967 (Bedford, 6 caps).
Debut v France, 26 February 1966.
Born: 12 August 1940.
Educated: Cheltenham College, Trinity College (Dublin), Oxford University.
Clubs: Trinity College (Dublin), Oxford University (Blue 1964), Bedford, Barbarians.

Bob Hearn first appeared for England in their disastrous season of 1966. But late the following year, when he was approaching the peak of his rugby career with six caps to his name and having been tipped for more, he lay critically ill after breaking his neck during the Midland & Home Counties match against New Zealand on 28 October 1967. The injury was caused when he launched himself to tackle Ian MacRae. The impact of the clash left him lying paralysed from the neck down with a broken spinal cord. He survived and fought his way back, relearned how to walk and returned to his teaching career at Haileybury, where he taught economics.

His autobiography *Crash Tackle* was published in 1972 and is a very informative and sometimes heartrending story, reliving his career, the traumas and eventual victory over his disability. He was manager of the Nomads (English schoolboys) tour of Africa in 1972. He was the Irish Universities middleweight boxing champion in 1963.

HEATH
Arthur Howard, JP MP

Full-back. 1876 (Oxford University, 1 cap).
Debut v Scotland, 6 March 1876.
Born: 29 May 1856, Newcastle under Lyme, Staffordshire; Died: 24 April 1930, London.
Educated: Clifton College, Oxford University.
Club: Oxford University (Blues 1875-9).

Heath played cricket for Oxford University, Gloucestershire, Middlesex and Staffordshire. He served in World War One as a lieutenant-colonel on the staff of the Royal Field Artillery Regiment and was mentioned in despatches by the Secretary of State for War in 1917. He contested Hanley for the Conservative Party, losing in 1892 and 1895 and winning in 1900. He lost his seat in 1906 but returned as MP for Leek in 1910.

HEATON
John, JP

Centre. (Waterloo, 1935-1947, 9 caps).
Debut v Wales, 19 January 1935.
Born: 30 August 1912.

Educated: Cowley Grammar School (St Helens), Liverpool University.
Clubs: Liverpool University, Nottingham, Waterloo, Barbarians, Lancashire (66 appearances)

Heaton was at Liverpool University from 1930 to 1936 and made history as their first undergraduate to play rugby for England. He scored three penalty-goals against Scotland in 1939 to give England a 9-6 victory in the Calcutta Cup. He has the unique record of having England's longest international career — 13 seasons from 1935 to 1947 — and captained his country as a 39-year-old, after a lapse of 12 years. His cousin, Dickey Guest, is also an England international and they played together in six internationals either side of World War Two. He captained Lancashire after the war, after helping them to the County Championship title in 1934-5.

Heaton played cricket for Liverpool University and appeared in a one-day wartime match for Nottinghamshire against Derbyshire at Trent Bridge in July 1944. He ran in the 100 yards at the university sports day in 1931.

HENDERSON
A.P.

Hooker. 1947-1949 (Edinburgh Wanderers, 9 caps).
Debut v Wales, 18 January 1947.
Born: Kirkintilloch, Scotland.
Educated: Taunton School, Cambridge University.

Clubs: Cambridge University (Blues 1945-7), Edinburgh Wanderers.

His only try for England was against Scotland on 15 March 1947, in the 24-5 Calcutta Cup win.

HENDERSON
Robert Samuel Findlay (Sir), KCMG CB

Forward. 1882-1885 (Blackheath, 5 caps).
Debut v Wales, 16 December 1882.
Born: 11 December 1858, Calcutta; Died: 5 October 1924, Millbank, London.
Educated: Bedford School, Fettes College, Edinburgh University.
Clubs: Blackheath, St Mary's Hospital.

He scored a try on his debut in the 'unofficial' Championship season of 1882-3. Sir Robert served in World War One, being mentioned in despatches in 1917. He spent much of his service life abroad, including service in the South African War of 1901-02. Awarded the CB in 1917 and the KCMB in 1919.

HENNICKER-GOTLEY
Anthony Lefroy Henniker

Scrum-half. 1910-1911 (Oxford University, 6 caps).
Debut v France, 3 March 1910.
Born: 2 March 1887; Died: May 1972.
Educated: Tonbridge School, Oxford University.
Clubs: Oxford University (Blue 1909), Blackheath, Barbarians, Surrey, Kent.

A lawyer called to the Bar in 1923, he served in World War One in East Africa and in World War Two with the Royal Air Force Volunteer Reserve. He lived in Southern Rhodesia (now Zimbabwe) in 1911. A clever little player, he went on the 1910 British Lions tour of Argentina.

HEPPELL
W.G.

Prop. 1903 (Devonport Albion, 1 cap).
Debut v Ireland, 14 February 1903.
Clubs: Devonport Albion, Devon.

HERBERT
A. John

Flanker. 1958-1959 (Wasps, 6 caps).
Debut v France, 1 March 1958.
Born: 1 January 1933.
Educated: Marling School, Fettes College, Cambridge University.
Clubs: Cambridge University (Blues 1954-6, latterly as captain), Wasps.

Herbert went on the Oxford-Cambridge tour of South America in 1955 and captained Wasps from 1958 until 1961. He moved to Australia and taught history at Geelong Prep School. He was also employed by ICI. He made his debut against France in England's biggest win over them since 1914. A splendid tackler and handler, he could always be relied upon to give good cover.

HESFORD
Robert J. ('Bob')

Number 8. 1981-1985 (Bristol, 1981-1985, 10 caps).
Debut v Scotland, 21 February 1981.
Born: 26 March 1952, Blackpool.

Educated: Borough Road College, Arnold School (Blackpool), Durham University.

Clubs: UAU, British Universities, Wasps, Bristol United, Bristol, Barbarians, Durham, East Midlands, Gloucestershire.

Bob Hesford's debut for England was made as a replacement for the injured N.C. Jeavons, who was also making his debut that day when England won the Calcutta Cup. He also appeared in the Calcutta Cup victory of 1985, when England won 10-7. He comes from a sporting family: his father, Bob, kept goal in the 1938 FA Cup Final for Huddersfield Town; and his brother Iain, also a goalkeeper, played for Blackpool. His other brother, Steve, played Rugby Union for Fleetwood before switching codes to play for

Bob Hesford

Warrington RL, for whom he has now scored over 1,000 points. As a 40-year-old, Bob was coaxed out of retirement to make an appearance for Whitehall, the club he coaches, when the Bristol-based club were suffering an injury crisis.

Nigel Heslop

HESLOP
Nigel John

Right-wing. 1990-1992 (Orrell, 10 caps).
Debut v Argentina, 3 November 1990.
Born: 4 December 1963, Hartlepool

Educated: Rainford High School (St Helens).

Clubs: Liverpool, Waterloo, Orrell, Lancashire (over 12 appearances).

Nigel Heslop began playing rugby at the age of 14 and represented England Colts against France in 1980. In 1986 he suffered a dislocated elbow but recovered to reach the very top in the game. He went on the England 'B' trip to Spain in the summer of 1989, played for an England XV v an Italian XV in 1990 and went on the England tour of Argentina that year. A police officer stationed at Newton-le-Willows, he was in England's 1991 World Cup squad but, having played in two matches, he was not chosen for the Final against Australia. His brother plays Rugby League for Leeds Polytechnic. Nigel Heslop helped Lancashire to the 1990 County Championship. In England's 1992 Grand Slam success he made one appearance, coming on as a replacement against Wales.

HETHERINGTON
James Gilbert George

Full-back. 1958-1959 (Northampton, 6 caps).
Debut v Australia, 1 February 1958.
Born: 3 March 1932.

Educated: Churcher's School (Petersfield), Cambridge University.

Clubs: Trojans, Cambridge University (Blue 1955), Northampton, East Midlands, Hampshire.

Hetherington scored a penalty-goal in each of his first two international matches. He went on the Oxford-Cambridge tour of South America in 1955.

HEWITT
Edwin Newbury

Full-back. 1951 (Coventry, 3 caps).
Debut v Wales, 20 January 1951.
Born: 22 April 1924.

Educated: Barker Butts School, Coventry Technical College.

Clubs: Coventry, Sphinx, Vikings, Warwickshire.

Hewitt marked his international debut by converting Rittson-Thomas's try in the 23-5 defeat by Wales. He played in three games that season with England finishing bottom for the second successive time in the Five Nations Championship.

HEWITT
Walter W.

Forward. 1881-1882 (Queen's House, 4 caps).
Debut v Wales, 19 February 1881.
Club: Queen's House.

Besides playing rugby, Walter Hewitt was also a very good oarsman.

HICKSON
John Lawrence

Forward. 1887-1890 (Bradford, 6 caps).
Debut v Wales, 8 January 1887.
Born: 1860; Died: 4 August 1920.

Clubs: Bingley, Bradford, Barbarians, Yorkshire (28 appearances, captain 1889-90).

Hickson captained England in their 6-0 win over Scotland in March 1890, which set up two late wins in the Championship which began the recovery process to give England a share in the title. He was also capped in the 1888 side that did not play. In 1895, five years after Hickson won his last England cap, Bradford helped form the Northern Union. There is no record of him playing Northern Union rugby but in 1884 he helped Bradford win their first trophy when they beat Hull 5-3 in the Yorkshire Challenge Cup.

HIGGINS
A.Reginald

Flanker. 1954-1959 (Liverpool, 13 caps).
Debut v Wales, 16 January 1954.
Born: 11 July 1930, Widnes; Died: 29 December 1979, Frodsham.

Educated: Wade Deacon High School (Widnes), Leeds University.

Clubs: Leeds University, UAU, Army, Combined Services, Liverpool, Barbarians, Lancashire (57 caps), North-West Counties.

A very powerful runner with the ball, not easily stopped, Higgins is Liverpool's most capped player. His international debut try came in the match against France in February 1955. Two years later he was a member of the side which won the Grand Slam, Triple Crown and Calcutta Cup and altogether he scored 13 tries for England.

Reg Higgins

Whilst on National Service in the Royal Signals he played for the Army against the RAF and Royal Navy in 1954 but on the British Lions' tour to South Africa the following year he sustained a knee injury in one of the Test Matches and did not play again until 1956. In April 1957 he played for the International XV which met Wales in a match arranged to raise money so that Cardiff could stage the 1958 Empire Games. And he appeared for the North-West Counties against New Zealand in February 1954 and was in Calcutta Cup-winning teams in 1954, 1955 and 1957. His father and an uncle were both Rugby League internationals.

HIGNELL
Alastair James

Full-back. 1975-1979 (Cambridge University, Bristol, 14 caps).
Debut v Australia, 31 May 1975.
Born: 4 September 1955, RAF Hospital, Ely, Cambridgeshire.

Educated: Denstone College, Cambridge University.

Clubs: Cambridge University (Blues 1974-9), Bristol United, Bristol.

Alastair Hignell played rugby for England Under-19s against Scotland, Wales and France in 1972-3 and went on the England tour of Australia in 1975.

He was also a well-known cricketer, gaining his Cambridge Blue and playing 137 games for Gloucestershire between 1974 and 1983. The Cricket Society voted him the most promising young cricketer of the year in 1974 and he scored 117 not out for England Schools against Indian Schools at Edgbaston. He went on to play in four matches in the England Under-19 XI

Alastair Hignell

— three in 1973 and one against the Australian Schools in 1974.

He is now a sports commentator and has worked for both BBC and ITV, being associated with the latter for the 1991 World Cup.

HILL
Basil Alexander (Sir), KBE CB DSO JP

Forward. 1903-1907 (Blackheath, 9 caps).
Debut v Ireland, 14 February 1903.
Born: 23 April 1880; Died: 31 July 1960.
Educated: Newenheim College (Heidelburg), Royal Naval Engineering College (Keyham).
Clubs: Army, United Services (Portsmouth), Blackheath, Barbarians, Kent.

Hill, who helped Kent to the County Championship in 1904, was a major general in the Army. He played for the Army three times, all against the Royal Navy, and represented the Army on the RFU from 1926 to 1939. He was an International Board member in 1938 and president of the RFU from 1937 to 1939. He was also a two-handicap golfer.

He served with the Royal Marines Artillery from 1897 and fought at the famous Siege of Tsingtau in 1914. In World War One he fought at Gallipoli, was mentioned in despatches three times, awarded the DSO in 1917, the CB in 1937 and was made a Knight of the British Empire in 1941. From 1942 to 1947 he was Colonel Commandant of the REME. He was a JP in Surrey.

HILL
Richard John

Scrum-half. 1984-1991 (Bath, 22 caps).
Debut v South Africa, 2 June 1984.
Born: 4 May 1961, Birmingham.
Educated: Bishop Wordsworth School (Salisbury), Exeter University.
Clubs: Salisbury, Bath.

Richard Hill, who represented England Students and the English Universities, is a member of the great Bath side of the 1980s which has won the premier KO Cup seven times — a distinction he shares with Gareth Chilcott — and the Courage First Division Championship once. He thus played in Rugby Union's first League and Cup double-winning side in 1989 and was voted Whitbread Player of the Month in November that year.

He went on the England tour of South Africa in 1984, playing in both Tests, and appeared for the Five Nations v Overseas XV at Twickenham in 1986.

He was captain during England's violent clash with Wales in Cardiff in 1987 and was one of the players banned following that game. Hill, who has skippered England four times, was recalled to the England squad in November 1989 after an absence of more than two years. In the summer of 1990 he had a knee operation but made a complete recovery and appeared in the 1991 World Cup Finals. He is a financial consultant by profession.

HILLARD
Ronald Johnstone, CMG

Prop. 1925 (Oxford University, 1 cap).
Debut v New Zealand, 3 January 1925.
Born: 6 May 1903, Durham.
Educated: St Paul's School, Oxford University.
Clubs: Oxford University (Blues 1923-4), Old Paulines, Barbarians.

He was awarded Companion of the Order of St Michael and St George in 1950.

HILLER
Robert ('Bob')

Full-back. 1968-1972 (Harlequins, 19 caps).
Debut v Wales, 20 January 1968.
Born: 14 October 1942, Woking.
Educated: Bec School, Birmingham University, Oxford University.
Clubs: Oxford University (Blue 1965), Harlequins, Surrey (68 appearances).

Employed as a schoolmaster, he was once England's most capped full-back and drop-goal scorer. He scored on every England appearance and captained his country seven times, the first in 1969. Hiller used the old-fashioned 'toe-ender' style of place kicking. He was on the England tour of Canada in 1967 and the British Lions' tours of South Africa in 1968 and Australia and New Zealand in 1971. He made nine appearances on the South African tour but did not play in any of the Tests. He also gained a cricket Blue whilst at Oxford.

HIND
Alfred Ernest

Wing. 1905-1906 (Leicester, 2 caps).
Debut v New Zealand, 2 December 1905.
Born: 7 April 1878, Preston; Died: 21 March 1947, Leicester.
Educated: Uppingham School, Cambridge University.
Clubs: Cambridge University (Blue 1900), Leicester, Nottingham, Midland Counties.

Hind, who also won athletics Blues (1898-1901) and ran the 100 yards in 9.8 seconds on two occasions, also played cricket for Nottinghamshire. He went on the 1903 British Lions tour of South Africa, before he was capped by England. He played for Midland Counties against New Zealand in 1905. He was a solictor.

HIND
Guy Reginald

Prop/Hooker. 1910-1911 (Blackheath, 2 caps).
Debut v Scotland, 19 March 1910.
Born: 4 April 1887, Stoke-on-Trent; Died: 8 November 1970.
Educated: Haileybury and Imperial Service College.
Clubs: Guy's Hospital, Blackheath, Barbarians, Kent.

The son of a doctor, he was uncapped when chosen for the British Lions tour of New Zealand in 1908. He also played for London v South Africa in 1912 and went on the Anglo-Welsh tour of Australia in 1908.

HOBBS
Reginald Francis Arthur, CB CMG DSO

Forward. 1899-1903 (Blackheath, 2 caps).

Richard Hill

Bob Hiller

Debut v Scotland, 11 March 1899.
Born: 30 January 1878; Died: 10 July 1953.

Educated: Wellington College, Royal Military Academy (Woolwich).

Clubs: Army, Blackheath, Barbarians, Kent.

Hobbs was the top athlete at Woolwich in 1897. He served in the Royal Engineers, reaching the rank of brigadier-general, and played for the Army against the Royal Navy in 1907. He served in the South African War of 1899-1902 and was awarded the DSO in 1902. During World War One he was mentioned in despatches five times. He was awarded the Companion of the Order of St Michael and St George in 1915, and the CB in 1931. He was the father of Reginald Geoffrey Stirling Hobbs and had two other sons, both of whom were killed during World War Two.

HOBBS
Reginald Geoffrey Stirling ('Pooh'), CB DSO OBE

Lock. 1932 (Richmond, 4 caps).
Debut v South Africa, 2 January 1932.
Born: 8 August 1908.

Educated: Wellington School, Royal Military Academy (Woolwich).

Clubs: Army, Richmond, Barbarians, Kent.

The son of Reginald Francis Arthur Hobbs, he played ten times for the Army, against the Royal Navy, RAF and French Army, and in 1931 he was a member of 11th Field Brigade's MacIlwaine Cup-winning team.

He served during World War Two and was awarded the DSO in 1942, the OBE in 1944, the CB in 1946 and the Croix de Guerre in 1958. In 1955 he was promoted to major-general in the Royal Artillery and whilst GOC of 1st Division he was elected a junior vice-president the RFU, and in 1961-62, whilst president of the Regular Commissions Board, he succeeded Tom Voyce as president of the RFU. From 1953 to 1967 he acted as chairman and later president of the Royal Artillery RFC. He had two brothers, both of whom were killed in World War Two.

HODGES
Harold Augustus

Prop. 1906 (Nottingham, 2 caps).
Debut v Wales, 13 January 1906.
Born: 22 January 1886, Mansfield Woodhouse; Died: 22 March 1918, near Mons (killed in action).

Educated: Roclareston House (Nottingham), Sedburgh School, Oxford University, the Sorbonne.

Clubs: Oxford University (Blues 1905-08, later captain), Nottingham, Blackheath, Midland Counties.

He taught at Tonbridge School from 1904 to 1914, served in World War One in the 3rd Monmouthshire Regiment

and was twice mentioned in despatches. He lost his life in the 1918 retreat on the Amiens front near Ham, whilst serving with the 11th South Lancashires.

His death, said some, was one of the great tragedies of the war. He was wounded whilst serving as a lieutenant with 'D' company on 5 May 1915. On 16 April 1916, he was captain of 'D' company and distinguished himself in preventing a serious explosion in an outbreak of fire in an ammunition dump at Forceville, and received the thanks of the divisional commander. He was described as a magnificent man. A fine athlete, he had a strong character, which exercised the highest influence amongst his officers and men, in which he was universally loved. He played cricket for Nottinghamshire in 1911.

HODGKINSON
Simon David

Full-back. 1989-1991 (Nottingham, 13 caps).
Debut v Romania, 13 May 1989.
Born: 15 December 1962, Bristol.

Educated: Stamford School, Trent Polytechnic (Nottingham).

Clubs: Nottingham, Barbarians.

In 1989-90, Simon Hodgkinson was leading scorer in the Five Nations Championship with 42 points (ten penalties and six conversions). He is only the 15th player to score more than 40 points in a Championship season and holds the record for most conversions for England, overhauling Dusty Hare's total of 44 with his kick in the final minute against Ireland in March

Simon Hodgkinson

1991. He kicked a world-record seven penalties against Wales in January 1991, a record he held for only four months until Mark Wyatt kicked eight in Canada's defeat of Scotland. He scored a record number of points — 60 — in the 1991 Five Nations Championship and against Argentina in November 1990, he scored 23 points, breaking a national record which had stood since 1911. He was a member of England's 1991 World Cup Final team. At club level, Hodgkinson is Nottingham's leading scorer with 315 points (three tries, 42 conversions, 72 penalties and one drop-goal). He represented British Polytechnics, England Students and the Under-23 and 'B' teams, has played for an England XV and was a Midlands Under-15 cricketer. He gained a BA in business studies and was a master at Trent College, teaching economics. Now he works for a finance company. His father played for Thornbury RFC of Bristol and Scarborough RFC.

HODGSON
John McDonald

Flanker or Number 8. 1932-1936 (Northern, 7 caps).
Debut v South Africa, 2 January 1932.
Born: 13 February 1909; Died: April 1970.
Clubs: Northern (Newcastle), Leicester, Northumberland, Northumberland/Durham.

Hodgson featured in the side which won the 1932 International Championship and was a member of the Triple Crown team in 1934, his last cap being awarded in 1936. He was on the British Lions' tour of Australia and New Zealand in 1930, when he was the only Lion of that year to win international honours for Britain before his first cap for England. He played in ten matches in New Zealand, scoring one try.

He captained the Northern club and played for Northumberland/Durham against New Zealand in 1935. He served during World War Two, fighting in Turkey. As well as playing rugby, he was a two-handicap golfer. Brother-in-law of J.T.W.Berry.

HODGSON
Stanley Arthur Murray

Hooker. 1960-1964 (Durham City, 11 caps).
Debut v Wales, 16 January 1960.
Born: 14 May 1928.
Clubs: Durham City, Barbarians, Durham County.

Hodgson was in the Triple Crown and Calcutta Cup teams of 1960 and went on the British Lions tour of South Africa in 1962. He had to retire from the game because of cartilage problems early in the 1970s.

HOFMEYR
Murray Bernard

Full-back/Fly-half. (Oxford University, 1950, 3 caps).
Debut v Wales, 21 January 1950.
Born: 9 December 1925, Pretoria, South Africa.
Educated: Pretoria High School, Rhodes University, Grahamstown, Oxford University.
Clubs: Oxford University (Blues 1948-50), Harlequins, Barbarians, Northern Transvaal.

Hofmeyr scored a conversion on his debut and from his three international matches he totalled two conversions and a penalty goal. He was chosen to play for England in 1950, when much controversy surrounded the side which contained one All Black and many Dominion players, mainly South African. He went on the Oxford rugby tour to France in 1950. Hofmeyr, who also won a cricket Blue at Oxford, was the best friend of Brian Boobbyer, the England centre. Hofmeyr's brother was a pioneer of Moral Rearmament in South Africa, the movement which Brian Boobbyer joined, giving up all sport to do so.

HOGARTH
Thomas Bradley

Forward. 1906 (Hartlepool Rovers, 1 cap).
Debut v France, 22 March 1906.
Born: 1877; Died: 1961.
Clubs: Hartlepool Creelers, Hartlepool Rovers, West Hartlepool, Leicester, Gray's Athletic, Durham City, Durham County.

Hogarth, who scored a try on his debut, had an unusually late call-up to earn his only cap. As well as rugby he played soccer for Huddersfield Town and Southampton, probably as an amateur as no records of him as a professional can be found by either club.

HOLFORD
G.

Lock. 1920 (Gloucester, 2 caps).
Debut v Wales, 17 January 1920.
Born: 1886.
Educated: Linden School.
Clubs: Gloucester, Gloucestershire.
Holford gained his first cap as a 34-year-old.

HOLLAND
David

Forward. 1912 (Devonport Albion, 3 caps).
Debut v Wales, 20 January 1912.
Born: 1886, Gloucester; Died: 7 March 1945, Gloucester.
Clubs: Devonport Albion, Gloucester, Oldham RL.

He scored only one try, against Scotland in the Calcutta Cup match of 1912,

which England lost 8-3. He served in World War One on HMS Colossus.

HOLLIDAY
Thomas E.

Full-back. 1923-1926 (Aspatria, 7 caps).
Debut v Scotland, 17 March 1923.
Born: 13 July 1898; Died: 19 July 1969.
Clubs: Aspatria, Cumberland and Westmorland, Oldham RL.

Thomas Holliday

He appeared in the final two matches of the 1923 Grand Slam season — the first as replacement for the injured Gilbert — and he was a member of the successful Calcutta Cup side. On the British Lions tour of South Africa in 1924, he was injured in the very first match. He skippered Cumberland and Westmorland to their County Championship victory over Kent in 1924.

HOLMES
Cyril Butler

Wing. 1947-1948 (Manchester, 3 caps).
Debut v Scotland, 15 March 1947.
Born: 11 January 1915.
Educated: Wrekin College, Manchester University, Royal Military College (Sandhurst).
Clubs: Manchester, Army, North West Counties, Lancashire (27 appearances).

Holmes scored a try on his international debut in the Calcutta Cup win and kicked two conversions to end his scoring feat in the 1949 matches against Ireland and France. At Sandhurst he played both soccer and rugby against Aldershot Services and he was a member of the Lancashire side that won the 1947 RU County Championship. Employed as a director in the family oil company, he served in World War Two in the Army PT Corps and as a CSM and sergeant-major instructor at Sandhurst. He was also one of England's most outstanding sprinters of his era, being AAA sprint champion and running for Great Britain in the 100 metres at the 1936 Olympics in Berlin. He set Empire Games records in the 100 yards (9.7 seconds) and 220 yards (21.2 seconds) at Sydney in 1938.

HOLMES
Edgar

Forward. 1890 (Manningham, 2 caps).
Debut v Scotland, 1 March 1890.
Born: 1863.

Clubs: Manningham, Yorkshire (25 appearances, captain 1890-91).

Manningham were one of the clubs who helped form the Northern Union in 1895. That club later disbanded and eventually became Bradford City AFC. Edgar Holmes would have played rugby on the Valley Parade ground that is now used for soccer.

HOLMES
Walter Alan

Prop. 1950-1953 (Nuneaton, 16 caps).
Debut v Wales, 21 January 1950.
Born: 10 September 1925, Nuneaton.

Educated: Vicarage Street School (Nuneaton).

Clubs: Nuneaton, Barbarians, Warwickshire.

Holmes, the Nuneaton club's most capped player, skippered them from 1952 to 1955.

He was in the Calcutta Cup-winning teams of 1951, 1952 and 1953 and the 1953 Championship-winning side, England's first outright title since 1937.

HOLMES
William Barry

Full-back 1949 (Cambridge University, 4 caps).
Debut v Wales, 15 January 1949.
Born: 6 January 1928, Buenos Aires, Argentina; Died: 10 November 1949, Salta, Argentina.

Educated: St George's School (Buenos Aires), Cambridge University.

Clubs: Cambridge University (Blues 1947-8), Richmond, Barbarians.

In his four England international matches he scored two conversions, against Ireland and France. In 1949 he returned to Argentina and won two caps against France for his native country. Within two months on his return home he died from typhoid fever.

HOOK
William Gordon

Full-back. 1951-1952 (Gloucester, 3 caps).
Debut v Scotland, 17 March 1951.
Born: 21 December 1920, Gloucester.

Educated: Sir Thomas Rich's School (Gloucester).

Clubs: Gloucester, Gloucestershire.

Hook, who joined Gloucester as a 15-year-old, scored on his international debut when he converted D.F.White's try — his only England score — in the 1951 Calcutta Cup win. He played 2nd XI cricket for Gloucestershire and represented the county at athletics. He has a son who played for Rosslyn Park. Hook served in the North African campaign during World War Two.

HOOPER
Charles Alexander

Centre. 1894 (Middlesex Wanderers, 3 caps).
Debut v Wales, 6 January 1894.
Born: 6 June 1869, Stonehouse, Gloucestershire; Died: 16 September 1950, Buckinghamshire.

Educated: Clifton College, Cambridge University.

Clubs: Cambridge University (Blue 1890), Richmond, Gloucester, Barbarians, Middlesex Wanderers, Gloucestershire, Middlesex (captain 1895-96).

A solicitor, he was a member of England's first four-three quarters line against Wales in what was also their only win during the 1894 campaign. He emigrated to Hong Kong in 1914 and served in the Hong Kong Special Police Force during World War One.

HOPLEY
Frederick John Van der Byl, DSO

Flanker. 1907-1908 (Blackheath, 3 caps).
Debut v France, 5 January 1907.
Born: 28 August 1883, Grahamstown, South Africa; Died: 16 August 1951, Salisbury, Rhodesia.

Educated: Harrow School, Cambridge University.

Clubs: Cambridge University, Blackheath, Villagers (South Africa), Barbarians, Kent.

He was the public school heavyweight boxing champion of 1901-02 and also played cricket and athletics. The son of Mr Justice Hopley, he was chosen as reserve for the South African tour of the British Isles and France in 1912-13. He was School's PT advisor to the Rhodesian Government. Hopley served during World War One as a lieutenant in the Grenadier Guards, twice being mentioned in despatches. He was awarded the DSO for 'conspicuous gallantry', despite being wounded at Beaumont Hamel.

HORDERN
Peter Cotton, AFC

Flanker or Number 8. 1931-1934 (Gloucester, 4 caps).
Debut v Ireland, 14 February 1932.
Born: 13 May 1907.

Educated: Brighton College, Oxford University.

Clubs: Oxford University (Blue 1928), Newport, Gloucester, Blackheath, Barbarians, Devon, North Midlands, Hampshire.

Hordern, who was coached by Ernie Hammett at Brighton College, was on the British Lions tour of Argentina in 1936. Employed as a school teacher at Monmouth and Bromsgrove Schools, he was appointed secretary of appointments board at Birmingham University in 1945, and elected as warden of Chancellor's Hall from 1945 to 1963. He served during World War Two as an RAF flying instructor. He was awarded the Air Force Cross in 1944. On his debut he was one of six new caps in the England team.

HORLEY
Charles Henry

Forward. 1885 (Swinton, 1 cap).
Debut v Ireland, 7 February 1885.
Born: 1861, Pendlebury; Died: 10 May 1924, Birkdale.

Clubs: Pendlebury R, Swinton, Lancashire (16 appearances).

Horley was employed by the Yorkshire and Lancashire Railways, based in Manchester.

HORNBY
Albert Neilson ('Monkey'), JP

Back. 1877-1882 (Manchester, 9 caps).
Debut v Ireland, 5 February 1877.
Born: 10 February 1847, Blackburn; Died: 17 December 1925, Parkfield, Nantwich, Cheshire.

Educated: Harrow School.

Clubs: Preston Grasshoppers, Manchester, Lancashire.

Monkey Hornby, the prominent English back of his era, scored a try on his international debut, in which he was one of England's two threequarters in the first 15-a-side rugby international, between England and Scotland at Kennington Oval in 1877, five days before his 30th birthday.

Hornby excelled at many sports. He was a fine boxer and was equally at home with a gun or in the saddle, although in March 1900 he was thrown from his mount whilst riding with the South Cheshire Hounds, breaking three ribs. He played five times for North v South but refused to play in the 1883 rugby international against Scotland because it coincided with his plans for a shooting weekend. He was never selected again. He was a member of the RFU committee and a very strict referee.

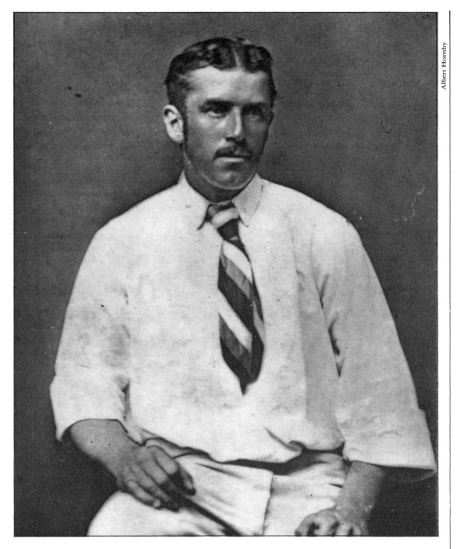

Albert Hornby

He also turned out occasionally for Blackburn Rovers at soccer.

A captain in the East Cheshire Militia, he also distinguished himself as captain of England, at both rugby and cricket. Indeed, Hornby was one of the most famous cricketers of his day. Associated with Lancashire CCC from 1867 to 1899, he skippered them for nearly 20 seasons and was later president.

In 1864, at the age of 17, he played for Harrow against Eton at Lord's and was the smallest player at that time ever to play in a public school XI, at 5ft 3in and weighing under 6st, despite growing into a very powerful man. He was also an ambidextrous cricketer.

He appeared frequently for the Gentleman against the Players, as well as for the North, and played for England against Australia, as captain in 1883. For the MCC against Derbyshire at Lord's in 1885, he was credited with a hit for eight, four being for an overthrow. He also played for Cheshire and the Free Foresters, as well as Blackburn. And he took part in two overseas tours: to the USA and Canada with R.A.Fitzgerald's team in 1872; and as a member of Lord Harris' side which toured Australia in 1878-9.

By all accounts he was a model cricketer and very popular. He was one

the first of the great Test players and the first to captain England at both cricket and rugger concurrently, in 1882. He retired from county cricket in August 1899, after 31 years but did not make his last first-class appearance until 1906, at the age of 59. Altogether he scored over 16,000 first-class runs.

On 15 October 1884, he was elected president of the Lancashire Amateur Cricket Association, and member of the MCC committee. He had several sons, one of whom was a 1st XI player for Elstree School in 1893-4. His third son was invalided home whilst serving with the Cheshire Regiment in South Africa. Monkey's elder brother was also a cricketer and soccer player and another brother, W.H.Hornby, was an MP.

Hornby is buried in Acton Cemetary, Nantwich, where a memorial has been placed which includes a testimony to his devotion to sport, particularly cricket. This takes the form of a carving of a bat, a wicket and a ball, engraved on a sloping slab of Sicilian Marble.

HORROCKS-TAYLOR
John Philip

Fly-half. 1958-1964 (Cambridge University, Leicester, Middlesbrough, 10 caps).
Debut v Wales, 18 January 1958.
Born: 27 October 1934, Halifax.

Educated: Heath Grammar School, Cambridge University.
Clubs: Cambridge University (Blues 1956-7), Halifax, Wasps, Leicester, Middlesbrough, Barbarians, Yorkshire (61 appearances, sometimes captain).
Horrocks-Taylor, who played in one Test on the British Lions' tour of Australia and New Zealand in 1959, is counted by the Halifax club as their most capped player because he was also with them, playing in the holidays, when he first appeared for England.

HORSFALL
Edward Luke

Flanker. 1949 (Harlequins, 1 cap).
Debut v Wales, 15 January 1949.
Born: 11 August 1917, Huddersfield;
Died: 1 June 1981.
Educated: Giggleswick School.
Clubs: Huddersfield, Bedford, Gloucester, Headingley, Harlequins, Percy Park, Cardiff, RAF, Combined Service, Yorkshire (6 appearances), Hampshire.
During World War Two he served as a squadron leader in the RAF. He remained in the RAF until 1967 and retired with the rank of wing commander, then went into teaching. He was also a very able skier, winning a Norwegian gold medal for cross county skiing.

HORTON
Anthony Lawrence ('Pinkey')

Prop. 1965-1967 (Blackheath, 7 caps).
Debut v Wales, 16 January 1965.
Born: 13 July 1938.
Educated: Stoneyhurst College.
Clubs: Royal Marines, Blackheath, Warlingham (Surrey), Van der Stol (South Africa), Barbarians, Surrey, London Counties.
A tight-head prop, he became something of an expert in assisting and supporting his line-out players. Employed in the wine trade, he did his National Service in the Royal Marines (45 Commando) from 1957-1959. He went on the British Lions tour to South Africa 1968, playing in 12 matches and the last three Tests. He lived in South Africa for a time.

HORTON
John Philip

Fly-half. 1978-1984 (Bath, 13 caps).
Debut v Wales, 4 February 1978.
Born: 11 April 1951, St Helens.
Educated: Cowley School, Didsbury College.
Clubs: St Helens, Sale, Bath, Bristol, Lancashire (30 appearances), Somerset.
John Horton shares, with R.Hiller, A.G.B.Old and C.R.Andrew, the record of most drop-goals (two) by one player in an England match. Horton scored two against France in 1980. He is second in the overall table of England players,

John Horton

with four drop-goals, and shares, with A.G.B.Old, the record of most drop-goals against France (*see above*). A much-travelled player, who was in the Calcutta Cup-winning team of 1978, he played for North-West Counties against Fiji in 1970, at the age of 19, for South-West Counties against Australia in 1975 and for the North Midlands against Australia in 1975 and against Argentina in 1976. In 1978 he represented an England XV against the United States. He returned to play for Lancashire after his Somerset days.

HORTON
Nigel Edgar

Lock. 1969-1980 (Moseley, Toulouse, 20 caps).
Debut v Ireland, 8 February 1969.
Born: 13 April 1948.
Educated: Wheeler's Lane Secondary Modern School (Birmingham).
Clubs: King's Norton, Birmingham Police, Moseley, Toulouse (France), Wasps, North Midlands.

Nigel Horton

Horton was capped as a 20-year-old. He was in the Moseley side which was runners-up to Gloucester in the first RU KO Cup, a match which saw him dismissed for felling Gloucester's Dick Smith after only four minutes. He was captain of Moseley for a spell amd also played some games for the Wasps whilst commuting from Toulouse. A police-man, he is also an able water-polo player.

HOSEN
Roger Wills

Full-back or Wing. 1963-1967 (Bristol, Northampton, 10 caps).
Debut v New Zealand, 25 May 1963.
Born: 12 June 1933, Falmouth.
Educated: Falmouth School, Loughborough College.
Clubs: Penryn, Loughborough Colleges, UAU, Plymouth Albion, Wasps, Cheltenham, Bristol, Northampton, Barbarians, Hampshire, Midland Counites, Cornwall (54 appearances).

When he made his international debut at the age of nearly 30, it was the end of a long wait for Hosen, who had first played in an England trial in 1954. He had good positional sense and was good at long-range place-kicking. He was the only tourist to be made a 'Player of the Year' by the *Rugby Almanack of New Zealand*, when he scored 30 of England's 45 points in the five games of the New Zealand tour of May 1963.

Hosen scored a Championship record 38 points in 1967, the year he was a member of a Calcutta Cup-winning team. He played cricket for Cornwall between 1955 and 1969 and represented the Minor Counties against the South Africans in 1965. A schoolmaster, he taught at Northampton Grammar School, Warwick College and Cheltenham College, where he was also in charge of rugby.

HOSKING
Geoffrey Robert d'Aubrey

Lock. 1949-1950 (Devonport Services, 5 caps).
Debut v Wales, 15 January 1949.
Born: 11 March 1922.
Educated: Cheltenham College.
Clubs: Devonport Services, Royal Navy.
During World War Two he reached the rank of captain in the Royal Marines. He later worked in Australia as a farmer.

HOUGHTON
Samuel

Full-back. 1892-1896 (Runcorn, 2 caps).
Debut v Ireland, 6 February 1892.
Born: 16 August 1870, Runcorn; Died: 17 August 1920, Runcorn.
Clubs: Runcorn, Birkenhead W, Runcorn RL, Cheshire.

HOWARD
Peter Dunsmore

Number 8/Flanker. 1930-1931 (Old Millhillians, 8 caps).
Debut v Wales, 18 January 1930.
Born: 20 December 1908, Maidenhead; Died: 25 February 1965, Lima, Peru.
Educated: Mill Hill School, Oxford University.
Clubs: Old Millhillians, Oxford University (Blues 1929-30).

Peter Howard fought back to fitness after a very bad leg injury, which nearly ended his career in sport, to became one of the country's leading wing-forwards of his time. He left university in 1931, without having obtained a degree of any kind, and accepted the post of national secretary of the New Youth Movement after being offered the same by Sir Oswald Moseley. He stood as New Party candidate at Bristol in the General Election of 1931.

Married to Doris Metaxa, French junior lawn tennis champion and Wimbledon ladies doubles winner of 1932 (with J.Sigart), Howard was a regular rugby correspondent for the *Sunday Express* and also wrote for the *Daily Express* and *Evening Standard*. He left Fleet Street to devote his life to the Oxford group of the Moral Rearmament movement. He wrote 16 books and 14 plays.

HUBBARD
George Cairns ('Scatter')

Back. 1892 (Blackheath, 2 caps).
Debut v Wales, 2 January 1892.
Born: 23 November 1867; Died: 18 December 1931, Eltham.
Educated: Tonbridge School.
Clubs: Blackheath, Barbarians, Kent.

Hubbard, who scored 71 tries in 121 appearances for Blackheath, scored a try on his international debut in what turned out to be an excellent season for England, who won the Triple Crown. Hubbard was one of eight new caps to represent England in the match against Wales. He retained his place in the next match but was not picked for the final match at Raeburn Place against Scotland. He is the father of John C.Hubbard. He also played cricket for Kent. He was capped in the 1888 England side that did not play. A stockbroker by profession.

HUBBARD
John Cairns

Full-back. 1930 (Harlequins, 1 cap).
Debut v Scotland, 15 March 1930.
Born: 27 June 1902.
Educated: Tonbridge School.
Clubs: Tonbridge, Harlequins, Barbarians, Kent.

The son of George C.Cairns, also an England international, he originally planned to join the Blackheath club as his father had played for them in the late-nineteenth century, but joined Harlequins when Blackheath informed him that he failed to reach the standard they required of him. He was well known for wearing gloves on wet days. He was a member of the Stock Exchange for over 50 years, from 1921 to 1972.

HUDSON
Arthur

Wing. 1906-1910 (Gloucester, 8 caps).
Debut v Wales, 13 January 1906.
Born: 27 October 1882, Gloucester; Died: 27 July 1973.
Clubs: Gloucester, Devonport, Harwich, Royal Navy, Combined Services, Gloucester.

Hudson, who weighed over 13 stones, achieved a remarkable record of scoring ten tries in his eight international appearances. Employed as a railway official, he was a contemporary of D.R. ('Dai') Gent. A very clever and resourceful wing threequarter, he scored a try on his international debut and his four tries in the England-France game on 22 March 1906 created a new record for an Englishman, despite the fact that he was not originally selected for the match. He scored 41 tries for Gloucester in 1905-06 and later became secretary of that club, a position he held for 40 years.

HUGHES
George Edgar

Forward. 1896 (Barrow, 1 cap).
Debut v Scotland, 14 March 1896.
Born: 24 February 1870, Otley; Died: 6 October 1947, Walney in Barrow.
Clubs: Barrow, Otley, Lancashire (15 appearances), Yorkshire.

Hughes made one appearance for Yorkshire, against Durham in 1897, after moving to the Otley club. He worked in the shipbuilding industry in Barrow.

HULME
Frank Croft (Frankie)

Half-back. 1903-1905 (Birkenhead Park, 4 caps).
Debut v Wales, 10 January 1903.
Born: 31 August 1881.
Educated: Birkenhead School.
Clubs: Birkenhead Park, Blackheath, Liverpool, Barbarians, Cheshire.

Along with 'Toggie' Kendall, Hulme developed a great half-back partnership in the days when specialised half-back positions were virtually unheard of. He went on the British Lions tour of Australia and New Zealand in 1904, when the Lions won all 13 games, including three Tests, in Australia but lost the first-ever Test between Britain and the All Blacks. He also played for Cheshire against New Zealand in 1905.

HUNT
James Thomas

Forward. 1882-1884 (Manchester, 3 caps).
Debut v Ireland, 6 February 1882.
Clubs: Preston Grasshoppers, Manchester, Lancashire.

He was the brother of Robert and William Hunt and played alongside Robert in the England-Ireland match at Lansdowne Road on his debut, Robert scoring a try in that match.

HUNT
Robert

Back. 1880-1882 (Manchester, 4 caps).
Debut v Ireland 30 January 1880.
Born: 21 January 1856; Died: 19 March 1913.
Educated: Preston Grammar School, Owen's College.
Clubs: Preston Grasshoppers, Manchester, Blackheath, Lancashire.

A GP in Blackburn, he played in the England-Ireland match with his brother James at Lansdowne Road in 1882. His brother William was also an England international.

HUNT
William Henry

Forward. 1876-1878 (Manchester, 4 caps).
Debut v Scotland, 6 March 1876.
Born: 11 May 1854, Preston.
Preston Grasshoppers, Manchester, Lancashire.

Brother of James and Robert, he had an army career and commanded the 5th Lancashire Artillery. He won the Lance v Sword mounted section at the 1889 Royal Military Tournament.

HUNTSMAN
Robert Paul

Prop. 1985 (Headingley, 2 caps).
Debut v New Zealand, 1 June 1985.
Born: 5 May 1957, Beverley.
Educated: Hymers College (Hull), Bulmershe College (Reading).
Clubs: Maidenhead, Headingley, Wasps, Yorkshire (12 appearances), Northern Division.

He went on England's tour of New Zealand in 1985 and appeared in both Tests, his only caps. He is a PE teacher.

HURST
Andrew Charles Brunel

Wing. 1962 (Wasps, 1 cap).
Debut v Scotland, 17 March 1962.
Born: 1 October 1935, Cairo.
Educated: The Dragon School (Oxford), Abbotsholme School, Oxford University.
Clubs: Oxford University (no Blue), Wasps, Barbarians, Middlesex.

Hurst served in the Royal Navy during his National Service, being based in

Malta for a time. He was on the Oxford-Cambridge tour of the Far East in 1957.

HUSKISSON
Thomas Frederick, MC MBE

Lock Forward. 1937-1938 (Old Merchant Taylor's, 8 caps).
Born: 1 July 1914.
Debut v Wales, 16 January 1937.
Educated: Merchant Taylor's School.
Clubs: Old Merchant Taylors, Army, London Counties, Eastern Counties, Lancashire.

Huskisson made his international debut in the 1937 Triple Crown campaign and was also a member of the 1939 Calcutta Cup-winning side. He also went on the British Lions tour of Argentina in 1936. During World War Two he served with the Duke of Wellington's Regiment and was awarded the Military Cross and bar in 1940 and the MBE in 1945.

HUTCHINSON
Frank, MC

Fly-half. 1909 (Headingley, 3 caps).
Debut v France, 30 January 1909.
Born: 1885 Wakefield; Died: 5 March 1960, Leeds.
Educated: Leeds Grammar School.
Clubs: Old Leodiensians, Headingley, Yorkshire (13 appearances).

Hutchinson marked his international debut with a try. He played cricket for Yorkshire 2nd XI. Awarded the Military Cross in 1919 after serving in World War One.

HUTCHINSON
James E.

Wing. 1906 (Durham City, 1 cap).
Debut v Ireland, 10 February 1906.
Born: 1884.
Educated: Bernard Castle School.
Clubs: Durham City, Northumberland.

Employed as a farmer, he had a deformed hand due to a childhood accident with a harvester.

HUTCHINSON
W.C.

Half-back. 1876-1877 (Royal Indian Engineering College, 2 caps).
Debut v Scotland 6 March 1876.
Born: 1856; Died: late-1800s in India.
Educated: Christ's College (Finchley), Royal Indian Engineering College.
Club: Royal Indian Engineering College.

He had a career in the British Army, serving mainly in India it is believed. A very unselfish player, he nevertheless scored two tries against Ireland in 1877.

HUTCHINSON
William Henry Heap ('The Baron')

Forward. 1875-1876 (Hull & East Riding, 2 caps).

Debut v Ireland, 15 February 1875.
Born: 31 October 1850; Died: 4 July 1929, Brough.
Educated: Rugby School.
Clubs: Hull & East Riding, Yorkshire (11 appearances, captain in 1873).

One of the last players to appear in the old 20-a-side teams, he played in the first England-Ireland match at Kennington Oval. Hull went on to help form the Northern Union in 1895. The Baron, as he was known, was the first player to be capped from a Yorkshire club by England and his cap was with the old Hull & East Riding club. He was a fine, strapping forward.

HUTH
Henry

Full-Back. 1879 (Huddersfield, 1 cap).
Debut v Scotland, 10 March 1879.
Born: 1859; Died: December 1929, London.
Educated: London International College.
Clubs: Huddersfield, Yorkshire (15 appearances).

A wool merchant, he played cricket for the Gentlemen of the North and was one of three brothers who played county rugger for Yorkshire. His brothers M. and Frank also played for Huddersfield before the club went on to help form the Northern Union in 1895.

HYDE
John Phillip

Wing. 1950 (Northampton, 2 caps).
Debut v France, 25 February 1950.
Born: 8 June 1930.
Educated: Wellingborough Grammar School.
Clubs: Northampton, Army, Combined Services, Barbarians, Midlands.

Hyde replaced I.J.Botting. The previous year he had appeared in the first of the England '19 Group' matches. He served in the Northamptonshire Regiment and played six times for the Army, against the Royal Navy, RAF and French Army. He was employed as a school teacher.

HYNES
William Baynard

Lock. 1912 (United Services (Portsmouth), Royal Navy, 1 cap).
Debut v France, 8 April 1912.
Born: 1889; Died: 2 March 1968.
Clubs: United Services (Portsmouth), Royal Navy.

Hynes was a director of Naval intelligence attached to the Royal Canadian Navy from 1931 to 1933. He served in World War One and also in World War Two. His decorations include Officer of US Legion of Merit (1945), Distinguished Service Order (1921), Com-

mander British Empire (1943). He was also awarded the Bronze Medal of the Royal Humane Society. A barrister, he was called to the Bar in 1938.

IBBITSON
Ernest Denison

Lock. 1909 (Headingley, 4 caps).
Debut v Wales, 16 January 1909.
Born: 1 February 1882, Leeds; Died: circa 1955-6 in Canada.
Educated: Wesley College (Sheffield).
Clubs: Headingley, Yorkshire.

He made two appearances for Yorkshire, the first against Monmouth in 1905. He was employed in the woollen industry.

IMRIE
Henry Marshall

Wing. 1905-1907 (Durham City, 2 caps).
Debut v New Zealand, 2 December 1905.
Born: 1877; Died: 16 October 1938, Middleton St George, Durham.
Clubs: Durham YMCA, Durham City, Durham County.

He made his debut against the first All Blacks at Crystal Palace but had to wait until 1907 for his second and last cap, when he scored a try against Ireland at Lansdowne Road.

INGLIS
Rupert Edward

Forward. 1886 (Blackheath, 3 caps).
Debut v Wales, 2 January 1886.
Born: 17 April 1864; Died: 18 September 1916, Ginschy (killed in action).
Educated: Rugby School, Oxford University.
Clubs: Oxford University (Blues 1883-4), Blackheath, Middlesex.

A clergyman who was ordained in 1899, he was the son of Sir John Inglis, the defender of Lucknow. All his caps were won in 1886, against Wales, Ireland and Scotland, winning two and drawing with the 'Auld enemy' at Raeburn Place. He served during World War One as chaplain to the forces and lost his life at the age of 52 whilst trying to bring in the wounded under heavy fire.

IRVIN
Samuel Howell

Full-back. 1905 (Devonport Albion, 1 cap).
Debut v Wales, 14 January 1905.
Born: 1880 Hartlepool; Died: 1939, Oldham.
Clubs: Hartlepool Old Boys, Devonport Albion, Devon, Oldham RL.

ISHERWOOD
Francis William Ramsbottom

Forward. 1872 (Ravenscourt Park, 1 cap).
Debut v Scotland, 5 February 1872.
Born: 16 October 1852; Died: 30 April 1888, Southsea.

Educated: Rugby School, Oxford University.

Clubs: Oxford University (Blue 1871), Ravenscourt Park.

He scored England's first conversion against Scotland on his debut international in 1872. He played cricket for Oxford (Blue 1872), Essex CCC.

Sources say that he worked somewhere in the Carpathian Mountain region.

JACKETT
Edward John

Full-back. 1905-1909 (Leicester, Falmouth, 13 caps).
Debut v New Zealand, 2 December 1905.
Born: 4 July 1882, Falmouth; Died: 1935, Middlesbrough.

Clubs: Falmouth, Leicester, Devonport Albion, Transvaal (South Africa), De Beers (South Africa), Kimberley (South Africa), Dewsbury RL, Cornwall (52 appearances).

Jackett made his debut for England against the first All Blacks, at the Crystal Palace in 1905, the same year that England won the Calcutta Cup. He was one of only three men to play in all five England games in 1905-06. He scored only two conversions for his country, both against France in 1909, in a 22-0 win. He went on the British Lions' tour of Australia and New Zealand in 1903 and was a member of the Cornwall side which represented Britain in the Olympics in 1908, winning the silver medal against Australia. In 1903 he played for Transvaal against the British Lions. Jackett was famed for finding touch within a foot of his intended spot. He was also cycling champion of Cornwall. Employed as a theatre manager, he was also an artists' model.

JACKSON
A.H.

Half-back. 1878-1880 (Blackheath, 2 caps).
Debut v Ireland, 30 January 1880.
Clubs: Guy's Hospital, Blackheath.

He scored 22 tries in 37 appearances for Blackheath between 1877 and 1881. He was a powerful, clever player. It is said that he had 'a good drop with either foot and absolutely chock-full of pluck and resource'. It is said that on occasion he could be a 'selfish' player, inclined to run with the ball when a pass would have been a better choice.

JACKSON
Barry S.

Prop/Flanker. 1970 (Broughton Park, 2 caps).
Born: 9 August 1937.
Debut v Scotland, 21 March 1970.
Clubs: Broughton Park, Lancashire (50 appearances).

He won his first cap when he replaced B.R.West in the Calcutta Cup match at Murrayfield in 1970. He was the first player to be capped from the Broughton Park club.

JACKSON
Peter Barrie

Right-wing. 1956-1963 (Coventry, 20 caps).
Debut v Wales, 21 January 1956.
Born: 22 September 1930, Birmingham.
Educated: King Edward VI School (Birmingham).

Clubs: Old Edwardians, Coventry, Aldershot Services, Army, North Midlands, Warwickshire.

Peter Jackson is one Coventry player who will leave his mark in the record books. A magnificent runner with the ball, he is Coventry's record cap holder, overtaking Ivor Price who previously held the record with 12 caps. In December 1950, at the age of 20, Jackson appeared in an England trial at Otley, whilst with Old Edwardians, but failed to progress and it was to be six years before he gained a full cap.

His greatest moment came in the international between England and Australia in 1958, when he dived over the try-line to give England victory in the final minute of the match. He was displaced in 1960 but recalled to play in the 1963 International Championship, when he was in his mid-30s.

In 1954 and 1955 he played three times for the Army whilst serving in the Royal Signals; and in 1962 he captained Warwickshire to their fourth County Championship win in five years. He went on the British Lions' tour to Australia and New Zealand in 1959 and scored a try in the Fourth Test. He works in the export packing business.

JACKSON
Walter Jesse

Centre. 1894 (Halifax, 1 cap).
Debut v Scotland, 17 March 1894.
Born: 16 March 1870, Gloucester; Died: 1 December 1958, Halifax.
Clubs: Gloucester, Halifax.

Walter Jackson was the first international player from Gloucester, but won his cap whilst at Halifax, whom he joined in 1893, 'so that he could pursue his career as a boilermaker'. After Halifax joined the Northern Union in 1895, he played only one more season for them. He lost an eye in a work accident before the beginning of the 1896-7 season and had to retire after scoring ten tries and one goal (34 points in all) in his 37 appearances for the club. He became second-team coach. Jackson made five appearances for Yorkshire RFU in 1894, making his debut against Lancashire.

JACOB
Frederick

Forward. 1897-1899 (Cambridge University, 8 caps).

Debut v Wales, 9 January 1897.
Born: 4 January 1873, Northbourne, Kent; Died: 1 September 1945, India.
Educated: Sandwich School, Cambridge University, Gottingen University, London University.

Clubs: Thanet Wanderers, Cambridge University (Blues 1895-6), Blackheath, Richmond, Cheltenham, Gloucester, Barbarians, Kent.

He also won a polo Blue. Employed as a teacher, he taught at Cheltenham College, Felstead and Bradfield College.

JACOB
Herbert Percy

Wing. 1924-1930 (Blackheath, 5 caps).
Debut v Wales, 19 January 1924.
Born: 12 October 1902.
Educated: Cranleigh School, Oxford University.

Clubs: Oxford University (Blues 1923-5), Blackheath.

He scored a try on his international debut for England. Employed as a master at Cranleigh School and Worksop College, he was much interested in golf and was secretary of the Royal Blackheath Golf Club. The last surviving player from England's first Grand Slam side, he now lives in Australia.

JACOB
Philip Gordon

Half-back. 1898 (Blackheath, 1 cap).
Debut v Ireland, 5 February 1898.
Born: 14 May 1875, India.
Educated: Bedford Grammar School, Cambridge University.

Clubs: Cambridge University (Blues 1894-6), Blackheath, Kent.

He was employed in the Accountant General's office, based in the Punjab.

JACOBS
Charles Ronald

Prop. 1956-1964 (Northampton, 29 caps).
Debut v Wales, 21 January 1956.
Born: 28 October 1928, Whittlesey, Cambridgeshire.
Educated: Oakham School, Nottingham University.

Clubs: Northampton, Barbarians, East Midlands.

Jacobs, Northampton's most capped player, appeared in the Calcutta Cup-winning teams of 1956, 1957, 1960, 1961 and 1964 (as captain) and in the Triple Crown teams of 1957 and 1960. An RFU selector and East Midlands CB representative, he is a farmer.

JAGO
Raphael Anthony

Scrum half. 1906-1907 (Devonport Albion, 5 caps).
Debut v Wales, 13 January 1906.
Born: 20 January 1882, Chaddock, Dorset.

Clubs: Devonport Albion, Devon (59 appearances).

Jago, who made 320 appearances for Devonport Albion between 1899 and 1919, scored a try in his second international match, against Ireland in 1906, his only score for his country. He was a blacksmith by trade. He helped Devon win the County Championship in 1906.

JANION
Jeremy Paul Aubrey George

Centre/Wing. 1971-1975 (Bedford, 13 caps).
Debut v Wales, 16 January 1971.
Born: 25 September 1946, Bishop's Stortford.
Educated: St Edmund's College (Ware).
Clubs: Saffron Waldon, Bedford, Richmond, Barbarians, London Counties, Eastern Counties.

A hefty winger, Janion played for England Under-25s against Fiji in 1970 and toured Japan and the Far East in 1971. He is employed in the brewing industry.

JARMAN
J. Wallace

Forward. 1900 (Bristol, 1 cap).
Debut v Wales, 6 January 1900.
Born: 15 July 1872; Died: September 1950, Vancouver, Canada.
Clubs: Merchant Venturers, Bristol, Gloucestershire.

Jarman was selected to tour Australia with the British Lions in 1899 before he gained his full England international cap; when that cap was awarded he became the first player to be capped from his club, Bristol. He emigrated to Canada in 1920 and remained there until his death.

JEAVONS
Nicholas Clive

Flanker. 1981-1983 (Moseley, 14 caps).
Debut v Scotland, 21 February 1981.
Born: 12 November 1957, Calcutta, India.
Educated: Berkhamstead Prep School, Wolverhampton Grammar School, Tettenhall College, Wolverhampton Polytechnic.
Clubs: Moseley, Barbarians, Midlands.

He was replaced by R.Hesford on his international debut in the Calcutta Cup win over Scotland in 1981, but returned to the side in the next game against the Irish at Lansdowne Road. He was on the British Lions' tour of New Zealand in 1983 and went to Argentina with England in 1981 (playing in both Tests) and to Canada and the USA in 1983. He also played for England Students against Argentina, for England Under-23s against France in 1977 and on the tour of France in 1978.

Nick Jeavons

Dickie Jeeps

JEEPS
Richard Eric Gautrey ('Dickie'), CBE JP

Scrum half. 1956-1961 (Northampton, 24 caps).
Debut v Wales, 21 January 1956.
Born: 25 November 1931.
Educated: Bedford Modern School, Cambridge University.
Clubs: Cambridge University (no Blue), Northampton, Barbarians, London Counties, Eastern Counties.

Dickie Jeeps is said to be one of the finest scrum-halves of this century and he was most certainly one of the most respected and loved of England international players. He captained England 13 times and his 24 caps was a record for a scrum-half. Jeeps went on the British Lions' tour of South Africa in 1955, before being capped by England, and his 13 Lions Test appearances include four before his first appearance for England, a record which only Bill McBride has surpassed. The only uncapped player on that Lions tour to South Africa, he later succeeded Jeff Butterfield as captain of the side. In 1962 he was appointed captain of the Lions side which toured South Africa again.

He played in the International XV which met Wales on 6 April 1957, in a match organised to raise funds for the staging of the Empire Games in Cardiff in 1958. He was an RFU selector from 1965 to 1971 and president from 1976 to 1977 (the first time that an Eastern Counties member had achieved rugby's highest honour). He also played cricket for Cambridgeshire. A fruit farmer, he later became chairman of the Sports Council and served as a county councillor and a JP.

JEFFREY
George Luxton

Forward. 1886-1887 (Blackheath, 6 caps).
Debut v Wales, 2 January 1886.
Born: 1863; Died: 4 November 1937.
Educated: St John's Wood School, Cambridge University.
Clubs: Cambridge University (Blues 1884-5), Harlequins, Blackheath, Barbarians, Middlesex.

Jeffrey scored only one try for England, on 5 March 1887 when he scored the try which enabled England to draw the match against Scotland at Manchester. It was his last appearance for England, although he was also capped in the side of 1888 that did not play. He was a stockbroker.

JENNINS
Christopher Robert

Centre. 1967 (Waterloo, 3 caps).
Debut v Australia, 7 January 1967.
Born: 5 February 1942.
Educated: Rydal School, Liverpool University.

Clubs: Waterloo, Lancashire (34 appearances).
He appeared in the England side which beat Ireland 8-3 at Lansdowne Road, their first victory over the Irish since 1962. He graduated from Liverpool as a Bachelor of Commerce and is employed as a chartered accountant.

JEWITT
J.H.

Lock. 1902 (Hartlepool Rovers, 1 cap).
Debut v Wales, 11 January 1902.
Clubs: Hartlepool Rovers, Durham County, Broughton Rangers RL.
Jewitt went to play Rugby League for Broughton Rovers in 1902-03.

JOHNS
William Alexander

Forward. 1909-1910 (Gloucester, 7 caps).
Debut v Wales, 16 January 1909.
Born: 1 February 1882, Gloucester.
Educated: Sir Thomas Rich's School (Gloucester).
Clubs: Gloucester, Gloucestershire.

Johns scored his first England try against France at Leicester in the 22-0 win on 30 January 1909, his only score for England. He appeared in three of the four matches in the 1910 Championship-winning season which saw the opening of Twickenham. He wrote an article entitled 'How to Lead Rugby Forward' in the *The Empire Annual for Boys* for 1913.

JOHNSTON
William R.

Full-back. 1910-1914 (Bristol, 16 caps).
Debut v Wales, 15 January 1910.
Educated: Colston's School (Bristol).
Clubs: Bristol, Gloucester.

He once held the record as England's most capped full-back, playing either side of World War One and appearing in two of the three Championship-winning matches of 1910, the season which saw the opening of Twickenham. He was also in the Grand Slam and Calcutta Cup-winning side of 1913 and shared in the Triple Crown triumph of 1914.

JONES
Frederick Phelp.

Wing. 1893 (New Brighton, 1 cap).
Debut v Scotland, 4 March 1893.
Born: 1873; Died: 14 August 1944.
Educated: Wallasey Grammar School.
Clubs: New Brighton, Birkenhead Park.

JONES
Herbert Arthur

Lock. 1950 (Barnstaple, 3 caps).
Debut v Wales, 21 January 1950.
Born: 22 August 1918, Landkey, Barnstaple.
Clubs: Barnstaple, Devon.

He was probably one of the greatest forwards ever to come out of the West Country, despite the fact that he won only three caps. He captained Barnstaple and played for Devon from 1946 to 1952. He was a farmer.

JORDEN
Anthony Mervyn

Full-back. 1970-1975 (Cambridge University, Blackheath, Bedford, 7 caps).
Debut v France, 18 April 1970.
Born: 28 January 1947, Radlett, Hertfordshire.

Tony Jorden

Educated: Monmouth School, Cambridge University.
Clubs: Cambridge University (Blues 1968-9), Upper Clapton, Blackheath, Bedford, Barbarians, Eastern Counties.

Jorden, a reliable two-footed full-back, scored one penalty-goal and converted two tries by Spencer and Taylor on his international debut. A member of the 1973 and 1975 Calcutta Cup-winning teams, he scored a total of five conversions and four penalty-goals for England. He captained Eastern Counties in 1971, played for them in the 1975 County Championship Final and was their CB representative. He also won a cricket Blue and made 60 appearances for Essex CCC between 1966 and 1970. He was president of the Hawks club in 1970. He took charge of the Wasps for a spell in February 1992 after their coach resigned.

JOWETT
Donald

Forward. 1889-1891 (Heckmondwike, 6 caps).
Debut v Maoris, 16 February 1889.
Born: 4 December 1866, Bradford; Died: 27 August 1980, Hekmondwike, near Bradford.
Clubs: Heckmondwike, Heckmondwike RL, Yorkshire (31 appearances).

His only score for England was when he converted a try by J.W.Dyson in the match against Scotland on 1 March 1890, when he was one of five Yorkshire players in the side. A licensee, he was a relative of E.E.Booth (New Zealand, 1905-1907).

JUDD
Philip Edward

Prop. 1962-1967 (Coventry, 22 caps).
Debut v Wales, 20 January 1962.
Born: 8 April 1934.
Educated: Broad Street School (Coventry).
Clubs: Broad Street Old Boys, Coventry, RAF, Barbarians, Warwickshire.

His 442 senior appearances were a Coventry club record until 1972, when George Cole surpassed it. He went on the England tours of Australia and New Zealand in 1962 and Canada 1967. He was also a county water polo and squash player. Employed as a pattern maker. He had played in ten England trials before being awarded his first cap.

KAYLL
Henry Edward

Full-back. 1878 (Sunderland, 1 cap).
Debut v Scotland, 4 March 1878.
Born: 16 July 1855, Sunderland; Died: 14 February 1910, Vancouver, Canada.
Educated: Richmond School (Yorkshire).
Clubs: Sunderland, Durham County.

Kayll was one of six brothers who played for the Sunderland club. The English pole vault champion, he set a world record vault of 11ft 1in in 1877. A farmer, he emigrated to Canada.

KEELING
John Hugh

Hooker. 1948 (Guy's Hospital, 2 caps).
Debut v Australia, 3 January 1948.
Born: 28 October 1925.
Club: Guy's Hospital.

KEEN
Brian Warwick

Prop-forward. 1968 (Newcastle University, 4 caps).
Debut v Wales, 20 January 1968.
Born: 1 June 1944.
Educated: Hardyes School (Dorchester).
Clubs: Dorchester, Newcastle University, Northern, Moseley, Barbarians.
Keen is Dorchester's first international

player of modern days. As an agricultural student at Newcastle University, he represented Northumberland in the County Championship and won a place in the England team after only one trial match. He is the son of Don Keen, Dorchester's 'A' XV captain in 1948-9 and now president of the club. Brian Keen has also played in the full-back position and was reputed to be the fastest front-row forward in first-class rugby. He was in the 1968 Calcutta Cup-winning team.

KEETON
George Haydn

Hooker. 1904 (Leicester, 3 caps).
Debut v Wales, 9 January 1904.
Born: 13 October 1878; Died: 7 January 1949, Menton, France.
Educated: Oakham School, Cambridge University.
Clubs: Cambridge University (Blues 1899-1900), Richmond, Leicester, Midland Counties.

Employed as a headmaster, he held many posts including those at such famous schools as Fettes College and Reading School. He has the distinction of being buried in the same cemetery in Menton, on the French Riviera, as the legendary William Webb Ellis and Percy Carpmael, founder of the Barbarians.

KELLY
Geoffrey Arnold

Prop. 1947-1948 (Bedford, 4 caps).
Debut v Wales, 18 January 1947.
Born: 9 February 1914.
Educated: Perse School.
Clubs: Letchworth, Bedford, Barbarians, East Midlands, Eastern Counties.

He appeared in the 1947 season, when England shared the Championship and won the Calcutta Cup.

KELLY
Thomas Stanley

Lock/Prop. 1906-1908 (London Devonians, 12 caps).
Debut v Wales, 13 January 1906.
Born: 1882, Tiverton.
Educated: Blundell's School.
Clubs: Exeter, London Devonians, Devon.

A civil servant, he was in Calcutta Cup-winning teams in 1906, 1907 and 1908.

KEMBLE
Arthur Twiss

Forward. 1885-1887 (Liverpool, 3 caps).
Debut v Wales, 3 January 1885.
Born: 3 February 1862, Sebergham, Carlisle; Died: 13 March 1925, Park Cottage, Crawley Down, Sussex.
Educated: Appleby Grammar School (Westmorland).
Clubs: Liverpool, Lancashire (22 appearances), Leicestershire.

Third son of the Rev N.F.Y.Kemble of Allerton, Liverpool, and a member of a well-known theatrical family, Kemble had few superiors in the scrummage and was an all-round sportsman. He played cricket for Liverpool from 1883 until May 1899, when he resigned due to business pressures, and kept wicket for Lancashire for 20 seasons from July 1885 to 1905. He also played for Liverpool and District against Cambridge University in 1895 and against Cumberland in 1889. He served on the committees of both the Lancashire and Sussex CCCs and in 1899 took a team to the Canary Islands, winning all three matches. In later years he was honorary secretary of the Copthorne Golf Club in Sussex. Chairman of Garston District Council in 1901, he was also a member of Liverpool City Council and chairman of the Garston Overseers. He was admitted as a solicitor in 1891. He died of sceptic pneumonia, aged 63.

KEMP
Dudley Thomas

Number 8. 1935 (Blackheath, 1 cap).
Debut v Wales, 19 January 1935.
Born: 18 January 1910.
Educated: King Edward VI School (Southampton).
Clubs: Trojans, Blackheath, Barbarians, Hampshire (51 appearances including one post-war).

Kemp was also a first-class referee, who took charge of many county games and Barbarian matches, plus a final trials match and the Combined Services against South Africa at Twickenham in 1951. One of the few former playing internationals to have taken up so many duties, he was also president of the RFU from 1969 to 1970, an International Board representative from 1971 to 1977, secretary of Hampshire RFU from 1946 to 1967, team secretary from 1946 to 1953 and president from 1973 to 1977.. He represented the Railway Athletic Association in 1930 and the Territorial Army in 1937 and played cricket for Hampshire 2nd XI in 1949.

KEMP
Thomas Arthur

Fly-half. 1937-1948 (Richmond, 5 caps).
Debut v Wales, 16 January 1937.
Born: 12 August 1915.
Educated: Denstone College, Cambridge University.
Clubs: Cambridge University (Blue 1936), St Mary's Hospital, Richmond, Manchester, Army, Barbarians, London Counties, Lancashire, Middlesex.

Thomas Kemp was said to be one of the finest kickers of a ball ever to occupy the position of stand-off half in an England XV. In 1948, however, he declined to play against Ireland and there ended his international career. He captained the St Mary's Hospital side that in 1939 won the Hospitals' Cup for a record sixth time.

He represented Cambridge University on the RFU from 1953 and was a selector from 1955 to 1962. President of the RFU from 1971 to 1972 and chairman of the RFU Centenary Congress at Cambridge University in 1970. He served in the RAMC.

KENDALL
Percy Dale ('Toggie').

Fly-half/Scrum Half. 1901-1903 (Birkenhead Park, 3 caps).
Debut v Scotland, 9 March 1901.
Born: 21 August 1878, Prescot; Died: 25 January 1915, Ypres (killed in action).
Educated: Elleray School (New Brighton), Tonbridge School, Cambridge University.
Clubs: Cambridge University (no Blue), Blackheath, Birkenhead Park, Cheshire (later as captain).
Kendall captained England against Scotland in 1903 and with Frank Hulme developed a great half-back partnership in the days when specialised half-back positions were virtually unknown. He played for Cheshire against the New Zealanders in 1905. A legend in his own right both on and off the rugby field, he served during World War One with the King's Liverpool Regiment. Employed as a solicitor.

KENDALL-CARPENTER
John MacGregor, CBE

Number 8/Prop. 1949-1954 (Oxford University, Bath, 23 caps).
Debut v Ireland, 12 February 1949.
Born: 25 September 1925, Cardiff; Died: 23 May 1990.
Educated: Truro School, Oxford University.
Clubs: Oxford University (Blues 1948-50), Bath, Penzance & Newlyn, Barbarians, Cornwall (28 appearances).
A very speedy wing-forward, he captained every side for which he played, including skippering England in 1951. Chairman of the IRFB and president of the RFU, he also served on the RFU schools committee and was chairman of the Rugby World Cup organising committee. He was awarded the CBE in 1989 for services to rugby. A schoolmaster, he taught at Cranbrook and Eastbourne College and was headmaster at Wellington School, Somerset. During World War Two he served in the Royal Naval Volunteer Reserve.

KENDREW
Douglas Andrew ('Joe'), DSO
CBE KCMG

Prop. 1930-1936 (Leicester, 10 caps).
Debut v Wales, 18 January 1930.
Born: 22 July 1910.
Educated: Uppingham School.
Clubs: Woodford, Leicester, Army,

Joe Kendrew

Ulster, Combined Services, Barbarians, Eastern Counties.

Kendrew, who went on the British Lions' tour of New Zealand and Australia in 1930, served in the Leicester Regiment, made seven appearances for the Army, against the Royal Navy and the RAF. He also played for Ulster against New Zealand in 1935. He served in World War Two and won the DSO in 1943 (later gaining three bars), the CBE in 1944, the CB in 1958 and the KCMG in 1963. He was Governor of Western Australia.

KENNEDAY
Robert Day

Wing. 1949 (Camborne School of Mines, 3 caps).
Debut v Ireland, 12 February 1949.
Born: 14 August 1925; Died: May 1979, Rhodesia.
Educated: Camborne School of Mines.
Clubs: Rhodesia, Camborne School of Mines, Cornwall (11 appearances).
He won all three England caps whilst a member of the School of Mines club and was a member of the 1949 Calcutta Cup-winning side. Employed as a mining engineer, he was killed in an ambush whilst living in Rhodesia, now Zimbabwe.

KENT
Charles Philip

Centre. 1977-1978 (Rosslyn Park, 5 caps).
Debut v Scotland, 15 January 1977.
Born: 4 August 1953, Bridgwater.
Educated: Blundell's School, Oxford University.

Charles Kent

Clubs: Oxford University (Blues 1972-5), Rosslyn Park, Bridgwater Albion, Somerset.
Kent scored a try on his international debut, his only score for England. He also scored three tries for England Under-23s against Japan in 1977.

KENT
Thomas

Forward. 1891-1892 (Salford, 6 caps).
Debut v Wales, 3 January 1891.
Born: 19 June 1864, Nottingham; Died: 29 January 1928.
Clubs: Salford, Lancashire.
He appeared in the England side of 1892, which captured the Triple Crown without conceding a single score, and he was on the British Lions' tour of Australia and New Zealand in 1888. A builder by trade.

KERSHAW
Cecil Ashworth

Scrum-half. 1920-1923 (United Services (Portsmouth), Royal Navy, 16 caps).
Debut v Wales, 17 January 1920.
Born: 3 February 1895; Died: 1 November 1972.
Educated: Wharfedale School (Ilkley), Royal Naval College (Osborne), Royal Naval College (Dartmouth).
Clubs: United Services (Portsmouth), Blackheath, Royal Navy, Harlequins, Barbarians, Yorkshire.
A captain in the Royal Navy, the son of Sir Lewis Kershaw KCSI, he was never on a losing England side, his worst experience being a drawn game with France in 1922. He retired from international football after the 1923 Grand Slam season and holds the record, along with W.J.A.Davies, of 14 half-back appearances. Kershaw played in the centenary match at Rugby School in 1923 and for Harlequins in their 21-11 defeat of the Olympic champions, the United States, in 1924. He also fenced for Great Britain in the 1920 Olympics in Antwerp and was an able cricketer and hockey player.
During World War One he served in submarines around the Baltic region and in World War Two he was on the Naval planning staff for the D-Day landings.

KEWLEY
Edward

Forward. 1874-1878 (Liverpool, 7 caps).
Debut v Scotland, 23 February 1874.
Born: 20 June 1852, Farnham, Buckinghamshire; Died: 17 April 1940, Winchester, Hampshire.
Educated: Marlborough College.
Clubs: Liverpool, Lancashire.
Kewley was the first Northern club player to captain England, against Ireland in 1877, in the first 15-a-side international. He was a vice-president of RFU from 1878 to 1879. He played cricket for Marlborough and Lancashire and was secretary of Liverpool CC in 1893. In his cricket days with Marlborough he was said to have 'very good defence'.

KEWNEY
Alfred Lionel, OBE

Forward. 1906-1913 (Leicester, 16 caps).
Debut v Wales, 13 January 1906.
Born: 1883; Died: 16 December 1959.
Clubs: Rockcliff, Leicester, Barbarians, Northumberland.
A fiery Northumbrian, he was held in particularly high regard by Welsh players, who nicknamed him 'Kicking Ginger'.

KEY
Alan, OBE TD

Scrum-half. 1930-1933 (Old Cranleighans, 2 caps).
Debut v Ireland, 8 February 1930.
Born: 4 June 1908; Died: 2 July 1989.
Educated: Cranleigh School.
Clubs: Old Cranleighans, Honourable Artillery Company, London Counties, Barbarians, Middlesex.
A former England Schools hockey player, Key was a versatile, skilful rugby player. He went on five successive Easter tours of South Wales with the Barbarians, on one occasion appearing as an emergency threequarter. He made his international debut when Wilf Sobey withdrew from the side to play Ireland in 1930, and he became the first player to be capped direct from the Old Cranleighans Club. He last appeared for England at Twickenham in 1933 when, at the tenth attempt, Wales beat England for the first time on that ground. He served during World War Two and was mentioned in despatches in 1940 and awarded the OBE in 1945. He was founder-manager of the Army Kinema Corporation. He reached the rank of lieutenant-colonel.

KEYWORTH
Mark

Flanker. 1976 (Swansea, 4 caps).
Debut v Australia, 3 January 1976.
Born: 19 February 1948, Bridgnorth.
Educated: Ellesmere College (Shropshire), Cirencester Agricultural College.
Clubs: Swansea, Aberystwyth, North Midlands, Shropshire.
Keyworth, who was at Ellesmere College at the same time as Bill Beaumont, was on the losing side in all four England appearances. He is a farmer.

KILNER
Barron, JP

Forward. 1880 (Wakefield Trinity, 1 cap).
Debut v Ireland, 30 January 1880.
Born: 11 October 1853, Dewsbury; Died: 28 December 1922, Wakefield.
Clubs: Wakefield Trinity, Yorkshire (10 appearances).
Kilner was Wakefield's first international player after appearing in the North v South trial. He became manager of Wakefield in 1899, after the club

had helped form the Northern Union four years earlier. A leading referee, administrator and president of the Yorkshire Union, he was one of the touch-judges for the Yorkshire-New Zealand match in 1905.

KINDERSLEY
Richard Stephen

Forward. 1882-1885 (Exeter, 3 caps).
Debut v Wales, 16 December 1882.
Born: 27 September 1858; Died: 26 September 1932.
Educated: Clifton College, Oxford University.
Clubs: Oxford University (Blues 1882-3), Exeter, Devon.

Kindersley scored the first of his two international tries against Scotland in 1884, his second coming against Wales in 1885, and he never appeared on a losing England side. That first try led to a suspension of fixtures between the two countries and the forming of the International Board after the Scots claimed that there had been a knock-back on their side; since England had the advantage, the try was allowed. He gained rowing Blues 1880 and 1881. He taught at Radley College and Eton College.

KING
Ian

Full-back. 1954 (Harrogate, 3 caps).
Debut v Wales, 16 January 1954.
Born: 1923.
Educated: Loretto College.
Clubs: Harrogate, Yorkshire (51 appearances, captain 1949-1950).

He scored a penalty-goal and a conversion in the game against Ireland on 13 February 1954, his only score of any kind for England. He helped Yorkshire win the County Championship in 1953.

KING
John Abbott

Number 8. 1911-1913 (Headingley, 12 caps).
Debut v Wales, 21 January 1911.
Born: 21 August 1883, Leeds; Died: 9 August 1916, Guillemont, France (killed in action).
Educated: Giggleswick School.
Clubs: Durbanville (South Africa), Headingley, Barbarians, Yorkshire 1906-1913 (36 appearances, captain 1911-13).

He was England's smallest international player, often referred to as a 'pocket Hercules'. He was, though, a courageous rugby footballer, who broke two ribs in the England-Scotland game in 1912, returning for the first game of the 1913 season against South Africa.

KING
Quentin Eric Moffitt Ayres

Wing. 1921 (Army, 1 cap).
Debut v Scotland, 19 March 1921.

Born: 8 July 1895 Bedford; Died: 30 October 1954.
Educated at St Edward's School (Oxford).
Clubs: Blackheath, Army, Barbarians.

He scored a try on his international debut, playing in one game of the 1921 Grand Slam season to help England win the Calcutta Cup. During World War One he served as a major in the Royal Field Artillery and after the war appeared in three games for the Army, against the Royal Navy in 1921 and 1923, and against the RAF in 1921.

KINGSTON
Peter

Scrum Half. 1975-1979 (Gloucester, 5 caps).
Debut v Australia, 24 May 1975.
Born: 24 July 1951, Lydney.
Educated: Lydney Grammar School, St Paul's College (Cheltenham).
Clubs: Lydney, Moseley, Gloucester, North Midlands, Gloucestershire.

Kingston played for Lydney whilst on vacation from college. A PE teacher, his first appointment was at a Birmingham school and he played for Moseley during

that time, beginning in the 3rd XV, before moving to a position at Penhill Secondary School in Swindon, when he joined Gloucester. He went on the England tour of Australia in 1975, where he won his first cap, and played in both Tests. He was a good all-round natural rugby player who also played for Gloucestershire in the 1975 County Championship Final.

KITCHING
Alfred Everley

Lock. 1913 (Blackheath, 1 cap).
Debut v Ireland, 8 February 1913.
Born: 6 May 1889; Died: 17 March 1945.
Educated: Oundle School, Cambridge University.
Clubs: Cambridge University (Blues 1910-11), Blackheath, Barbarians.

He served during World War One with the East African Field Force.

KITTERMASTER
Harold James

Fly half. 1925-1926 (Harlequins, 7 caps).
Debut v New Zealand, 3 January 1925.
Born: 7 January 1902; Died: 28 March 1967, Broughton-by-Bigger, Scotland.

Harold Kittermaster

Educated: Rugby School, Oxford University.

Clubs: Oxford University (Blues 1922-4), Harlequins.

Kittermaster scored a try on his international debut against the All-Blacks, when he was one of five Harlequins in the side. His debut try was said to be 'the try of the match'. His only other try was scored in the 1926 England-France match at Twickenham. He was a teacher and later headmaster, mainly at Rugby School and Sherbourne, two rugger 'nurseries'.

KNIGHT
Frederick P.

Flanker. 1909 (Plymouth, 1 cap).
Debut v Australia, 9 January 1909.

Clubs: Devonport, Plymouth, Devon, Plymouth RL.

Employed as a draughtsman at HM Dockyard Plymouth, he was one of ten new caps in the England side which met Australia in 1909, in the last international match to be played at Blackheath.

KNIGHT
Peter Michael

Full-back/Wing. 1972 (Bristol, 3 caps).
Debut v France, 26 February 1972.
Born: 7 October 1947, Bristol

Educated: Bristol Cathedral School, Durham University, St Luke's College (Exeter).

Clubs: Bristol United, Bristol, Gloucestershire.

Knight first played rugby as an 11-year-old in 1959, at Bristol Cathedral School. He made steady progress and played for Bristol Public and Grammar Schools and for Bristol United as a 16-year-old. At Durham University he played as a full-back and at St Luke's College reverted to the wing, playing in that position in most games during his four years there.

Knight played for Bristol during his vacations and his first full season with the club did not come until 1971-2, when he was leading try scorer with 27. He went on the England tour to South Africa in 1972 and was a member of Bristol's 1972-3 RFU Club KO Cup runners-up team. He made a poor international debut at the Stade Colombes in February 1972; a week later he turned out for Gloucestershire in their Championship semi-final against Middlesex, scoring a try. He played in three County Championship Finals for Gloucestershire and was on the winning side once, in 1972.

In 1974 he said that he was not enjoying the game any more and decided to retire. His last appearance for Bristol came in the first match of the 1974-5 season, against Redruth in the opening match of Bristol's South West tour. A PE teacher at Sherborne School and Clifton College.

KNOWLES
Edward

Forward. 1896-1897 (Millom, 2 caps).
Debut v Scotland, 14 March 1896.
Born: 1868; Died: 17 March 1945.

Clubs: Millom, Cumberland, Millom RL.

Knowles was a member of the Cumberland side which finished runners-up in the 1896 County Championship.

KNOWLES
Thomas Caldwell

Fly half. 1931 (Birkenhead Park, 1 cap).
Debut v Scotland, 21 March 1931.
Born: 6 May 1908; Died: 12 December 1985.

Educated: Ampleforth College.

Clubs: Birkenhead Park, Barbarians, Cheshire (52 appearances).

Knowles went on the British Lions tour of Australia and New Zealand in 1930, one of six uncapped players in the squad. He also toured Argentina with the Lions in 1936. He also played for Combined Cheshire/Lancashire against NSW 'Waratahs' and for Combined Cheshire/Lancashire against South Africa. He was a vice-president of Cheshire RFU. During World War Two he served with the RAF and besides rugby he played a lot of golf, a left-handed player who holed-in-one at Dunedin.

KRIGE
J.A.

Centre. 1920 (Guy's Hospital, 1 cap).
Debut v Wales, 17 January 1920.
Born: 6 June 1897; Died: 27 September 1946.

Educated: Victoria College (Stellenbosch, South Africa).

Clubs: Guy's Hospital, Barbarians.

His selection against Wales prompted considerable adverse criticism from the media, who castigated the selectors for choosing a South African. No further South Africans were selected in the next few years and this decision could certainly have cost him further caps. His brother, P.J.Krige, also played for Guy's Hospital.

LABUSCHAGNE
Nicholas Arthur

Hooker. 1953-1955 (Harlequins, Guy's Hospital, 5 caps).
Debut v Wales, 17 January 1953.
Born: 26 May 1931, Durban, South Africa.

Educated: Hilton College (Cape Town, South Africa), Cape Town University.

Clubs: Guy's Hospital, Harlequins, Middlesex, Western Province (South Africa), Natal (South Africa), Barbarians.

Labuschagne was the last of the so-called 'colonial' players to be selected by England. A dental surgeon, he

appeared in the 1952 England trials whilst a student at Guy's. A member of the 1955 Calcutta Cup-winning team. He is president of Natal RFU and a founder member of the South African Barbarians.

LAGDEN
Ronald Owen

Lock. 1911 (Richmond, 1 cap).
Debut v Scotland, 18 March 1911.
Born: 21 November 1889, Maseru, Basultoland; Died: 1 March 1915, St Eloi, France (killed in action).

Educated: Mr Pellat's School (Swanage), Marlborough College, Oxford University.

Clubs: Oxford University (Blues 1909-11), Richmond.

He converted two tries on his international debut to help England secure the Calcutta Cup. He taught at Harrow School and during World War One served as a captain and later as a major, being mentioned in despatches in 1915, shortly before he lost his life. He won Blues at cricket (1909-12), hockey (1910-11) and rackets (1909).

LAIRD
Henri Colin Campbell

Fly Half. 1927-1929 (Harlequins, 10 caps).
Debut v Wales, 15 January 1927.
Born: 3 August 1908.

Educated: Nautical   College (Pangbourne).

Clubs: Harlequins, Barbarians, Middlesex.

Laird celebrated the fact that he was England's youngest-ever player, at 18 years and 134 days old, by helping defeat the Welsh 11-9 on his debut. His first try came in the second match of that year, when he ran over for a try against the Irish; he did the same again in the next match against the Scots, but England lost the Calcutta Cup match on that occasion. A member of the 1928 Grand Slam side, scoring two tries, in total he scored five tries for England in his ten matches. Laird had the ability to kick equally well with either foot.

LAMBERT
Douglas

Wing. 1907-1911 (Harlequins, 7 caps).
Debut v France, 5 January 1907.
Born: 4 October 1883, Cranbrook; Died: 13 October 1915, Loos (killed in action).

Educated: St Edward's School (Oxford), Eastbourne College.

Clubs: Harlequins, Barbarians, Middlesex.

Along with George Lindsay, Lambert shares the distinction of scoring five tries, a world record, on his international debut. In 1911 he equalled the record of scoring most points in an international match, with 22 against France; as a Five Nations Championship record it remained his alone until Jonathan Webb equalled it with 22 points against Ireland in 1992; only F.McCormack (with 24 points for New Zealand v Wales in 1969) has now scored more in an international match. Lambert scored a total of eight tries for England, successfully converted eight tries and kicked two successful penalty-goals. His 46 points from seven games was an England record up to World War One.

Yet despite these impressive statistics, Lambert was selected for his England debut only because the original wing had cried off and, indeed, he was not selected for the next match. He was a superb place-kicker and his tackle was said to be devastating, always downing his man. Yet he began as a soccer player with Eastbourne College (turning to rugby when they switched codes in 1900) and also turned out for the famous Corinthians. Rugby lost one of its best when he was killed in World War One as a lieutenant in the Buffs; sadder still was the fact that his son was born just two months after he lost his life.

LAMPOWSKI
Michael Stanley

Scrum-half 1976 (Headingley, 4 caps).
Debut v Australia, 3 January 1976.
Born: 4 January 1953, Scunthorpe.
Educated: St Bede's School (Scunthorpe).
Clubs: Headingley, Wakefield RL.

Lampowski also represented Notts-Lincs-Derbys RU side. He signed for Wakefield in a Leeds hotel, in a blaze of publicity in 1977. An electrician by trade, a severe knee injury ended his career after making 154 appearances for Wakefield, scoring 135 points. He played in the Challenge Cup Final at Wembley against Widnes on 5 May 1979.

LAPAGE
Walter Nevill, OBE

Wing. 1908 (United Services (Portsmouth), Royal Navy, 4 caps).
Debut v France, 1 January 1908.
Born: 5 February 1883; Died: 17 May 1939.
Educated: Royal Naval College (Greenwich).
Clubs: United Services (Portsmouth), Royal Navy, Surrey.

Lapage scored a try on his international debut and two altogether. A versatile wing-threequarter, he was one of the first products of the Royal Navy RFU which was formed in 1907. He served during World War One in the Navy.

LARTER
Peter John

Lock. 1967-1973 (Northampton, RAF, 24 caps).
Debut v Australia, 7 January 1967.
Born: 7 September 1944.

Peter Larter

Educated: Churston Ferrers Grammar School (Brixham).
Clubs: Weston-super-Mare, Northampton, RAF, Combined Services, Barbarians, Leicestershire.

A first-class place-kicker, he scored one try and one penalty-goal for England and was in Calcutta Cup-winning teams of 1968 and 1969. He went on the British Lions' tour of South Africa in 1968, appearing in the Second Test, and on England tours of Canada in 1967 and South Africa in 1972. An RAF technician, he represented them at rugby and basketball.

LAW
Archibald Fitzgerald (Sir), KBE

Forward. 1877 (Richmond, 1 cap).
Debut v Scotland, 5 March 1877.
Born: 1853; Died: 26 June 1921.
Educated: Wellington College, Oxford University.
Clubs: Oxford University (Blue 1875), Richmond, Middlesex.

A barrister, called to the Bar in 1879, he was knighted in 1908. He also served on the judicial committee.

LAW
Douglas Edward

Prop. 1927 (Birkenhead Park, 1 cap).
Debut v Ireland, 12 February 1927.
Born: 12 October 1902.
Educated: Birkenhead School.
Clubs: Birkenhead Park, Cheshire.

Law toured Argentina with the RFU in 1927 and played for Cheshire in that year's County Championship Final. He attended the banquet which celebrated Birkenhead Park's centenary on 19 November 1971.

LAWRENCE
Henry Arnold (Hon.)

Forward. 1873-1875 (Richmond, 4 caps).
Debut v Scotland, 3 March 1873.
Born: 17 March 1848; Died: 16 April 1902, Minchinhampton.
Educated: Wellington College.
Club: Richmond.

The son of the 1st Baron Lawrence, he was an RFU vice-president from 1875 to 1876 and captained England against Scotland in 1874.

LAWRIE
Percy William

Wing. 1910-1911 (Leicester, 2 caps).
Debut v Scotland, 19 March 1910.
Born: 26 September 1888, Lutterworth; Died: 27 December 1956, Leicester.
Educated: Wyggeston School,
Clubs: Leicester, Barbarians, Leicestershire, Midlands.

He served in both world wars, with the Royal Artillery as a lieutenant in 1914-18 and with the Home Guard in World War Two.

LAWSON
Richard Gordon

Number 8. 1925 (Workington, 1 cap).
Debut v Ireland, 14 February 1925.
Born: 1 September 1901; Died: 3 January 1961, Cockermouth.
Educated: St Bees School.
Clubs: Workington, Cumberland (60 appearances).

Brother of Thomas Lawson, he served in both world wars. In World War One he was shot down over France whilst serving in the Royal Flying Corps and remained a PoW; in World War Two he served as a captain at a coastal defence battery in England.

LAWSON
Thomas Mattocks

Flanker. 1928 (Workington, 2 caps).
Debut v New South Wales, 7 January 1928.
Born: 1900, Cockermouth; Died: 21 October 1951, Workington.
Educated: St Bees School.
Clubs: Workington, Cumberland (50 appearances).

He was the brother of Richard Lawson, who also played for England and Workington. Thomas Lawson was also a welterweight boxing champion.

LEADBETTER
Michael Morris

Lock. 1970 (Broughton Park, 1 cap).
Debut v France, 18 April 1970.
Born: 25 July 1947.
Clubs: Broughton Park, Barbarians, North West Counties, Lancashire (33 appearances), Rochdale Hornets RL.

Leadbetter, who played in Lancashire's 1972-3 County Championship side, joined Rochdale Hornets in 1974. He is employed as a printer.

LEADBETTER
Victor H.

Lock. 1954 (Edinburgh Wanderers, 2 caps).
Debut v Scotland, 20 March 1954.
Born: September 1929, Northamptonshire.
Educated: Kettering Grammar School, Cambridge University.
Clubs: Cambridge University (Blues 1951-2), Edinburgh Wanderers.

He played in the 1954 Calcutta Cup-winning team.

LEAKE
William Robert Martin

Half-back. 1891 (Harlequins, 3 caps).
Debut v Wales, 3 January 1891.
Born: 31 December 1865, Ceylon; Died: 14 November 1942.
Educated: Clifton College, Dulwich College, Cambridge University.
Clubs: Cambridge University (Blues 1885-7), Old Alleynians, Harlequins, Barbarians, Surrey.

A clergyman and schoolteacher, he taught at Dulwich College. He was Harlequins' first international player and an original member of the Barbarians.

LEATHER
George

Forward. 1907 (Liverpool, 1 cap).
Debut v Ireland, 9 February 1907.
Born: 22 February 1881; Died: 2 January 1957, Liverpool.
Educated: Liverpool College.
Clubs: Liverpool, Lancashire (14 appearances).

A chartered accountant, he was the cousin of Wilfred Stoddart. His two sons, W.H. and W.J. Leather, won Blues whilst at Cambridge University.

LEE
Frederick Hugh

Forward. 1876-1877 (Marlborough Nomads, 2 caps).
Debut v Scotland, 6 March 1876.
Born: 4 September 1855; Died: 6 February 1924, Aberdeen.
Educated: Marlborough College, Oxford University.
Clubs: Oxford University (Blues 1874-7), Marlborough Nomads.

Fred Lee scored a try on his international debut against Scotland. He played cricket for Worcestershire and Suffolk and was a solicitor and registrar.

LEE
Henry

Full-back. 1907 (Blackheath, 1 cap).
Debut v France, 5 January 1907.
Born: 8 December 1882, Batley, Yorkshire; Died: 11 January 1933, Leeds.
Educated: Tettenhall College, Cambridge University.
Clubs: Cambridge University (Blue 1904), Guy's Hospital, Blackheath, Barbarians, Kent.

During World War One he served as a captain in the Royal Army Medical Corps. He had a strange death, being found dead in his car in mysterious circumstances.

LE FLEMING
John

Back. 1887 (Blackheath, 1 cap).
Debut v Wales, 8 January 1887.
Born: 23 October 1865; Died: 9 October 1942, Montreux.
Educated: Tonbridge School, Cambridge University.
Clubs: Cambridge University (Blues 1884-6), Blackheath, Barbarians, Kent.

A teacher at his old school, Tonbridge, he was a very enthusiastic sportsman, being AAA's 120-yards hurdles champion in 1887 and gaining his athletics Blue for the hurdles (1886-8) and hammer (1887). He played cricket for Kent from 1890 to 1909 and was a very able ice skater. During World War One he served with the Queen's Own Regiment.

Jason Leonard

LEONARD
Jason

Prop. 1990-1992 (Saracens, Harlequins, 19 caps).
Debut v Argentina, 28 July 1990.
Born: 14 August 1968, Barking, London.
Educated: Warren Comprehensive School (Chadwell Heath).
Clubs: Barking, Saracens, Harlequins, Essex, Eastern Counties, London Counties.

Whilst Jason Leonard was with Barking, the club won the Essex Colts Cup and he was capped by England Colts, having already played for Essex, Eastern Counties and London. He was also a promising junior athlete at the discus, javelin and shot. He helped Saracens win the English Second Division title in 1988-9, played in the Eastern Counties' Under-21 County Championship team and went with England Under-21 to Romania but did not play.

Leonard played for England 'B' in 1989, with two caps against Fiji and France, and was on the bench against the Soviet Union. He joined the Harlequins in 1990 and went on the England tour of Argentina that year, making his full debut in the First Test, and to Australia and Fiji in 1991 before playing in the World Cup Final. He followed up that memorable experience with a regular place in the 1992 Grand Slam team. He is a self-employed builder.

LESLIE-JONES
Frederick Archibald, CBE

Centre. 1895 (Richmond, 2 caps).
Debut v Wales, 5 January 1895.
Born: 9 July 1874; Died: 24 January 1946.
Educated: Hereford Cathedral School, Bromsgrove School, Oxford University.
Clubs: Oxford University (Blues 1894-6), Blackheath, Richmond, Barbarians, Somerset (captain 1900-01).

A clergyman and schoolmaster, he taught at Marlborough College and a number of other establishments. Author of *A View of English History*, during World War One he served in the Indian Defence Force. He scored a try on his international debut.

LEWIS
Alec Ormonde

Flanker. 1952-1954 (Bath, 10 caps).
Debut v South Africa, 5 January 1952.
Born: 20 August 1920, Brighton.
Educated: Royal Masonic School (Bushy).
Clubs: Old Masonians, Wells, Army, Swindon, Bath, Somerset (captain 1951-2), Mendip, Plymouth Albion, Sale.

Alec Lewis played soccer and rugby as a border at the Royal Masonic School, Bushy, before joining the London Rifle Brigade as a Territorial. He represented the Army at fencing at the Royal Tournament, and during World War Two served in the Rifle Brigade and with the 8th Army. In 1942 he took part in the battle before El Alamein, going on to fight through North Africa, Sicily and Italy in some of the toughest battles of the war.

As the company sergeant-major he was accompanying his CO on a reconnaissance mission when he stepped on an anti-personnel mine and was shipped to convalesce in Palestine, where he took up soccer again. Demobbed at the age of 27, he worked for a petrol company in Swindon and joined Swindon Town FC as an amateur, playing in their colts side, during which time he had a county trial at lawn tennis.

Eventually he drifted back to rugby and played for Swindon RFC before work forced a move to Bath. He joined the local club in 1948 and became captain in 1950-51 (the season they won 27 matches), winning his first caps as a blind-side flanker at the age of 31. He was a member of England's International Championship team of 1952-3 and the Calcutta Cup-winning sides of 1952 and 1953. He played for Bath until 1956 before going into semi-retirement, turning out for Mendip and then Plymouth Albion's 2nd XV and also in a handful of matches for Sale's junior team. He became a Sale selector and then fixtures secretary. Returning to Bristol, he was elected to the Somerset committee and was a county selector. He is now an honorary life member and was president in 1972-73.

In 1971 he was appointed an England selector and 'stand-in' chairman and manager of the England tour of South Africa that year, seeing his side victorious against the Springboks at Ellis Park, Johannesburg. He continues to serve his beloved Bath, assisting in small activities such as car parking on match days until being elected club president.

LEYLAND
Roy ('Bus'), OBE

Wing/Centre. 1935 (Waterloo, 3 caps).
Debut v Wales, 19 January 1935.
Born: 6 March 1912, Wigan; Died: 4 January 1984, Pewsey.

Educated: Wigan Grammar School, Liverpool University.

Clubs: Wigan Old Boys, Liverpool University, Waterloo, Leicester, Richmond, Army, Combined Services, Barbarians, Lancashire, Hampshire.

Leyland was in the Education Corps when he represented the Army eight times, against the Royal Navy and the RAF. He was in Lancashire's County Championship side of 1934-5 and toured South Africa with the British Lions in 1938. He was a school teacher before serving in World War Two with the BEF at Dunkirk and then with the Parachute Regiment. He represented the Army on the RFU from 1964. A lieutenant-colonel, he was awarded the OBE in 1957.

Roy Leyland

LINNETT
Mark Stuart

Prop. 1989 (Moseley, 1 cap).
Debut v Fiji, 4 November 1989.
Born: 17 February 1963, Rugby.

Clubs: Rugby, Moseley, Barbarians.

Linnett played for England Colts in 1981, for the Under-23s in 1984 and won one England 'B' cap in 1988. He scored a try on his international debut and went on the England tour of Argentina in 1990. In April 1991 he played in the Rolls-Royce-President's XV (Andy Turner memorial match). A policeman, he is a qualifed PT instructor.

LIVESAY
Robert O'Hara, CMG DSO

Half-back. 1898-1899 (Blackheath, 2 caps).
Debut v Wales, 2 April 1898.
Born: 27 June 1876; Died: 23 March 1946.

Educated: Wellington College, Royal Military College (Sandhurst).

Clubs: Blackheath, Army, Barbarians, Kent.

During the South African war of 1899-1902, he was awarded the Queen's and King's Medals. He also served during World War One, was mentioned in despatches six times and awarded the CMG in 1919 as well as the French Legion d'Honneur and the American DSM, eventually reaching the rank of brigadier-general. He played cricket for Kent.

LLOYD
Robert Hoskins

Centre. 1967-1968 (Harlequins, 5 caps).
Debut v New Zealand, 4 November 1967.
Born: 3 March 1943.

Educated: Cheltenham College.

Clubs: Clifton, Harlequins, Barbarians, Surrey.

Lloyd scored two tries on his international debut and was in the 1968 Calcutta Cup-winning team. He was chosen to tour South Africa with the British Lions in 1968 but was unable to do so because of exams. He is a civil engineer.

LOCKE
Harold Meadows

Centre. 1923-1927 (Birkenhead Park, 12 caps).
Debut v Scotland, 17 March 1923.
Born: 1898; Died: 23 March 1960, Birmingham.

Educated: Birkenhead School.

Clubs: Birkenhead Park, Civil Service, Cheshire.

A strong runner with the ball, Locke was one of the great centre three-quarters of the period. He scored his only try for England against Wales on 19 January 1924 and was in the Calcutta Cup-winning teams of 1923 and 1924.

In November 1923 he played in the Rugby School centenary match for England/Wales v Scotland/Ireland. He helped Cheshire to their first County Championship semi-final in 1922 and skippered them to another in 1927 as well as playing against the New Zealanders in 1924-5.

LOCKWOOD
Richard Evison ('Dicky')

Back. 1887-1894 (Heckmondwike, 14 caps).
Debut v Wales, 8 January 1887.
Born: 11 November 1867, Crigglestone, Wakefield; Died: 10 November 1915, Leeds.
Clubs: Dewsbury, Heckmondwike, Yorkshire (46 appearances, captain 1892-4), Wakefield Trinity RL, Dewsbury RL.

Dicky Lockwood, who captained England, had speed and was a very accurate kicker. His tackling was said to be 'very sure' and he was probably one of the finest all-round three-quarters of his time. As a 17-year-old with Dewsbury, Lockwood was known as 'Little Dicky, The World's Wonder'. He signed for Heckmondwike in 1889, at the same time as England's 19st forward Don Jowett. He first played for Yorkshire when he was 19 and joined Wakefield Trinity in 1895, at the time of the split which led to the Northern Union. He stayed with the club until 1903 and played for Dewsbury again until his retirement. He made 15 appearances for Yorkshire whilst at Dewsbury, his remaining county appearances being made whilst he was with Heckmondwike. He appeared for the North v the South.

LOGIN
Spencer Henry Metcalf, CVO

Full-back. 1875 (Royal Naval College (Dartmouth), 1 cap).
Debut v Ireland, 13 December 1875.
Born: 24 September 1851; Died: 22 January 1909.
Educated: Wellington College, Royal Naval College (Dartmouth).
Club: Royal Naval College (Dartmouth).

Login had a career in the Royal Navy in which he reached the rank of rear admiral. He was commander of a number of battleships before World War One and was made a Commander of the Royal Victorian Order in 1905. He was one of the founder members of the Royal Navy RFU in 1906.

LOHDEN
Frederick Charles, OBE JP

Forward. 1893 (Blackheath, 1 cap).
Debut v Wales, 7 January 1893.
Born: 13 June 1871; Died: 13 April 1954, Cheam.
Educated: Durham School.

Clubs: Hartlepool Rovers, Blackheath, Barbarians, Durham Counties, Surrey.

Lohden, who scored a try on his international debut against Wales in Cardiff, was awarded the OBE 1919. A very active gentleman, he shared in the London badminton doubles championship in 1921, played lawn tennis for Surrey and was chairman of the LTA in 1933 and a vice-president in 1934, representing Great Britain on the ILTF in the latter year. He was mayor of Sutton and Cheam, and a JP there.

LONGLAND
Raymond John

Prop. 1932-1938 (Northampton, 19 caps).
Debut v Scotland, 19 May 1932.
Born: 29 December 1908; Died: 21 September 1975.

Raymond Longland

Clubs: Olney, Buckingham, Bedford, RAF, Northampton, Combined Services, East Midlands, Barbarians.

Longland, who was probably one of England's greatest prop forwards, was in the Calcutta Cup teams of 1932, 1933, 1936 and 1937 and the Triple Crown sides of 1934 and 1937. He served in the RAF during World War Two.

LOWE
Cyril Nelson, MC DFC

Wing. 1913-1923 (Cambridge University, Blackheath, 25 caps).
Debut v South Africa, 4 January 1913.
Born: 7 October 1891, Holbeach, Lincolnshire; Died: 6 February 1983, Surrey.
Educated: Dulwich College, Cambridge University.
Clubs: Cambridge University (Blues 1911-13), Old Alleynians, Richmond, Blackheath, West of Scotland, Surrey.

A little giant of a man — he stood just 5ft 6in tall and weighed 8st 7lb — Cyril Lowe was strong and beautifully poised. He scored eight tries in the Championship-winning season of 1913-14 which beat the record previously held by V.M.H.Coates, who scored six. In all Lowe played in 25 consecutive matches for England and scored 17 tries and one drop-goal. He is Blackheath's most capped player and was once England's most capped player. He played in Calcutta Cup teams of 1913, 1914, 1920, 1921 and 1922 and Triple Crown sides of 1913, 1914 and 1921.

The son of a Lincolnshire cleric, he served during World War One in the 1st Reserve Horse Transport, RASC, before volunteering for the Royal Flying Corps. A report claimed that he shot down 31 enemy aircraft, but official records credit him with nine. He was awarded the MC and DFC for gallantry. He played soccer at Dulwich until 16 and was an excellent all-round sportsman at cricket, athletics, swimming and boxing. Lowe represented the RAF on RFU and was a selector from 1934 to 1938.

LOWRIE
Frederick William.

Forward. 1889-1890 (Wakefield Trinity, 2 caps).
Debut v Maoris, 16 February 1889.
Born: 1 March 1868, Wakefield; Died: 9 August 1902, Leeds.
Educated: Wakefield Collegiate School.
Clubs: Wakefield Trinity, Batley, Batley RL, Yorkshire (27 appearances).

He made his debut for Yorkshire against Lancashire and made 15 appearances for the county whilst with Wakefield, the remainder whilst with Batley RFC. A licensee by trade, he played in the North against the South international trial match of 1888, in two trials in 1889, and two in 1890.

LOWRY
Wilfrid Malbon

Wing. 1920 (Birkenhead Park, 1 cap).
Debut v France, 31 January 1920.
Born: 14 July 1900; Died: 4 July 1974, Heswall.
Educated: Leys School.
Clubs: Old Leysians, Birkenhead Park, Waterloo, Cheshire.

Lowry played in the 1921-2 Cheshire side which reached the County Championship semi-finals for the first time in their history. A winger with speed enough to take advantage of any opening, no matter how small, in the history of the Cheshire RFU (published in 1976) it stated that 'he had the extraordinary experience of being selected against Wales and photographed with the team, but was withdrawn just before the kick-off in favour of H.L.Day, whose style of play was thought to be more suited to the heavy conditions'.

He served during World War Two with the Royal Artillery and reached the rank of lieutenant. He attended the banquet which celebrated the centenary of Birkenhead Park RFC on 19 November 1971.

LOZOWSKI
Robert Andrew Peter

Centre. 1984 (Wasps, 1 cap).
Debut v Australia, 3 November 1984.
Born: 18 November 1960, London.
Educated: Gunnersbury School.
Clubs: Old Gaytonians, Wasps, Barbarians.

Son of a Polish father and Italian mother, Lozowski played for England Under-23s in 1984 and the England 'B'

team in 1989 and appeared in the London side which beat the Australians 21-10 in 1988. He has suffered a broken leg on no less than three occasions. He is employed as a sales manager. His brother-in-law, Steve Moriarty, played for Harlequins and Surrey.

LUDDINGTON
William George Ernest

Prop/Lock. 1923-1926 (Devonport Services, 13 caps).
Debut v Wales, 20 January 1923.
Born: 8 February 1894; Died: 10 January 1941 (killed in action).
Clubs: Devonport Services, Royal Navy, Devon.

Luddington, who was in the Calcutta Cup and Triple Crown teams of 1923 and 1924, made two scores for England

William Luddington

— a conversion against Scotland (17 March 1923) and a drop-goal against Scotland (21 March 1925). He served during World War Two as a Naval master-at-arms and was killed in the Mediterranean.

LUSCOMBE
Francis

Forward. 1872-1876 (Gipsies, 6 caps).
Debut v Scotland, 5 February 1872.
Born: 1846, Died: 17 July 1926.
Educated: Tonbridge School.
Club: Gipsies.

Luscombe, who captained England against Ireland on 13 December 1875 and against Scotland on 6 March 1876, was one of the main people involved in the acceptance of Scotland's challenge to play the first international in 1871. A racehorse owner and an original member of the RFU in 1871, he was a vice-president from 1877 to 1878. Brother of Sir John Luscombe.

LUSCOMBE
John Henry, (Sir), JP

Forward. 1871 (Gipsies, 1 cap).
Debut v Scotland, 27 March 1871.
Born: 1848, Cuckfield; Died: 3 April 1927, Worth Sussex.
Educated: Tonbridge School.
Club: Gipsies.

Brother of Francis Luscombe, he was the longest lived of England's first international team which met Scotland in 1871. He was chairman of Lloyds Bank, London, and chairman of Lloyds Register of Shipping from 1921. He was a JP in Sussex, HM Lieutenant for the City of London and High Sheriff in 1913. He was knighted in 1902.

LUXMOORE
Arthur Fairfax Charles Coryndon, (Sir), KC PC KT JP

Forward. 1900-1901 (Richmond, 2 caps).
Debut v Scotland, 10 March 1900.
Born: 27 February 1876; Died: 25 September 1944, Hammersmith, London.
Educated: King's School (Canterbury) Cambridge University.
Clubs: Cambridge University (Blues 1896-7), Richmond, Kent, Barbarians.

A Lord Justice, he was called to Bar in 1899. Liberal candidate for the Isle of Thanet in the 1924 General Election, he was appointed a King's Council in 1919 and a Privy Councillor in 1938. He was knighted in 1929. A member of the 1900 Calcutta Cup-winning team.

LUYA
Humphrey Fleetwood

Lock. 1948-1949 (Waterloo, Headingley, 5 caps).
Debut v Wales, 17 January 1948.
Born: 3 February 1918.
Educated: Merchant Taylor's School (Crosby).
Clubs: Waterloo, Carlisle, Headingley, Barbarians, Lancashire.

Luya was a prisoner-of-war, captured in Crete during World War Two. In the international matches of 1948 he was one of only four players to be ever-present.

LYON
Arthur

Back. 1871 (Liverpool, 1 cap).
Debut v Scotland, 27 March 1871.
Born: 4 August 1852; Died: 4 December 1905, New Zealand.
Educated: Rugby School.
Clubs: Liverpool, Lancashire.

Lyon played in the first international between Scotland and England in 1871, one of the players who learned the game at Rugby School.

LYON
George Hamilton d'Oyly, KCB CB

Full-back. 1908-1909 (United Services (Portsmouth), Royal Navy, 2 caps).
Debut v Scotland, 21 March 1908.
Born: 3 October 1883, Cupra, India; Died: 20 August 1947, Sussex.
Educated: King's School (Bruton).
Clubs: United Services (Portsmouth), Royal Navy, Barbarians, Surrey (23 appearances), Hampshire.

A member of the 1908 Calcutta Cup team, he captained England against Australia in January 1909, a team that contained ten new caps. Affectionately known as 'Torpedo', he was a hard-tackling player who would almost certainly have won more caps but for a demanding naval career. A founder

member of the Royal Navy RFU in 1906, he also played cricket for the Navy and for Hampshire. He reached the rank of admiral and was awarded the CB in 1936 and the KCB in 1940. During World War One he served on HMS Monarch at the Battle of Jutland.

McCANLIS
Maurice Alfred

Centre. 1931 (Gloucester, 2 caps).
Debut v Wales, 17 January 1931.
Born: 17 June 1906, Quetta, India.
Educated: Cranleigh School, Oxford University.
Clubs: Oxford University (Blues 1926-7), Old Cranleighans, Gloucester, Blackheath, Northampton, Barbarians, Gloucestershire, Kent.

McCanlis, a member of the Gloucestershire sides that won the County Championship 1930-1932, also gained cricket Blues (1926-8) and played county cricket for Surrey and Gloucestershire. He taught at Cheltenham College and was secretary of the North Cotswold Hunt in 1969.

McFADYEAN
Colin William

Centre. 1966-1968 (Moseley, 11 caps).

Colin McFadyean

Debut v Ireland, 12 February 1966.
Born: 11 March 1943.

Educated: Loughborough Colleges.

Clubs: Loughborough Colleges, UAU, Bristol, Moseley, Somerset (22 appearances, captain 1965-9).

A most popular player, in his last season as an international McFaydean captained England in two consecutive drawn matches at Twickenham. He was fast and ingenious in his attacking play and a reliable member of the team under pressure in defence. He had an eventful Lions tour of Australia and New Zealand in 1966, scoring a try in the last Test against New Zealand, in total scoring eight tries and a conversion, and breaking his nose against Canterbury. He was in the Moseley side which finished runners-up in the first RFU KO Cup Final. In 1967 he was employed as a PE lecturer at Alsagar Training College.

MacILWAINE
Alfred Herbert, MC DSO

Prop/Lock. 1912-1920 (United Services (Portsmouth), Hull and East Riding, 5 caps).
Debut v Wales, 20 January 1912.
Born: 27 March 1889; Died: 1983, South Africa.

Educated: Clifton College.

Clubs: Hull and East Riding, Army, United Services (Portsmouth), Harlequins, Yorkshire (37 appearances, captain 1913-14).

MacIlwaine began playing rugby whilst with the 2nd Northumbrian Brigade, RFA (TA) in 1912, as a 23-year-old subaltern. He was gazetted into the RFA and whilst serving in County Tipperary turned out for Monkstown RFC and later represented the Combined Services against South Africa. He played four times for the Army, against the Royal Navy three times and the RAF, captaining the side twice. He was Yorkshire's last captain before the outbreak of World War One, during which he was awarded the DSO and the Croix de Guerre. During World War Two he was a major in command of a South Rhodesia Light Battalion. In 1925 he retired from active rugby and presented a silver cup to the Royal Artillery RFC for inter-brigade competiton. It became known as the MacIlwaine Cup. After leaving the army he farmed in the Inyanga Mountains of Rhodesia. There were eight years between England caps. In April 1922 he played for Harlequins Past against Harlequins Present in aid of the King Edward VII Hospital Fund.

MACKIE
Osbert Gadesden

Centre. 1897-1898 (Wakefield Trinity, Cambridge University, 2 caps).
Debut v Scotland, 13 March 1897.

Born: 23 August 1869, Wakefield; Died: 25 January 1927, Redcar, Yorkshire.

Educated: Haileybury and Imperial Service College, Cambridge University.

Clubs: Cambridge University (Blues 1895-7), Wakefield Trinity, Barbarians, Yorkshire.

He played in the South against North international trial match in 1897-8. He went on the British Lions tour of South Africa in 1896 and made his Yorkshire debut against Cumberland in 1894. A clergyman, he was ordained in 1899.

MacKINLAY
James Egan Harrison

Forward. 1872-1875 (St George's Hospital, 3 caps).
Debut v Scotland, 5 February 1872.
Born: 17 December 1850, Guildford; Died: 1 July 1917.

Educated: Rugby School.

Club: St George's Hospital.

James MacKinlay was a surgeon.

MacLAREN
William

Back. 1871 (Manchester, 1 cap).
Debut v Scotland, 27 March 1871.

Club: Manchester RFC.

Brother of James MacLaren, RFU president from 1882 to 1884, and uncle of A.C.MacLaren, the Lancashire and England cricketer, he played in the first international match between Scotland and England.

MacLENNAN
Roderick Ross Forrest

Prop. 1925 (Old Merchant Taylor's, 3 caps).
Debut v Ireland, 14 February 1925.
Born: 23 December 1903, Glasgow.

Educated: Merchant Taylor's School.

Clubs: Old Merchant Taylor's, Headingley, London Scottish, Middlesex.

During World War Two he served in Army intelligence. He was public schools middleweight boxing champion in 1912.

McLEOD
Norman Frederick

Forward. 1879 (Royal Indian Engineering College, 2 caps).
Debut v Scotland, 10 March 1879.
Born: 30 June 1856, Madras, India; Died: 20 April 1921, Kensington, London.

Educated: Clifton College, Royal Indian Engineering College.

Club: Royal Indian Engineering College.

He was probably employed as a civil engineer on the Indian railways.

MADGE
Richard John Palmer

Scrum-half. 1948 (Exeter, 4 caps).
Debut v Australia, 3 January 1948.
Born: 19 December 1914.

Educated: Exeter School.

Clubs: Exeter, Devon.

Madge served in the Middle East and in Italy with the Royal Artillery. He was a member of the Exeter side which lost only two matches in 1945-6.

MALIR
Frank William Stewart

Centre. 1930 (Otley, 3 caps).
Debut v Wales, 18 January 1930.
Born: 4 August 1905, India; Died: 22 January 1974, York.

Educated: Heriot's School, Stanley House (Bridge of Allan), Woodhouse Grove School (Apperley Bridge).

Clubs: Otley, Yorkshire (45 appearances, captain 1930-31).

Malir won his first cap along with fellow Otley player, A.H.Bateson. They were the first two international players from that club.

MANGLES
Roland Henry, DSO CMG CB

Forward. 1897 (Richmond, 2 caps).
Debut v Wales, 9 January 1897.
Born: 9 February 1874; Died: 29 September 1948.

Educated: Marlborough College.

Clubs: Richmond, Army, Barbarians, Surrey.

Mangles served in the South African War and was awarded his DSO in 1902. During World War One he was mentioned in despatches on eight occasions. He attained the rank of brigadier-general and was awarded the CMG in 1919 and the (CB) in 1924. He was the son of Ross L.Mangles, one of only four civilians to have been awarded the VC.

MANLEY
Donald Charles ('Dick')

Flanker. 1963 (Exeter, 4 caps).
Debut v Wales, 19 January 1963.
Born: 17 February 1932, Devon.

Educated: Hele's School (Exeter).

Clubs: Exeter, Barbarians, Devon (56 appearances).

Manley played for Devon Colts before joining Exeter and spent 13 seasons with that club, making over 450 appearances and captaining the side. His Devon appearances spanned the period 1954 to 1967 (although he did not play in 1964 and 1965) and he played 12 times for the Barbarians. He appeared in seven England trials spread over a period of six years and was a member of the 1963 International Championship-winning side. From his debut in first-class rugby he appeared against every major touring

Dick Manley

the following season. He played for England Under-19s as a schoolboy and won an Under-23 cap in the 40-3 win over Tonga in October 1974. His full England debut came in the First Test of the 1975 tour of Australia. Mantell, who made 120 appearances for Nottingham before retiring in 1987, also skippered the Midlands club and joined their coaching staff in October 1991. An accountant, his father ran a stationery business in Reigate. He plays club cricket.

MARKENDALE
Ellis T.

Forward. 1880 (Manchester Rangers, 1 cap).
Debut v Ireland 30, January 1880.
Born: November 1856.
Educated: Uppingham School.
Clubs: Manchester Rangers, Lancashire.

Markendale scored a try on his only international appearance.

MARQUES
Reginald William David

Lock. 1956-1961 (Cambridge University, Harlequins, 23 caps).
Born: 9 December 1932, Hertford.
Debut v Wales, 21 January 1956.

Educated: Yandle Court School, Tonbridge School, Cambridge University.

Reginald Marques

side that visited England up to January 1963. A cabinet maker in Exeter, he was later on the Exeter RFC committee.

MANN
William Edgar, DSO

Forward. 1911 (United Services (Portsmouth), Army, 4 caps).
Debut v Wales, 21 January 1911.
Born: 19 January 1885; Died: 14 February 1969.
Educated: Marlborough College, Royal Military Academy (Woolwich).
Clubs: United Services (Portsmouth), Army, Surrey.

Mann scored only once for England, a try in the 37-0 win over France in January 1911 at Twickenham. He played for the Army against the Royal Navy in 1911 and served in the Royal

Field Artillery during World War One, being awarded the DSO in 1917. The son of Sir Edward Mann, he also played cricket for Worcestershire.

MANTELL
Neil Dennington

Lock. 1975 (Rosslyn Park, 2 caps).
Debut v Australia, 24 May 1975.
Born: 13 October 1953, Reigate.
Educated: Reigate Grammar School.
Clubs: Rosslyn Park, Nottingham, Surrey.

Mantell played in his school XV for four years, captaining them in his final year, and during one period the school had a run of 56 games undefeated. He joined Rosslyn Park in March 1973, straight from school, and made his 1st XV debut against United Services (Portsmouth)

Clubs: Cambridge University (Blues 1954-7), Army, Combined Services, Harlequins, Barbarians, Hertfordshire, Surrey.

Marques was an excellent line-out jumper and at 6ft 5in was reputed to be the tallest player in British representative rugby. He played at number 8 on the Barbarians tour of South Africa in 1957-8 and was on the Lions tour of Australia and New Zealand in 1959, making 18 appearances including two Tests. He also toured Canada with the Barbarians in 1956-7. With fellow Harlequin and Oxford Blue John Currie, he played in 22 consecutive international matches for England, a record before they went their separate ways in 1961. He also toured Canada and South Africa with the Barbarians and played in the International XV which met Wales in April 1957, in a match arranged to raise funds so that the Empire Games could be staged in Cardiff the following year.

At university he studied for a degree in engineering and did his National Service in the Royal Engineers, playing three times for the Army in 1954, against the Royal Navy, RAF and French Army. His father was Australian and his mother Welsh, from Llanelli. He played cricket for Hertfordshire and was a crewman on the yacht 'Sovereign' in the 1966 America's Cup Challenge. He is a civil engineer.

MARQUIS
John Campbell

Scrum half. 1900 (Birkenhead Park, 2 caps).
Debut v Ireland, 3 February 1900.
Born: 1876; Died: 28 January 1928, Birkenhead.
Clubs: Birkenhead Park, Barbarians.

Marquis was employed in the shipping industry.

MARRIOTT
Charles John Bruce

Forward. 1884-1887 (Blackheath, 7 caps).
Debut v Wales, 5 January 1884.
Born: 15 July 1861, Rensham, Suffolk; Died: 25 December 1936, Ipswich.
Educated: Blackheath Proprietory School, Tonbridge School, Cambridge University.
Clubs: Cambridge University (Blues 1881-3), Gipsies, Blackheath, Middlesex.

Charles Marriott represented Cambridge University on the RFU from 1897 to 1907, becoming RFU secretary in 1904, and in response to a special invitation, he implemented the first serious coaching scheme at Cambridge. His efforts, particularly in relation to the forwards, undoubtedly hastened the end of Oxford's domination of the Varsity match and the 1886 game saw Cambridge gain the first of four successive victories over the Dark Blues, due

solely to Marriott's influence. He was also secretary of the Queen's club. During World War One he served as a captain in the RASC. He edited *The Rugby Game and How To Play It* and his brother 'Trojan' captained Guy's to victory in the 1885 Hospitals Cup Final.

MARRIOTT
Ernest Edward

Forward. 1875 (Manchester, 1 cap).
Debut v Ireland, 13 December 1875.
Born: 15 January 1857; Died: 1917.
Educated: Rugby School.
Clubs: Manchester, Lancashire.

The son of Henry Marriott, he was a founder of Manchester RFC in 1860, and later was to become the club's first president. He did not have a very distinguished playing career but did much to influence the birth of the Manchester club.

MARRIOTT
Victor Robert

Flanker. 1963-1964 (Harlequins, 4 caps).
Debut v New Zealand, 25 May 1963.
Born: 29 January 1938.
Educated: Balham Grammar School.
Clubs: Harlequins, Army, Combined Services, London Counties, Surrey.

Marriott served with the Army Education Corps and played for the Army against the Royal Navy in 1961 and 1962 and against the RAF in 1962 He went on England's tour of Australia and New Zealand in 1962-3, playing in two Tests against the All Blacks.

MARSDEN
George Herbert

Fly-half 1900 (Morley, 3 caps).
Debut v Wales, 6 January 1900.
Born: 16 October 1880, Morley; Died: 7 July 1948, Lytham St Annes, Lancashire.
Clubs: Morley, Yorkshire (11 appearances), Bradford RL.

It is stated that he was one of the founding members of the Fylde club in 1919. He joined Bradford RL in 1900 and made 173 appearances for them before retiring in 1906. He played for Yorkshire at both League and Union codes, being selected for the RL side in 1904. He also played for England v Other Nationalities at Bradford Park Avenue in January 1905.

MARSH
Henry, CIE

Forward. 1873 (Royal Indian Engineering College, 1 cap).
Debut v Scotland, 3 March 1873.
Born: 8 September 1850; Died: 25 April 1939.
Educated: Stacpoole's School (Kingstown), Royal Indian Engineering College.
Club: Royal Indian Engineering College.

He worked as a civil engineer in India and was awarded the CIE in 1900.

MARSH
James H.

Wing. 1892 (Swinton, 1 cap).
Debut v Ireland, 6 February 1892.
Died: 1 August 1928.
Educated: Edinburgh Institute, Edinburgh University.
Clubs: Edinburgh Institute FP, Edinburgh University, Swinton, Lancashire (12 appearances).

James Marsh is the only player to be capped by both England and Scotland. He played for the Scots twice in 1889, whilst at Edinburgh University.

MARSHALL
Howard, OBE

Half-back. 1893 (Blackheath, 1 cap).
Debut v Wales, 7 January 1893.
Born: 20 December 1870, Sunderland; Died: 9 October 1929, Westminster.
Educated: Eltham School, Cambridge University.
Clubs: Cambridge University (no Blue), Barnard Castle, Sunderland, St Bartholomew's Hospital, Blackheath, London, Kent, Barbarians.

Howard Marshall went on the British Lions' tour of South Africa in 1891, before being capped by England, and scored eight tries in one game on the tour. He scored three tries in his only international appearance for England. A surgeon at Cirencester Hospital, he was awarded the OBE in 1920.

MARSHALL
Murray Wyatt

Forward. 1873-1878 (Blackheath, 10 caps).
Debut v Scotland, 3 March 1873.
Born: 1853; Died: 28 July 1930.
Educated: Wellington College.
Clubs: Blackheath, Surrey.

Murray Marshall was once England's record cap holder and also captained the side. He was a member of the Surrey CCC committee.

MARSHALL
Robert Mackenzie, DSC

Lock. 1938-1939 (Oxford University, 5 caps).
Debut v Ireland, 12 February 1938.
Born: 18 May 1919; Died: 12 May 1945 (killed in action).
Educated: Giggleswick School, Oxford University.
Clubs: Oxford University (Blues 1936-8), Scarborough, Harlequins, Barbarians.

Marshall, who was once hailed as the 'new Wavell Wakefield', scored a try on his international debut and was said to be one of the best forwards ever to wear a Harlequin shirt. He would certainly have gained many more caps had the war not claimed his life. He served as a lieutenant in the RNVR and won a bar to his DSC.

MARTIN
Christopher Ronald
Full-back. 1985 (Bath, 4 caps).
Debut v France, 2 February 1985.
Born: 27 June 1961.
Clubs: Penryn, Bath, Cornwall (20 appearances).
Martin was in the 1985 Calcutta Cup side and the following year helped Bath to equal Leicester's record of three successive JPS Cup Final victories.

MARTIN
Nicholas O.
Lock. 1972 (Harlequins, 1 cap).
Debut v France, 26 February 1972.
Born: 1946.
Educated: Cambridge University.
Clubs: Cambridge University (Blues 1965-7), Harlequins, Bedford, Barbarians
He made his international debut when he replaced Tony Neary. The following year he went on the England tour to Argentina. His Barbarians debut came at Cardiff in April 1974.

MARTINDALE
Samuel Airey
Lock. 1929 (Kendal, 1 cap).
Debut v France, 1 April 1929.
Born: 5 May 1905.
Clubs: Kendal, Cumberland and Westmorland.
He was on the British Lions' tour of Australia and New Zealand in 1930 and was also a county water polo player.

MASSEY
Edward John
Scrum half. 1925 (Leicester, 3 caps).
Debut v Wales, 17 January 1925.
Born: 2 July 1900; Died: 30 April 1940, Woking.
Educated: Ampleforth College.
Clubs: Liverpool, Leicester, Leicestershire, Lancashire (17 appearances), Barbarians.
Massey, who broke his collarbone in the match against Scotland in 1925, was a member of the Leicestershire side which won the County Championship that year. A farmer, he served during World War Two with the RASC.

MATHIAS
John Lloyd
Lock. 1905 (Bristol, 4 caps).
Debut v Wales, 14 January 1905.
Born: 1878; Died: 21 November 1940.
Clubs: Bristol, Gloucestershire.
Mathias made 187 appearances for Bath and played for them against the 1905 New Zealanders.

MATTERS
John Charles
Wing. 1899 (Royal Naval Engineering College (Keyham), 1 cap).
Debut v Scotland, 11 March 1899.
Born: 1879; Died: 24 April 1949, Surrey.
Clubs: Royal Naval Engineering College (Keyham), Devon, Barbarians.
A member of the Devon side which in 1899 won the County Championship for the first time, his international career was cut short through injury. He served in the Royal Navy during World War One and reached the rank of rear admiral.

MATTHEWS
John Robert Clive
Lock. 1949-1952 (Harlequins, 10 caps).
Debut v France, 26 February 1949.
Born: 14 June 1922, Hastings.
Educated: Sutton Valence School.
Clubs: Guy's Hospital, Royal Navy, Combined Services, Harlequins, London Counties, Middlesex (captain 1950-53), Barbarians.
He played in the 1949 and 1952 Calcutta Cup-winning sides and captained London Counties against the South Africans in 1952. A dental surgeon, he served during World War Two in the RNVR as a surgeon-lieutenant and was stationed at Murmansk. He was attached to the naval mission to Moscow from 1944 to 1945.

MAUD
Philip, CMG CBE
Forward. 1893 (Blackheath, 2 caps).
Debut v Wales, 7 January 1893.
Born: 8 August 1870; Died: 28 February 1947.
Educated: Leamington College, Royal Military College (Woolwich).
Clubs: Royal Engineers, Blackheath, Kent, Barbarians.
He reached the rank of brigadier-general in the Royal Engineers, serving on the North-West Frontier in 1889. Awarded CMG 1903, he served during World War One and was awarded the CBE in 1919. He holds the record of 24 appearances for Barbarians, sharing this distinction with M.P.Atkinson and F.Stout.

MAXWELL
Andrew William
Centre. 1975-1978 (New Brighton, Headingley, 8 caps).
Debut v Australia, 24 May 1975.
Born: 3 March 1951, West Kirby.
Educated: Caldy Grange Grammar School.
Clubs: New Brighton, Headingley, Yorkshire.
Maxwell, who captained New Brighton in their centenary season in 1974-5, was

on the England tour of Australia in 1975. He was a solid type of player who was not afraid to attack.

MAXWELL-HYSLOP
John Edgar
Flanker. 1922 (Oxford University, 3 caps).
Debut v Ireland, 11 February 1922.
Born: 31 March 1899; Died: 10 December 1990.
Educated: Wellington College, Oxford University.
Clubs: Oxford University (Blues 1920-21, later as captain) Richmond, Sussex.
At the time of his death in 1990, aged 91, he was England's oldest surviving international player. He scored a try on his international debut. During World War One he served as a second lieutenant in the Royal Field Artillery and in World War Two he was an RAF fitter before being transferred to the intelligence section. A schoolmaster, he taught at Rottingdean School from 1923 to 1961.

MAYNARD
Alfred Frederick
Hooker. 1914 (Cambridge University, 3 caps).
Debut v Wales, 17 January 1914.
Born: 23 March 1894, Kent; Died: 13 November 1916, Beaumont Hamel (killed in action).
Educated: Seaford School, Durham School, Cambridge University.
Clubs: Cambridge University (Blues 1912-13), Harlequins, Durham City, Durham County.
He served World War One in the Royal Naval Division and took part in the assault on Gallipoli in 1915 but was killed a year later, fighting in France. A burly second-row forward he was part of England's Triple Crown, Championship, Grand Slam and Calcutta Cup side of 1914 and would probably have won more caps had war not intervened.

MEIKLE
Graham William Churchill
Wing. 1934 (Waterloo, 3 caps).
Debut v Wales, 20 January 1934.
Born: 14 October 1911, Waterloo.
Educated: St Bees College, Cambridge University.
Clubs: Cambridge University (no Blue), Waterloo, Lancashire (15 appearances), Leicester, Barbarians.
Brother of Stephen Meikle, he taught at King Edward's School in Birmingham and later at Wellington College. He scored two tries on his England debut, equalling the feat of his brother in 1929.

MEIKLE
Stephen Spencer Churchill
Fly-half. 1929 (Waterloo, 1 cap).
Debut v Scotland, 16 March 1929.

Born: 6 July 1904; Died: 4 June 1960, Liverpool.

Educated: St Bees School.

Clubs: Waterloo, Lancashire (57 appearances), Barbarians.

Brother of Graham, he scored a try on his international debut, a feat which was later repeated by his brother in 1934. He represented Lancashire on the RFU from 1955 to 1960 and was a leading referee in the county. He played for Combined Cheshire/Lancashire against NSW 'Waratahs' in 1927-8.

MELLISH
Frank Whitmore, MC JP

Flanker. 1920-1921 (Blackheath, 6 caps).
Debut v Wales, 17 January 1920.
Born: 26 April 1897, Rondesbosch, South Africa; Died: 21 August 1965, England.

Educated: Wynberg Boys' High School, Rondesbosch Boys' High School.

Clubs: Cape Town Highlanders, Villagers, Blackheath, Western Province, Barbarians.

After winning his England caps, Mellish returned to South Africa and played in two Tests for the Springboks in New Zealand in 1921 and in all four Tests against the British Lions in 1924. He represented South Africa on the RFU from 1945 to 1946 and was selector and manager of the South African tour to the British Isles and France in 1951. During World War One he served in German South-West Africa and was later with the South African Heavy Artillery, reaching the rank of colonel and being awarded the MC in 1916. In World War Two he was with the South African Armoured Division.

MELVILLE
Nigel David

Scrum-half. 1984-1988 (Wasps, 1984-1988, 13 caps).
Debut v Australia, 3 November 1984.
Born: 6 January 1961, Leeds.

Educated: Aireborough Grammar School, North-East London Polytechnic.

Clubs: Otley, Wakefield, Yorkshire (30 appearances, captain 1985-6), Wasps, Barbarians.

Nigel Melville had the unusual distinction of captaining England on his debut. Indeed, he has skippered almost every team for which he has played and at 20 led the England 'B' side in France in 1981. He also skippered the Under-23s tour to Romania in 1982 and went on England tours to Argentina in 1981, to the USA and Canada in 1982 and on the British Lions' tour of New Zealand in 1983. He played in only one match (in which he scored two tries) on that trip before suffering a spinal injury.

Whilst at Aireborough Grammar

Nigel Melville

School he played for England Under-19s against France at Otley on 17 April 1979. He was also first-choice scrum-half in the England Under-19 side which went through Australia unbeaten and played for Northern Schools against Australian Schools. He has also played for Yorkshire Under-16s, North-East Counties Under-16s, the North of England, Yorkshire Under-19s, England Schools and England Colts. In 1984 he was injured playing for Major Stanley's XV against Oxford University.

Melville was the mastermind behind the 'Yorkshire Tries for Charity' World Cup relay which took place on 29 August 1991, a day of fun and frolic organised to promote RU in Yorkshire and which benefited charity. He is the son of Harry, a well-known Otley winger.

MERRIAM
Lawrence Pierce Brooke (Sir), MC JP

Lock. 1920 (Blackheath, 2 caps).
Debut v Wales, 17 January 1920.

Born: 28 January 1894; Died: 27 July 1966, London.

Educated: St Paul's School, Oxford University.

Clubs: Oxford University (Blue 1913), Blackheath, Barbarians.

At Oxford, Merriam also won Blues for swimming and water polo. He served during World War One with the Rifle Brigade, was twice wounded and mentioned in despatches. He was awarded the MC in 1916 and knighted in 1949. He was a JP in Essex.

MICHELL
Arthur Tompson

Half-back. 1875-1876 (Oxford University, 3 caps).
Debut v Ireland, 15 February 1875.
Born: 16 September 1853; Died: 13 August 1923.

Educated: Rugby School, Oxford University.

Clubs: Oxford University (Blues 1871-4), Ravenscourt Park.

Michell scored a try on his international

debut and his England cap is now in the RFU Museum. At Rugby School he edited three volumes of the register and at Oxford University won the sculls in 1884. A clergyman, ordained in 1879, he was the son of the Revd Richard Michell, who was principal of Hertford College, Oxford.

MIDDLETON
Bernard Boswell
Forward. 1882-1883 (Birkenhead Park, 2 caps).
Debut v Ireland, 6 February 1882.
Born: 25 December 1858; Died: 22 October 1947.
Educated: Marlborough College.
Clubs: Marlborough Nomads, Birkenhead Park, Cheshire.

MIDDLETON
John Alan, OBE
Full-back. 1922 (Richmond, 1 cap).
Debut v Scotland, 18 March 1922.
Born: 11 January 1894.
Educated: St Andrew's College (Dublin).
Clubs: Wanderers, Richmond, Army.
Middleton, who was in the 1922 Calcutta Cup side, played for the Army six times, against the Royal Navy, the RAF and the French Army. He served in World War One with the RASC and was posted to Egypt in 1924. In 1941 he was captured in Italy but escaped from a PoW camp in 1943. When he retired after 35 years' military service, he had reached the rank of colonel. Middleton, who also had an Irish qualification, played in the final England trial match at Twickenham in 1922. He was instrumental in the formation of the Aldershot Services side.

MILES
John Henry
Wing. 1903 (Leicester, 1 cap).
Debut v Wales, 10 January 1903.
Born: 1880, Grimsby; Died: 23 January 1953.
Educated: Medway Street School (Leicester).
Clubs: Medway Athletic, Stoneygate, Leicester, Northampton, Midlands.
A farmer, he was the first player to be capped direct from Leicester RFC. He was also a capable referee and took charge of the Ireland-France and France-Wales matches in 1913, and the Wales-French match the following year. He was a member of the Leicester side which won the Midlands Counties Cup in 1903, 1904 and 1905.

MILLETT
Harry
Full-back. 1920 (Richmond, 1 cap).
Debut v France, 31 January 1920.
Born: 2 April 1892, London; Died: 26 May 1974.

Educated: University School, Hampstead.
Clubs: Guy's Hospital, Richmond, Harlequins, Middlesex, London Counties, Barbarians.
A surgeon at Guy's Hospital, he was a bit on the small side but played the game of his life for London against the South Africans in 1912. He served during World War One with the Royal Marines and was mentioned in despatches fighting at Gallipoli.

MILLS
Frederick William
Full-back. 1872-1873 (Marlborough Nomads, 2 caps).
Debut v Scotland, 5 February 1872.
Born: 5 May 1849, Chertsey; Died: 2 February 1904, London.
Educated: Marlborough College.
Clubs: Marlborough Nomads, Bradford, Yorkshire.
A solicitor, he made one appearance for Yorkshire, against Durham in 1874.

MILLS
Stephen Graham Ford
Hooker. 1981-1984 (Gloucester, 5 caps).
Debut v Argentina, 30 May 1981.
Born: 25 February 1953, Cirencester.
Clubs: Gloucester, Barbarians.

Mills captained England 'B' against France 'B' in 1980 and played for the South-West and South the same year. He was a member of the Gloucestershire side that finished runners-up in the 1977-8 County Championship and that same season he played for Gloucester when they beat Leicester in the RFU Club KO Cup. Mills later captained Gloucester, leading the side that shared the JPS Cup with Moseley in 1981-2.

MILLS
William Alonzo
Number 8/Lock. 1906-1908 (Devonport Albion, 11 caps).
Debut v Wales, 13 January 1906.
Born: 2 February 1879, Devonport.
Clubs: Devonport Albion, Devon.
Mills scored his first international try in the 16-6 defeat by Ireland in February 1906, then followed it with further tries, in the next match against Scotland and then against France the same year.

MILMAN
Dermot Lionel Kennedy (Sir), Bt
Number 8. 1937-1938 (Bedford, 4 caps).
Debut v Wales, 16 January 1937.
Born: 24 October 1912; Died: 13 January 1990.
Educated: Uppingham School, Cambridge University.

Clubs: Cambridge University (no Blue), Bedford, Edinburgh Wanderers, East Midlands (14 appearances), Barbarians.
Sir Dermot Milman is one of a small band of international rugby players from Cambridge University who never gained a rugby Blue. He played in four internationals as a back-row forward whilst associated with the Bedford club, including one match in 1937 when England regained the Triple Crown. Milman was one of seven men to play in all England's international matches in 1938, although a year earlier he had been seriously injured in the match against Wales. He played cricket for Cambridge University and Bedfordshire and served in World War Two with the RASC, being mentioned in despatches.

As a UK Council officer, he was stationed in Italy, South America and Pakistan from 1946. Later he was a master at Epsom College. In 1962 he succeeded his father as 8th Baronet Milman.

MILTON
Cecil Henry

Centre. 1906 (Camborne School of Mines, 1 cap).
Debut v Ireland, 10 February 1906.
Born: 7 January 1884; Died: 1961.
Educated: Bedford Grammar School, Camborne School of Mines.
Clubs: Camborne School of Mines, Cornwall (10 appearances), Barbarians.

The son of Sir William, his brother J.G. was also an England international and Camborne School of Mines player. Another brother, N.W., was not an international but won Blues at Oxford University in 1905-07.

MILTON
J.G. ('Jumbo')

Forward. 1904-1907 (Camborne School of Mines, 5 caps).
Debut v Wales, 9 January 1904.
Born: 1 May 1885;
Died: 15 June 1915.
Educated: Bedford Grammar School, Camborne School of Mines.
Clubs: Camborne School of Mines, East Midlands, Cornwall (18 appearances), Barbarians.

Milton played a full international season whilst still at Bedford School. Son of Sir William and brother of Cecil Henry, he had another brother, N.W., who was not an international player but gained Blues whilst at Oxford University (1905-07). J.G.Milton won his first cap when he was 18 and he became the first player to follow his father into an England team. He emigrated to South Africa around 1907, at the age of 22.

MILTON
William Henry (Sir), KCMG KCVO

Back. 1874-1875 (Marlborough Nomads, 2 caps).
Debut v Scotland, 23 February 1874.
Born: 3 December 1854, Marlow; Died: 6 March 1930.
Educated: Marlborough College.
Club: Marlborough Nomads.

Sir William Milton was the first man to play rugby for one country and cricket for another. He played for England at rugger when the game was 20-a-side, in 1874; and in 1888 he captained South Africa on their entry into Test Cricket. He was the father of Cecil Henry and J.G, both England internationals, J.G. being the first player to follow his father into an England side. Another son, N.W., was not an international but won Blues at Oxford University (1905-07). Sir William was secretary to Cecil Rhodes from 1890 to 1896. He was awarded the KCVO in 1910.

MITCHELL
Frank

Forward. 1895-1896 (Blackheath, 6 caps).
Debut v Wales, 5 January 1895.
Born: 13 August 1872, Market

Frank Mitchell

Weighton; Died: 11 October 1935, Lewisham.
Educated: St Peter's School (York), Cambridge University.
Clubs: Cambridge University (Blues 1893-5), Blackheath, Kent, Sussex, Barbarians.

Frank Mitchell, who scored with a conversion on his international debut, was a remarkable sportsman, a triple Blue who played rugby and cricket for England and cricket for South Africa as well as serving on the Barbarians committee.

He began the South African War as a private but was later promoted to lieutenant with the Yorkshire Dragoons, with whom he fought at Boshof and Schwartz Koffeefontein, winning the Queen's Medal. He returned to play cricket for the strong Yorkshire side but then went back to South Africa, where he remained in business until 1914. During World War One he served with the West Riding RFA, being promoted to the rank of lieutenant-colonel.

Mitchell won an athletics Blue for the shot putt in 1896 and captained the Cambridge University CC tour of the USA in 1895. Whilst captaining Cambridge in the 1896 Varsity match he caused an uproar by ordering a bowler to give away extras so that Oxford would not have to follow-on. His action led to the law being changed so that enforcing the follow-on became voluntary.

In 1898 he toured South Africa with Lord Hawke's team, when he opened the innings, and after the Boer War he captained South African teams to England in 1904 and 1912. He also played cricket for MCC, Buckinghamshire and Transvaal. The Badminton Library Series contains his book *Rugby Football*.

MITCHELL
William Grant (Willie)

Full-back. 1890-1893 (Richmond, 7 caps)
Debut v Wales, 15 February 1890.
Born: 23 May 1865; Died: 14 January 1905, Canada.
Educated: Bromsgrove School, Cambridge University.
Clubs: Cambridge University (Blue 1886), Guy's Hospital, Richmond, Middlesex, Barbarians.

Willie Mitchell played in all 19 matches of the British Lions' tour to South Africa in 1891 and at Kimberley he won the Second Test with his goal from a mark.

According to an 1887 edition of the *Guy's Hospital Gazette*, he was 'quite an unorthodox player, he tackled by the hand, shoulders, arm or jersey and often fly-kicked the ball into touch (soccer-style) 30 or 40 yards away instead of picking it up. Frequently he turned up at an international match without any kit — even boots!'

In 1887 he won an athletics Blue for the shot putt and also played soccer, cricket, golf, billiards, tennis, racquets and hurdling. He was an original member of the Barbarians. He joined the Yukon gold rush in Alaska and died of phthisis in 1905.

MOBBS
Edgar Robert, DSO

Wing-Centre. 1909-1910 (Northampton, 7 caps).
Debut v Australia, 9 January 1909.
Born: 29 June 1882, Northampton; Died: 29 July 1917, Zillebeke (killed in action).
Educated: Bedford Modern School.
Clubs: Olney, Northampton, East Midlands, Barbarians.

The first big match in which Edgar Mobbs played was for Bedford against the New Zealanders in 1905. He scored a try on his international debut, captained Northampton from 1907 to 1913, represented East Midlands on the RFU and skippered the Barbarians against Wales at Cardiff in a wartime fundraising match in 1915. He was also on the Barbarians and RFU committees.

He was the son of Oliver Mobbs and, like his brothers, Noel and Herbert, he was employed by the Pytchley Autocar Company, Edgar being manager of their Market Harborough branch. His retirement from rugby was marked by a public testimonial with around 400 admirers being gathered together at Northampton Town Hall.

Another measure of how high Mobbs was regarded is the fact that he was immortalised by the staging of an annual encounter between the Barbarians and an East Midlands XV, in what is known as the 'Edgar Mobbs Memorial Match'. The first such game was staged on 10 February 1921, less than four years after he met his death in a fearless way which was characteristic of the man.

When war broke out, Mobbs applied for a commission. He was refused because of his age — he was 32 — and so returned to Northampton to raise his own corps. Known as 'D' Company, 7th Northamptonshire Regiment, it included a number of rugby players and many other sportsmen. More than 400 volunteers served with 'Mobbs' Army', with only 85 surviving. Mobbs steadily earned promotion to major and in the 1917 New Year's Honours list he was awarded the DSO as a lieutenant-colonel. At the time he was recovering from a shrapnel wound to a shoulder, from a shell which had killed his orderly and others. In the Messines battle he was struck in the chest by another piece of shrapnel but escaped serious injury.

Mobbs rose to the rank of colonel and upon the opening of the great offensive of 31 July 1917, he received orders with the Sherwood Foresters to take two lines of enemy trenches. His attack managed to secure the first trench but he was then held back by a machine-gun in a redoubt on the second trench. Mobbs was rallying his men for a charge on the trench when he was cut down in a hail of bullets. Mortally wounded, he was able to write out a map reference of the gun so that a messenger could send it back to HQ. The messenger was also killed minutes later and another messenger was also shot, but the information was finally delivered. The Northamptons were under heavy fire that first day of the bloody battle of Passchendaele and Mobbs was the only officer to be killed, although six others were seriously wounded. His action was said to be one of the most heroic of the war.

MOBERLEY
William Octavius

Back. 1872 (Ravenscourt Park, 1 cap).
Debut v Scotland, 5 February 1872.
Born: 14 November 1851 Shoreham; Died: 2 February 1914, Cornwall.
Educated: Rugby School, Oxford University.
Clubs: Oxford University (Blues 1871-3), Clifton, Ravenscourt Park, Gloucestershire.

Although he appeared for England under the banner of the Ravenscourt club, Moberley was also captain of Oxford University at the time. He played cricket for Oxford, although he did not gain a Blue, and for Gloucestershire from 1876 to 1883 and again in 1886. He taught at Clifton College from 1874 until 1913.

MOORE
Brian Christopher

Hooker. 1987-1992 (Harlequins, Nottingham, 40 caps).
Debut v Scotland, 4 April 1987.
Born: 11 January 1962, Birmingham.
Educated: Crossley and Porter High School (Halifax), Nottingham University.
Clubs: Old Crossleyans, Roundhay, Nottingham University, Nottingham, Harlequins, Barbarians.

Brian Moore, a member of England's 1991 World Cup Final team and their 1991 and 1992 Grand Slam sides, graduated from Nottingham University with a law degree and went on to skipper Nottingham RUFC. He played for England v Japan in 1986 (no caps were awarded) and was voted Whitbread/*Rugby World* Player of the Year for 1989-90.

Earlier he had represented England Students against Fiji in 1982 and toured Italy, Romania and Spain with the England Under-23 side. He went to the Far East with England Students in 1983 and led England 'B' on his first appearance, against Italy in April 1985. On the British Lions tour of Australia in 1989 he played in three Tests. His other representative honours include an

Brian Moore

England XV in 1989-90, and England's tours of Argentina in 1990 and Australia and Fiji in 1991.

In May 1991 he escaped a ban by the RFU after receiving a four months suspended prison sentence and a fine of £500 after pleading guilty to assault in a Nottingham public house. A 57-man committee sat in his judgement for his conduct but decided to take no action. A solicitor by profession, Moore currently works as a corporate financier.

MOORE
Edward James, CB

Forward. 1883 (Blackheath, 2 caps).
Debut v Ireland, 5 February 1883.
Born: 25 May 1862; Died: 7 March 1925, Lewisham.
Educated: Epsom College, Oxford University.
Clubs: Oxford University (Blues 1882-3), St Bartholomew's Hospital, Blackheath, Kent.
A GP at Blackheath, he served in World

War One as a lieutenant-colonel in the RAMC and was mentioned in despatches. He received the CB in 1911.

MOORE
Norman J.N. Hope

Forward. 1904 (Bristol, 3 caps).
Debut v Wales, 9 January 1904.
Born: 1877, Lewisham; Died: 8 March 1938, Skipton.
Clubs: Bath, Bristol, Gloucestershire, Somerset.
Norman Moore made 231 appearances for Bristol between 1901 and 1910. He scored two tries against Ireland in 1904.

MOORE
Philip Brian Cecil (Lord), GCVO KCB CMG PC

Number 8. 1951 (Blackheath, 1 cap).
Debut v Wales, 20 January 1951.
Born: 6 April 1921.
Educated: Dragon School (Oxford),

Cheltenham College, Oxford University.
Clubs: Oxford University (Blues 1945-6), Blackheath, Oxfordshire, Barbarians.
Lord Moore, who also played cricket for Oxfordshire and won a hockey Blue in 1946, served during World War Two with 106 Squadron (Bomber Command). Captured after being shot down over Germany, he was a prisoner-of-war from 1942 to 1945.

In 1947 he entered the Admiralty and was Assistant Private Secretary to the First Lord of the Admiralty from 1950 to 1951, then Principal Private Secretary from 1957 to 1958. British High Commissioner to Singapore from 1963 until 1965, he was awarded the CMG. He became Private Secretary to Her Majesty the Queen and was made a peer in 1986. He was also employed by the Crown as Keeper of Her Majesty's Archives.

MOORE
William Kenneth Thomas

Scrum-half. 1947-1950 (Leicester, 7 caps).
Debut v Wales, 18 January 1947.
Born: 24 February 1921.
Educated: Wyggeston School (Leicester).
Clubs: Old Wyggestonians, Devonport Services, Leicester, Royal Navy, Cornwall, Leicestershire, Barbarians.
He served in World War Two in the Royal Navy and also played in two Victory internationals against Scotland. He is a member of the East Midlands and Staffordshire Referees' Society.

MORDELL
Robert John

Flanker. 1978 (Rosslyn Park, 1 cap).

Bob Mordell

Debut v Wales, 4 February 1978.
Born: 2 July 1951, Twickenham.
Educated: Thames Valley Grammar School.
Clubs: Wasps, Rosslyn Park, Oldham RL, Kent Invicta RL.

He joined Kent Invicta (later Southend Invicta) as coach for a fee of £13,500 and after apparently disappearing from the Rugby League scene he was reinstated by the International Board for 1990-91 and after a spell with Richmond Thamesians he rejoined Rosslyn Park.

MORFITT
Samuel

Back. 1894-1896 (West Hartlepool, 6 caps).
Debut v Wales, 6 January 1894.
Born: December 1868, Kingston upon Hull; Died: 1 January 1954, Kingston upon Hull.
Clubs: West Hartlepool, Hull Kingston Rovers (remaining when Hull KR changed to RL in 1897), Durham Counties, Yorkshire.

The first player to be capped by England from West Hartlepool, he scored a try on his international debut.

MORGAN
James Rydiard

Hooker. 1920 (Hawick, 1920, 1 cap).
Debut v Wales, 17 January 1920.
Born: 1890 Cockermouth, near Workington; Died: 29 April 1961, Hawick, Scotland.
Club: Hawick.

It is believed that his England cap is still the property of the Hawick club, to whom it was presented.

MORGAN
William George Derek

Number 8. 1960-1961 (Medicals, Newcastle, 9 caps).
Debut v Wales, 16 January 1960.
Born: 30 November 1936, Gwent.
Educated: Lewis School (Pengam), Durham University.
Clubs: Medicals, Newbridge, Percy Park, Monmouthshire, Northumberland, Barbarians.

Although being born in Wales — and his friendly Welsh accent is still clear today — he opted to play for England, making his debut, strangely enough, against Wales. He managed the England tour of New Zealand in 1985 and was secretary of the Newbridge club. He is a dental surgeon.

MORLEY
Alan John, MBE

Wing. 1972-1975 (Bristol, 7 caps).
Debut v South Africa, 3 June 1972.
Born: 25 June 1950, Bristol.
Educated: Colston's School (Bristol).
Clubs: Bristol, Gloucestershire, Barbarians.

Dewi Morris

Alan Morley made over 516 appearances for Bristol between 1959 and 1986, helped them to the 1973 RFU Club KO Cup Final and played for Gloucestershire in that year's County Championship Final. He also held the world record of 475 first-class tries; and England's most tries in any tour match — four in Western Australia in 1975 — a record shared with P.Preece. He went on the England tour to South Africa in 1972 and scored on his debut. He was awarded the MBE in 1985.

MORRIS
Alfred Drummond Warrington, CB CMG OBE

Forward. 1909 (United Services (Portsmouth), Royal Navy, 3 caps).
Debut v Australia, 9 January 1909.
Born: 1883; Died: 24 March 1962, London.
Educated: Alverstoke School.
Clubs: United Services (Portsmouth), Royal Navy, Barbarians.

Morris made his England debut in the same match as Edgar Mobbs. He enlisted in the Royal Navy in 1899 and served during World War One with the Royal Navy Air Division before joining the RAF. He was awarded the OBE in 1918, the CMG in 1919 and the CB in 1943. During World War Two he was an air commodore. He represented the RAF on the RFU from 1923 to 1925 and again from 1927 to 1945.

MORRIS
Colin Dewi

Scrum-half. 1988-1992 (Liverpool St Helens, 9 caps).
Debut v Australia, 5 November 1988.
Born: 9 February 1964, Crickhowell, Wales.
Educated: Brecon, Crewe and Alsager College.
Clubs: Winnington Park, Liverpool St Helens, Orrell, Lancashire.

Dewi Morris, who scored a try on his full England debut, progressed from junior rugby to international level within six months. He played twice for England 'B' in 1988 and went on the full England tour to Argentina in 1990. In 1992, after an absence of three years, he was recalled to the side and played in every game in that year's Grand Slam success. Playing for the North against the Australians in October 1988, he scored the winning try two minutes from time. He has broken his nose three times. A distillery production controller. He played for Gwent Schools in an Under-19 County Cricket Final.

MORRISON
Percy Henderson

Back. 1890-1891 (Cambridge University, 4 caps).
Debut v Wales, 15 February 1890.
Born: 30 July 1868; Died: 12 July 1936.
Educated: Loretto School, Cambridge University.
Clubs: Cambridge University (Blues 1887-90), Northern, Northumberland, Barbarians.

Percy Morrison scored only one try for England, in a 3-0 win over Ireland on 15 March 1890. He read medicine at Cambridge but decided not to take his final examinations. During World War One he was a special police constable.

MORSE
Sydney

Back. 1873-1875 (Marlborough Nomads, 3 caps).
Debut v Scotland, 3 March 1873.
Born: 1 June 1854; Died: 27 January 1929.
Educated: Marlborough College.
Clubs: Marlborough Nomads, The Law Club (Harlequins).

Morse was a solicitor.

MORTIMER
William

Forward. 1899 (Marlborough Nomads, 1 cap).
Debut v Wales, 7 January 1899.
Born: 2 May 1874; Died: 31 October 1916, Crowborough.
Educated: Marlborough College, Cambridge University.
Clubs: Cambridge University (Blues 1895-6), Marlborough Nomads, Blackheath, Kent, Lancashire, Barbarians.

William Mortimer was chosen to tour South Africa with the British Lions in 1896, before he gained a full international cap. He won hockey Blues (1895-6) and went on the Cambridge University CC tour of the United States in 1895.

MORTON
Harold James Storrs

Prop. 1909-1910 (Blackheath, 4 caps).
Debut v Ireland, 13 February 1909.
Born: 31 January 1886, Sheffield; Died: 3 January 1955, Whitechapel.

Educated: Uppingham School, Cambridge University.
Clubs: Cambridge University (Blue 1908), London Hospital, United Hospitals, Blackheath, Kent, Barbarians.
Morton served during World War One as a captain in the RAMC.

MOSS
F.

Forward. 1885-1886 (Broughton, 3 caps).
Debut v Wales, 3 January 1885.
Club: Broughton.

MULLINS
Andrew Richard

Prop. 1989 (Harlequins, 1 cap).
Debut v Fiji, 4 November 1989.

Born: 12 December 1968, Eltham, London.
Educated: Dulwich School, Durham University.
Clubs: Old Alleynians, Durham University, Harlequins, Barbarians.

Andy Mullins shares his birthdate with Harlequins and England colleague Will Carling, with whom he played in the same university and England Under-18 schools teams. Mullins, who had a year in the army between school and Durham University, represented England Under-23s in 1986 and made his England 'B' debut against Australia in 1988. During his playing career he has suffered a broken nose and has broken bones in his foot. He is an accountant. He was the London Schools breaststroke swimming champion. He recently completed 100 first-team appearances for the Harlequins.

Andy Mullins

MYCOCK
Joseph

Lock. 1947-1948 (Sale, 5 caps).
Debut v Wales, 18 January 1947.
Born: 17 January 1916.

Educated: Giggleswick School.

Clubs: Sale, Vale of Lune, Harlequins, RAF, Combined Services, Lancashire (56 appearances), Barbarians.

He captained England on his international debut and was in the 1947 Calcutta Cup-winning team. During World War Two he served in the RAF.

MYERS
Edward, MC

Centre. 1920-1925 (Bradford, 18 caps).
Debut v Ireland, 14 February 1920.
Born: 23 September 1895, USA; Died: 29 March 1956, Bradford.

Educated: Leeds University.

Clubs: Headingley, Leicester, Bradford, Yorkshire (42 appearances, captain 1921-2 and in 1924-5.

Edward Myers

He scored a try on his international debut and is the Bradford club's most capped player. Originally capped as a centre, then as a fly-half, he was a member of the 1923-4 Championship side. He was chosen for the match against France in 1921, but did not play due to a family bereavement. He was born of Yorkshire parents in the USA and served during World War One with the West Yorkshire Regiment, being wounded on three occasions. He joined the Bradford club after the war and was later its captain. A cool player, he seldom appeared ruffled.

MYERS
Harry

Scrum-half. 1898 (Keighley, 1 cap).
Debut v Ireland, 5 February 1898.
Born: 3 February 1875, Leeds; Died: 19 December 1906, Keighley.

Clubs: Bramley, Keighley, Yorkshire (28 appearances).

Myers made his international debut as a late replacement for an injured player. When Keighley changed codes in 1900, he also turned to play League rather than Union. He died of a spinal injury sustained in the Rugby League match at Dewsbury on 3 November 1906.

NANSON
William Moore Bell

Forward. 1907 (Carlisle, 2 caps).
Debut v France, 5 January 1907.
Born: 12 December 1880, Carlisle; Died: 4 June 1915, El Krithia (killed in action).

Educated: Lowther Street School (Carlisle).

Clubs: Carlisle, Cumberland, Oldham RL.

He scored a try on his international debut and in 1908 moved into Rugby League with Oldham. He served in the South African War with the Border Regiment, and during World War One with the Manchester Regiment in Egypt and Gallipoli. Posted missing in El Krithia, he was declared dead a year later. In South Africa he gained both the Queen's and King's Medals.

NASH
Edward Henry

Half-back. 1875 (Richmond, 1 cap).
Debut v Ireland, 15 February 1875.
Born: 20 December 1854; Died: 18 September 1932.

Educated: Rugby School, Oxford University.

Clubs: Oxford University (Blues 1874-5), Richmond.

Nash scored on his international debut with an excellent drop-goal. He also won a hockey Blue and was one of the founding committee members of the Hockey Association, one of the HA's two trustee and its second president from 1892 to 1896. He was also one of five vice-presidents from 1890 to 1892 and again from 1897 to 1932. He played hockey for Ealing and Middlesex and at centre-half for the South against the North. Nash proposed the toast to the Chairman, the Rt Hon Lord Desborough, KCVO — at the Hockey Association banquet at the Hotel Russell in London, on the occasion of the 1908 Olympic Games.

NEALE
Bruce Alan

Lock. 1951 (Rosslyn Park, 3 caps).
Debut v Ireland, 10 February 1951.
Born: 15 September 1923.

Educated: Emmanuel School (Battersea).

Clubs: Rosslyn Park, Army, Combined Services, London Combination, Durham County, Surrey.

Neale served with the Royal Artillery and made 17 appearances for the Army between 1948 and 1953, against the Royal Navy, RAF and French Army. After his military service he was employed by ICI. He was a member of England's 1951 Calcutta Cup-winning team.

NEALE
Maurice Edward

Centre. 1912 (Blackheath, 1 cap).
Debut v France, 8 April 1912.
Born: 1886 Bristol; Died: 9 July 1967, Bristol.

Clubs: Blackheath, Bristol, Barbarians.

One of three Bristol players in the British Lions' party to South Africa in 1910, Maurice Neale had never appeared in an English trial and yet completed the tour as leading try-scorer. In the match against a Border XV he became only the second Briton on an official tour to score a hat-trick of tries, his overall total being ten tries from 14 matches. He appeared in the England trial of 1911 before winning his only cap in Paris.

NEAME
Stuart

Forward. 1879-1880 (Old Cheltonians, 4 caps).
Debut v Scotland, 10 March 1879.
Born: 15 June 1856; Died: 16 November 1936, Bromley.

Educated: Cheltenham College.

Clubs: Old Cheltonians, Blackheath, Kent.

He was president of the Cheltonian Society from 1921 to 1922.

NEARY
Anthony

Flanker. 1971-1980 (Broughton Park, 43 caps).
Debut v Wales, 16 January 1971.
Born: 25 November 1949, Manchester.

Educated: De la Salle College (Salford), Liverpool University.

Clubs: UAU, British Universities, Broughton Park, Lancashire (73 appearances).

Tony Neary played at both Under-15 and Under-19 levels for England Schools and for England Under-25s against Fiji in 1970. He first toured in 1971, when he went with England to Japan and the Far East, after winning his first full cap against Wales in January that year. The following year he went on the England tour to South Africa, where they won only one Test match; and in 1973 to New Zealand where they again won only one Test.

He was on the British Lions tour of South Africa in 1974 and the Lions tour of New Zealand in 1977, when he played in the final Test. Neary has also played for North-West Counties against South Africa and Fiji, and he was in Lancashire's 1973 County Championship side. At one time he was England's most capped player and he is still the most capped from the Broughton Park club.

His wife Linda (neé Higson) is the girl who sang *I'd Like to Buy the World a Coke* in the 1971 TV advertisement for Coca-Cola. In 1990 the film was remade with Linda as lead singer and included her husband and children,

Keely and Daniel. A solicitor by profession, Neary is a partner, with Fran Cotton and Steve Smith in the *Cotton Traders'* leisurewear firm.

NELMES
Barry George
Prop. 1975-1978 (Cardiff, 6 caps).
Debut v Australia, 24 May 1975.
Born: 17 April 1948, Bristol.
Educated: Portway Secondary Modern School.
Clubs: Bristol, Cardiff, Barbarians.
Nelmes, scored a try when England won the Calcutta Cup in 1978. He was captain of Cardiff in 1978-9 and played for the Barbarians against the 1977 British Lions.

Barry Nelmes

Tony Neary

NEWBOLD
Charles Joseph, DSO
Hooker. 1904-1905 (Blackheath, 6 caps).
Debut v Wales, 9 January 1904.
Born: 12 January 1881, Tunbridge Wells; Died: 26 October 1946.
Educated: Uppingham School, Cambridge University.
Clubs: Cambridge University (Blues 1902-03), Wanderers, Blackheath, Kent, Barbarians.

He appeared on a winning England side only once in six international matches. He served in World War One as a lieutenant-colonel in the Royal Engineers, was mentioned in despatches three times and awarded the DSO in 1917. He was managing-director of the Arthur Guinness company and chairman of the Brewers Association.

NEWMAN
Sydney Charles
Full-back. 1947-1948 (Oxford University, 3 caps).
Debut v France, 19 April 1947.
Born: 27 July 1919.

Educated: Christian Brothers College (Pretoria, South Africa), Witwatersrand University (South Africa), Oxford University.

Clubs: Oxford University (Blues 1946-7), Barbarians.

He served with the South African Army during World War Two and was wounded and then captured in Libya and held as a PoW from 1942 until 1945. He was awarded the 1939-45 Star, Africa Star, War Medal (1939-45) and Africa Service Medal.

NEWTON
Arthur Winstanley

Wing. 1907 (Blackheath, 1 cap).
Debut v Scotland, 16 March 1907.
Born: 12 September 1879; Died: sometime during World War One.
Clubs: Blackheath, Army, Barbarians.

Newton served in the Dublin Fusiliers and played for the Army twice, both against the Royal Navy.

NEWTON
Philip Arthur

Forward. 1882 (Blackheath, 1 cap).
Debut v Scotland, 4 March 1882.
Born: 11 April 1860; Died: 25 December 1946.
Educated: Blackheath Proprietory School, Oxford University.
Clubs: Oxford University (Blues 1879-80), Blackheath, Kent.

NEWTON-THOMPSON
John Oswald, DFC

Scrum-half. 1947 (Oxford University, 2 caps).
Debut v Scotland, 15 March 1947.
Born: 2 December 1920, London; Died: 3 March 1974, Africa.
Educated: Diocesan College (Rondebosch, South Africa), Cape Town University (South Africa), Cambridge University, Oxford University.
Clubs: Cambridge University (Blues 1937-8), Oxford University (Blues 1945-6, also captain), Barbarians.

Newton-Thompson, who also gained a cricket Blue for Oxford in 1946 and played for Western Province against MCC in 1948-9, was South Africa's representative on the RFU in 1947-8. He served in World War Two with the South African Air Force and reached the rank of captain. His decorations included the 1939-45 Star, Italy Star, War Medal (1939-45) and Distinguished Flying Cross. He was a South African United Party MP from 1961 to 1974 and the brother of C.L.Newton-Thompson. He was killed in an air crash.

NICHOL
William

Forward. 1892 (Brighouse Rangers, 2 caps).
Debut v Wales, 2 January 1892.

Born: 30 October 1868, Raistrick, Yorkshire; Died: 10 April 1922, Brighouse.
Club: Brighouse Rangers.

He scored a try on his international debut and turned to Rugby League when the Brighouse club helped form the Northern Union in 1895. He worked as a licensee.

NICHOLAS
Philip Leach

Wing. 1902 (Exeter, 1 cap).
Debut v Wales, 11 January 1902.
Born: 30 May 1876; Died: 31 January 1952, Barnstaple.
Educated: Monmouth School, Oxford University.
Clubs: Oxford University (Blues 1897-9), Exeter, Devon, Barbarians.

Nicholas was a member of the Devon side which won the County Championship in 1900-01, the season he played for the Rest of England. A clergyman, he was ordained in 1908.

NICHOLSON
Basil Ellard

Centre. 1938 (Harlequins, 2 caps).
Debut v Wales, 15 January 1938.
Born: 1 January 1913.
Educated: Whitgift School.
Clubs: Old Whitgiftians, Harlequins, Surrey, Barbarians.

He was on the British Lions tour of South Africa in 1938 and scored one try for England, against Ireland in February 1938. During World War Two he was a lieutenant-colonel in the Royal Engineers and was involved in the D-Day invasion plans.

NICHOLSON
Edward Sealy, MBE

Hooker. 1935-1936 (Leicester, 5 caps).

Edward Nicholson

Born: 10 June 1912.
Died: 16 March 1992, Beccles.
Educated: Marlborough College, Woodham College (Oxford), Oxford University.
Clubs: Oxford University (Blues 1931-4), Guy's Hospital, Rosslyn Park, Leicester, Blackheath, Surrey, Barbarians.

He first came to the attention of the England selectors during the 1934-5 season, playing in the second trial game, and was chosen for the Rest against England. A GP at Beccles, he served during World War Two as an RAF squadron leader.

NICHOLSON
Ellist Tennant

Wing. 1900 (Birkenhead Park, 2 caps).
Debut v Wales, 6 January 1900.
Born: 13 December 1871; Died: 1 December 1953.
Educated: Liverpool College.
Clubs: Liverpool, Birkenhead Park, Lancashire (22 appearances), Cheshire.

He scored a try on his international debut.

NICHOLSON
Thomas

Wing. 1893 (Rockcliff, 1 cap).
Debut v Ireland, 4 February 1893.
Clubs: Rockcliffe, Northumberland, Wigan RL.

He made his Rugby League debut for Wigan against St Helens on 4 November 1899 and last played for the club on 23 February 1901 against Leigh. In 1899-1900 he made 19 appearances and scored four tries; in 1900-1901, ten appearances and two tries.

NINNES
Barry Francis

Lock. 1971 (Coventry, 1 cap).
Debut v Wales, 16 January 1971.
Born: 23 March 1948, St Ives.
Educated: Hayle Grammar School, Camborne Technical College.
Clubs: St Ives, Coventry, Cornwall (24 appearances), Warwickshire.

He played for Coventry when they won the RFU Club KO Cup in 1972-3.

NORMAN
Douglas James

Hooker. 1932 (Leicester, 2 caps).
Debut v South Africa, 2 January 1932.
Born: 12 June 1897; Died: 27 December 1971.
Educated: Medway School.
Clubs: Medway Athletic, Leicester, Lancashire, Barbarians.

He was president of the Liecestershire Schools Rugby Union. Served during World War One with the Royal Artillery and in World War Two in the Home Guard.

NORTH
Eustace Herbert Guest

Forward. 1891 (Blackheath, 3 caps).
Debut v Wales, 3 January 1891.
Born: 4 November 1868; Died: 17 March 1942.

Educated: St Paul's School, Blackheath Proprietory School, Oxford University.

Clubs: Oxford University (Blues 1888-90), Blackheath, Sussex, Kent, Barbarians.

He played cricket for Oxford Authentics and was chairman of the Prep Schools Association from 1920 to 1928, then treasurer from 1931 to 1942.

NORTHMORE
S.

Fly half. 1897 (Millom, 1 cap).
Debut v Ireland, 6 February 1897.
Clubs: Millom, Cumberland, Broughton Rangers RL.

NOVAK
Michael John

Wing. 1970 (Harlequins, 3 caps).
Debut v Wales, 28 February 1970.

Mike Novak

Born: 27 September 1947, Stratford upon Avon.
Educated: Eastbourne Grammar School.
Clubs: Eastbourne, Harlequins, Surrey, Sussex.

Novak scored a try on his international debut. He was a big, fast winger with a good swerving movement.

NOVIS
Anthony Leslie, MC

Centre. 1929-1933 (Blackheath, 7 caps).
Debut v Scotland, 16 March 1929.
Born: 22 September 1906.

Educated: Epsom College, Oxford University.

Clubs: Oxford University (Blue 1927), Blackheath, Army, Combined Services, Headingley, Surrey, Barbarians.

Novis, a natural ball-player and resolute runner, began his career as a fly-half at Epsom and Oxford University, moving into the centre when he joined Blackheath. On the British Lions 1930 tour, he was leading try-scorer with 12 in New Zealand and four in Australia. In Sydney he scored the only British try of the game.

He was a Regular Army officer in the Leicestershire Regiment and made 14 appearances for the Army, against the RAF, French Army and Royal Navy, between 1929 and 1935. He helped his regiment to an Army Cup Final. An injury sustained early in 1933-4 put him out for the rest of the season but he captained the Combined Services against New Zealand in 1935. He served during World War Two, was twice wounded and retired in 1945 with the rank of lieutenant-colonel.

OAKELEY
Francis Eckley

Scrum half. 1913-1914 (United Services (Portsmouth), Royal Navy, 4 caps).
Debut v Scotland, 15 March 1913.
Born: 5 February 1891, Hereford; Died: 11 December 1914 (killed in action at sea).

Educated: Hereford School, Eastman's School, Royal Naval College (Osborne), Royal Naval College (Dartmouth).

Clubs: United Services (Portsmouth), Royal Navy.

He joined the Royal Navy in 1908 and was a lieutenant in submarines when he was presumed drowned during World War One. He was in the Calcutta Cup teams of 1913 and 1914 and played in three games of the 1914 Triple Crown, Championship and Grand Slam season.

OAKES
Robert Frederick

Forward. 1897-1899 (Hartlepool Rovers, 8 caps).
Debut v Wales, 9 January 1897.
Born: 1873, Hartlepool; Died: 23 October 1952, Leeds.

Clubs: Hartlepool Trinity, Hartlepool Rovers, Headingley, Durham County.

Born at Hartlepool Barracks, the son of an army sergeant, he worked mainly in the administration of the Yorkshire RFU, being secretary (1907-1947) and president (1922-1924) and representing Yorkshire on the RFU from 1920 to 1945. He was an England selector from 1929 to 1939, an International Board member from 1936 and president of the RFU from 1933 to 1934. He skippered the Hartlepool club from 1894 to 1899.

OAKLEY
Lionel Frederick Lightborn

Centre. 1951 (Bedford, 1 cap).
Debut v Wales, 20 January 1951.
Born: 24 January 1925; Died: 1981.

Educated: Bedford School, Bedford.

Clubs: Army, Bedford, East Midlands, Barbarians.

During World War Two he served with the Royal Artillery, then with the 2nd battalion of the Indian Airborne Division.

OBOLENSKY
Prince Alexander ('Obo' or 'The Flying Slav')

Wing. 1936 (Oxford University, 4 caps).
Debut v New Zealand, 4 January 1936.
Born: St Petersburg, Russia, 17 February 1916; Died: 29 March 1940, Norfolk.

Educated: Trent College, Oxford University.

Clubs: Oxford University (Blues 1935-37), Rosslyn Park, Barbarians.

The only Russian to play rugby for England, he was the son of Prince Alexis Obolensky, an officer of the Tsar's Imperial Horse Guards. He came to England as a child, following the Russian Revolution when his family, finding their privileged position under threat, sent him to England. He was still a Russian national when he won his first Oxford Blue in 1935, and as an undergraduate he was first chosen to play for England in 1936, against the touring All Blacks.

At first, quite a controversy raged around a Russian being chosen to play for England, despite him taking out nationalisation papers. He is one of only a select band of players to have had a try named after him. 'Obolensky's Try' — his second of the match — came against the All Blacks at Twickenham just before half-time in England's 13-0 win in January 1936. In 1939-40 he became vice captain of Rosslyn Park, the club he had joined upon leaving Oxford.

A pioneer of lightweight rugby boots, he held claims to have scored most tries in a representative match, with 17 for the RFU against a Brazilian XV on 31 August 1936, on an RFU tour of South America.

He was the first international player to lose his life in World War Two when his Hawker Hurricane crashed landed in East Anglia whilst on a training flight. A well respected and much loved sportsman, his tragic death was mourned by many.

Prince Obolensky

Alan Old

OLD
Alan Gerald Bernard

Fly half. 1972-1978 (Middlesbrough, Leicester, Sheffield, 16 caps).
Debut v Wales, 15 January 1972.
Born: 23 September 1945, Middlesbrough.
Educated: Acklam Hall Grammar School (Middlesbrough), London University, Durham University.
Clubs: London University, Durham University, Middlesbrough, Leicester, Sheffield, Yorkshire (69 appearances, captain 1982-4).

Alan Old captained his school soccer side and played alongside his brother Chris (a future Yorkshire and England fast bowler) for the Acklam Hall School rugby side which won Morpeth Sevens. He went to Queen Mary College, London, where he played for London University, and then to Durham University for a year, appearing for them in the UAU Championship semi-final against Bangor. He began his club rugby with Middlesbrough and appeared for the North-Eastern Counties against South Africa in 1970.

In September 1972, Old took up a teaching appointment at Worksop College, and he joined Leicester before returning to Middlesbrough and then switching to Sheffield.

He went on the England tour of South Africa in 1972 and on the British Lions tour of South Africa in 1974, scoring 37 points for the Lions against SW District, the most by a Lions player in a single tour match and a record by any player on a tour of South Africa. He scored most dropped-goals against France in 1978, with two, a feat equalled by J.P.Horton in 1980.

In 1971-2, Old played for Yorkshire with three other Middlesbrough players, an all-time record for the club who previously had never more than two players in the county side at the same time. Old is Middlesbrough's most capped player and in 1971-2 he was top points scorer for the club with 180 in 16 matches. He scored his 100th point for Yorkshire when he kicked the final penalty-goal against Westmorland and Cumberland at Kendal 1974-5, on his 32nd appearance. In his first 14 games for Yorkshire he scored only 12 points but the total increased rapidly when, in 1972, he succeeded Bradford's Phil Carter as the side's goal-kicker.

Old became the North's director of coaching and then Divisional Technical Administrator (North) of the RFU. He made one appearance for Warwickshire CCC in 1969, declining an invitation to join them on a permanent basis, and also turned out for Durham CCC.

OLDHAM
W.L.

Forward. 1908-1909 (Coventry, 2 caps).
Debut v Scotland, 21 March 1908.
Clubs: Coventry, Midland Counties.
Oldham was the first player to be capped from Coventry.

OLVER
Christopher John

Hooker. 1990-1991 (Northampton, 2 caps).
Debut v Argentina, 3 November 1990.
Born: 23 April 1962, Manchester.
Educated: Rossall School (Lancashire), Borough Road College.
Clubs: Sandbach, Harlequins, Northampton.

Olver made his England debut against an Italian XV in 1990 but no caps were awarded. He took over from David Cooke as captain of the Harlequins in 1986 and two years later led their JPS Cup-winning team. He represented London Division, captained England 'B', went on the 1990 tour to Argentina and made one appearance in the 1991 World Cup. He has suffered a dislocated shoulder on two occasions. Also a fine cricketer (hitting three consecutive sixes on one occasion), he is a seven-handicap golfer and also enjoys fly fishing and shooting. He is a teacher at Northampton School.

O'NEILL
A.

Forward. 1901 (Teignmouth, Torquay Athletic, 3 caps).
Debut v Wales, 5 January 1901.
Clubs: Teignmouth, Torquay Athletic, St Bartholomew's Hospital, Devon.
O'Neill was Torquay Athletic's first international player and 'a master in the art of the dribbling game'.

John Orwin

OPENSHAW
William Edward

Half-back. 1879 (Manchester, 1 cap).
Debut v Ireland, 24 March 1879.
Born: 1851; Died: 15 February 1915, Warrington.
Educated: Harrow School.
Clubs: Manchester, Lancashire.

In 1869, Openshaw was in the Harrow soccer XI and ten years later was capped by England at rugby. He won the 880 yards and mile whilst at Harrow School and played cricket against Eton in 1869 and 1870, scoring 45 runs with an average of 11.25 and taking two wickets for 24 runs. He also played for Harrow Wanderers CC and between 1879 and 1882 appeared for Lancashire CCC, without much success, and for the Gentlemen of Cheshire. He worked as a merchant in Manchester.

ORWIN
John

Lock. 1985-1988 (Gloucester, RAF, Bedford, 14 caps).
Debut v Romania, 5 January 1985.
Born: 20 March 1954.

Clubs: Gloucester, RAF, Bedford, Morley.

Orwin played in the 1985 Calcutta Cup-winning side. After completing his RAF service he became a licensee and in 1991-2 was assistant coach with the Morley club.

OSBORNE
Richard R.

Back. 1871 (Manchester, 1 cap).
Debut v Scotland, 27 March 1871.
Born: 20 May 1848, Yorkshire; Died: 4 November 1926, Rochdale.
Educated: Hurstpierpoint College.
Clubs: Rochdale, Manchester, Lancashire.

Osborne played in the first international match between Scotland and England. He was a solicitor and brother of John, a famous jockey and racehorse trainer. His cap and England shirt is apparently on display in the Manchester clubhouse .

OSBORNE
Sidney Herbert

Forward. 1905 (Oxford University, 1 cap).
Debut v Scotland, 18 March 1905.
Born: 26 February 1880, London; Died: 15 July 1939.
Educated: Fettes College, Oxford University.
Clubs: Oxford University (Blues 1900-02), Harlequins, Middlesex, Cumberland.

A head teacher, he is also said to have played for St Bee's.

OTI
Christopher

Wing. 1988-1991 (Cambridge University, Nottingham, Wasps, 9 caps).
Debut v Scotland, 5 March 1988.
Born: 16 June 1965, London.
Educated: Millfield School, Durham University, Cambridge University.
Clubs: Cambridge University (Blues 1986-7), Wasps, Barbarians.

Chris Oti, who scored three tries on his England home debut, against Ireland, in March 1988, and four tries against Romania in 1989, has been unlucky with injuries which have certainly prevented more caps. He had a successful operation to mend knee ligaments in March 1988 but had to return home from the British Lions tour of Australia in 1989 due to injury. He played for England 'B' in 1987 and for an England XV v Italy in 1989-90 (no caps were awarded). He went on the England tour of Australia and Fiji in 1991 and was a member of that year's World Cup squad. Oti holds the Millfield School 100 metres record of 10.8 seconds, achieved as a 17-year-old, and scored

Chris Oti

two tries in the 1987 Varsity match. On his debut for the Barbarians he scored four tries against East Midlands. A chartered surveyor, he later worked for the Bank of England.

OUGHTRED
Bernard

Scrum half. 1901-1903 (Hartlepool Rovers, 6 caps).
Debut v Scotland, 9 March 1901.
Born: 22 August 1888, Hartlepool; Died: 12 November 1949.
Educated: Hartlepool Grammar School, King Edward VI School (Birmingham).
Clubs: Old Edwardians, Hartlepool Rovers, Hull & East Riding, Barrow, Westmorland, Durham County, Yorkshire (12 appearances, later as captain), Barbarians.
A member of the Calcutta Cup teams of 1901 and 1902, he served in the Royal Navy during World War One and fought at the Battle of Jutland. An architect by profession. He helped Durham win the County Championship in 1902 and captained Hartlepool Rovers in 1901.

OWEN
John Ernest

Lock. 1963-1967 (Coventry, 14 caps).
Debut v Wales, 19 January 1963.
Born: 21 September 1939.
Educated: Brocksford Hall School (Derbyshire), Oundle School, Cambridge University.
Clubs: Cambridge University (Blue 1961), Blackheath, Coventry, Warwickshire, Barbarians.
Owen, a notable line-out performer, scored a try on his international debut and played in the Calcutta Cup and Championship-winning side of that year. In 1963, when England became the first Home country to tour New Zealand, they moved on to Australia and Owen appeared in the Test at Sydney, the only Test in which he was fit to play.
He also gained an athletics Blue at Cambridge. Employed in the market research department of a Coventry car-manufacturing company.

OWEN-SMITH
Harold Geoffrey Owen ('Tuppy')

Full-back. 1934-1937 (St Mary's Hospital, 10 caps).
Debut v Wales, 20 January 1934.
Born: 18 February 1909, Cape Town, South Africa; Died: 28 February 1990, South Africa.
Educated: Diocesan College (Rondebosch, South Africa); Cape Town University (South Africa), Oxford University.
Clubs: Oxford University (Blues 1932-3), St Mary's Hospital, Barbarians, Hampshire.
Owen-Smith captained England three times and also represented his native South Africa in the Test series against England in 1929. A noted all-round sportsman, he achieved distinction as a brilliant full-back who played in the Triple Crown-winning teams of 1934 and 1937. His casual manner on the field was a snare for the unwary and he proved adventurous. Despite his lack of inches, he had a bone-crushing tackle.
He won Blues at Oxford for athletics (1931-2) and boxing (1931-2) and played cricket for South Africa. During World War Two he served in the South African Medical Corps, seeing action in the Middle East. After the war he took up practice as a GP in Rondebosch.

PAGE
John Jackson

Scrum-half. 1971-1975 (Bedford, Northampton, 5 caps).
Debut v Wales, 16 January 1971.
Born: 16 April 1947, Brighton.
Educated: Cambridgeshire High School, Cambridge University.
Clubs: Old Cantabrigians, Cambridge University (Blues 1968-70), Bedford, Northampton.
'Jacko' Page, who played rugby for Cambridgeshire, Eastern Counties and England Schools, first appeared for Bedford just before he went to university. He played for England Under-25s against Fiji in 1970 and on a Combined Oxford-Cambridge tour of South America, he caught hepatitis. His father played soccer and cricket for Sussex and was a travelling salesman for a Nottingham-based firm which meant that the family moved house quite regularly. Page was employed by a Northampton bank and later as an engineer.

PALLANT
John Noel

Number 8. 1967 (Nottingham, 3 caps).
Debut v Ireland, 11 February 1967.
Born: 24 December 1944.
Educated: High Pavement Grammar School, Loughborough Colleges.
Clubs: Loughborough Colleges, UAU, Nottingham, Midland Counties.
Pallant was a county basketball player and All-England Schools hammer throw champion in 1958. He taught at Merchant Taylor's School in 1968.

PALMER
Alexander Croydon, OBE

Wing. 1909 (London Hospital, 2 caps).
Debut v Ireland, 13 February 1909.
Born: 2 July 1887, Dunedin, New Zealand; Died: 16 October 1963.
Educated: Waitaki Boys' High School (New Zealand), Otago University (New Zealand).
Clubs: London Hospital, Harlequins, Eastern Counties, Barbarians.
Palmer, who was a major in the RAMC during World War Two, and a surgeon in gynaecological and obstetrics at King's Hospital, London, scored two tries and a conversion on his international debut.

PALMER
F.H.

Wing. 1905 (Richmond, 1 cap).
Debut v Wales, 14 January 1905.
Born: 6 August 1877.
Educated: Bedford Grammar School.
Clubs: Richmond, Middlesex, Barbarians.

PALMER
Godfrey Vaughan, CBE TD OBE

Wing. 1928 (Richmond, 3 caps).
Debut v Ireland, 11 February 1928.
Born: 21 February 1900; Died: 28 April 1972.
Educated: Monmouth School, Royal Military Academy (Sandhurst).
Clubs: Cross Keys, Harlequins, Richmond, Combined Services, Hampshire, Barbarians.
Palmer scored two tries against France in 1928, then retired from international rugby before the 1929 season. He served in the Queen's Regiment, represented the Army 12 times, against the RAF, French Army and Royal Navy. He was awarded the OBE and the US Legion of Merit in 1944 and the CBE and TD in 1945, in which year he became the first governor of the British zone of occupied Vienna. He reached the rank of brigadier.

PALMER
John Anthony

Centre. 1984-1986 (Bath, 3 caps).
Debut v South Africa, 2 June 1984.
Born: 13 February 1957, Malta.
Educated: Prior Park College (Bath), St Mary's College (Twickenham).
Club: Bath.
He went on the England Under-23 tour of Canada and the USA in 1977 and on the England 'B' tour of Romania in 1978. He captained the Bath side which won the JPS Cup for the third successive time in 1986, equalling the record set by Leicester in 1981. He is a school teacher.

PARGETTER
Thomas Alfred

Lock. 1962-1963 (Coventry, 3 caps).
Debut v Scotland, 17 March 1962.
Born: 21 July 1932.
Educated: King Edward VI School (Stratford upon Avon), Cambridge University.
Clubs: Cambridge University (no Blue), Moseley, Coventry, Warwickshire, Midland Counties.
A member of the Warwickshire side that won the County Championship in 1962. Employed as a baker, he also played cricket for Warwickshire 2nd XI.

PARKER
Graham Wilshaw, OBE TD

Full-back. 1938 (Gloucester, 2 caps).
Debut v Ireland, 12 February 1938.
Born: 11 February 1912, Bristol.
Educated: the Gloucester Crypt School, Cambridge University.
Clubs: Cambridge University (Blues 1932-5), Gloucester, Blackheath, Gloucestershire (15 appearances), Barbarians
Parker scored a penalty-goal and converted six out of seven tries on his international debut, a record for a first match for England. He also holds the England record for most conversions in an international, a distinction shared with J.E.Greenwood. He won cricket Blues and also played for Gloucestershire CCC from 1935 to 1951 and was secretary from 1968 to 1969. A teacher, he worked at Dulwich College and later at Blundell's School. Parker skippered Cambridge University against the New Zealanders in 1935. He was a member of the Gloucestershire side that won the County Championship in 1937.

PARKER
Sydney

Forward. 1874-1875 (Liverpool, 2 caps).
Debut v Scotland, 23 February 1874.
Born: 3 October 1853; Died: 21 May 1897, London.
Educated: Rugby School.
Clubs: Liverpool, Lancashire.
Fifth son of the 6th Earl of Macclesfield, he was a tea planter.

PARSONS
Ernest Ian, DFC

Full-back. 1939 (RAF, 1 cap).
Debut v Scotland, 18 March 1939.
Born: 24 October 1912, Christchurch, New Zealand; Died: 14 October 1940, Italy (killed in action).
Educated: Christchurch Boys' High School (New Zealand), Canterbury University (New Zealand).
Clubs: Hull & East Riding, Yorkshire (6 appearances).
A member of the 1938 Calcutta Cup-winning side, he played in England's last international match before the outbreak of World War Two, during which he was killed whilst serving as a pilot-officer with Bomber Command.

PARSONS
Michael James

Lock. 1968 (Northampton, 4 caps).
Debut v Wales, 20 January 1968.
Born: 13 March 1943.
Educated: King's School (Canterbury).
Clubs: Oxford City, Northampton, Oxfordshire (over 25 appearances).
He won his first cap after only one trial match and was in the Calcutta Cup team of 1968. In 1965 he helped Oxfordshire become the first 'southern group' county to reach the County Championship semi-finals, a feat they repeated 12 months later. He is a farmer.

PATTERSON
William Michael

Centre. 1961 (Sale, 2 caps).
Debut v South Africa, 7 January 1961.
Born: 11 April 1936, Newcastle upon Tyne.
Educated: Sale Grammar School.
Clubs: Sale, Wasps, Cheshire, Barbarians.
A member of the 1961 Calcutta Cup-winning side, he went on the British Lions tour of New Zealand in 1959 before gaining his first England cap. He toured Canada with England in 1967 and captained North-West Counties against South Africa in November 1960.

PATTISSON
Richard Murrills

Forward. 1883 (Blackheath, 2 caps).
Debut v Ireland, 5 February 1883.
Born: 5 August 1860, Tonbridge; Died: 28 November 1948.
Educated: Tonbridge School, Cambridge University.
Clubs: Cambridge University (Blues 1881-2), Gipsies, Blackheath.
A barrister, he was called to Bar in 1888.

PAUL
J.E.

Forward. 1875 (Royal Indian Engineering College, 1 cap).
Debut v Scotland, 8 March 1875.
Club: Royal Indian Engineering College.

PAYNE
Arthur Thomas

Number 8. 1935 (Bristol, 2 caps).
Debut v Ireland, 9 February 1935.
Born: 11 November 1908; Died: 7 June 1968.

Clubs: Bristol, Gloucestershire.

He made 163 appearances for the Bristol club between 1931 and 1938.

PAYNE
Colin Martin

Lock. 1964-1966 (Harlequins, 10 caps).
Debut v Ireland, 8 February 1964.
Born: 19 May 1937.

Educated: Sherborne School, Oxford University.

Clubs: Oxford University (Blue 1960), Harlequins, Warwickshire, Surrey, Barbarians.

Payne, who was employed as a television engineer, was captain of the Harlequins from 1962 to 1964.

PAYNE
John Henry

Half-back. 1882-1885 (Broughton, 7 caps).
Debut v Scotland, 4 March 1882.
Born: 19 March 1858, Broughton; Died: 24 January 1942, Victoria Park, Manchester.

Educated: Manchester Grammar School, St John's College, Cambridge University.

Clubs: Cambridge University (Blue 1879), Broughton, Lancashire (23 appearances, later as captain).

John Payne was considered to be one of the most 'scientific' half-backs of his time, credited with bringing about many of the reforms introduced for the purification of rugby football. He played for Withington FC, which was then absorbed by the Broughton club, and represented Lancashire on the RFU. Son of John Brown Payne, a well-known cricketer in the north, John Henry Payne kept wicket for Broughton CC, Cambridge University and Lancashire, was a Somerset Exhibitioner and as a solicitor was a member of Payne, Galloway & Payne of Manchester, specialising in workmen's compensation.

PEARCE
Gary Stephen

Prop. 1979-1988 (Northampton, 35 caps).
Debut v Scotland, 3 February 1979.
Born: 2 March 1956.

Educated: Mandeville County School (Aylesbury).

Clubs: Aylesbury, Northampton, Buckinghamshire, Midlands, Barbarians.

Gary Pearce is England's most capped prop. He went on the tours to the Far East in 1979, to Argentina in 1981, to South Africa in 1984 and to New

Gary Pearce

Zealand in 1985. He also played for an England XV v Canada in 1983, but no caps awarded. In 1991 he was a member of Northampton's Pilkington Cup Final team. He is a surveyor.

PEARSON
A.W.

Full-back. 1875-1878 (Blackheath, 7 caps).
Debut v Ireland, 15 February 1875).
Born: 1854.
Educated: Blackheath Proprietory School.
Clubs: Guy's Hospital, Blackheath.

An excellent place-kicker, he converted one of England's two tries on his international debut. He never worked at Guy's Hospital and entered only to play in the Hospital Cup games, being a member of their 1885 Cup-winning team. In 1880 he went to Australia to farm.

PEART
Thomas George Anthony Hunter

Number 8. 1964 (Hartlepool Rovers, 2 caps).
Debut v France, 22 February 1964.
Born: 10 September 1936.
Educated: Sedbergh School.
Clubs: Blackheath, Army, Hartlepool Rovers, Durham County, Barbarians.

Peart played four games for the Army, against Royal Navy, RAF and French Army. He was captain of Hartlepool Rovers in 1964.

PEASE
Frank Ernest

Forward. 1887 (Hartlepool Rovers, 1 cap).
Debut v Ireland, 5 February 1887.
Born: 17 January 1864, Darlington; Died: 27 June 1957.
Educated: Harrow School.
Clubs: Darlington, Hartlepool Rovers, Durham County, Barbarians.

Pease, who was 93 when he died, was one of the original members of the Barbarians club.

PENNY
Sidney Herbert

Hooker. 1909 (Leicester, 1 cap).
Debut v Australia, 9 January 1909.
Born: 1875; Died: 1965.
Clubs: Leicester, Midland Counties (68 appearances).

Sid Penny set up a record of individual consecutive appearances for both club and county by appearing in 246 consecutive matches for Leicester and in 68 matches for the Midlands. In all he made 500 appearances for Leicester.

PENNY
W.J.

Full-back. 1878-1879 (United Hospitals, 3 caps).
Debut v Ireland, 11 March 1878.
Clubs: King's College Hospital, United Hospitals.

He scored a try on his international debut to become the first full-back to score for England.

PERCIVAL
Lancelot Jefferson (Revd), KCVO

Forward. 1891-1893 (Rugby, 3 caps).
Debut v Ireland, 7 February 1891.
Born: 22 May 1869; Died: 22 June 1941, Woking.
Educated: Clifton College, Oxford University.
Clubs: Oxford University (Blues 1889-91), Rugby, Midlands, Barbarians.

Percival became the Rugby club's first international player, although being capped whilst at Cambridge University. He was a minister, being ordained in 1895. He played cricket for Herefordshire between 1895 and 1901 and was made a KCVO in 1936.

PERITON
Harold Greaves

Flanker. 1925-1930 (Waterloo, 21 caps).
Debut v Wales, 17 January 1925.
Born: 8 March 1901; Died: April 1980.
Educated: Merchant Taylor's School (Crosby).
Clubs: Waterloo, Lancashire (64 appearances), Barbarians.

Waterloo's most capped player and the club's first international to be capped by England, Periton was of Irish descent. A great scrummaging forward, he had a unique niche in rugby football as the only Irishman to have captained England (four times) against his native country. A stockbroker by profession, during World War Two he served as an RAF liaison officer. He was in the 1928 Grand Slam team.

PERROTT
Edward Simcocks

Forward. 1875 (Old Cheltonians, 1 cap).
Debut v Ireland, 15 February 1875.
Born: 16 September 1852; Died: 22 April 1915.
Educated: Cheltenham College.
Clubs: Old Cheltonians, Middlesex.

Perrott moved to China to set up in business and after retirement he went to live somewhere in Montgomeryshire.

PERRY
David Gordon

Number 8. 1963-1966 (Bedford, 15 caps).
Debut v France, 23 February 1963.
Born: 26 December 1937.
Educated: Clifton College, Cambridge University.

Clubs: Cambridge University (Blue 1958), Harlequins, Bedford, London Counties, Surrey, Barbarians.

A member of the 1963 Championship and Calcutta Cup teams, he scored his first England try against Wales in January 1964 and captained England against Wales, Ireland, France and Scotland 1965. He scored another try against Wales in 1966. A member of the Oxford-Cambridge tour of the USA in 1959. He did his National Service in the Parachute Regiment.

PERRY
Samuel Victor

Lock. 1947-1948 (Cambridge University, Waterloo, 7 caps).
Debut v Wales, 18 January 1947.
Born: 16 July 1918.
Educated: King George V School (Southport), Cambridge University.
Clubs: Cambridge University (Blues 1946-7), Waterloo, Lancashire (12 appearances).

He was employed at Birmingham University.

PETERS
James ('Darkie')

Fly half. 1906-1908 (Plymouth, 5 caps).
Debut v Scotland, 16 March 1907.
Born: 1880 Salford; Died: March 1954.
Educated: Knowle School (Bristol).
Clubs: Knowle, Plymouth, Devon, Somerset, Barrow RL.

He scored England's only try on his debut against Scotland and made his own little niche in rugby history when he ran on to the field at Blackheath against Scotland in 1906 and became the first coloured man to play rugby for England. He was employed in the dockyards at Devonport and changed from the Union to the League code, when he joined Barrow in 1913.

PHILLIPS
Charles

Forward. 1880-1881 (Birkenhead Park, 3 caps).
Debut v Scotland, 28 February 1880.
Born: 14 August 1857; Died: 11 September 1940.
Educated: Rugby School, Oxford University.
Clubs: Oxford University (Blues 1876-9), Birkenhead Park, Cheshire.

Phillips was a solicitor.

PHILLIPS
Malcolm Stanley

Centre/Wing. 1958-1964 (Flyde, 25 caps).
Debut v Australia, 1 February 1958.
Born: 3 March 1935.
Educated: Arnold School (Blackpool), Oxford University.
Clubs: Oxford University (Blues 1956-9), Lancashire (captain 1962-5), Barbarians.

He learned rugby under the guidance of former Lancashire centre Bill Howarth, at Arnold School, joined Fylde whilst still at school and in 1958 became the club's first international capped direct from them, despite already having won caps whilst at Oxford University. He became an England selector and is still actively involved in the administration side in the north of England. He scored a try on his international debut and whilst serving in the Army represented BAOR at rugby and athletics. Once England's record cap holder and a member of the Barbarians committee, in November 1960 he played for North-West Counties against South Africa.

PICKERING
Arthur Stanley

Centre. 1907 (Harrogate, 1 cap).
Debut v Ireland, 9 February 1907.
Born: 24 March 1885, Dewsbury; Died: 17 February 1969.
Educated: Sedbergh School.
Clubs: Harrogate, Old Dewsburians, Headingley, Yorkshire (27 appearances, captain 1907-09), Barbarians.
He also represented Yorkshire at golf and was employed in the wool trade.

PICKERING
Roger David Austin

Scrum half. 1967-1968 (Bradford, 6 caps).
Debut v Ireland, 11 February 1967.
Born: 15 June 1943.
Educated: Whitecliffe Mount Grammar School (Cleckheaton), Hull University.
Clubs: Bradford, Yorkshire (52 appearances, captain 1968-9), Dax (France), Barbarians.
Whilst working as a schoolteacher in France, he played for the Dax club, where he partnered the French international, Pierre Albaladejo. He came out of retirement in 1975 when he led Yorkshire president Dennis Fox's XV against Giggleswick School in a match to celebrate the school's 500th year and 100 years of rugby there. In 1989 he joined the management team at Bradford and Bingley RFC.

PICKLES
Reginald Clarence Werrett, MC

Full-back. 1922 (Bristol, 2 caps).
Debut v Ireland, 11 February 1922.
Born: 11 December 1895.
Clubs: Bristol, Gloucestershire.
He was awarded the Military Cross in 1917, whilst on wartime service with the Royal Engineers.

PIERCE
Richard

Forward. 1898-1903 (Liverpool, 2 caps).
Debut v Ireland, 5 February 1898.
Born: 30 May 1875.
Educated: Charterhouse School.

Clubs: Liverpool, Lancashire (34 appearances), Barbarians.

PILKINGTON
William Norman, DSO

Wing. 1898 (Cambridge University, 1 cap).
Debut v Scotland, 12 March 1898.
Born: 26 July 1877; Died: 8 February 1935.
Educated: Clifton College, Cambridge University.
Clubs: Cambridge University (Blues 1896-7), St Helens Recreation, Lancashire, Blackheath, Barbarians.
Pilkington, who was the public schools hurdles champion in 1896, won athletics Blues for the 100 yards from 1897 to 1899. During World War One he served as a major in South Lancashire Regiment, was mentioned in despatches on three occasions, awarded the DSO in 1916 and a bar to that medal in 1919.

PILLMAN
Charles Henry ('Cherry'), MC

Flanker. 1910-1914 (Blackheath, 18 caps).
Debut v Wales, 15 January 1910.
Born: 8 January 1890; Died: 13 November 1955.
Educated: Tonbridge School.
Clubs: Blackheath, Kent, Barbarians.
Pillman created the custom, at scrummages, of detaching himself quickly from the side of the pack once opponents had heeled the ball, his fast pace enabling him to attack the opposing player before a move could be initiated.
He made his England debut as a 20-year-old in the first international to be played at Twickenham, in England's first Championship-winning season since 1892. A tall, slim figure, he was an all-round footballer and an excellent reader of the game. He was in the England side which won the Championship on four occasions before the outbreak of World War One, during which he won the Military Cross whilst serving with the Dragoon Guards. (His brother, Robert, also an England international, was killed in the conflict). In World War Two he was area flour officer for the South-East Division.
On the British Lions tour of South Africa in 1910, he was leading scorer with 65 points but broke a leg against Scotland in 1914, which ended his international career. He captained Blackheath in 1919-20 and played golf for the South of England against the North.

PILLMAN
Robert Lawrence

Flanker. 1914 (Blackheath, 1 cap).
Debut v France, 13 April 1914.
Born: 9 February 1893, Sidcup; Died: 9 July 1916, Armentieres.

Educated: Merton Court School (Sidcup), Rugby School.
Clubs: Blackheath, Kent, London Counties.
A solicitor, he was the brother of Charles, also an England international. He played in the last international, against France in Paris, before the outbreak of World War One. He died from his wounds whilst serving with the Royal West Kent Regiment. A scratch golfer.

PINCH
John

Forward. 1896-1897 (Lancaster, 3 caps).
Debut v Wales, 4 January 1896.
Born: 1871, Lancaster; Died: 1946, Lancaster.
Clubs: Lancaster, Lancashire (12 appearances).

PINCHING
William Wyatt ('Nipper')

Forward. 1872 (Guy's Hospital, 1 cap).
Debut v Scotland, 5 February 1872.
Born: 24 March 1851, Gravesend; Died: 16 August 1878.
Educated at King's College School (Wimbledon), Cheltenham College.
Club: Guy's Hospital (captain 1870-7).
Employed as senior surgeon on the SS *Eldorado*, he lost his life when he was washed overboard in a gale. Known as 'Conchy Bill', because of his long nose, or 'Nipper'.

PITMAN
Isaac James, KBE MP

Wing. 1922 (Oxford University, 1 cap).
Debut v Scotland, 18 March 1922.
Born: 14 August 1901, Kensington; Died: 1 September 1985, London.
Educated: Summer Field School (Oxford), Eton College, Oxford University.
Clubs: Oxford University (Blue 1921), Harlequins.
He also won Blues for athletics and skiing in 1922. A forceful right-wing, he was public schools middleweight boxing champion in 1919. Served during World War Two in the RAF and, as chairman of Royal Society of Teachers, he designed the initial teaching alphabet. He was awarded the KBE in 1961 and was Conservative MP for Bath from 1945 to 1964. A Director of the Bank of England, he worked for the Treasury between 1943 and 1945. He was the first Old Etonian to play for England at rugby.

PLUMMER
Kenneth Clive

Wing. 1969-1976 (Bristol, 4 caps).
Debut v Wales, 12 April 1969.
Born: 17 January 1947.
Clubs: Penryn, Bristol, Cornwall (52 appearances).
Employed as a car mechanic.

Francis Poole

POOLE
Francis Oswald

Forward. 1895 (Oxford University, 3 caps).
Debut v Wales, 5 January 1895.
Born: 17 December 1870; Died: 22 May 1949.
Educated: Cheltenham College, Oxford University.

Clubs: Oxford University (Blues 1891-4), Gloucester, Sunderland, Gloucestershire, Durham County, Barbarians.

He also won Blues at water polo (1892-5). A clergyman, he was ordained in 1895 and spent his life as curate in many areas of the country.

POOLE
Robert Watkins

Full-back. 1896 (Hartlepool Rovers, 1 cap).
Debut v Scotland, 14 March 1896.
Born: 4 November 1874, Hartlepool; Died: circa 1930-31.
Clubs: Hartlepool Old Boys, Hartle-pool Rovers, Durham County, Barbarians, Broughton Rangers RL.

The son of an army sergeant, he also won two England caps at Rugby League after changing codes in 1903.

POPE
Edward Brian

Scrum half. 1931 (Blackheath, 3 caps).
Debut v Wales, 17 January 1931.
Born: 29 June 1911.
Educated: Uppingham School, Cambridge University.
Clubs: Cambridge University (Blue 1932), Blackheath, Barbarians.
He was in the RAF during World War Two.

PORTUS
Garnet Vere

Fly half. 1908 (Blackheath, 2 caps).
Debut v France, 1 January 1908.
Born: 7 June 1883, Australia; Died: June 1954.
Educated: Maitland High School (Australia), Sydney University (Australia), Oxford University.
Clubs: Oxford University (no Blue), Blackheath, Barbarians.

He scored a try on his international debut. A clergyman, he was ordained in 1911. He returned to live in Australia and wrote many books, mainly about politics.

POULTON
Ronald William (later POULTON-PALMER)

Wing. 1909-1914 (Oxford University, Liverpool, 16 caps).
Debut v France, 30 January 1909.
Born: 12 September 1889, Oxford; Died: 4 May 1915, Ploegsteer, Belgium (killed in action).
Educated: Dragon School (Oxford), Rugby School, Oxford University.
Clubs: Oxford University (Blues 1909-11), Harlequins, Liverpool, East Midlands.

Ronald Poulton-Palmer has a special place in the history of the game, for he dominated the rugby world in the period before World War One, captaining England four times and scoring four tries in the last international before the war, against France in Paris. He began playing rugger whilst at Rugby School and appeared in the 1st XV from the age of 16. He scored five tries in the 1910 Varsity match, won a hockey Blue and was an excellent cricketer.

He served during World War One as a lieutenant in the Royal Berkshire Regiment and was killed by a sniper's bullet on the night of the 4 May 1915. He was the first officer of the regiment to fall and the Bishop of Pretoria (Dr Furse) officiated at his funeral at the battalion cemetery on the western edge of Plugstreet Wood, by the side of the Messines Road. His gravestone reads:

'His was the joy that made people smile, when they met him'. Many sources state that he died on 5 May 1915, but 4 May is recorded in the *Great War* records published by the Royal Berkshire Regiment.

His father was a professor of zoology at Oxford and he changed his name from Poulton to Poulton-Palmer when his uncle (G.W.Palmer) died in 1913 because implicit of his inheritance was a change of name which he adopted once his international career had finished, although he never lived to succeed the estate.

Poulton's last rugby match was played whilst his regiment was spending four days at Steenwerck and a game was staged at Port de Nieppe between the 4th and 48th Divisions. The latter side, which was victorious, was captained by Poulton-Palmer of the 1/4th Battalion.

POWELL
David Lewes

Prop. 1966-1971 (Northampton, 11 caps).
Debut v Wales, 15 January 1966.
Born: 17 May 1942, Rugby.
Educated: Daventry Grammar School.

David Powell

Clubs: Long Buckby, Rugby, Northampton, East Midlands, Barbarians.

A farmer, he went on the British Lions tour of Australia and New Zealand in 1966, when they lost all the Tests against the All Blacks.

PRATTEN
William Edgar

Lock. 1927 (Blackheath, 2 caps).
Debut v Scotland, 19 March 1927.
Born: 29 May 1907.
Educated: Marlborough College.
Clubs: Blackheath, Sidcup, Kent, Barbarians.

In 1927, Pratten helped Kent become the first south-east county to win the County Championship. During World War Two he served as a major in the Royal Artillery. The nephew of R.d'A Patterson.

PREECE
Ivor, JP

Fly half. 1948-1951 (Coventry, 12 caps).
Debut v Ireland, 14 February 1948.
Born: 15 December 1920, Coventry.
Clubs: Coventry, Warwickshire, Midland Counties, Barbarians.

Ivor Preece

A skilful and tactically-minded stand-off half and an excellent kicker of drop-goals, Ivor Preece is credited as the last player ever to drop a goal worth four points. This occurred in the Hartlepool Rovers v R.F.Oakes' International XV at Hartlepool in 1948. Preece was the Coventry club's record England cap holder with 12, until P.B.Jackson passed his tally. He was on the British Lions tour of Australia and New Zealand 1950 and is the father of Peter Preece, also an England international player. He became a JP in 1964.

PREECE
Peter Stuart

Wing-Centre. 1972-1976 (Coventry, 12 caps).
Debut v South Africa, 3 June 1972.
Born: 15 November 1949, Coventry.
Educated: King Henry VIII School (Coventry).
Clubs: Coventry, Warwickshire, Barbarians.

His first complete season in the Coventry 1st XV was in 1971-2, when he was top scorer with 32 tries, and the

following season he was a member of the side which won the RFU Club KO Cup. He played in regional trial held at Coventry in December 1971, for the Midland Counties side, and went on the England tour to South Africa in 1972. In Australia in 1975 he scored most tries (along with Alan Morley) in any tour match when he went over the line four times against New South Wales. He played cricket for Kenilworth, as well as golf, tennis and squash. A building society official, he is the son of Ivor Preece, also an England international.

PREEDY
Malcolm

Prop. 1984 (Gloucester, 1 cap).
Debut v South Africa, 2 June 1984.
Born: 15 September 1960, Gloucester.
Educated: Hucclecote Secondary School.
Club: Long Levens, Gloucester, Gloucestershire.

Preedy was a member of the Gloucester side which shared the RFU Club KO Cup with Moseley in 1981-2. That season he also played in the Gloucestershire side that reached the County Championship semi-finals.

PRENTICE
Frank Douglas

Number 8. 1928 (Leicester, 3 caps).
Debut v Ireland, 11 February 1928.
Born: 1897; Died: 3 October 1962.
Educated: Wyggeston School (Leicester).
Clubs: Westleigh, Leicester, Leicestershire, Barbarians.

Captain of the British Lions touring party to Australia and New Zealand in 1930 — the first occasion on which they were called 'Lions' — he was the last Englishman for 50 years to lead a Lions side. He was the side's second most prolific scorer in New Zealand, when the tourists won 20 of their 28 games, including one Test, scoring 624 points to 318. He retired as a player in 1931, becoming a national selector from 1932 to 1947. He continued to work as an administrator until ill health forced him to resign in 1962. In 1936, he was manager of the tour to Argentina and took over as secretary of the RFU at the end of World War Two, during which he had served as a lieutenant-colonel in the RASC. During World War One he was with the Royal Artillery.

PRESCOTT
Robert Edward ('Robin')

Flanker. 1937-1939 (Harlequins, 6 caps).
Debut v Wales, 16 January 1937.
Born: 3 April 1913; Died: 18 May 1975, Dartmouth.
Educated: Wells House Prep School, Marlborough College, Oxford University.
Clubs: Oxford University (Blues 1928-32), Harlequins, Army, Combined

Services, Guildford, Middlesex, Barbarians.

Prescott captained the English Services rugby team against Wales at Swansea in November 1943. He went on the RFU tour of South America in 1936 and was an England selector from 1949 to 1959 and vice president from 1962 until becoming paid secretary of the RFU the following year. He also represented Oxford University on the RFU in 1951-2. The son of Ernest Prescott (RFU president 1920-22) and the nephew of Curly Hammond. He left Rugby Union altogether in 1973, when he went to live in a house built for him in part of a garden belonging to Mark Sugden, the Wanderers and Ireland international. He sang in a choral society and was a solicitor by profession.

PRESTON
Nicholas John

Centre. 1979-1980 (Richmond, 3 caps).
Debut v New Zealand, 24 November 1979.
Born: 5 April 1948, Prestwich.

Nick Preston

Educated: Lancaster Grammar School, Nottingham University.
Club: Richmond.

PRICE
Herbert Leo, MC

Flanker. 1922-1923 (Harlequins, 4 caps).
Debut v Ireland, 11 February 1922.
Born: 21 June 1899; Died: 18 July 1943, Manchester.
Educated: Bishop's Stortford College, Oxford University.
Clubs: Oxford University (Blues 1920-21), Leicester, Harlequins, Surrey (12 appearances), Leicestershire, Barbarians.

Price had the distinction of being selected to play rugby and hockey for England on the same day (18 March 1922); he chose to play in the England-Scotland rugby match. He recorded one of the fastest tries in an international match when he went over the line straight from the kick-off against Wales in 1923 without an opponent touching the ball. He played 12 times for England at hockey (1921-4), won Blues for hockey (1921-2) and water polo (1919-22) and also played cricket for Oxford University.

PRICE
John

Lock. 1961 (Coventry, 1 cap).
Debut v Ireland, 11 February 1961.
Club: Coventry.

Price did not have a long rugby career in the UK as he emigrated to Australia.

PRICE
P.L.A.

Half-back. 1877-1878 (Royal Indian Engineering College, 3 caps).
Debut v Ireland, 5 February 1877.
Educated: Royal Indian Engineering College.
Club: Royal Indian Engineering College.

PRICE
Thomas William

Prop. 1948-1949 (Cheltenham, 6 caps).
Debut v Scotland, 20 March 1948.
Born: 26 July 1914; Died: 12 July 1991.
Educated: St Mark's School.
Clubs: Gloucester, Cheltenham, Gloucestershire, Barbarians.

Price is Cheltenham's most capped player.

PROBYN
Jeffrey Alan

Prop. 1988-1992 (Wasps, 33 caps).
Debut v France, 16 January 1988.
Born: 27 April 1956, London.
Educated: London Nautical School (Stamford Street).
Clubs: Old Albanians, Ilford Wander-

Jeff Probyn

John Pullen

ers, Streatham-Croydon, Richmond, Wasps, Askeans (summer 1991, played one game), Wasps again, Hertfordshire, Surrey, Middlesex, London.

Jeff Probyn, a member of the 1991 and 1992 Grand Slam sides, had a traumatic experience in the early days of his international career, when he was carried off with concussion in the England-Ireland match in 1989. He played for England 'B' v France, for the World XV v South Africa (1st Test) in 1989 and for the Home Unions v France, also in 1989. He went on the England tour of Argentina in 1990 and the tour of Australia and Fiji in 1991. He was a member of the 1987 and 1991 World Cup squads, although he did not play in the first tournament. In April 1986 he was a member of the Wasps team which lost to Bath in the JPS Cup Final. He enjoys sailing, shooting and fishing and has a brother who also plays rugby. Probyn's early schooling was intended for a career in the Merchant Navy but instead he joined the family furniture manufacturing business.

PROUT
Derek Henry

Wing. 1968 (Northampton, 2 caps).
Debut v Wales, 20 January 1968.
Born: 10 November 1942.

Educated: Cornwall Technical College, Loughborough Colleges.

Clubs: Launceston, Redruth, Loughborough Colleges, UAU, Northampton, South-West Counties, Cornwall (41 appearances), Barbarians.

His inclusion for his debut brought the number of Northampton players in the England team that day to five. A PE teacher, he is also a Volleyball Association coach.

PULLIN
John Vivian

Hooker. 1966-1976 (Bristol, 42 caps).

Debut v Wales, 15 January 1966.
Born: 1 November 1941, Australia.

Educated: Thornbury Grammar School, Cirencester Agricultural College.

Clubs: Bristol Saracens, Bristol, Gloucestershire, Barbarians.

Pullin shared, with Ken Kennedy (Ireland), the record of the world's most capped hooker (49 including seven British Lions caps). He also held the record of 42 caps for England, which stood until Tony Neary overtook it. Pullin captained England 13 times and holds the distinction of leading a home union to victories over South Africa, Australia and New Zealand. He went on England tours to Canada (1967), South Africa (1972, as captain), New Zealand (1973, as captain) and Australia (1975); and British Lions tours of South Africa in 1968, playing in 11 matches which included the 2nd, 3rd and 4th Tests, and Australia and New Zealand in 1971, appearing in all four Tests in New Zealand. He played for Bristol in the 1972-3 RFU Club KO Cup Final and toured South Africa with the Barbarians in 1968 as well as playing for them against New Zealand in 1973. He is a farmer.

PURDY
Stanley John

Flanker. 1962 (Rugby, 1 cap).
Debut v Scotland, 17 March 1962.
Born: 6 February 1936.

Educated: Lawrence Sheriff School (Rugby), Nottingham University.

Clubs: Nottingham University, UAU, Rugby, Army, Combined Services, Fylde, Warwickshire, Barbarians.

He was in the Education Corps and played four times for the Army in 1959-60, against the Royal Navy and the RAF. His last appearance for Rugby FC came in May 1972, when the club played in their annual match against the twin town of Evereux (Normandy). The French won 7-6 and Purdy played in the unaccustomed role of full-back.

PYKE
James

Forward. 1892 (St Helens Recreation, 1 cap).
Debut v Wales, 2 January 1892.
Born: 8 February 1866, St Helens; Died: 17 May 1941, St Helens.

Clubs: St Helens Recreation, Lancashire (15 appearances).

PYM
John Alfred, MC

Scrum half. 1912 (Blackheath, 4 caps).
Debut v Wales, 20 January 1912.
Born: 25 March 1891; Died: 9 February 1969.

Educated: Cheltenham College, Royal Military Academy (Woolwich).

Clubs: Blackheath, Kent, Barbarians.

Pym scored a try on his international debut and would have surely won many more caps but for an army career which took him to India at the end of 1912. He served during World War One as a Royal Artillery captain, seeing action in India, being wounded and mentioned in despatches on two occasions as well as winning the Military Cross and Bar. He took to farming in New Zealand, where he remained until his death.

QUINN
James Patrick

Centre. 1954 (New Brighton, 5 caps).
Debut v Wales, 16 January 1954.
Born: 19 February 1930, Widnes, Lancashire; Died: 18 January 1986, Leicester.

Educated: Wade Deacon High School (Widnes), Sheffield City Training College.

Clubs: Aldershot Services, Army, Car-

Mike Rafter

negie Hall, Harrogate, Hampshire, New Brighton, Lancashire (36 appearances), Leeds R.L.

Quinn went on the British Lions tour of South Africa in 1955 before changing codes to join Leeds in 1956, gaining Cup winners' medals with them in 1956 and 1959 (as captain). He was a fine centre who had energy for a sudden burst of speed, and a tremendous tackler who nearly always managed to bring down his man. A lawn tennis coach, as well as a swimming coach, he represented the Royal Military Police in the 1949 modern pentathlon championships. A rugby correspondent for the *Sunday Express* and BBC Radio Merseyside, he died in a car crash whilst driving home from the England-Wales international in 1986.

RAFTER
Michael

Flanker. 1977-1981 (Bristol, 17 caps).
Debut v Scotland, 15 January 1977.
Born: 31 March 1952, Bristol.

Educated: St Brendan's College (Bristol), St Luke's College (Exeter).

Club: Bristol.

In September 1963, Rafter entered senior school, where he met teacher Elqyn Price, who was to play an influential part in Rafter's rugby career. A nephew of Mike Pegler, Rafter's first love as a young boy was Bristol City AFC and he also enjoyed playing squash. He went on the England rugby tour to Japan, Fiji and Tonga in 1979, after playing for the England Under-19s and Under-23s. He also went with Gloucester on their trip to Rhodesia in 1976 and played for Gloucestershire when they won the 1983 County Championship. One of 11 children (six boys, five girls), he is now a teacher at Filton High School, Bristol. He is the nephew of former England player Sam Tucker.

RALSTON
Christopher Wayne

Lock. 1971-1975 (Richmond, 22 caps).
Debut v Scotland, 27 March 1971.

Born: 25 May 1944, London.

Educated: King William's College (Isle of Man).

Clubs: Richmond, Middlesex (captain 1977-80), London Counties.

Ralston, who was the 1,000th player to be capped by England, scored his country's first four-point try, against Ireland in 1972. He played for the Barbarians against Llanelli in 1972-3, went on the British Lions tour of South Africa in 1974, played for London Division v New Zealand in 1979 and that same year led Middlesex to the County Championship. He played in five Finals, three of them on the winning side. He is employed in the advertising industry.

RAMSDEN
Harold E.

Forward. 1898 (Bingley, 2 caps).
Debut v Scotland, 12 March 1898.

Clubs: Bingley, Yorkshire (14 appearances).

Ramsden made his Yorkshire debut against Lancashire in 1897 and his last appearance was against Cumberland in 1899. He was employed in the woollen industry.

RANSON
John Matthew

Wing. 1963-1964 (Rosslyn Park, 7 caps).
Debut v New Zealand, 25 May 1963.
Born: 26 July 1938.

Educated: Birmingham University.

Clubs: Durham City, Rosslyn Park, Headingley, Selby, Durham Counties, Middlesex, North Midlands, Barbarians.

He scored a try on his international debut. Employed as a teacher at Durham School and later at Birmingham University, in 1958 he joined the Arthur Guinness company.

RAPHAEL
John Edward

Wing. 1902-1906 (Old Merchant Taylor's, 9 caps).
Debut v Wales, 11 January 1902.
Born: 30 April 1882, Belgium; Died: 11 June 1917, Belgium.

Educated Merchant Taylor's School, Oxford University.

Clubs: Old Merchant Taylor's, Oxford University (Blues 1901-04), Surrey.

Raphael captained England and went on the RFU tour of Argentina in 1910. He also gained Blues at water polo (1902-04) and cricket (1903-05) and played cricket for Surrey from 1903 to 1906. A barrister, called to the Bar in 1908, he contested Croydon for the Liberal Party in the 1909 by-election. He served during World War One with the Duke of Wellington's Regiment and was wounded whilst fighting on Messines Ridge on 7 June 1917. He died

four days later. His name was a by-word for grace and elusiveness on the rugby field during the early part of the century.

RAVENSCOURT
John J.

Forward. 1881 (Birkenhead Park, 1 cap).
Debut v Ireland, 5 February 1881.
Born: 11 June 1857; Died: 18 August 1902, Argentina.

Educated: Rugby School, Oxford University.

Clubs: Oxford University (Blues 1877-8), Birkenhead Park, Cheshire.

RAWLINSON
William Cecil W.

Forward. 1876 (Blackheath, 1 cap).
Debut v Scotland, 6 March 1876.
Born: 17 December 1855; Died: 14 February 1898, Northampton.

Educated: Clifton College, Royal Military Academy (Sandhurst).

Club: Blackheath.

He was a major in the Lincolnshire Regiment.

REDFERN
S

Prop. 1984 (Leicester, 1984, 1 cap).
Debut v Ireland, 18 February 1984.

Clubs: Leicester; Sheffield.

Redfern made his international debut as a replacement for C. White. He was in Leicester's JPS Cup runners-up team in 1983.

REDMAN
Nigel Charles

Lock. 1984-1991 (Bath, 11 caps).
Debut v Australia, 3 November 1984.
Born: 16 August 1964, Cardiff.

Educated: Priory Comprehensive School (Weston-super-Mare), South Bristol Technical College.

Clubs: Weston-Super-Mare, Bath.

Redman played for England Colts in 1983, for England 'B' in 1986 and appeared in the first World Cup in 1987. He went on the 1990 tour of Argentina and on the tour to Australia and Fiji in 1991. He played in Bath's Pilkington Cup winning teams of 1983, 1984 and

Nigel Redman

1992. He has a younger brother who plays at Number 8 for Weston-super-Mare.

REDMOND
Gerald Francis

Number 8. 1970 (Cambridge University, 1 cap).
Debut v France, 18 April 1970.
Born: 23 March 1943.
Educated: St Luke's College, Cambridge University.
Clubs: Western Hornets, Cambridge University (Blues 1969-71), Bedford, St Luke's College, Weston-super-Mare, Bristol, Eastern Counties, Somerset (20 appearances).

REDWOOD
Brian William

Scrum half. 1968 (Bristol, 2 caps).
Debut v Wales, 20 January 1968.
Born: 6 February 1939.
Educated: Bristol Grammar School, Exeter University.
Clubs: Bristol, Gloucestershire.
Despite having only one good eye, he scored a try on his international debut and later became an England selector. He was employed at Rolls-Royce.

REES
Gary William

Flanker. 1984-1991 (Nottingham, 21 caps).
Debut v South Africa, 9 June 1984.
Born: 2 May 1960, Long Eaton, Derbyshire.

Educated: Trent College.
Clubs: Nottingham, Barbarians.
Rees, who joined Nottingham in 1978 as a full-back, went on the England Under-23 tours to Italy in 1982 and Romania in 1983. He played for the Midlands v New Zealand in 1983, was a member of England's 1987 World Cup party and toured Australia in 1988 and Australia and Fiji in 1991. In 1989-90 he played for the Barbarians against New Zealand, and in April 1991 appeared in the Rolls-Royce v President's XV game in memory of Andy Turner. He also played hockey and cricket at county schoolboy level. Employed in banking as a financial advisor.

REEVE
James Stanley Roope

Left-wing. 1929-1931 (Harlequins, 8 caps).
Debut v France, 1 April 1929.
Born: 12 September 1908, Kensington; Died: 6 November 1936.
Educated: Rugby School, Cambridge University.
Clubs: Cambridge University, Harlequins, Barbarians.
Reeve was also a noted hurdler and a keen cricketer, but he is one of a small group of Oxbridge internationals who never won a rugby Blue. A popular member of any side, he went on the British Lions tour to Australia and New Zealand in 1930 and scored a try in the Lions' First Test victory over the New Zealanders; in all he scored eight tries on the tour. A speedy, long-striding, natural left-winger, he had the ability to swerve off his left foot, enabling him to deceive opponents. The son of Judge Roope Reeve, he was a barrister and lost his life in a traffic accident.

REGAN
Martin

Fly half. 1953-1956 (Liverpool, 12 caps).
Debut v Wales, 17 January 1953.
Born: 24 September 1929, St Helens.
Educated: St Helens Catholic Grammar School, West Park Grammar School (St Helens), St Mary's College (Twickenham).
Clubs: St Helens, Liverpool, Blackheath, Lancashire (49 appearances), Barbarians, Warrington RL.
A quick, well-balanced fly half, Regan was a classy player 'who oozed style' as one Rugby League official described him. Employed as a PE teacher, he made 64 appearances for Warrington, scored 14 tries and 15 goals.

RENDALL
Paul Anthony George ('Judge').

Prop. 1984-1991 (Wasps, 28 caps).
Debut v Wales, 17 March 1984.

Born: 18 February 1954, London.
Educated: St Joseph's School (Slough).
Clubs: Slough, Buckinghamshire, Wasps, Askeans, Middlesex, Southern Counties, London Division, Barbarians.

Rendall, who was a member of the 1987 and 1991 World Cup squads, played for England 'B' against France in 1981 and went on the England tour of Argentina that year but sprained his shoulder in the first game and was unable to play again on the tour. He was in the England 'B' side against Italy in 1982, when he also turned out against the USA in a game for which no caps were awarded, and played for an England XV v Canada in 1983, for the World XV v New Zealand in Tokyo 1987, and for an International XV v South Africa in 1989, when he appeared in two Tests. He captained Wasps in 1982-3 and was in London Counties' 1990 Toshiba Divisional Championship side. He is a self-employed engineer. In 1991-2 he was coach at Bracknell RUFC.

REW
Henry

Lock. 1929-1934 (Blackheath, 9 caps).
Debut v Scotland, 16 March 1929.
Born: 11 November 1906; Died: 11 December 1940, Libya.
Educated: Exeter School.
Clubs: Exeter, Blackheath, Army, Devon, Barbarians.

Rew joined the Army in 1928, when he became a commissioned officer in the Royal Tank Corps. The following year, without appearing in an England trial, he won his first cap and by the time he was picked for the British Lions tour to Australia and New Zealand in 1930, he had four caps to his credit. He was a muscular, powerful scrummager, whose technique earned him the respect of his opponents. In 1934 he was a member of the England side which won the Triple Crown. He left England for India in 1935, to run a small arms school, and served mainly in France during World War Two, although it was at Tripolitania in Libya where he died of wounds, when he was a Tank Corps major.

REYNOLDS
Frank Jeffrey

Fly half. 1937-1938 (Old Cranleighans, 3 caps).
Debut v Scotland, 20 March 1937.
Born: 2 January 1916, China.

Educated: Cranleigh School, Royal Military Academy (Sandhurst).

Clubs: Old Cranleighans, Army, Blackheath, Kent, Barbarians.

Reynolds had a very safe pair of hands, was pin-point accurate in his line-kicking and always cheerful. He was one of three Old Cranleighans who went on the British Lions visit to South Africa in 1938 but in the Second Test he was badly injured and unable to play again on the tour. He played hockey for Kent and also appeared for that county's 2nd XI at cricket. He served during World War Two with the Duke of Wellington's Regiment and was mentioned in despatches twice. Whilst on tour in 1938 he had met a South African girl, whom he married. They eventually returned to Southern Africa and settled in Salisbury, where he later went into hotel management.

REYNOLDS
Shirley

Forward. 1900 (Richmond, 4 caps).
Debut v Wales, 6 January 1900.
Born: 1874; Died: 9 January 1946, Epsom.

Clubs: Christ's Hospital, Richmond, Barbarians.

RHODES
John

Forward. 1896 (Castleford, 3 caps).
Debut v Wales, 4 January 1896.
Clubs: Castleford, Yorkshire (15 appearances), Hull Kingston Rovers RL.

He switched to Northern Union with Hull Kingston Rovers in 1897.

RICHARDS
Dean

Number 8. 1986-1992 (Leicester, 31 caps).

Dean Richards

Debut v Ireland, 1 March 1986.
Born: 11 July 1963, Nuneaton.

Educated: John Cleveland College (Hinckley).

Clubs: Roanne (France), Leicester, Barbarians, Leicestershire, Midlands.

Policeman Dean Richards, who is now England's most capped number-eight, was the first England forward to score two tries on his debut since H.Wilkinson did so against Wales in 1929. Richards played for England Schools at lock and made his debut for the Under-23s against Romania. Richards went on the British Lions tour of Australia in 1987, playing in three Tests, and appeared in the 1987 World Cup. He suffered a recurring dislocated shoulder in 1989-90, an injury that ruled him out of England's International Championship side that season. In September 1990 he played for England against the Barbarians (no caps awarded) and toured Australia and Fiji in 1991. In 1990-91 he was named 'Whitbread/*Rugby World* Player of the Year. He played in the 1991 and 1992 Grand Slam sides. Richards captained Leicester for two years until the end of 1990-91. His father played for Nuneaton and in the 1990 World Cup.

RICHARDS
Ernest Edward

Scrum half. 1929 (Plymouth Abion, 2 caps).
Debut v Scotland, 16 March 1929.
Born: 11 March 1905, Plymouth.

Clubs: Penryn, Plymouth Albion, Devon, London Highfield RL.

He served in the Royal Navy and later worked as a bricklayer.

RICHARDS
Joseph

Forward. 1891 (Bradford, 3 caps).
Debut v Wales, 3 January 1891.
Clubs: Bradford, Yorkshire (12 appearances).
He made his Yorkshire debut against Lancashire and his last appearance against Somerset.

RICHARDS
Stephen Brookhouse

Hooker. 1965-1967 (Richmond, 9 caps).
Debut v Wales, 16 January 1965.
Born: 28 August 1941, West Kirby.
Educated: Clifton College, Oxford University.
Clubs: Oxford University (Blue 1962), Richmond, Bristol, Sheffield, Middlesex.
A solicitor, he went on the Oxford-Cambridge tour of East Africa, Rhodesia and South Africa in 1963 and the England tour of Canada in 1967.

RICHARDSON
James Vere

Centre. 1928 (Birkenhead Park, 5 caps).
Debut v New South Wales, 7 January 1928.
Born: 16 December 1903.
Educated: Uppingham School, Oxford University.
Clubs: Oxford University (Blue 1925), Birkenhead Park, Richmond, Cheshire (21 appearances), Middlesex, Barbarians.
In his only international season, England recorded five wins in five matches for the first time in their history and he scored 23 points, including eight conversions, which equalled the record for a season set by Len Stokes in 1881. In 1927-8 he played for Combined Cheshire-Lancashire v NSW 'Waratah's'. He also won cricket and hockey Blues in 1925 and played for Essex CCC from 1924 to 1926. During World War Two he served as a major in the Royal Artillery. In November 1971, Richardson, who was a stockbroker, attended the banquet celebrating Birkenhead's centenary.

RICHARDSON
William Ryder

Half-back. 1881 (Manchester, 1 cap).
Debut v Ireland, 5 February 1881.
Born: 1861; Died: 30 July 1920.
Educated: Manchester Grammar School, Oxford University.
Clubs: Oxford University (Blue 1881), Manchester, Lancashire.
He was the first schoolboy to be capped for England, making his first appearance whilst still at Manchester Grammar School. During World War One he served as a lieutenant in the West Yorkshire Regiment. He was the secretary of Royal St George Golf Club, Sandwich, from 1900 to 1920, taking office when the club abandoned its completely amateur administration and appointed a full-time secretary. He lived in Sandwich and was appointed at a salary of £350 per annum.

RICKARDS
Cyril Henry

Forward. 1873 (Gipsies, 1 cap).
Debut v Scotland, 3 March 1873.
Born: 11 January 1854; Died: 25 February 1920.
Educated: Rugby School, Cheltenham College, Royal Military Academy (Woolwich).
Club: Gipsies.

RIMMER
Gordon

Scrum half. 1949-1954 (Waterloo, 12 caps).
Debut v Wales, 15 January 1949.
Born: 28 February 1925, Southport.
Educated: King George V School (Southport).
Clubs: Wigan Old Boys, Waterloo, Lancashire (78 appearances), North-West Counties.
He played for the British Lions on their tour of New Zealand in 1950 and captained North-West Counties against the New Zealanders in February 1954. During World War Two he served with the Fleet Air Arm. He was employed in the brewing industry and later worked as a sports outfitter. He played golf for Lancashire.

RIMMER
Lawrence Ivor

Flanker. 1961 (Bath, 5 caps).
Debut v South Africa, 7 January 1961.
Educated: Birkenhead School, Oxford University.
Clubs: Oxford University (Blue 1958), Old Birkonians, Bath, Cheshire, Dorset, Wiltshire, North-West Counties.
Rimmer played for the North-West Counties against South Africa in November 1960. A school teacher, he also played cricket for the Authentics and Free Foresters and went on the 1959 Oxford-Cambridge tour to the Far East.

RIPLEY
Andrew George

Number 8. 1972-1976 (Rosslyn Park, 24 caps).
Debut v Wales, 15 January 1972.
Born: 1 December 1947.
Educated: Greenway Comprehensive School (Bristol), University of East Anglia.
Clubs: Rosslyn Park, Middlesex, Barbarians.
Andy Ripley is Rosslyn Park's most capped player and president in 1989-

Andy Ripley

90. He went on the British Lions tour of South Africa in 1974 and the England tours of South Africa in 1972 and Australia in 1975. He began playing rugby as a 19-year-old — playing soccer until then — and broke many of his bones before retiring in 1989.

His other sporting talents extend to being a British Canoe Union instructor, basketball player, triathlon champion, member of Polytecnic Harriers (for whom he recorded some fast AAA 400-metre hurdle times, reaching the semi-final 1978) and he also plays tennis, sails and water skis. He worked for the United Bank of Kuwait as a deputy general manager and is the author of *Rugby Rubbish* (published 1985) with a second book due to be published in 1992.

He has two businesses, *DART* a teaching company for chartered accountants (Ripley is a chartered accountant) and *Incredibly Fit Co*, which markets rugby gear. He is a director of the Esprit Health Club in London and, being able to speak fluent French, he provided commentary on the 1991 World Cup for

French TV. He writes a regular sports column for a Sunday newspaper and produced an award-winning video (*Andy Ripley's Workout for Men*). His charity work provides him with an involvement with the Bristol Sporting Association for the Disabled and Sports Aid Foundation, as well as the Aston Charity Trust for Homeless People.

RISMAN
Augustus Beverley Walter

Fly-half-Centre. 1959-1961 (Loughborough Colleges, 8 caps).
Debut v Wales, 17 January 1959.
Born: 23 November 1937, Salford.

Educated: Cockermouth Grammar School, Loughborough Colleges, Manchester University.

Clubs: Loughborough Colleges, UAU, Cumberland, North-West Counties, Lancashire (24 appearances), Leigh RL, Leeds RL.

On the British Lions tour of Australia and New Zealand in 1959, he played as a fly-half in four Tests before chipping an ankle bone on the eve of the 2nd Test against New Zealand, recovering to play in the final Test. He turned out for North-West Counties against the South Africans in November 1960 and played lawn tennis for the UAU and Cumberland. The son of Gus Risman, who also played Rugby League, he was said to be one of the most 'complete' players of his day. In 1968 he gained a Challenge Cup winners' medal with Leeds and played full-back for Great Britain in five internationals, captaining the British side which played in the World Cup. In his last Rugby League Test match, against New Zealand, he kicked seven goals. He is a school master.

RITSON
John Anthony Sydney, DSO OBE MC TD

Forward. 1910-1913 (Northern, 8 caps).
Debut v France, 12 February 1910.
Born: 18 August 1887; Died: 16 October 1957, Guildford.

Educated: Uppingham School, Durham University, Edinburgh University.

Clubs: Northern, Northumberland, Barbarians.

He went on the British Lions tour of New Zealand in 1908, before he was capped by England. He worked as an HM Mines inspector and served in World War One as a major in the Durham Light Infantry. He was mentioned in despatches twice and awarded the Military Cross in 1917, the DSO in 1918 and the OBE in 1935.

RITTSON-THOMAS
George Christopher

Flanker. 1951 (Oxford University, 3 caps).
Debut v Wales, 20 January 1951.

Born: 18 December 1926.

Educated: Dragon Prep School (Oxford), Sherborne School, Oxford University.

Club: Oxford University (Blues 1949-50).

He scored a try on his international debut, won a swimming Blue in 1949 and was an Olympic trialist. He worked for Lloyds Bank.

ROBBINS
Graham Leslie

Number 8. 1986 (Coventry, 2 caps).
Debut v Wales, 18 January 1986.
Born: 24 September 1956, Sutton Coldfield.

Educated: Fairfax High School.

Clubs: Coventry, Midlands.

A former England Colts player, he was out of rugby for over a year due to a cartilage injury which needed two major operations to mend. He played for England 'B' against Ireland in 1985.

ROBBINS
Peter George Derek

Flanker. 1956-1962 (Oxford University, Moseley, Coventry, 19 caps).
Debut v Wales, 21 January 1956.
Born: 21 September 1933.

Educated: Bishop Vesey Grammar School (Sutton Coldfield), Oxford University.

Clubs: Oxford University (Blues 1954-7, captain 1957), Moseley, Coventry, Warwickshire, Barbarians.

A school teacher, Peter Robbins is Moseley's most capped player. He went on the Oxford-Cambridge tour of the USA and Canada in 1955, to the Argentine in 1956 and to East Africa and Rhodesia in 1957 and on the visit to East Africa and South Africa in 1963 as manager. He also played for the International XV which met Wales in April 1957, in a match organised to raise funds so that Cardiff could stage the Empire games in 1957. He retired from rugby in 1965 and went to live in France, working as a director of an industrial cleaning company, when he was a regular broadcaster on Radio Monte Carlo. A rugby correspondent for the *Financial Times* and *Observer* newspapers, he was a public relations manager of a London property company in the mid 1970s.

ROBERTS
Alan Dixon, MC

Wing. 1911-1914 (Northern, 8 caps).
Debut v Wales, 21 January 1911.
Born: 1887; Died: 1 September 1940.

Educated: Durham School, Cambridge University.

Clubs: Cambridge University, Northern, Northumberland, Barbarians.

Roberts scored a try on his international debut and five altogether in his eight appearances for England. A solicitor by profession, he served in World War One

as a private with the Royal Fusiliers and was wounded and awarded the Military Cross when a temporary second lieutenant attached to the Welch Regiment in which he later served as a captain.

ROBERTS
Ernest William, OBE

Forward. 1901-1907 (Royal Naval College, 6 caps).
Debut v Wales, 5 January 1901.
Born: 14 November 1878, Lowestoft; Died: 19 November 1933, Manchester.

Educated: Framlingham School, Merchant Taylor's School (Crosby), Royal Navy Engineering College (Keyham), Royal Naval College (Dartmouth).

Clubs: Royal Naval College (Dartmouth), Royal Navy, Devon, Barbarians.

Roberts was the first services player to captain an international team, when he skippered England against Scotland in 1907. He was a member of the Devon side which won the County Championship in 1901 and one of the founder members of Royal Navy RFU in 1906. He represented the Navy on the RFU committee, was a Navy selector and became secretary of the Royal Navy RFU when he retired from playing. Amongst his contemporaries were J.C.Matters and S.F.Coopper. In the Navy, he reached the rank of rear admiral and served during World War One with the Grand Fleet.

ROBERTS
Geoffrey Dorling ('Khaki'), OBE QC

Forward. 1907-1908 (Harlequins, 3 caps).
Debut v Scotland, 16 March 1907.
Born: 27 August 1886; Died: 7 March 1967.

Educated: Rugby School, Oxford University.

Clubs: Oxford University (Blues 1907-08), Harlequins, Exeter, Devon, Barbarians.

Called to Bar in 1912, he served in the Devonshire Regiment during World War One, reached the rank of major, was mentioned in despatches five times and was later Deputy Assistant Adjutant General. He was Recorder of Exeter from 1932 to 1946, when he was appointed as one of the prosecutors at the Nuremburg War Crimes trials, and Recorder of Bristol from 1946 to 1960. 'Khaki' Roberts, who also won a tennis Blue, played for Harlequins Past v Harlequins Present in a match in aid of King Edward VII Hospital Fund in April 1922.

ROBERTS
James

Left-wing. 1960-1964 (Sale, 8 caps).
Debut v Wales, 16 January 1960.
Born: 25 June 1932.

Educated: Millhill School, Cambridge University.

Clubs: Cambridge University (Blues 1952-4), Old Millhillians, Sale, Middlesex, Barbarians.

Roberts, who scored two tries on his international debut, spent more than a decade in top flight rugger. Before business took him north he regularly turned out for the Old Millhillians club.

ROBERTS
Reginald Sidney

Hooker. 1932 (Coventry, 1 cap).
Debut v Ireland, 13 February 1932.
Born: 1911, Coventry.

Clubs: Coventry, Warwickshire, Huddersfield RL.

He moved into Rugby League with Huddersfield in 1932.

ROBERTS
Samuel

Full-back. 1887 (Swinton, 2 caps).
Debut v Wales, 8 January 1887.
Club: Swinton.

ROBERTS
Victor George

Flanker. 1947-1956 (Penryn, Harlequins, 16 caps).
Debut v France, 19 April 1947.
Born: 6 August 1924, Penryn.

Educated: Falmouth Grammar School.

Clubs: Harlequins, Penryn, Swansea, Cornwall (45 appearances), Barbarians.

Penryn's most capped player, he scored a try on his international debut and captained England twice. A skilful, organised wing-forward with a very safe pair of hands at the line-out, he went on the British Lions tour of Australia and New Zealand in 1950. He was a member of the Barbarians committee. During World War Two he served as a lieutenant in the RNVR and was later employed as a Customs and Excise officer.

ROBERTSHAW
Albert Rawson

Back-Centre. 1886-1887 (Bradford, 5 caps).
Debut v Wales, 2 January 1886.
Born: 1861, Bradford; Died: 17 November 1920.

Clubs: Bradford, Yorkshire (9 appearances).

Albert Robertshaw's conception of centre-threequarter play, which he introduced around 1886, has endured down the years. He was with Bradford when they helped to form the Northern Union in 1895. He was the brother of Percy Robertshaw, also of Bradford, who was picked to play for England in 1888 but never made an appearance because of the dispute over the formation of the International Board.

ROBINSON
Arthur

Forward. 1889-1890 (Blackheath, 4 caps).
Debut v Maoris, 16 February 1889.
Born: 8 November 1865, Darlington; Died: 9 April 1948.

Educated: Cheltenham College, Cambridge University.

Clubs: Cambridge University (Blues 1886-7), Hartlepool Rovers, Blackheath, Middlesex.

He was also 'capped' in the 1888 England side which did not play. A barrister, he was called to the Bar in 1890. He played cricket for Durham CC.

ROBINSON
Ernest T.

Hooker. 1954-1961 (Coventry, 4 caps).
Debut v Scotland, 20 March 1954.
Born: 17 January 1929.

Club: Coventry.

One of four new caps in the England side which met the Scots in 1954, he had a seven-year gap between appearances. Employed as an engineer.

ROBINSON
George Carmichael ('Tot'), JP

Wing. 1897-1901 (Percy Park, 8 caps).
Debut v Ireland, 6 February 1897.
Born: 1876; Died: 29 May 1940.

Educated: Dame Allan's School (Newcastle upon Tyne).

Clubs: Gosforth, Percy Park, Northumberland, Blackheath, Barbarians.

George Robinson, the first of a line of Northumberland players to win England caps, scored a try in each of his first five international matches and altogether scored eight tries in eight matches for England. He represented Northumberland on the RFU from 1923 to 1940, was an England selector from 1921 to 1929 and RFU president from 1939 to 1940. A scratch golfer. He was a JP from 1932 to 1940.

ROBINSON
John James

Forward. 1893-1902 (Headingley, 4 caps).
Debut v Scotland, 4 March 1893.
Born: 28 June 1872, Burton upon Trent; Died: 3 January 1959, Leeds.

Educated: Appleby Grammar School, Cambridge University.

Clubs: Cambridge University (Blue 1892), Headingley, Burton, Midlands, Yorkshire (7 appearances), Barbarians.

Robinson won his second cap ten years after his first international appearance, an interval between caps which is still an England record, although J.E. Williams equalled it in 1965. He became the first international from Headingley, although he was also a Cambridge undergraduate at the time.

A solicitor, he also won a cricket Blue in 1894.

ROBINSON
Richard Andrew ('Andy')

Flanker. 1988-1989 (Bath, 7 caps).
Debut v Australia, 12 June 1988.
Born: 3 April 1964, Taunton.

Educated: Loughborough Colleges.

Clubs: Loughborough Students, Taunton, Bath, South-West Division.

One of the best ball-winners in the game, Andy Robinson had early representative experience with Somerset Under-19s and West of England Schools. He suffered a broken knee cap whilst at Loughborough but captained Loughborough Students to the 1986 UAU title. He made his debut for Bath when they inflicted Pontypool's first home defeat for 20 years. Robinson played in the 1990 and 1992 Pilkington Cup-winning sides and succeeded Stuart Barnes as Bath's captain in June 1991.

Andy Robinson

He was Whitbread's Player of the Year in 1989, and in 1990 he toured Argentina with the British Lions, led the South-West Division and skippered the England 'B' team which beat Namibia. His father captained Somerset and the Royal Navy and was coach of Somerset; his brother Sean plays for Saracens; and another brother, Peter, turns out for Taunton. Andy Robinson is a PE teacher.

ROBSON
Alan

Hooker. 1924-1926 (Northern, 5 caps).
Debut v Wales, 19 January 1924.
Clubs: Northern, Northumberland.

He is the brother-in-law of Herbert Whitley, also a Northern and England player.

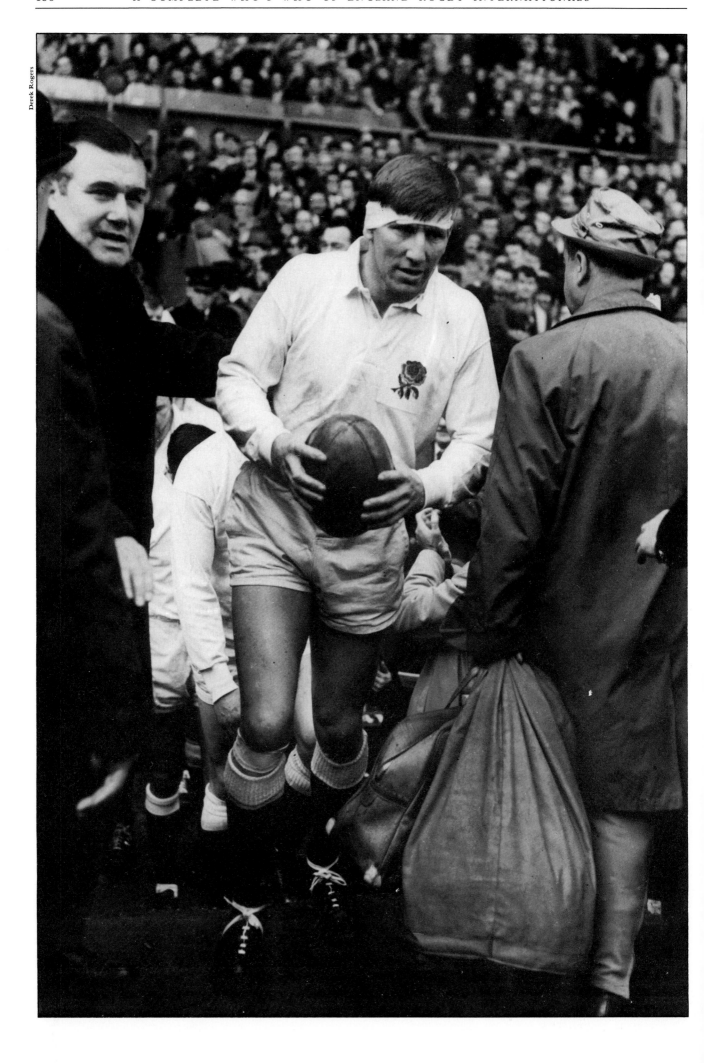

Derek Rogers

ROBSON
Matthew

Centre. 1930 (Oxford University, 4 caps).
Debut v Wales, 18 January 1930.
Born: 16 December 1908; Died: 30 November 1983, Edinburgh.
Educated: George Heriot's School, Oxford University.
Clubs: Heriot's FP, Oxford University (Blue 1929), Blackheath, Northumberland, Barbarians.

He worked in the Colonial Office, and served in World War Two with the Royal West African Frontier Force. His try and drop-goal won the 1929 Varsity match for Oxford.

RODBER
Timothy Andrew Keith

Number 8. 1992 (Northampton, 2 caps).
Debut v Scotland, 18 January 1992.
Born: 2 July 1969, Richmond, Yorkshire.
Educated: Churchers School, Oxford Polytechnic.
Clubs: Oxford Old Boys, Petersfield, Army, Northampton.

Tim Rodber had an unhappy debut, being taken from the field against Scotland suffering from a spinal injury. When he won his first full cap, Rodber was at Sandhurst on an officer training course. He was due to join his regiment, the Green Howards, as a second-lieutenant in August 1992. A former England Under-21 international, he played for an England XV against Italy in 1990 and the same year went on the England tour to Argentina, playing against Tucuman, Cuyo and Cordoba. In 1990 he also won an England 'B' cap against France and in 1991 added 'B' caps against Namibia, Ireland and France again. He broke ribs playing against Plymouth Albion in 1989. Rodber, who can play at either lock, flanker or number-8, was in the Northampton side which lost to the Harlequins in the 1991 Pilkington Cup Final. He also played for Hampshire Schools at cricket and hockey.

ROGERS
Derek Prior ('Budge'), OBE

Flanker. 1961-1969 (Bedford, 34 caps).
Debut v Ireland, 11 February 1961.
Born: 20 June 1935.
Educated: Bedford School.
Clubs: Bedford, East Midlands, Barbarians.

Derek Rogers, who could pass the ball with pin-point accuracy, was the leading loose-forward in English rugby during the 1960s. Once England's record cap holder, Rogers joined Bedford when he left school, immediately made the 1st XV and is, inevitably, the club's most capped player.

His first trial was in December 1959, at Banbury, and he scored a try on his international debut, in Dublin. He went on the British Lions tour of South Africa in 1962, playing in 12 matches — although only two were Tests — and led the England team in 1969, to win his 34th cap. An England selector, he was one of the youngest men to serve in that role. Awarded OBE for services to rugby, he is an executive of an engineering firm.

ROGERS
John Henry

Forward. 1890-1891 (Moseley, 4 caps).
Debut v Wales, 15 February 1890.
Died: 1922.
Educated: Bromsgrove School.

Clubs: Moseley Woodstock, Moseley, Midland Counties, Barbarians.

He was the first Moseley player to win an England cap.

ROGERS
Walter Lacey Yea, DSO

Forward. 1905 (Blackheath, 2 caps).
Debut v Wales, 14 January 1905.
Born: 20 September 1878; Died: 10 February 1948.
Educated: Rugby School, Oxford University.
Clubs: Oxford University (Blues 1898-1900), Army, Blackheath, Kent, Barbarians.

John Rogers

He served during World War One with the Royal Field Artillery and Royal Horse Artillery. A major, he was mentioned in despatches three times, awarded the DSO in 1918 and eventually reached rank of lieutenant-colonel. He played for the Army against the Royal Navy in 1908.

ROLLITT
David Malcolm

Number 8. 1967-1975 (Bristol, 11 caps).
Debut v Ireland, 11 February 1967.
Born: 24 March 1943, Wombwell, Barnsley.
Educated: Barnsley Grammar School, Bristol University, Loughborough Colleges.
Clubs: Loughborough Colleges, UAU, Bristol, Wakefield, Richmond, Gloucestershire.
He played eight times for England during his first two international seasons of 1967 and 1969 but was then ignored until the England-Scotland game in 1974-5 and went on the England tour to Australia later that year. He played in Bristol's 1972-3 RFU Club KO Cup Final team and in that season's County Championship Final for Gloucestershire. A school teacher.

RONCORONI
Anthony Dominic Sebastian, MC

Lock. 1933 (West Herts, Richmond, 3 caps).
Debut v Wales, 21 January 1933.
Born: 16 March 1908; Died: 20 July 1953.
Educated: Rossall School.
Clubs: West Herts, Richmond, East Midlands, Midland Counties, Surrey.
Before World War Two he was the financial advertisement manager of the *Morning Post* newspaper and later joined *The Scotsman*. During the war he served in the Royal Artillery, reaching the rank of major. He was taken prisoner in Italy, after serving in the Western Desert, but after two years he escaped and joined a commando battery in France, where he was awarded the Military Cross. He was wounded in the D-Day landings in June 1944. He joined the *Financial Times* in 1946 and died seven years later, after a long, painful illness.

ROSE
W.Marcus H.

Full-back. 1981-1987 (Cambridge University, Coventry, Harlequins, 10 caps).
Debut v Ireland, 7 March 1981.
Educated: Loughborough Grammar School, Durham University, Cambridge University.
Clubs: Cambridge University (Blues 1979-81), Leicester, Coventry, Rosslyn Park, Harlequins.
A chartered surveyor, he scored a try on his international debut.

Marcus Rose

ROSSBOROUGH
Peter Alec

Full-back. 1971-1975 (Coventry, 7 caps).
Debut v Wales, 16 January 1971.
Born: 30 June 1948, Coventry.
Educated: King Henry VIII School (Coventry), Durham University.
Clubs: Old Coventrians, Durham University, UAU, British Universities, Coventry, Durham County, Warwickshire.
He scored a penalty-goal on his international debut and played for England Under-25s against Fiji in 1970. He captained Coventry and was in their 1972-3 RFU Club KO Cup-winning team. He is a solicitor.

ROSSER
David William Albert

Centre. 1965-1966 (Wasps, 5 caps).
Debut v Wales, 16 January 1965.
Born: 27 March 1940, Portsmouth.
Educated: Rochdale Grammar School, Cambridge University.

Clubs: Old Rochdalians, Cambridge University (Blues 1962-4), Manchester, Army, Wasps, London Welsh, Hampshire (20 appearances), Barbarians.
He served in the Education Corps, played for the Army five times (against the Royal Navy and the RAF) and went on the Oxford-Cambridge tours of Africa in 1963 and Argentina in 1965. He teaches English.

ROTHERHAM
Alan

Half-back. 1882-1887 (Richmond, 12 caps).
Debut v Wales, 16 December 1882.
Born: 31 July 1862; Died: 30 August 1898.
Educated: Uppingham School, Oxford University.
Clubs: Oxford University (Blues 1882-1884), Coventry, Richmond, Middlesex (captain 1886-87).
Within two years of leaving school, Rotherham was a key player in the England team. He was, without doubt,

the innovator of half-back play as we know it and, along with Harry Vassall, he revolutionised rugby football. A barrister, he was called to the Bar in 1888. A cousin of Arthur Rotherham.

ROTHERHAM
Arthur

Scrum half. 1898-1899 (Richmond, 5 caps).
Debut v Scotland, 12 March 1898.
Born: 27 May 1869; Died: 3 March 1946.
Educated: Uppingham School, Cambridge University.
Clubs: Cambridge University (Blues 1890-91), St Thomas's Hospital, Richmond, Coventry, Surrey, Midland Counties, Barbarians.
Cousin of Alan Rotherham, he was often described as a 'heroic' half-back. He was the assistant medical officer to London asylums.

ROUGHLEY
David F.K.

Centre. 1973-1974 (Liverpool, 3 caps).
Debut v Australia, 17 November 1973.
Born: 10 December 1947, Warrington.
Educated: Beaumont School (Warrington).
Clubs: Liverpool, Lancashire (34 appearances).

ROWELL
Robert Errington

Lock. 1964-1965 (Leicester, 2 caps).
Debut v Wales, 18 January 1964.
Born: 29 August 1939.
Educated: Wymondham College, Loughborough Colleges.
Clubs: Loughborough Colleges, Leicester, Fylde, Waterloo, Leicestershire, Lancashire, Barbarians.
He is a school master.

ROWLEY
Alfred J.

Number 8. 1932 (Coventry, 1 cap).
Debut v South Africa, 2 January 1932.
Born: 1908, Coventry.
Club: Coventry.

ROWLEY
Hugh Campbell

Forward. 1879-1882 (Manchester, 9 caps).
Debut v Scotland, 10 March 1879.
Born: 1854.
Educated: Manchester Grammar School.
Clubs: Manchester, Cheshire, Lancashire.
His family were the founders of Lancashire CCC.

ROYDS
Percy Molyneux Rawson, (Sir), CMG MP

Back. 1898-1899 (Blackheath, 3 caps).
Debut v Scotland, 12 March 1898.

Born: 1874; Died: 25 March 1955.
Educated: Eastmans Naval School (Southsea), Royal Naval College (Greenwich).
Clubs: United Services (Portsmouth), Blackheath, Kent, Barbarians.
A Naval rear admiral, he was decorated for rescuing diplomats from Peking during the 1900 rebellion. In World War One he was commander of HMS Canterbury at Zeebrugge and the Battle of Jutland, was mentioned in despatches and awarded the Legion d'Honneur and the CMG in 1917. From 1937 to 1945 he was Conservative MP for Kingston-on-Thames.
He scored a try on his international debut and was president of Royal Navy RFU in 1923, an England selector from 1928 to 1931, an RFU trustee from 1929 to 1955 and president from 1927 to 1928. He was also an International Board member from 1927 to 1949 and represented the Royal Navy on the RFU from 1920 to 1928. Also a referee, he took charge of Wales v France in 1921 and France v Ireland in 1923. Author of many books which specialised on the laws of rugby football, his *The History of the Laws of Rugby Football* was published in 1949.

ROYLE
A.V.

Full-back. 1889 (Broughton Rangers, 1 cap).
Debut v Maoris, 16 February 1889.
Clubs: Broughton Rangers, Lancashire (12 appearances).

RUDD
Edward Lawrence

Wing. 1965-1966 (Liverpool, 6 caps).
Debut v Wales, 16 January 1965.
Born: 28 September 1944, Liverpool.
Educated: St Edward's College (Liverpool), Oxford University.
Clubs: Oxford University (Blues 1963-4), Liverpool, Lancashire (13 appearances), Barbarians.
He has a career in banking.

RUSSELL
Richard Forbes

Forward. 1905 (Leicester, 1 cap).
Debut v New Zealand, 2 December 1905.
Born: 5 April 1879; Died: 30 May 1960, Isle of Man.
Educated: St Peter's School (York), Cambridge University.
Clubs: Cambridge University (no Blue), Leicester, Castleford, Yorkshire (13 appearances), Cork.
A school teacher, he was the nephew of Sir Timothy O'Brien a Middlesex and England cricketer. He served during World War One as a special constable in the Isle of Man.

RUTHERFORD
Donald

Full-back. 1960-1967 (Percy Park, Gloucester, 14 caps).
Debut v Wales, 16 January 1960.
Born: 22 September 1937.
Educated: Tynemouth High School.
Clubs: Percy Park, Preston Grasshoppers, St Luke's College, Wasps, Gloucester, Northumberland, Barbarians.
Percy Park's most capped player, he scored two penalty-goals on his international debut and went on the British Lions tour of Australia in 1966. He was technical administrator to the RFU in 1969 and the RFU coaching organizer. He is a school teacher.

RYALLS
Henry John

Forward. 1885 (New Brighton, 2 caps).
Debut v Wales, 3 January 1885.
Born: 12 December 1858; Died: 17 October 1949.
Educated: Birkenhead School.
Clubs: New Brighton, Cheshire.
He scored a try on his international debut. His England cap is now with the New Brighton club. He served in the military during World War One.

RYAN
Dean

Number 8. 1990 (Wasps, 1990, 2 caps).
Debut v Argentina, 28 July 1990.
Born: 22 June, 1966, Tuxford, Notts.
Clubs: Newark, Saracens, Wasps, London Division.
Dean Ryan was selected for England 'B' v France in 1988 but had to withdraw through injury. The following year he suffered a fractured left arm for the second time, against Cardiff. He represented London in their 21-10 win over the Australians in 1988 and was a member of Wasps' Championship side of 1989-90. Ryan scored a try on his full England debut, which came on the tour of Argentina in 1990. He stands 6ft 6in tall and was a regular soldier in the Royal Engineers but is now in civilian life as a builder. In 1991 he toured Australia with London.

RYAN
Peter Henry

Flanker. 1955 (Richmond, 2 caps).
Debut v Wales, 22 January 1955.
Born: 1 October 1930.
Educated: Harrow School, Cambridge University.
Clubs: Cambridge University (Blues 1952-3), Richmond, London Counties, Middlesex (captain 1959-61), Barbarians.
Peter Ryan played in the annual Harrow-Eton cricket match at Lord's in 1949.

SADLER
Edward H.

Flanker. 1933 (Army, 2 caps).

Debut v Ireland, 11 February 1933.
Born: 1912.

Clubs: Army, Oldham RL.

He scored a try on his international debut. Whilst serving with the Royal Signals he made seven appearances for the Army, against the Royal Navy, RAF and French Army. He joined Oldham RLFC in 1933.

SAGAR
John Warburton

Full-back. 1901 (Cambridge University, 2 caps).
Debut v Wales, 5 January 1901.
Born: 6 December 1878; Died: 10 January 1941, Bournemouth.

Educated: Durham School, Cambridge University.

Clubs: Cambridge University (Blues 1899-1900), Castleford, Durham County, Yorkshire, Barbarians.

A school teacher, he made one appearance for Yorkshire, against Cumberland in 1900.

SALMON
James Lionel Broome

Centre. 1985-1987 (Harlequins, 12 caps).
Debut v New Zealand, 1 June 1985.
Born: 16 October 1959, Hong Kong.

Educated: Wellington College.

Clubs: Blackheath, Athletic, Wellington (New Zealand), Harlequins, Kent.

A teacher at Wellington College, Salmon went to New Zealand in 1979 and was capped for that country — against Fiji in 1980 and against Romania and France in 1981 — before returning to Great Britain. When the International Board changed the qualification rules he was also capped by England, making his debut, coincidentally, on the tour to New Zealand in 1985. Salmon, who also played for New Zealand 'colts' sides, is only the third player to play for England and another International Board country.

SAMPLE
Charles Herbert, OBE

Full-back. 1884-1886 (Cambridge University, 3 caps).
Debut v Ireland, 4 February 1884.
Born: 22 November 1862; Died: 2 June 1938.

Educated: Edinburgh Academy, Cambridge University.

Clubs: Cambridge University (Blues 1882-4), Durham County, Northumberland.

Sample scored on his international debut when he converted W.N.Bolton's try to give England victory by one goal to nil. He also played cricket for Northumberland. During World War One, he served as district commissioner on Northern Counties Board for Agriculture and Fisheries and was awarded the OBE in 1918.

SANDERS
Donald Louis ('Sandy')

Prop. 1954-1956 (Harlequins, 9 caps).
Debut v Wales, 16 January 1954.
Born: 6 September 1924, Fulham.

Clubs: Ipswich YMCA, Harlequins, London Counties, Eastern Counties, Barbarians.

Jamie Salmon

'Sandy' Sanders

Donald Sanders served as RFU president and treasurer, was chairman of the RFU selectors in 1971 and managed the England team that toured Fiji and New Zealand in 1973. During World War Two he served in the RNVR and his international appearances included the Calcutta Cup sides of 1954 and 1956.

SANDERS
Frank Warren

Hooker. 1923 (Plymouth Albion, 3 caps).
Debut v Ireland, 10 February 1923.
Born: 24 January 1893; Died: 22 June 1953.

Clubs: Devonport Dockyard Sports Club, Plymouth Albion, (captain against New Zealand in 1922)

A member of England's 1923 Grand Slam side, Frank Sanders had a long career with the Civil Service Sports Association, being a founder member of the Plymouth area association when it was formed in 1927. He was involved with various sub-committees concerning bowls, cricket, football and grounds, and at the 1928 annual meeting was elected to the grounds committee and the main management until February 1931, when he was elected ground steward. He served in that post until February 1937 and was membership secretary from 1946 to 1948. During that period he was also chairman of the rugby and bowls sections and secretary of the bowling club from 1943 to 1950. He was captain of that club in 1951. Sanders first settled in Plymouth 1916, later spending two years at Invergordon before returning to Plymouth. He was employed in Devonport Dockyard as a chargehand of pattern makers.

SANDFORD
Joseph Ruscombe Poole

Centre. 1906 (Marlborough Nomads, 1 cap).
Debut v Ireland, 10 February 1906.
Born: 5 March 1881; Died: 19 July 1916, Khartoum.

Educated: Allhallows School, Marlborough College, Oxford University.

Clubs: Oxford University (Blues 1902-3), Marlborough Nomads, Devon.

Sandford, who was also a hockey Blue in 1903, worked extensively in the Civil Service in the Sudan and was acting Governor of Omdurman in 1916.

SANGWIN
Roger Dennis

Centre. 1964 (Hull & East Riding, 2 caps).
Debut v New Zealand, 4 January 1964.
Born: 2 December 1937.

Educated: Sedbergh School.

Clubs: Hull & East Riding, Yorkshire (24 appearances), Barbarians.

Sangwin is the Hull & East Riding club's most capped player. He is an architect by profession.

SARGENT
Gordon A.F.

Prop. 1981 (Gloucester, 1 cap).
Debut v Ireland, 7 March 1981.
Born: 18 October 1949, Gloucester.

Educated: Lydney Grammar School.

Clubs: Lydney, Gloucester, Barbarians, Gloucestershire.

Sargent made his international debut when he replaced Gloucester teammate Phil Blakeway. In September 1989, he organised a charity rugby match in aid of local orphan children. The game had 15 full international players in the Invitation XV which played a Forest of Dean Combination XV. The game was held at Lydney's ground — the club Sargent managed in 1991-2 — and more than 1,000 spectators helped raise around £2,000.

SAVAGE
Keith Frederick

Right-wing. 1966-1968 (Northampton, 13 caps).

Debut v Wales, 15 January 1966.
Born: 24 August 1940.

Educated: Leamington College for Boys (Leamington Spa), Loughborough Colleges.

Clubs: Loughborough Colleges, Northampton, Harlequins, East Midlands.

A PE teacher, he went on the England tour of Canada in 1967 and on the British Lions tour of Australia and New Zealand in 1966, when he scored six tries. On the Lions' 1968 trip to South Africa he played in 11 games and scored three tries.

SAWYER
Charles Montague

Back. 1880-1881 (Broughton Park, 2 caps).
Debut v Scotland, 28 February 1880.
Born: 1856, Broughton, Manchester; Died: 30 March 1921, Ormskirk, Lancashire.

Keith Savage

Clubs: Broughton Wasps, Broughton Park, Lancashire.

A right-handed batsman and fastish bowler, he played cricket for Lancashire, making two appearances as an amateur in 1884 with a top score of 11 not out against Surrey at The Oval on his first-class debut.

SAXBY
Leslie Eric

Flanker. 1932 (Gloucester, 2 caps).
Debut v South Africa, 2 January 1932.
Born: 19 May 1900.
Educated: Reading School.
Club: Gloucester.

SCHOFIELD
John W.

Forward. 1880 (Manchester Rangers, 1 cap).
Debut v Ireland, 30 January 1880.
Born: March 1858; Died: 3 May 1931.
Educated: Uppingham School.
Clubs: Manchester Rangers, Lancashire.

He was employed as a stockbroker.

SCHOLFIELD
John Arthur

Centre. 1911 (Preston Grasshoppers, 1 cap).
Debut v Wales, 21 January 1911.
Born: 6 April 1888; Died: 14 September 1967.
Educated: Sedbergh School, Cambridge University.
Clubs: Cambridge University (Blues 1909-10), Manchester Rangers, Preston Grasshoppers, Harlequins, Lancashire, Barbarians.

Employed as an insurance broker, he also played cricket for Lancashire 2nd XI in 1908 and captained Royal Birkdale Golf Club. During World War One he was a captain in the Manchester Regiment and was wounded and captured. He scored a try on his international debut.

SCHWARZ
Reginald Oscar, MC

Fly half. 1899-1901 (Richmond, 3 caps).
Debut v Scotland, 11 March 1899.
Born: 4 May 1875, Kent; Died: 18 November 1918, France.
Educated: St Paul's School, Cambridge University.
Clubs: Cambridge University (Blue 1893), Richmond, Middlesex, Barbarians.

Schwartz was also a fine cricketer, playing for Oxfordshire in 1899 and 1900, for Middlesex from 1901 to 1905 and appearing in five Tests for South Africa against England 1904-1907) and four Tests against Australia (1910-1911). One of South Africa's best leg-spin and googly bowlers, he also played for Transvaal. A stockbroker by profession, he served in World War One and was

wounded, mentioned in despatches and won the MC. He died of influenza shortly after Armistice Day.

SCORFIELD
Edward Scafe

Lock. 1910 (Percy Park, 1 cap).
Debut v France, 3 March 1910.
Born: 21 March 1882, North Shields; Died: 1966.
Educated: Royal Grammar School (Newcastle upon Tyne).
Clubs: Percy Park, Northumberland.

Scorfield was employed as a cartoonist, first with the *Newcastle Chronicle*, then with the *Sydney Bulletin* (Australia), holding the post of art director of the publication from the mid-1920s until his retirement in the 1950s. He was a member of Tyneside Rowing Club from 1906 to 1925.

SCOTT
Charles Tillard

Forward. 1900-1901 (Blackheath, 4 caps).
Debut v Wales, 6 January 1900.
Born: 26 August 1877; Died: 6 November 1965.
Educated: Tonbridge School, Cheltenham College, Cambridge University.
Clubs: Cambridge University (Blue 1899), London Hospital, Blackheath, Kent, Barbarians.

Scott served during World War Two as a major in the Home Guard. He played cricket for Cambridgeshire.

SCOTT
Edward Keith

Centre. 1947-1948 (St Mary's Hospital, Redruth, 5 caps).
Debut v Wales, 18 January 1947.
Born: 14 June 1918, Truro, Cornwall.
Educated: Clifton College, Oxford University.
Clubs: Oxford University (no Blue but played XV), St Mary's Hospital, Redruth, Harlequins, London Counties, Cornwall (19 appearances), Barbarians.

Edward Scott, the son of Frank Scott, captained England three times. He also played in the Victory internationals against the Kiwis and Wales. He played cricket for Oxford University in 1938, for Gloucestershire in 1937, for the Minor Counties in 1949 and toured Canada with MCC in 1951.

SCOTT
Frank Sholl

Wing. 1907 (Bristol, 1 cap).
Debut v Wales, 12 January 1907.
Born: 9 January 1886, Australia; Died: 4 February 1952.
Educated: Epsom College.
Clubs: Bristol, Devon, Gloucestershire.

Father of Edward Keith Scott, he worked as a GP in Australia and then moved to the UK, practising in Cornwall from

1918 to death. He served during World War One with the RAMC.

SCOTT
Harry

Full-back. 1955 (Manchester, 1 cap).
Debut v France, 26 February 1955.
Born: 7 November 1927, Batley, Yorkshire.
Educated: Stretford Junior Technical College, Salford Technical College.
Clubs: Eccles, United Services (Portsmouth), United Services (Chatham), Manchester, Lancashire (46 appearances, captain 1960-61), North-West Counties.

An enterprising player with safe hands and quick to turn defence into attack, he comes from a rugby-playing family. An engineering draughtsman, he played for North-West Counties against New Zealand in February 1954.

SCOTT
John Phillip

Number 8. 1978-1984 (Rosslyn Park, Cardiff, 30 caps).
Debut v France, 21 January 1978.
Born: 28 September 1954, Exeter.
Educated: Hele's Grammar School, Exeter College of Further Education, St Luke's College (Exeter).
Clubs: Exeter, Rosslyn Park, Cardiff.

Once England's most capped number 8, John Scott began his representative career at the age of 17, when he played for Devon in the County Championship, and he was still at school when he became the youngest forward ever to play in an England trial, still aged 17. Scott played for England Under-19s in 1972-3 (against Scotland, Wales and France), for the Under-23s against Italy in 1975, and went on the tour of Canada as captain in 1977. Then followed England's tour of the Far East in 1979, to Argentina in 1981 and to South Africa as captain in 1984. He also toured South Africa with Cardiff and he is the only man to captain the Cardiff club in four consecutive seasons (1980-84). In September 1981 he captained the Taverners' team in the Harlequins-Lords Taverners Sevens at Stoop Memorial Ground.

SCOTT
John Stanley Marshall

Full-back. 1958 (Oxford University, 1 cap).
Debut v France, 1 March 1958.
Born: 23 January 1935.
Educated: Leas School (Hoylake), Radley College, Oxford University.
Clubs: Birkenhead Park, Oxford University (Blues 1957-8), Harlequins, Cheshire, London Counties, Negri Sembilan Club.

A solicitor by profession, he also played cricket for Oxford University Authentics in 1958 and was a crew member of the America's Cup yachting challenger

'Sovereign' in 1964. He also had a short spell with the Negri Sembilan club of Malaya in 1956, whilst serving with the Gurkhas. He was commissioned into the 10th Gurkha Rifles in December 1954.

SCOTT
Mason Thompson

Half-back. 1887-1890 (Cambridge University, 3 caps).
Debut v Ireland, 5 February 1887.
Born: 20 December 1865; Died: 1 June 1916.
Educated: Craigmount School, Cambridge University.
Clubs: Cambridge University (Blues 1885-7), Northern, Blackheath, Northumberland, Barbarians.
Brother of William Martin Scott, he was the first player to be capped from the Northern RFC. A gentleman of considerable wealth, he left £130,000 in his will.

SCOTT
William Martin

Half-back. 1889 (Cambridge University, 1 cap).
Debut v Maoris, 16 February 1889.
Born: 27 March 1870; Died: 26 February 1944.
Educated: Craigmount School, Cambridge University.
Clubs: Cambridge University (Blue 1888), Blackheath, Northern, Northumberland, Barbarians.
Brother of Mason Thompson Scott, he also played cricket for Cambridge University. During World War One he was a major in the Royal Engineers. He was one of the first players to specialise in 'selling the dummy'.

SEDDON
Robert L.

Forward. 1887 (Broughton Rangers, 3 caps).
Debut v Wales, 8 January 1887.
Born: 1860 Yorkshire; Died: 15 August 1888, Australia.
Clubs: Broughton Rangers, Swinton, Lancashire (21 appearances).
Seddon was selected to captain the 1888 British Isles team to Australia and New Zealand but drowned whilst bathing in the Hunter River before the tour was properly under way. A.E.Stoddart took over as captain. Seddon was a popular and handsome player and a memorial was erected in his honour in Maitland, NSW, Australia.

SELLAR
Kenneth Anderson ('Monkey'), DSO DSC

Full-back. 1927-1928 (United Services (Portsmouth), Royal Navy, 7 caps).
Debut v Wales, 15 January 1927.

Born: 11 August 1906; Died: 15 May 1989, South Africa.
Educated: Royal Naval College (Dartmouth), Royal Naval College (Greenwich).
Clubs: United Services (Portsmouth), Royal Navy, Combined Services, Blackheath, London Counties, Hampshire, Barbarians.
Kenneth Sellar made his international debut for England as a 20-year-old, when his line-kicking and defence as a full-back were described as 'sensational'. Although not England's greatest full-back, he was certainly the most courageous and was always smiling, no matter what befell his team.

After he had helped England to the Grand Slam in 1928, his promising rugby career was interrupted when he followed his Royal Navy career. He served throughout World War Two and was in the leading landing craft on Sword Beach during the D-Day landings in Normandy. He was awarded the DSC in 1944 and the DSO after he led the assault of Walcheren Island in 1944.

He played rugby and cricket for the Royal Navy and was also a member of the Royal Yacht Squadron. After the war he became a stockbroker before emigrating to South Africa for health reasons in the early 1980s. He also played cricket for Sussex and MCC; and he scored 92 not out for the Barbarians against Richmond in 1928.

SEVER
Harold Sedgewick ('Hal')

Left-wing. 1936-1938 (Sale, 10 caps).
Debut v New Zealand, 4 January 1936.
Born: 3 March 1910.
Educated: Shrewsbury School.
Clubs: Sale, Cheshire, Barbarians.
Sever, who scored five tries in ten appearances for England, played for Combined Cheshire-Lancashire against South Africa in 1931-2 and for Combined Cheshire-Lancashire against New Zealand in 1935-6. A powerful, strong-running wing three-quarter, he scored a try on his international debut.

SHACKLETON
Ian Roger

Fly-half. 1969-1970 (Cambridge University, 4 caps).
Debut v South Africa, 20 December 1969.
Born: 17 June 1948, Shipley, Yorkshire.
Educated: Bradford Grammar School, Cambridge University.
Clubs: Cambridge University (Blues 1968-70), Harrogate, Bradford, Lavelanet (France), Yorkshire (9 appearances), Richmond.
Shackleton captained his school XV and he scored the winning try for Cambridge on his Varsity match debut. He joined Harrogate upon leaving school in 1967, then turned out for Bradford, and

played for Lavelanet when he went to work in the French textile industry. He first played for England as a 21-year-old, but refused to play county rugby for a time because he lived in London, although he did play an handful of games after leaving school. His early representative rugby was with Yorkshire Schools and the England Under-19 side. He is a school teacher.

SHARPE
Richard Adrian William, OBE

Fly-half 1960-1967 (Oxford University, Wasps, Redruth, 14 caps).
Debut v Wales, 16 January 1960.
Born: 9 September 1938, Mysore, South India.
Educated: Montpelier School (India), Blundell's School, Oxford University.
Clubs: Oxford University (Blues 1959-61), Redruth, Royal Navy, Wasps, Bristol, Cornwall (28 appearances), Barbarians.
Richard Sharpe made his mark on the game in a remarkable debut at Twickenham against Wales, when he was picked to play after A.B.W.Risman was injured. A blond Cornishman, he was blessed with great speed and remarkable fitness and succeeded R.E.G.Jeeps as England's captain, going on to lead his country five times. In 1962, in the British Lions match at Pretoria against Northern Transvaal, he was knocked unconscious by a flying tackle in the first six minutes of the game. He was carried off and a fractured cheek bone was diagnosed.

Redruth's most capped player, he served in the Royal Marines as a commando and his appearances for Cornwall include the 1967 County Championship semi-final against Surrey. He played for the Barbarians against New Zealand in 1964.

Sharpe was an assistant master at Sherborne from 1963 to 1968 and was also a rugby correspondent for the *Sunday Telegraph*. He was awarded the OBE in 1986. He is the nephew of I.J.Sharpe and the son of a former Wasps player, F.G.Sharpe.

SHAW
Cecil Hamilton

Forward. 1906-1907 (Moseley, 6 caps).
Debut v Scotland, 17 March 1906.
Born: 1 August 1879, Wolverhampton; Died: 13 November 1964.
Educated: Sedbergh School.
Clubs: Moseley, Midland Counties.
He was a captain in the Royal Engineers during World War One.

SHAW
Frederick

Forward. 1898 (Cleckheaton, 1 cap).
Debut v Ireland, 5 February 1898.
Club: Cleckheaton.

SHAW
James Fraser

Forward. 1898 (Royal Naval Engineering College (Keyham), 2 caps).
Debut v Scotland, 12 March 1898.
Born: 2 January 1878; Died: 23 July 1941.

Educated: King William's School (Isle of Man), Royal Naval Engineering College (Keyham).

Clubs: Royal Naval Engineering College (Keyham), Devon, Barbarians.

The father of actor Robert Shaw, his was a wholly Naval career. He served in World War One as an assistant engineer, then as an engineering captain on HMS Invincible, HMS Suffolk and later on HMS Cordelia. Shaw fought at the Battle of Heligoland and in the Falkland Islands and was mentioned in despatches in 1914.

SHEPPARD
Austin

Prop. 1981-1985 (Bristol, 2 caps).
Debut v Wales, 17 January 1981.
Born: 1 May 1950.

Club: Bristol.

Sheppard, who worked as an undertaker, made his international debut as a replacement for Fran Cotton.

SHERRARD
Charles William

Forward. 1871-1872 (Blackheath, 2 caps).
Debut v Scotland, 27 March 1871.
Born: 25 December 1849, London; Died: 1921.

Educated: Rugby School.

Clubs: Blackheath, Army.

Sherrard, who was in the Royal Engineers, had the distinction of becoming the first serving soldier, along with C.A.Crompton, to gain international honours when he played in the very first match between Scotland and England at Raeburn Place. He was awarded the South African War Medal with clasp and reached the rank of colonel.

SHERRIFF
George Albert

Number 8. 1966-1967 (Saracens, 3 caps).
Debut v Scotland, 19 March 1966.
Born: 29 May 1937.

Clubs: Saracens, London Counties, Middlesex, Barbarians.

Sherriff did not begin playing rugby until he was 24 years old and gained his first cap at 28. He had quite a short rugger career and remained with Saracens throughout.

SHEWRING
Harry Edward

Centre. 1905-1907 (Bristol, 10 caps).
Debut v Ireland, 11 February 1905.
Born: 26 April 1882; Died: 27 November 1960.

Educated: Colston School.

Clubs: Keynsham, Bristol, Somerset (45 appearances, captain 1907-08).

Shewring made 250 appearances for Bristol, scoring 67 tries for that club.

SHOOTER
John Henry

Forward. 1899-1900 (Morley, 4 caps).
Debut v Ireland, 4 February 1899.
Born: 25 March 1875, Nottingham; Died: 13 August 1922, Leeds.

Clubs: Morley, Hunslet RL.

A coalminer, he had a short career in the Union game before changing to the League code in 1900.

SHUTTLEWORTH
Dennis William, OBE ADC

Half-back. 1951-1953 (Headingley, 2 caps).
Debut v Scotland, 17 March 1951.
Born: 22 July 1928, Leeds.

Educated: Roundhay School (Leeds), Royal Military Academy (Sandhurst).

Clubs: Old Roundhegians, Roundhay, Headingley, Blackheath, Army, Combined Services, Halifax, Dover, Barbarians, Yorkshire (33 appearances).

Dennis Shuttleworth was commissioned into the Duke of Wellington's Regiment in December 1948, served in Korea and retired from the Army in 1983 with the rank of brigadier. In his early days he represented the Army 22 times, against the RAF, Royal Navy and French Army. In 1951-2, along with Evan Hardy, he played in the Calcutta Cup match, in what was an Army first, for both half-backs in an international came from the same regiment.

Shuttleworth played for Halifax at various times over the years and was with the Dover club in 1950. He was a Yorkshire selector in 1961-2 and 1962-3, Yorkshire committee member from 1978 to date, a member of the Army RFU committee and the Army representative on the RFU from 1962 to 1964 and from 1974 to 1985, and he was the 78th RFU president in 1985-6. In 1990 he was elected president of the Rugby Football Schools Union and he was the regional director of the 1991 Rugby World Cup.

SIBREE
Herbert John Hyde, MC

Scrum half. 1908-1909 (Harlequins, 3 caps).
Debut v France, 1 January 1908.
Born: 9 May 1885; Died: 20 August 1962, Tilehurst, Sussex.

Educated: Eltham College.

Clubs: Harlequins, London Counties, Middlesex, Barbarians.

During World War One, he was a captain in the Royal Norfolk Regiment (Artists' Rifles) and was awarded the Military Cross in 1916. In April 1922 he played for Harlequins Past against Harlequins Present in a match in aid of King Edward VII's Hospital Fund. He spent 50 years as a ship's broker before retiring in 1959.

SILK
Nicholas

Flanker. 1965 (Harlequins, 4 caps).
Debut v Wales, 16 January 1965.
Born: 26 May 1941, Lewes.

Educated: Lewes Grammar School, Oxford University.

Clubs: Oxford University (Blues 1961-3, captain 1963), Harlequins, St Thomas's Hospital, British Universities, Sussex (captain 1964-5).

His career was cut short in 1966 after knee injury prevented him from playing first-class rugby. A physiologist by profession.

SIMMS
Kevin Gerard

Centre. 1985-1988 (Cambridge University, Liverpool, Wasps, 15 caps).
Debut v Romania, 5 January 1985.
Born: 25 December 1964.

Educated: Cambridge University.

Kevin Simms

Clubs: Cambridge University (Blues 1983-5), Liverpool, Wasps.

He was replaced by G.H.Davies on his international debut against Romania, in the first game between the two countries at full level.

SIMPSON
Colin Peter

Wing. 1965 (Harlequins, 1 cap).

Debut v Wales, 16 January 1965.
Born: 21 September 1942.

Educated: Ipswich School, Royal Military Academy (Sandhurst).

Clubs: Ipswich, Army, Combined Services, Harlequins, Wolfhounds (Ireland), Suffolk, Eastern Counties, Barbarians.

Colin Simpson had the distinction of being capped whilst still a cadet at Sandhurst. He served in the Royal Anglian Regiment and represented the Army five times, against the Royal Navy and the RAF. He also played cricket for Suffolk.

SIMPSON
Paul Donald

Flanker. 1983-1987 (Bath, 3 caps).
Debut v New Zealand, 19 November 1983.
Born: 7 June 1958, Leeds.
Educated: Newcastle Polytechnic.
Clubs: Gosforth, Bath, Barbarians.

Paul Simpson, who played Rugby League at school, was a member of the Bath team which won the JPS Cup in 1986 to equal Leicester's record of three successive wins. He is a sales manager for Allied Dunbar in Bath.

SIMPSON
Thomas

Wing. 1902-1909 (Rockcliffe, 11 caps).
Debut v Scotland, 15 March 1902.

Clubs: Rockcliff, Northumberland, Barbarians.

Thomas Simpson, an accountant by profession, was secretary of the Northumberland RFU from 1925 to 1932.

SKINNER
Michael Gordon

Flanker. 1988-1992 (Harlequins, 21 caps).
Debut v France, 16 January 1988.
Born: 26 November 1958, Newcastle upon Tyne.
Educated: Walbottle Grammar School, Newcastle upon Tyne.
Clubs: Tynedale, Blaydon, Blackheath, Harlequins, Barbarians, Kent, London.

Mickey Skinner, who in the 1991 World Cup tournament was the only English forward to score a try, is unmistakable on the rugby field, his long hair probably making some retired players of the 'old school' blench today. Skinner began his career as a centre for Tynedale before being converted to an open side flanker with Blaydon Colts. He scored the winning try on his debut for Blaydon, at Stockton in 1975-6, despite a serious eye wound, and in his first season with Harlequins, in 1985-6, the club won the first of five successive Middlesex Sevens titles.

He made his England 'B' debut against France in 1987 and his full debut against the same country the following year. He suffered a broken nose in the first line-out against Ireland in 1988, but continued to play. Skinner went on the tours to Argentina in 1990, to Australia and Fiji in 1991, and was a member of the 1991 World Cup Final team. He was a member of the two victorious Grand Slam sides of 1991 and 1992.

He represented Kent in the 1985 County Championship Final and since joining the Quins has played for London Division regularly, helping them to Divisional Championship successes in 1988, 1989 and 1990. He

Paul Simpson

Mickey Skinner

served as an apprentice engineer with British Engines (in Byker, Newcastle) and is now employed as a freelance computer consultant. At Walbottle Grammar School, his PE teacher was former England prop, Colin White.

SLADEN
Geoffrey Mainwaring, DSO DSC

Centre. 1929 (United Services (Portsmouth), Royal Navy, 3 caps).
Debut v Wales, 19 January 1929.
Born: 3 August 1904.

Educated: Royal Naval College (Dartmouth).

Clubs: United Services (Portsmouth), Royal Navy, Hampshire.

Sladen represented the Royal Navy and Dorset at hockey, and both the Navy and Royal Marines at athletics. During World War Two he served on HMS Trident, was awarded the DSC in 1940, the DSO and bar in 1942 and was promoted to captain in 1946.

SLEMEN
Michael Anthony Charles

Wing. 1976-1984 (Liverpool St Helens, 31 caps).
Debut v Ireland, 6 March 1976.
Born: 11 May 1951, Liverpool.

Educated: St Edmund's College (Liverpool), St Luke's College (Exeter).

Clubs: St Luke's College (Exeter), Devon, Liverpool St Helens, Lancashire (36 appearances).

Michael Slemen was England's most capped wing and between 1976 and 1980 he played in every game in the Five Nations Championship and also made two international appearances against New Zealand. He was in the England Under-23 side which beat Tonga 40-4 in 1974 and went on the British Lions tour of South Africa in 1980. In the 1980 County Championship Final he scored a try for Lancashire.

In 1978-9, Slemen turned down offers to turn professional from both Widnes and Barrow RL clubs. He was coach to the Liverpool St Helens club before resigning in April 1991, in order to concentrate on his coaching duties with the England 'B' side. He is a teacher at Merchant Taylor's School, Crosby.

SLOCOCK
Lancelot Andrew Noel

Forward. 1907-1908 (Liverpool, 8 caps).
Debut v France, 5 January 1907.
Born: 25 December 1886; Died: 9 August 1916, Guillemont (killed in action).

Educated: Marlborough College.

Clubs: Liverpool, Lancashire (14 appearances).

Slocock, who was the Liverpool secretary later in his career, scored a try on his international debut. Employed in the cotton trade, he served with the King's Liverpool Regiment during World War One and reached the rank of second-lieutenant.

Mike Slemen

SLOW
Charles F.

Fly-half. 1934 (Leicester, 1 cap).
Debut v Scotland, 17 March 1934.
Born: 1911 Northampton; Died: 15 April 1939.
Clubs: Northampton, East Midlands.

In 1931-2, Slow played in the Midlands' famous victory over the third Springboks touring side, when they suffered their only defeat in 26 matches. He was serving with the RAF Volunteer Reserve when he was killed in a car accident.

SMALL
Harold Dudley

Flanker. 1950 (Oxford University, 4 caps).
Debut v Wales, 21 January 1950.
Born: 7 January 1922, South Africa.
Educated: Dundee High School (South Africa), Witwaterstrand University (South Africa), Oxford University.
Clubs: Oxford University (Blues 1949-50), Barbarians.

Small served as an engineer in the Merchant Navy during World War Two. He returned to his native South Africa in 1951 and was employed as a mining engineer.

SMALLWOOD
Alistair McNaughton

Wing. 1920-1925 (Leicester, 14 caps).
Debut v France, 31 January 1920.
Born: 18 November 1892, Alloa.

Alistair Smallwood

Educated: Royal Grammar School (Newcastle upon Tyne), Cambridge University.
Clubs: Cambridge University (Blue 1919), Gosforth Nomads, Northumberland, Leicester, Leicestershire.

A school teacher, he served during World War One as a lieutenant with the 5th Northumberland Fusiliers.

SMART
Colin Edward

Colin Smart

Prop. 1979-1983 (Newport, 17 caps).
Debut v France, 3 March 1979.
Born: 5 March 1950, Highbury.
Educated: Skinners School (Tunbridge Wells), Cardiff College.
Clubs: Newport, Kent.

He went on the England tour to the Far East in 1979 and to Argentina in 1981. He was invited to join the Welsh squad in 1974, but chose to play for England.

SMART
Sidney E.J.

Number 8. 1913-1920 (Gloucester, 12 caps).
Debut v South Africa, 4 January 1913.
Born: 1888.
Educated: Deacon's School (Gloucester).
Clubs: Gloucester, Gloucestershire.

Smart played in Gloucestershire's County Championship winning sides of 1920, 1921 and 1922.

SMEDDLE
Robert William

Wing. 1929-1931 (Cambridge University, 4 caps).
Debut v Wales, 19 January 1929.
Born: 14 July 1908.
Educated: Durham School, Cambridge University.
Clubs: Cambridge University (Blues 1928-31), Durham City, Blackheath, Durham County.

A stockbroker, Smeddle was an Army captain during World War Two. He played cricket for Durham County.

SMITH
C.C.

Wing. 1901 (Gloucester, 1 cap).
Debut v Wales, 5 January 1901.
Club: Gloucester.

SMITH
Dyne Fenton

Lock. 1910 (Richmond, 2 caps).
Debut v Wales, 15 January 1910.
Born: 21 July 1890, Brighton; Died: 28 August 1969.
Educated: Sherborne School.
Clubs: Richmond, Barbarians, Surrey.

Dyne Smith is the youngest forward to appear for a fully representative British side in an international match. He went on the British Lions tour of South Africa in 1910, played in 23 of the 24 matches, including three Tests, and celebrated his 20th birthday only a couple of days before making his Test debut. At 6ft 2in, he was the tallest player in the squad. He played for England in the first international to be staged at Twickenham, in 1910.

A stockbroker and foreign exchange specialist, he served with distinction as a major in the Royal Fusiliers during World War One.

SMITH
John Vincent, JP

Wing. 1950 (Cambridge University, Rosslyn Park, 4 caps).
Debut v Wales, 21 January 1950.
Born: 23 May 1926.
Educated: Marling School (Stroud), Cambridge University.
Clubs: Cambridge University (Blues 1948-50), Stroud, Rosslyn Park, Army, Gloucestershire, Barbarians.

John Smith, who was also an athletic Blue in 1949, is the Stroud club's most capped player. He served mainly in the Gloucestershire Regiment from 1944 to 1948 and played twice for the Army in 1948, against the RAF and the French Army.

He was the Gloucestershire CB representative from 1961 to 1971 and RFU president in 1982-3. A founder member of the Minchinhampton RFC, he was president in 1982 and also the Hawks Club president in 1950-51. He is the author of *Good Morning President* and *Rugby from the Top*. He was the Liberal Party candidate for Stroud in the 1966 General Election.

SMITH
Keith

Centre. 1974-1975 (Roundhay, 4 caps).
Debut v France, 2 March 1974.
Born: 19 November 1952, Leeds.
Educated: Cross Green School (Leeds).
Clubs: Moortown, Roundhay, Barbarians, Yorkshire (14 appearances), Wakefield Trinity RL.

Keith Smith, who scored a club record 318 points for Roundhay in 1972-3, played most of his club rugby as a fly-half. He played for England Under-23s v Japan and went on the England tour to Australia in 1975. He turned to Rugby League in 1977 and played for Wakefield Trinity until his retirement in September 1981. For Trinity he appeared in the 1979 RL Challenge Cup Final against Widnes; and he made his Rugby League debut for England in the European Championship match against Wales at Widnes in March 1979. He is a rent collector.

SMITH
Michael John Knight, OBE

Stand-off half. 1956 (Oxford University, 1 cap).
Debut v Wales, 21 January 1956.
Born: 30 June 1933, Broughton Astley, Leicestershire.
Educated: Stamford School, Oxford University.
Clubs: Oxford University (Blues 1954-5), Hinckley, Leicester, Leicestershire (15 appearances), Barbarians.

Mike Smith's international rugby career ended abruptly when, after a defeat by Wales, he was made something of a scapegoat. At cricket, though, the contrast could not have been greater, for Smith captained England 25 times at the summer game and played in 50 Tests altogether. He won cricket Blues at Oxford in 1954, 1955 and 1956 and also played for Leicestershire (28 appearances, 1951-5) and Warwickshire (430 appearances, 1956-75). He later served on the administrative side of cricket and his OBE was awarded for services to that game. Altogether he scored 39,832 first-class runs. His son, N.M.K.Smith, plays cricket for Warwickshire.

SMITH
Simon Timothy

Wing. 1985-1986 (Wasps, 9 caps).

Simon Smith

Debut v Romania, 5 January 1985.
Born: 29 April 1960, Baldock.
Educated: Gowerton Grammar School, King Edward VI School (Lichfield), Lancaster University, Cambridge University.
Clubs: Lichfield, Fylde, Cambridge University (Blues 1982-3), Wasps, Staffordshire, Lancashire, Glamorgan, Barbarians.

Simon Smith, who also won an athletics Blue at Cambridge, scored a try on his full international debut. Earlier he had played for England Secondary Schools in Australia in 1979, for the Under-19s against France at Otley the same year (whilst still at King Edward's School) and for England Under-23s. He went on the Cambridge University tour of Romania and Japan, and the England Students tour of the Far East. In 1984-5, Smith also played for the Barbarians and for London Division, both against the Australians. He was a member of the Wasps side that lost the 1986 JPS Cup Final to Bath.

SMITH
Stephen Rider

Scrum-half. 1959-1964 (Richmond, 5 caps).
Debut v Wales, 17 January 1959.
Born: 21 October 1934, India.
Educated: Eltham College, Cambridge University.
Clubs: Cambridge University (Blues 1958-9, also captain), Aldershot Services, Richmond, Hampshire (31 appearances), Barbarians.

Stephen Smith was assistant master at Harrow School before resigning to become a missionary in India with his wife Helen. He played for India against Ceylon in 1968 and appeared in the All-India rugby tournament at Bombay for five years, hanging up his boots — for the second time — in 1972. He skippered Hampshire for a while.

SMITH
Stephen James

Scrum-half. 1973-1983 (Sale, 28 caps).

Steve Smith

Debut v Ireland, 10 February 1973.
Born: 22 July 1951, Stockport.
Educated: King's School (Macclesfield), Loughborough Colleges.
Clubs: Wilmslow, Sale, Lancashire (16 appearances), Cheshire (captain 1972), Barbarians.

One of the real characters of the game and an outstanding player with a great sense of humour, Steve Smith was in and out of the England side over a ten-year period but still managed to win a record number of caps for a scrum-half and captained his country in 1982. He won his first representative honours in 1972, when he flew out to join the British Lions in South Africa, as a replacement for the injured Lionel Weston. Later that year he played for the North-West Counties in their memorable win over the New Zealanders. Smith, who appeared for Wilmslow during his college holidays before joining Sale, played for England Under-23s against Tonga in 1974. He first played for Cheshire as a 19-year-old and was captain in 1972. He has worked as a rugby correspondent of the *Today* newspaper and as a school teacher. He is a partner, with Fran Cotton and Tony Neary, of *Cotton Traders*.

SMITH
Trellevyn Harvey

Hooker. 1951 (Northampton, 1 cap).
Debut v Wales, 20 January 1951.
Born: 3 April 1920, Bedford.
Club: Northampton.

SOANE
Frank

Forward. 1893-1894 (Bath, 4 caps).
Debut v Scotland, 4 March 1893.
Born: 12 September 1866, Bath; Died: 1 April 1932.
Educated: Clifton House (Eastbourne).
Clubs: Oldfield Park, Bath, Somerset (45 appearances, captain 1896-9), Barbarians.

Frank Soane was the first England international to be capped from Bath, the club he skippered from 1890 to 1898. He was the Somerset secretary from 1893 to 1896 and president in 1902-03.

SOBEY
Wilfred Henry

Scrum Half. 1930-1932 (Old Millhillians, 5 caps).
Debut v Wales, 18 January 1930.
Born: 1 April 1905.
Educated: Mill Hill School, Cambridge University.
Clubs: Cambridge University (Blues 1925-6), Old Millhillians, London Counties, Hampshire, Barbarians.

Sobey went on the British Isles tour of Argentina in 1927 and was vice-captain of the British Isles tour party to New Zealand and Australia in 1930, when he was injured in the first match of the tour and took no further part. He was headmaster of Kingsfield Prep School.

SOLOMON
Bert ('Barney')

Centre. 1910 (Redruth, 1 cap).
Debut v Wales, 15 January 1910.
Born: 8 March 1885; Died: 30 June 1961.
Clubs: Treleigh Rangers, Redruth, Cornwall (26 appearances).

Bert Solomon was a legendary figure and one of the most exciting players of his era. He scored a try on his international debut and was a member of the Cornwall XV which won Olympic silver medal for rugby (representing Great Britain) against Australia in 1908. His son, Alfred, played for Camborne and appeared for Cornwall/Devon against the third Wallabies in 1947.

SPARKS
Robert Henry Ware

Prop. 1928-1931 (Plymouth Albion, 9 caps).
Debut v Ireland, 11 February 1928.
Born: 19 February 1899.
Clubs: Plymouth Albion, Civil Service, Devon.

He was employed in HM Dockyard and captained both Plymouth Albion and Devon.

SPEED
Harry

Forward. 1894-1896 (Castleford, 4 caps).
Debut v Wales, 6 January 1894.
Born: 19 August 1871, Castleford; Died: 3 July 1937, Castleford.
Clubs: Castleford, Yorkshire (25 appearances), Castleford RL.

He made his Yorkshire debut against Lancashire and played his last game against Glamorgan. His England cap is reputed to be at Castleford RFC. He was a licensee.

SPENCE
Frederick William, JP

Half-back. 1890 (Birkenhead Park, 1 cap).
Debut v Ireland, 15 March 1890.
Born: May 1867.
Educated: Fettes College.
Club: Birkenhead Park.

A civil servant, he emigrated to Australia and became a JP. He was awarded the Royal Humane Society Medal, one of the highest honours that can be awarded to a civilian, when he saved a person from drowning in Sydney Harbour.

SPENCER
Jeremy

Scrum-half. 1966 (Harlequins, 1 cap).
Debut v Wales, 15 January 1966.
Born: 27 June 1939.
Clubs: Harlequins, St Jean-de-Luz (France).

A player who, at first glance, appeared very frail, he was quite the opposite. He was also very agile. It was said that his home was a converted omnibus. A painter, he once had an exhibition of his work with the famous Spanish artist Juan Benito. His hobbies were weaving and gymnastic ballet.

SPENCER
John Sothern

Centre. 1969-1971 (Cambridge University, Headingley, 15 caps).
Debut v Ireland, 8 February 1969.
Born: 19 August 1947.
Educated: Cressbrook School (Kirby Lonsdale), Sedbergh School.
Clubs: Upper Wharfedale, Headingley, Barbarians, Yorkshire (2 appearances).

Spencer was head boy at Cressbrook and played for the Upper Wharfdale club whilst still at school. Not surprisingly he was capped by England Schoolboys. He skippered England Under-25s against Fiji in 1970 and went on the full tour to South Africa in 1972. He is a solicitor.

SPONG
Roger Spencer

Fly half. 1929-1932 (Old Millhillians, 8 caps).
Debut v France, 1 April 1929.
Born: 23 October 1906; Died: 27 March 1980.
Educated: Mill Hill School.
Clubs: Old Millhillians, Middlesex, Barbarians.

A composed, thoughtful player, he had abundant skills and tactical insight. He went on the British Isles tour of Australia and New Zealand in 1930, the first occasion on which the team were known as 'The Lions'. He was one of 16 English players in the party and scored five tries during the tour. Spong captained Old Millhillians in 1930-31 and was the club's chairman from 1967 to 1980.

SPOONER
Reginald Herbert

Wing. 1903 (Liverpool, 1 cap).
Debut v Wales, 10 January 1903.
Born: 21 October 1880, Litherland, near Bootle, Lancashire; Died: 2 October 1961, Woodhall Spa, Lincolnshire.
Educated: Marlborough College.
Clubs: Marlborough Nomads, Liverpool, Lancashire (10 appearances).

Reg Spooner was better known as one of the most stylish opening batsmen in the history of cricket. A tall, slim right-hander, he made his debut for Lancashire against Middlesex at Lord's in 1899 and when his career ended in 1923, he had scored 13,681 first-class runs (average 36.28) with 31 centuries (five of them of 200 or more) and held 132 catches.

He played ten times for England

between 1905 and 1912, hitting 119 against South Africa at Lord's in 1912. He was also invited to captain the tour of Australia with MCC in 1920-21, but declined because he felt he was not fit enough. He made 17 appearances for the Gentleman against the Players.

Spooner served in the Manchester Regiment during the Boer War (1900-1902) and made a good recovery from enteric fever; as a captain in the Lincolnshire Regiment on the Western Front during World War One, he was twice severely wounded and was awarded the Mons Star. But for these interruptions, his cricket statistics would be even more impressive.

He was president of Lancashire CCC from 1945 to 1946 and also played soccer for Lancashire. Two brothers and a father were also cricketers. He was assistant estate agent to Leonard Brassey of Northamptonshire, and later as land agent at the Earl of Londesborough's Blankney Estate in Lincolnshire. He died in a Lincolnshire nursing home a few days before his 81st birthday.

SPRINGMAN
Herman Henry

Forward. 1879-1887 (Liverpool, 2 caps).
Debut v Scotland, 10 March 1879.
Born: 1859, Liverpool; Died: 17 October 1936.
Educated: Craigmount School (Edinburgh).
Clubs: Liverpool, Lancashire.

Springman emigrated to the USA shortly after 1879, but returned in 1887 to be capped for a second time, a quite unusual circumstance. He was the brother of P.Springman (Oxford University).

SPURLING
Aubrey

Forward. 1882 (Blackheath, 1 cap).
Debut v Ireland, 6 February 1882.
Born: 19 July 1856; Died: 26 March 1945.
Educated: Blackheath Proprietory School.
Clubs: Blackheath, Kent.

Spurling was later the Blackheath treasurer. He was the brother of Norman, also an England international.

SPURLING
Norman

Forward. 1886-1887 (Blackheath, 3 caps).
Debut v Ireland, 6 February 1886.
Born: 15 February 1864; Died: 20 July 1919.
Educated: Blackheath Proprietory School.
Clubs: Blackheath, Kent.

Brother of Aubrey Spurling, Norman was first 'capped' in the 1888 team which did not play.

SQUIRES
Peter John

Wing. 1973-1979 (Harrogate, 29 caps).
Debut v France, 24 February 1973.
Born: 4 August 1951, Ripon, Yorkshire.
Educated: Ripon Grammar School, St John's College (York).
Clubs: Ripon, Harrogate, Yorkshire (56 appearances, captain 1979-82), Barbarians.

Peter Squires

Squires made a then record 29 appearances on the wing for England. He went on the tour to Australia in 1975 and the British Lions tour of New Zealand in 1977, when he made nine appearances including one Test). He made 49 appearances for Yorkshire CCC from 1972 to 1976. Employed as a school teacher.

STAFFORD
Richard Calvert (Dick)

Prop. 1912 (Bedford, 4 caps).
Debut v Wales, 20 January 1912.
Born: 23 July 1893, Bedford; Died: 1 December 1912, Bedford.
Educated: Bedford Modern School.
Club: Bedford.

His is one of the most tragic instances of an England rugby player losing his life. Dick Stafford died of spinal cancer when he was only 19, the youngest age at which an England international has died.

STAFFORD
William Francis Howard, CB

Forward. 1874 (Royal Engineers, 1 cap).
Debut v Scotland, 23 February 1874.
Born:19 December 1854;Died:8 August 1942.
Educated: Wellington College, Royal Military Academy (Sandhurst), Army.

Clubs: Royal Engineers, Rugby

Stafford was in the Royal Engineers and served in the Afghan War of 1878-80, being mentioned in despatches. The son of Major-General W.J.F.Stafford, who served in the South African war of 1899-1902, being awarded the King's and Queen's Medals. He retired from service as a brigadier-general in 1911, but returned at the age of 60 to serve in World War One, again being mentioned in despatches.

STANBURY
Edward

Flanker. 1926-1929 (Plymouth Albion, 16 caps).
Debut v Wales, 16 January 1926.
Born: 1897; Died: 1 May 1968, Plympton.
Clubs: Plymouth Albion, Devon, Barbarians.

Edward Stanbury

Stanbury's 16 international appearances are a record for a Devonian and also make him the Plymouth club's most capped player. He represented Devon on the RFU from 1963 to 1968, was on the Devon RFU committee from 1948 to 1968, secretary of the Devon union from 1949 to 1954 and its president from 1954 to 1957. He often used the expression, 'Good and hearty,' when asked to describe a match. He was good humoured and much liked. He was employed as a rates officer.

STANDING
G.

Forward. 1882 (Blackheath, 2 caps).
Debut v Wales, 16 December 1882.
Club: Blackheath.

Standing made 81 appearances for Blackheath between 1881 and 1885.

STANGER-LEATHES
Christopher Francis

Full-back. 1905 (Northern, 1 cap).
Debut v Ireland, 11 February 1905.
Born: 9 May 1881; Died: 27 February 1965.
Educated: Sherborne School.
Clubs: Northern, Northumberland.

Stanger-Leathes went on the British Isles tour of Australia and New Zealand in 1904, before gaining his full England cap. He skippered Northumberland at cricket and golf.

STARK
Kendrick James

Prop. 1927-1928 (Old Alleynians, 9 caps).
Debut v Wales, 15 January 1927.
Born: 18 August 1904.
Educated: Dulwich College.
Clubs: Old Alleynians, London Counties, Surrey.

He served during World War Two as a captain in the RASC and was mentioned in despatches.

STARKS
Anthony

Forward. 1896 (Castleford, 2 caps).
Debut v Wales, 4 January 1896.
Born: 11 August 1873, Castleford; Died: January 1952, Kingston upon Hull.
Clubs: Castleford, Yorkshire (13 appearances), Hull Kingston Rovers RL.

Starks, a licensee, switched codes to join Hull Kingston Rovers in 1897.

STARMER-SMITH
Nigel Christopher

Scrum-half. 1969-1971 (Harlequins, 7 caps).
Debut v South Africa, 20 December 1969.
Born: 25 December 1944, Cheltenham.
Educated: Magdalen College School (Oxford), Oxford University.
Clubs: Oxford University (Blues 1965-6), Harlequins, Surrey, Barbarians.

Starmer-Smith was reserve for England seven times before finally being capped five days before his 25th birthday. He played hockey for Oxford University and cricket for the TA and appeared in the Public School Wanderers team which reached the 1973 Middlesex Sevens Final. He was a teacher at Epsom College before moving to the BBC to become a regular rugby commentator. He is the editor of *Rugby World and Post* and author of the official history of the Barbarians which was published in 1977.

START
Sydney Philip

Scrum half. 1907 (United Services (Portsmouth), Royal Navy, 1 cap).
Debut v Scotland, 16 March 1907.
Born: 17 May 1879, Manchester; Died: 14 December 1969, Kent.
Educated: Manchester Grammar School, Royal Naval Engineering College (Keyham).
Clubs: United Services (Portsmouth), Devon, Surrey, Royal Navy.

Start joined the Royal Navy in 1894 and served during World War One. He was ADC to King George V in 1931 and eventually reached the rank of rear admiral. He played cricket for Cambridgeshire CCC.

STEEDS
John Harold

Hooker. 1949-1950 (Saracens, 5 caps).
Debut v France, 26 February 1949.
Born: 27 September 1916.
Educated: St Edward's School (Oxford), Cambridge University.
Clubs: Cambridge University (Blue 1938), Middlesex Hospital, Harlequins, Saracens, Middlesex, Barbarians.

Steeds was the first player to be capped for England direct from the Saracens club. During World War Two he served as a surgeon-lieutenant in the RNVR and broke his jaw and neck in an accident. He was registrar at the Middlesex Hospital from 1946 to 1950, after which he practised as a GP.

STEELE-BODGER
Michael Roland, CBE

Flanker. 1947-1948 (Cambridge University, 9 caps).
Debut v Wales, 18 January 1947.
Born: 4 September 1925.
Educated: Rugby School, Cambridge University, Edinburgh University.
Clubs: Cambridge University (Blues 1945-6), Edinburgh University, Harlequins, Moseley, Co-optimists, Barbarians.

Mickey Steele-Bodger

Steele-Bodger was a very versatile player who once appeared as a scrum-half for England. Injury curtailed his playing days but he has enjoyed a distinguished career as an administrator. He was an England selector from 1953 to 1968, an RFU trustee and president for 1973-4 and also chairman of the International Board. He was a vice-president of the Barbarians from 1973 to 1988, when he was elected that famous club's president, a position he currently holds. He was awarded the CBE in 1990.

STEINTHAL
Francis Eric

Centre. 1913 (Ilkley, 2 caps).
Debut v Wales, 18 January 1913.
Born: 21 November 1886, Bradford.
Educated: Bradford Grammar School, Oxford University.
Clubs: Oxford University (Blue 1906), Ilkley, Yorkshire (16 appearances).

Steinthal served during World War One as a captain in the Royal Fusiliers and was wounded in 1918. He was a school teacher who emigrated to the USA around 1947-8. He was assistant professor of German and French at the University of California from the mid-1950s.

STEVENS
Claude Brian ('Stack')

Prop. 1969-1975 (Penzance-Newlyn, Harlequins, 25 caps).
Debut v South Africa, 20 December 1969.
Born: 2 June 1941, Cornwall.
Educated: Leedstown High School (Cornwall), Cornwall Technical College.
Clubs: Penzance-Newlyn, Harlequins, Cornwall (83 appearances), Barbarians.

A farmer, he holds the record for most appearances for Cornwall and went on the British Lions tour of Australia and New Zealand in 1971.

STILL
Ernest Robert

Forward. 1873 (Oxford University, Ravenscourt Park, 1 cap).
Debut v Scotland, 3 March 1873.
Born: 14 July 1852; Died: 30 November 1931.
Educated: Rugby School, Oxford University.
Clubs: Oxford University (Blues 1871-3), Ravenscourt Park.

STIRLING
Robert Victor

Prop. 1951-1954 (Leicester, RAF, Wasps, 18 caps).
Debut v Wales, 20 January 1951.
Born: 4 September 1919, Lichfield; Died: 14 January 1990.
Clubs: RAF, Combined Services, Ayles-

'Stack' Stevens

tone St James, Leicester, Wasps, Kent, Barbarians.

Stirling was first capped at the age of 31 and went on to skipper England five times, playing in the 1954 Triple Crown team. He propped Eric Evans and their partnership became the nucleus of an England pack which was one of the most effective yet. Stirling served during World War Two, which saw his rise from flight-sergeant to wing commander. He represented the RAF as a heavyweight boxer from 1948 and joined Wasps in 1953, later becoming a vice-president of that club.

STODDART
Andrew Ernest

Back. 1885-1893 (Blackheath, 10 caps).
Debut v Wales, 3 January 1885.
Born: 11 March 1863, South Shields; Died: 3 April 1915, London.

Educated: Rev G.W.Oliver's School, St John's Wood School.

Clubs: Harlequins, Blackheath, Middlesex, Barbarians.

Andrew Stoddart is the only player to captain England and the British Isles at rugby and England at cricket. Indeed, he must be the only man who has remained behind to take part in a rugby tour of Australia and New Zealand immediately after a cricket tour there. He stayed in Australia after the 1887-

Andrew Stoddart

8 cricket tour to await the arrival of the British Isles squad, which he took over as captain after R.L.Seddon drowned.

Stoddart became the first player to kick a goal from a mark in international competition. He went on to captain England four times and on 15 March 1890, he led his country to a victory over the Irish which resulted in England sharing the International Championship with Scotland.

Stoddart played cricket for Middlesex and led England to victory over Australia in 1894-5. Altogether he played in 16 Tests for England, scoring 996 runs at an average of 35.57. His full first-class tally was 16,738 runs (average 32.13) and he scored 26 centuries and took 278 wickets. His final appearance for Middlesex in 1900 saw him score a mammoth 221 against Somerset at Lord's. For Hampstead against Stoics in 1885 he scored 485, then the highest score ever recorded. He toured Australia four times and the West Indies and America once each.

A stockbroker by profession, his end was tragic. His later years saw his health decline, he became depressed, and in April 1915 he shot himself through the head.

STODDART
Wilfred Bowring, JP

Forward. 1897 (Liverpool, 3 caps).
Debut v Wales, 9 January 1897.
Born: 27 April 1871, West Derby, Liverpool; Died: 8 January 1935, Grassendale, Liverpool.

Educated: Royal Liverpool Institute.

Clubs: Liverpool, Lancashire, Barbarians.

Wilfred Stoddart, who played for the now-defunct Dingle CC after leaving school and captained the Liverpool cricket and rugby teams, played 15 first-class matches for Lancashire CCC in 1898 and 1889, as well as appearing for MCC and the Gentlemen. For Lancashire he took 6 for 121 against Kent at Canterbury in 1898 and he was later a member of the Lancashire CCC committee. He was captain of the Royal Liverpool Golf Club in 1910 and president of the English Golf Union in 1926.

A member of Liverpool City Council — he was elected an alderman in 1929 — Stoddart was also on the Liverpool Northern Hospitals Committee. He was the managing director of a Liverpool tobacco company, and a merchant and shipowner. His death followed a short illness.

STOKES
Frederick

Forward. 1871-1873 (Blackheath, 3 caps).
Debut v Scotland, 27 March 1871.
Born: 12 July 1851, Blackheath; Died: 7 January 1928, Basingstoke.

Educated: Rugby School.

Clubs: Blackheath, Kent.

Stokes was England's very first captain, leading the side against Scotland at Raeburn Place in 1871. He was one of six brothers, of whom Lennard was also an England international. Fred Stokes also captained Blackheath and played cricket for Kent and for the Gentlemen against the Players. He was the RFU president in 1874-5, when he was only

24. A solicitor, he was the brother-in-law of J.F.Green, who was also an England international.

STOKES
Lennard

Back. 1875-1881 (Blackheath, 12 caps).
Debut v Ireland, 15 February 1875.
Born: 12 February 1856; Died: 3 May 1933.
Educated: Sidney College (Bath).
Clubs: Blackheath, Guy's Hospital.

Lennard Stokes had a reputation as an excellent place and drop-goal kicker — he dropped a goal from around 80 yards in the 1881 game against Scotland — and was said to be one of the most complete backs of his era. When he retired in 1881, so that he could concentrate on a medical career, he was the holder of a record 12 caps for England. His 17 conversions in internationals remains an English record.

He captained England on five occasions — he was the first English skipper against the Welsh in 1881 — and he also led Blackheath from 1876 to 1881, scoring 56 tries out of 136 by the entire team in 83 matches during his captaincy.

He was elected a member of the RFU committee in 1876 and served on it for over 50 years, being president from 1886 to 1888 and a trustee from 1926 to 1929. He played cricket for Kent, was United Hospital's sprint champion and a member of Guy's 1877 Hospital Cup-winning team. He was the brother of Fred Stokes and brother-in-law of J.F.Green.

According to an edition of *Guy's Gazette* in 1873, he was 'a faultless catch and field, and a very quick starter, and with his speed of foot, wonderful dodging powers, and clever "shoving off" was an extremely difficult man to tackle. An excellent place-kicker, he was also for several seasons the longest drop in the three kingdoms. Some of his drops at goal from difficult positons, when hemmed in by opponents, were simply marvellous. His tackling was not quite up to the standard of the rest of his play, as he frequently aimed too high, but his great speed often enabled him to rectify an error by a second attempt.'

STONE
Francis Le Strange, MC

Number 8. 1914 (Blackheath,, 1 cap).
Debut v France, 13 April 1914.
Born: 1886; Died: 7 October 1938.
Educated: Harrow School.
Clubs: Blackheath, London Counties, Barbarians.

Stone captained Blackheath in 1910-11. A solicitor by profession, he served during World War One with the King's Own Hussars.

STOOP
Adrian Dura, MC

Scrum-half/Fly-half. 1905-1922 (Harlequins, 15 caps).
Debut v Scotland, 18 March 1905.
Born: 27 March 1883, London; Died: 27 November 1957.
Educated: Dover College, Rugby School, Oxford University.
Clubs: Oxford University (Blues 1902-04), Harlequins, Surrey, Barbarians.

Adrian Stoop was in the Rugby School XV in 1900, when the Webb Ellis plaque was placed in the Doctor's Wall. He was noticed by Harlequins when their 'A' XV visited the school and he played his last game for the Quins against Eastbourne in 1938, aged 55.

Adrian Stoop

Indeed, he is the greatest name in the Harlequins' history: captain from 1906 to 1914, secretary from 1920 to 1938, and president from 1920 to 1949. His name is also immortalised in the Quins' Adrian Stoop Memorial Ground at Twickenham.

A notable tactician and an artist at the sideways tackle, Stoop was the mentor for Harlequins for many years. Unlucky with injuries — he broke his collar-bone twice, against United Services in 1907-1908, and against London Scottish the following season — it took him seven years to gain 15 England caps. Originally he intended to sign for Blackheath but remained loyal to Harlequins after joining that club.

He was an RFU selector from 1927 to

Adrian Stoop

1931, president in 1932-3, Central District representative from 1911 to 1933 and a member of the International Board in 1923. He also was a capable referee and took charge of the first Mobbs Memorial Match between the Barbarians and East Midlands in 1921. In April 1922 he captained Harlequins Past against Harlequins Present in aid of King Edward VII's Hospital Fund.

Stoop had a naturalised Dutch father and his mother was half Scots and half Irish. Stoop, who qualified as a barrister, was wounded in Mesopotamia during World War One whilst serving with the Queen's Royal West Surrey Regiment. He was awarded the Military Cross in 1919.

STOOP
Frederick MacFarlane ('Tim')

Centre. 1910-1913 (Harlequins, 4 caps).
Debut v Scotland, 19 March 1910.
Born: 17 September 1888, London; Died: 24 November 1972.
Educated: Rugby School.
Clubs: Harlequins, Surrey, Barbarians.

He played alongside his brother, Adrian Stoop, three times for England. A formidable three-quarter, he was taller and much heavier than his famous sibling. In April 1922 he played for Harlequins Past against Harlequins Present in aid of King Edward VII's Hospital Fund. A stock-broker, he served during World War One with the East Kent Regiment's Machine-gun Corps in Mesopotamia. He was wounded and mentioned in despatches.

STOUT
Frank Moxham, MC

Forward. 1897-1905 (Richmond, 14 caps).
Debut v Wales, 9 January 1897.
Born: 21 February 1877, Liverpool; Died: 30 May 1926, Sussex.
Clubs: Gloucester, Richmond, Gloucestershire (44 appearances), Barbarians.

Son of William Stout, who won the Diamond Sculls at Henley, he played alongside his brother, Percy, four times for England and went on the British Isles tours of Australia and New Zealand in 1899 and South Africa in 1903. He led the Lions on the 1899 tour after the Revd M.Mullineux stepped down after the First Test. Frank Stout played soccer for Gloucester before taking up rugby. He captained Richmond from 1903 to 1905 and served in World War One as a lieutenant in the Hussars, being mentioned in despatches 1916 and again in 1919.

STOUT
Percy Wyfold, DSO OBE

Wing. 1898-1899 (Richmond, 5 caps).
Debut v Scotland, 12 March 1898.
Born: 20 November 1875; Died: 9 October 1937.
Educated: Crypt Grammar School (Gloucester).
Clubs: Gloucester, Richmond, Bristol, Gloucestershire, Barbarians.

Son of William and brother of Frank, with whom he played four times in the England side, like his brother he played soccer first, turning out for the Corinthians and Gloucestershire. He served in World War One as an acting captain with the Machine Gun Corps, seeing action in Egypt. He was awarded the DSO in 1917, the OBE in 1919 and was mentioned in despatches on no less than five occasions. He was also awarded Order of the Nile (4th Class). His DSO came whilst he was serving in Gaza and the *War Illustrated* (Vol 7 p120) published his citation.

STRINGER
Nicholas Courtenay

Full-back. 1982-1985 (Wasps, 5 caps).
Debut v Australia, 2 January 1982.
Born: 4 October 1960.
Clubs: Wasps, Barbarians.

Nick Stringer

Stringer won his first cap as a replacement for Mike Slemen but was forced to retire from rugby in August 1988, at the age of 27, after suffering repeated concussion. He was advised that another blow to the head could have serious consequences. He was a member of the Wasps 1986 JPS Cup Final team and played for England Under-23s against the Netherlands (when he kicked ten out of ten successful kicks) and for England Students in 1980. He went on the England tour of Romania in 1983 and played for England 'B' against France in 1981. He was formerly on the groundstaff at Lord's cricket ground. He works in insurance.

STRONG
Edmund Linwood

Forward. 1884 (Oxford University, 3 caps).
Debut v Wales, 5 January 1884.
Born: December 1862; Died: 20 March 1945, India.
Educated: Edinburgh Academy, Oxford University.
Clubs: Weston, Oxford University (Blues 1881-3), Bath, Somerset.

A clergyman, ordained in 1887, he became curate of St John the Divine, Kennington. He gave great service to the Oxford University mission in Calcutta, where he enjoyed a lengthy career from 1894 until his death. He also played cricket.

SUMMERSCALES
George Edward

Forward. 1905 (Durham City, 1 cap).
Debut v New Zealand, 2 December 1905.
Born: 1879; Died: 31 December 1936, Durham.
Clubs: Durham City, Durham County.

Summerscales made his only appearance for England against the first New Zealand All Blacks at the Crystal Palace. He played 48 times for the county side from 1900 to 1909, and then made a single appearance in 1920, at the age of 41. He served in World War One.

SUTCLIFFE
John William

Wing. 1889 (Heckmondwike, 1 cap).
Debut v Maoris 16 February 1889.
Born: 14 April 1868, Shibden, near Halifax; Died: 7 July 1947.
Educated: St Thomas's School (Bradford).
Clubs: Bradford, Heckmondwike, Yorkshire (8 appearances).

John Sutcliffe, who scored a try and conversion on his international debut, remained with Heckmondwike until they changed to the Northern Union game. Sutcliffe changed codes altogether and began to play soccer. He joined Bolton Wanderers in September 1889 and later played for Millwall (April 1902), Manchester United (May 1903), Plymouth Argyle (close season 1904) and Southend United (1911-12). He was coach at Arnham in 1914 and became Bradford City's trainer in the close season of 1919.

He gained a rugby cap against the Maoris in 1889, becoming one of only three players to have played both codes for England. In soccer he was capped five times from Bolton Wanderers (against Scotland in 1895 and 1901; against Wales in 1893 and 1903; and against Ireland in 1895) and he played in the 1894 FA Cup Final. He played three times for the Football League and was a prolific batsman with Great Lever CC. His brother Charles, who was 22 years younger, kept goal for Leeds City, Rotherham and Sheffield United.

SWARBRICK
David William

Wing. 1947-1949 (Oxford University, 6 caps).
Debut v Wales, 18 January 1947.
Born: 17 January 1927
Educated: Kingswood School, Oxford University.
Clubs: Oxford University (Blues 1946-8), Blackheath, Midland Counties, Middlesex, Barbarians.

Swarbrick, who worked for chemical giants ICI, went on the Oxford-Cambridge University tour of Argentina in 1948. His career was a short one because he was forced to quit the game due to a head injury. He captained Blackheath from 1950 to 1952.

SWAYNE
Denys Harold

Flanker. 1931 (Oxford University, 1 cap).
Debut v Wales, 17 January 1931.
Born: 23 November 1909; Died: 9 September 1990.
Educated: Bromsgrove School, Oxford University.
Clubs: Oxford University (Blues 1930-31), St George's Hospital, Harlequins, London Counties, Herefordshire & Worcestershire, North Midlands, Middlesex, Gloucestershire.

One of three brothers (J.W.R. was also an England international) he served in World War Two in the RAMC and was wounded in the Normandy landings. After the war he became a GP in Stevenage. He also represented the United Hospitals at cricket.

SWAYNE
John Walter Rocke, MC TD

Number 8. 1929 (Bridgwater, 1 cap).
Debut v Wales, 19 January 1929.
Born: 27 May 1906; Died: June 1987.
Educated: Bromsgrove School.
Clubs: Bridgwater, Bromsgrove, Harlequins, Somerset.

One of three brothers (Denys was also an England international) he served during World War Two with the North Somerset Yeomanry. His Military Cross was awarded whilst fighting the Vichy French in 1941 in the Middle East. He served with the Territorial Army before the war and was mobilized to the Middle East early in 1940. After Palestine he was based in Huddersfield for a time. He skippered Bridgwater and Somerset and played squash and golf for Somerset, being president of the SW Golf Union in 1969.

SWIFT
Anthony Hugh

Left-wing. 1981-1984 (Swansea, 6 caps).
Debut v Argentina, 30 May 1981.
Born: 24 May 1959, Preston.
Educated: Hutton Grammar School.
Clubs: Swansea, Fylde, Bath, Barbarians.

Swift was a teammate of Gareth Roberts and Huw Davies for UMIST against Exeter in the 1980 UAU Cup Final. He played for England Under-23s and went on the England tours of Argentina in 1981 and the USA and Canada in 1982. He was in the Bath team which equalled Leicester's record when they won their third successive JPS Cup Final in 1986.

SYDDALL
James Paul

Lock. 1982-1984 (Waterloo, 2 caps).
Debut v Ireland, 6 February 1982.
Born: 7 March 1956.

Educated: De La Salle School (Salford).
Clubs: Waterloo, Lancashire (15 appearances), Barbarians.

Syddall played for England Under-19s against Wales in 1974 and was capped for England 'B' against France at Twickenham in 1981. He helped Lancashire win the County Championship from 1980-82, went on the England tour of Canada and the USA in 1982, playing in four of the eight games, and captained Waterloo in 1987-8. He missed much of the 1980-81 season due to a shoulder injury sustained in a county game and later suffered a broken arm in a motor accident. He made his debut for the Barbarians against the East Midlands in March 1982.

SYKES
Alexander Richard

Hooker. 1914 (Blackheath, 1 cap).
Debut v France, 13 April 1914.
Educated: Birkenhead School, Liverpool University.
Clubs: Liverpool University, Blackheath, Barbarians.

He studied architecture at Liverpool University and in 1912 was awarded a first-class certificate in this subject. With his brother, George Reginald, he played rugby for the university.

SYKES
Frank Douglas

Wing. 1955-1963 (Northampton, 4 caps).
Debut v France, 26 February 1955.
Born: 9 December 1927, Batley.
Educated: St Paul's College (Cheltenham).
Clubs: Huddersfield, Northampton, Yorkshire (79 appearances, captain 1957-8), Barbarians, Boston (USA).

Huddersfield's most capped player, he was a PE teacher at Northampton Grammer School from 1954 to 1955, having served with the RAEC as a sergeant in Singapore from 1947 until 1949. He emigrated to the USA and played for Boston RFC in Massachusetts. In 1972 he was president of the New England RFU.

SYKES
Patrick William

Scrum-half. 1948-1953 (Wasps, 7 caps).
Debut v France, 29 March 1948.
Born: 3 March 1925, Canada.
Educated: St John's School (Leatherhead), Cambridge University.
Clubs: Cambridge University (no Blue), Wasps, RAF, Combined Services, London Counties, Eastern Counties (16 appearances).

Sykes was in the 1952 Championship-winning side and played against every Home country. Four of his 'home' international shirts were exchanged with his respective opposite numbers and presented to Wasps along with an England jersey that he did not exchange. He played in the wartime Services international against the Kiwis in 1944. He joined Wasps upon leaving school and was vice president in 1955 and First XV captain from 1951 to 1955. He was chairman of the Middlesex selectors.

SYRETT
Ronald Edward

Flanker. 1958-1962 (Wasps, 11 caps).
Debut v Wales, 18 January 1958.
Born: 5 January 1931, Beaconsfield.

Educated: Royal Grammar School (High Wycombe) Wasps, High Wycombe, RAF, London Counties, Middlesex, Barbarians.

He played for Wasps from 1948 to 1963 and was vice captain in 1956-7. He is the brother-in-law of J.E.Woodward, also an England international. He was president of Buckinghamshire Referees' Society and a butcher until 1960, when he went into business in the retail sports trade.

TALLENT
John Arthur, CBE TD

Centre. 1931-1935 (Cambridge University, Blackheath, 5 caps).
Debut v Scotland, 21 March 1931.
Born: 8 March 1911, Christchurch.

Educated: Sherborne School, Cambridge University.

Clubs: Cambridge University (Blues 1929-31), Blackheath, Kent, East Midlands, Barbarians.

John Tallent

Tallent scored two tries on his international debut. He was a teacher at Stowe School from 1932 to 1936 and a member of the Stock Exchange from 1936 to 1939 and from 1946 to 1977. During World War Two he served with the Honorable Artillery Company as a lieutenant-colonel in the 118 Regiment. He was awarded the OBE (Military) in 1946 and his CB was awarded in 1960 for services to rugby. He was RFU president in 1959-60. and Central District CB representative in 1947.

TANNER
Christopher Champain, AM

Wing. 1930-1932 (Cambridge University, Gloucester, 5 caps).
Debut v Scotland, 15 March 1930.
Born: 24 June 1908; Died: 22 May 1941, Crete (killed in action).

Educated: Cheltenham College, Cambridge University.

Clubs: Cambridge University (Blue 1930), Richmond, Gloucester, Gloucestershire, Barbarians.

Tanner made his debut for the Barbarians against the East Midlands in 1929-30 and scored three tries. He was ordained in 1935 and became curate at Farnham, remaining there until 1937 when he took over the curacy of St Mary de Lode in Gloucester until 1939. He was the rector of Haselmere in 1939, when war broke out, and he then joined the Royal Naval Volunteer Reserve. He was killed in action whilst serving aboard HMS Fiji in the bloody battle that ensued off that island in 1941. He was awarded a posthumous Albert medal in 1942 for efforts in saving wounded sailors' when HMS Fiji was sunk. He lost his life shortly after an heroic deed which saved the life of one sailor who he managed to get aboard a rescue ship before exhaustion contributed to his own drowning. The Albert Medal is today known as the George Cross.

TARR
Francis Nathaniel

Centre. 1909-1913 (Leicester, 4 caps).
Debut v Australia, 9 January 1909.
Born: 14 August 1887; Died: 18 July 1915, Ypres (killed in action).

Educated: Stoneygate School (Leicester), Uppingham School, Oxford University.

Clubs: Oxford University (Blues 1907-09), Leicester, Headingley, Richmond, Midland Counties.

A solicitor, he was one of the first international players to join up on the first day of World War One.

TATHAM
William Meaburn

Forward. 1882-1884 (Oxford University, 7 caps).
Debut v Scotland, 4 March 1882.

Educated: Marlborough College, Oxford University.

Clubs: Marlborough Nomads, Oxford University (Blues 1881-3, later as captain).

A clergyman he was ordained in 1885 to become curate of St Saviour's in Folkestone until 1890. He then became curate of St Agnes in Dennington until 1892, when he went to Doncaster as the vicar of Cantley. During the South African War he was acting chaplain to the forces.

TAYLOR
Arthur Sneyd

Full-back. 1882-1886 (Blackheath, 4 caps).
Debut v Wales, 16 December 1882.
Born: 7 December 1859; Died: 31 July 1917.

Educated: Merchant Taylor's School, Cambridge University.

Clubs: Cambridge University (Blues 1879-81), Guy's Hospital, Blackheath, Kent.

He was one of three brothers who played for Blackheath (Harry was also an England international). According to *Guy's Gazette*, Arthur Taylor was 'a sure fielder and kicker, tackled very low, would gather himself together and shoot at his man like a streak of lightning, bringing him down with all of a heap'. He was a GP in Surbiton.

TAYLOR
Ernest William ('Little Billy')

Half-back. 1892-1899 (Rockcliff, 14 caps).
Debut v Ireland, 6 February 1892.
Born: 20 February 1869, Newcastle upon Tyne.

Clubs: Rockcliff, Northumberland, Barbarians.

An all-round sportsman, he was described as the 'Prince of Half-backs'. An England captain, he also captained the Whitley Bay Golf club and became a professional golfer. He also played cricket for Northumberland.

TAYLOR
Frank ('Sos')

Prop. 1920 (Leicester, 2 caps).
Debut v France, 31 January 1920.
Born: 5 May 1890; Died: October 1956.

Educated: Medway Street School (Leicester).

Clubs: Medway Old Boys, Medway Athletic, Leicester, Leicestershire, Midland Counties.

Brother of 'Tim' Taylor, he served during World War One with the Leicestershire Regiment.

TAYLOR
Frederick Mark ('Tim')

Fly-half. 1914 (Leicester, 1 cap).
Debut v Wales, 17 January 1914.

Born: 18 March 1888; Died: 1964.

Educated: Medway Street School (Leicester).

Clubs: Medway Old Boys, Medway Athletic, Leicester, Leicestershire, Midland Counties.

'Tim' Taylor was the brother of 'Sos' Taylor, also an England international.

TAYLOR
Henry Herbert

Half-back. 1879-1882 (Blackheath, 5 caps).
Debut v Scotland, 10 March 1879.
Born: 1 September 1858; Died: 25 May 1942.
Educated: Merchant Taylor's School.
Clubs: St George's Hospital, Blackheath, Kent.

Brother of Arthur Taylor (also an England international), he was the first English international to score three tries, setting this record in the 1881 match against the Irish. His first two tries were described as 'brilliant' by the Press. In all he scored six tries in five international appearances. He was surgeon at the Royal Alexandra Hospital for Children, and later held a post at the Sussex Eye Hospital.

TAYLOR
John T. ('Long John')

Centre 1897-1905 (West Hartlepool, 11 caps).
Debut v Ireland, 6 February 1897.
Born: 26 May 1876; Died: 8 September 1951, Ashington.
Clubs: Castleford, West Hartlepool, Durham County, Yorkshire (18 appearances, captain 1899-1900).

He captained every club for whom he played and was famous for his dropkicks. He was a licensee.

TAYLOR
Philip Joseph

Number 8. 1955-1962 (Northampton, 6 caps).
Debut v Wales, 22 January 1955.
Born: 6 June 1931, Wakefield.
Clubs: Wakefield, Army, Blackheath, Loughborough Colleges, Northampton, Yorkshire (54 appearances), Hertfordshire, Barbarians.

He served in the Duke of Wellington's Regiment and played for the Army three times in 1951, against the Royal Navy, RAF and French Army. He captained Northampton from 1961 to 1963 and was a teacher at Northampton Grammar School.

TAYLOR
Robert Bainbridge

Flanker. 1966-1971 (Northampton, 16 caps).

Bob Taylor

Debut v Wales, 15 January 1966.
Born: 30 April 1942.
Educated: Northampton Grammar School, King Alfred's College (Winchester).
Clubs: Northampton, Hampshire (10 appearances), East Midlands, Barbarians.

Bob Taylor was on the British Lions tour of South Africa in 1968 and played in 14 games, more than any other British forward. He captained the Lions twice in the provincial matches, winning both. Taylor captained England against Wales in 1970 and England-Wales against Scotland-Ireland in the RFU Centenary match. He taught PE at Wellingborough Grammar School from 1965 and played basketball for Northamptonshire. He played rugby for Hampshire whilst at college in Winchester.

TAYLOR (also known as KIRWAN-TAYLOR)
William John, OBE

Wing. 1928 (Blackheath, 5 caps).
Debut v New South Wales, 7 January 1928.

Born: 29 June 1905.
Educated: Epsom College, Cambridge University.
Clubs: Cambridge University (Blue 1926), Blackheath, Barbarians, Surrey.

He scored a try on his debut and also played cricket, turning out for MCC and the Crusaders. Awarded the OBE in 1946 after serving in World War Two as a lieutenant-colonel with the Rifle Brigade, he was also GSO with the 1st Airborne Division. He was also a member of the Kandahar and Marsden's ski clubs.

Mike Teague

TEAGUE
Michael Clive

Number 8/Flanker. 1985-1991 (Gloucester, 21 caps).
Debut v France, 2 February 1985.
Born: 8 October 1960.
Educated: Churchdown School (Gloucester).
Clubs: Cardiff, Gloucester Old Boys, Gloucester.

Mike Teague made his England debut as replacement for J.P.Hall. On the British Lions tour of Australia in 1989, he was unable to play in the First Test because of injury but appeared in the Second and Third Tests and was voted 'Player of the Series'.

Teague represented England at Under-23 and 'B' levels and went on the tours to South Africa in 1984, to Australia and Fiji in 1991 and played in the 1991 World Cup Final. He was carried off after a few seconds of England's match against Wales in 1989. He appeared for an International XV v South Africa in 1989 and for the Barbarians v Wales in October 1990. He also played for Gloucester in the 1982 JPS Cup Final. His grandfather played for Gloucestershire. Teague is a self-employed builder.

TEDEN
Derek Edmund

Prop. 1939 (Richmond, 3 caps).
Debut v Wales, 21 January 1939.
Born: 19 July 1916; Died: 15 October 1940, Friesian Islands (killed in action).
Educated: Taunton School.
Clubs: Richmond, Barbarians.
Teden, who scored a try on his international debut, served during World War Two as a pilot officer in the RAF.

TEGGIN
Alfred

Forward. 1884-1887 (Broughton Rangers, 6 caps).
Debut v Ireland, 4 February 1884.
Born: 22 October 1860, Broughton, Manchester; Died: 23 July 1941, Cleveleys, Blackpool.
Clubs: Broughton Rangers, Lancashire (19 appearances).
Teggin played cricket for Salford CC and Lancashire as a leg-spinner.

TETLEY
Thomas Spece

Back. 1876 (Bradford, 1 cap).
Debut v Scotland, 6 March 1876.
Born: 1856; Died: 15 August 1924.
Clubs: Bradford, Yorkshire (10 appearances).
Employed as a worsted spinner, he was the first England international capped from Bradford. He was also a very good 100 yards sprinter.

THOMAS
Charles

Forward. 1895-1899 (Barnstaple, 4 caps).
Debut v Wales, 5 January 1895.
Born: 1875; Died: 1935.

Charles Thomas

Clubs: Barnstaple Oaks, Barnstaple, Devon.
Charles Thomas is Barnstaple's most capped player.

THOMPSON
Peter Humphrey

Wing. 1956-1959 (Headingley, Waterloo, 17 caps).
Debut v Wales, 21 January 1956.
Born: 18 January 1929, Scarborough.

W.B. Thompson

Educated: Leeds Grammar School.

Clubs: Headingley, Waterloo, Yorkshire (47 appearances), Barbarians.

Peter Thompson captained the Headingley club in 1956-7.

THOMSON
George Thomas

Forward. 1878-1885 (Halifax, 9 caps).
Debut v Scotland,4 March 1878.
Born: 1857; Died: 31 October 1899, Australia.
Educated: Heath School (Halifax).
Clubs: Halifax, Yorkshire (29 appearances, captain 1881-4).

He helped Halifax win the first Yorkshire Cup Final, when they beat York 9-0 in December 1877. He was RFU vice-president from 1884 to 1887.

THOMSON
W.B.

Full-back. 1892-1895 (Blackheath, 4 caps).
Debut v Wales, 2 January 1892.
Born: 1871, Matabeleland, Southern Rhodesia.
Educated: Bedford Modern School.
Clubs: Lewisham Park, Blackheath, West of Scotland.

Thomson joined Blackheath during 1890-91 and played for West of Scotland after moving to Glasgow to work but helped Blackheath in important matches. He was described as 'fast, strong and full of resource'.

THORNE
John David

Hooker. 1963 (Bristol, 3 caps).
Debut v Wales, 19 January 1963.
Born: 1 January 1934.
Educated: Speedwell Secondary School.
Clubs: Bristol, Gloucestershire (over 20 appearances).

Thorne joined Bristol in 1955 and up to January 1963 had played in more than 230 games for the club. He made his first international trials appearance more than six years before his first cap. He was employed at a shoe manufacturers in Bristol.

TINDALL
Victor Ronald

Wing. 1951 (Liverpool University, 4 caps).
Debut v Wales, 20 January 1951.
Born: 1 August 1928.
Educated: Wallasey Grammar School, Liverpool University.
Clubs: Richmond, Liverpool University, New Brighton, RAF, Combined Services, Cheshire, Barbarians.

He was a consultant obstretician and gynaecologist, working at the United Cardiff Hospitals, he was a member of Cheshire Referees' Society from 1958 to 1964. He served in the RAF from 1952 to 1954.

TOBIN
Frank

Half-back. 1871 (Liverpool, 1 cap).
Debut v Scotland, 27 March 1871.
Born: 23 September 1849, Liverpool;
Died: 6 February 1927.
Educated: Rugby School, Cambridge University.
Clubs: Cambridge University (no Blue), Liverpool, Lancashire.

Captain of the Liverpool club from 1870 to 1872 and its president in 1912-14 and 1919-20, he played in the first international between Scotland and England in 1871. He was a cricket Blue at Cambridge from 1870 to 1872.

TODD
Alexander Findlater

Forward. 1900 (Blackheath, 2 caps).
Debut v Ireland, 3 February 1900.
Born: 20 September 1873; Died: 20 April 1915, Ypres.
Educated: Mill Hill School, Cambridge University.
Clubs: Cambridge University (Blues 1893-5), Blackheath, Kent (captain), Barbarians.

Alex Todd went on the British Isles tour of South Africa in 1896 and also played cricket for Berkshire in 1900 and again in 1910 and 1911. He was wounded during the South African War and during World War One served with the 3rd Battalion, Norfolk Regiment, being mentioned in despatches. He died from wounds received at Ypres.

TODD
R.

Forward. 1877 (Manchester, 1 cap).
Debut v Scotland, 5 March 1877.
Born: April 1847; Died: February 1927.
Educated: Allesley College (Manchester).
Clubs: Manchester, Lancashire.

TOFT
Henry Bert

Hooker. 1936-1939 (Waterloo, 10 caps).
Debut v Scotland, 21 March 1936.
Born: 2 October 1909; Died: 7 July 1987.
Educated: Manchester Grammar School, Manchester University.
Clubs: RAF, Broughton Park, Combined Services, Waterloo, Lancashire (61 appearances), Barbarians.

Toft, one of the greatest hookers of his day, taught at Manchester Grammar School, was an RFU selector in 1939 and served during World War Two with the RAF as a signals expert. After the war he was principal of Bath Technical College from 1948 to 1954. His Lancashire appearances spanned the years 1929 to 1938. He was a rugby correspondent for *The Observer* newspaper from 1952 to 1966.

John Toothill

TOOTHILL
John Thomas

Forward. 1890-1894 (Bradford, 12 caps).
Debut v Scotland, 1 March 1890.
Born: 1866, Bradford; Died: 29 June 1947, Bradford.
Clubs: Manningham, Bradford, York-shire (50 appearances, captain 1892-3 and 1894-5).

Toothill turned to Rugby League when Bradford helped form the Northern Union in 1895. He later became a licensee at a number of public houses in the Yorkshire region.

TOSSWILL
Leonard Robert, OBE

Forward. 1902 (Exeter, 3 caps).
Debut v Wales, 11 January 1902.
Born: 12 January 1880; Died: 3 October 1932.
Educated: Marlborough College.
Clubs: Marlborough Nomads, St Bartholomew's Hospital, Exeter, Devon, Barbarians.

Tosswill was a member of the Devon sides which won the County Championship in 1900-01 and met the Rest of England at Exeter in 1901-02. He served in World War One as a major with the RAMC, twice being mentioned in despatches. He was awarded the OBE in 1919 and was one of the first rugby broadcasters for BBC radio.

TOUZEL
Charles John Cliff

Forward. 1877 (Liverpool, 2 caps).
Debut v Ireland, 5 February 1877.
Born: 1855, Cheshire; Died: 23 August 1899.
Educated: Wellington College, Cambridge University.
Clubs: Cambridge University (Blues 1874-6), Blackheath, Liverpool, Lancashire.

In March 1888, Touzel was promoted to captain in the 3rd (Militia) Battalion of the Royal Welch Fusiliers.

TOWELL
Alan Clark

Centre. 1948-1951 (Bedford, 2 caps).
Debut v France, 29 March 1948.
Born: 1924.
Clubs: Leicester, Bedford.

Towell, who was a school teacher, captained Bedford.

TRAVERS
Basil Holmes ('Jika'), OBE

Flanker. 1947-1949 (Harlequins, 6 caps).
Debut v Wales, 18 January 1947.
Born: 7 July 1919, Australia.
Educated: Sydney C of E Grammar School (Australia), Sydney University, Oxford University.
Clubs: Oxford University (Blues 1946-7, captain), Harlequins, Barbarians, Northern Suburbs (Sydney).

Travers, who also won cricket, athletics and swimming Blues at Oxford, served during World War Two as a major with the Australian Infantry Division. He was mentioned in despatches and awarded the OBE (Military) in 1943. He is the author of *Let's Talk Rugby* (published in 1949) and *The Captain General* (1952). He taught at various Australian schools and colleges during the late 1940s and early '50s and in 1950 he captained New South Wales to victory over the British Lions.

TREADWELL
William Thomas

Hooker. 1966 (Wasps, 3 caps).
Debut v Ireland, 12 February 1966.
Born: 13 March 1939.
Educated: St Benedict's School (Ealing).
Clubs: Guy's Hospital, Wasps, London Counties, Surrey, Barbarians.

Treadwell is a dental surgeon in private practice.

TRICK
David Mark

Wing. 1983-1984 (Bath, 2 caps).
Debut v Ireland, 19 March 1983.
Born: 26 October 1960, Dartford.
Educated: Bryanston School.
Clubs: Plymouth Albion, Tavistock, Bath, Somerset, Barbarians.

Trick was a very speedy and efficient winger, who scored three tries for the England XV against Fiji in 1982. He played for England 'B' v Ireland in 1982 and went on the England tours of Argentina in 1981 and South Africa in 1984. In April 1986 he was a member of the Bath team which equalled Leicester's record of three successive JPS Cup Final victories. In 1980-81 he was voted Bath's most improved player. He is a stockbroker.

TRISTRAM
Henry Barrington

Full-back. 1883-1887 (Oxford University, 5 caps).
Debut v Scotland, 3 March 1883.
Born: 5 September 1861, Hartlepool; Died: 1 October 1946, Jersey.
Educated: Winchester College, Loretto School, Oxford University.
Clubs: Oxford University (Blues 1882-4), Durham City, Fettesian-Lorettonians, Newton Abbot, Durham County (2), Devon.

One of the first Wykehamists to gain a rugby Blue, in 1884 he was one of seven Lorettonians in the Oxford team. He also played cricket for Oxford University and Durham County and wrote *The History of Loretto School*.

TROOP
Carlton Lang, CBE

Number 8. 1933 (Aldershot Services, 2 caps).
Debut v Ireland, 11 February 1933.
Born: 10 June 1910, Malton.
Educated: St Peter's School (York), Royal Military Academy (Sandhurst).
Clubs: Harrogate Old Boys, Devonport Services, Richmond, Aldershot Services, Army, Hampshire, Barbarians.

Troop served with the BEF during World War Two and was later attached to the British Embassy in Stockholm. He was awarded the CBE (Military) in 1960 and emigrated to South Africa in 1967.

TUCKER
John Samuel (Sam)

Hooker. 1922-1931 (Bristol, 27 caps).
Debut v Wales, 21 January 1922.
Born: 1 June 1895; Died: 4 January 1973.
Educated: St Nicholas & St Leonard Church Schools (Bristol).
Clubs: Army, Gloucestershire, Barbarians, Bristol.

Not originally selected for the England-Wales match in 1930, he was flown from Bristol to Cardiff and arrived shortly before the kick-off, probably the first time that an England player had been flown to a match when required in an emergency. He was a great craggy gentleman, employed as a solicitor's clerk. He served World War One with the Royal Engineers and was wounded during the Battle of the Somme.

TUCKER
William Eldon

Forward. 1894-1895 (Blackheath, 5 caps).
Debut v Wales, 6 January 1894.
Born: 17 August 1872; Died: 18 October 1953.

William Tucker senior

Educated: Trinity College (Canada), Cambridge University.

Clubs: Cambridge University (Blues 1892-4), St George's Hospital, Blackheath, Kent, Barbarians.

He was the father of William Eldon (junior).

TUCKER
William Eldon, CVO MBE TD

Number 8. 1926-1930 (Blackheath, 3 caps).
Debut v Ireland, 13 February 1926.
Born: 6 August 1903.
Educated: Sherborne School, Cambridge University.
Clubs: Cambridge University (Blues 1922-5, captain), St George's Hospital, Blackheath, Middlesex, Barbarians.

William Tucker junior

The son of William Eldon (senior), he was a PoW from 1940 to 1943. He is the author of many books specializing in medicine. He was awarded the MBE in 1944, the CVO 1954, the TD in 1952 and was made a member of the Royal College of Surgeons in 1958.

TURNER
Dawson Palgrave

Forward. 1871-1875 (Richmond, 6 caps).
Debut v Scotland, 27 March 1871.
Born: 15 December 1846; Died: February 1909, Tunbridge Wells.
Educated: Rugby School, Richmond.
Club: Richmond.

Dawson Turner played in the first international between Scotland and England in 1871 at Raeburn Place and was the only player to have appeared in all of England's first six matches. He could not win a regular place in the Rugby School XV, yet he became one of the Richmond club's leading forwards. In later life he enjoyed a distinguished army career.

TURNER
Edward Beadon, BEM

Forward. 1875-1878 (St George's Hospital, 3 caps).
Debut v Ireland, 13 December 1875.
Born: September 1854; Died: 30 June 1931.
Educated: Uppingham School.
Clubs: Old Uppinghamians, St George's Hospital, Middlesex.

Brother of George Turner, he was on the RFU committee from 1878 to 1879.

TURNER
George Robertson (Sir), KBE CB

Forward. 1876 (St George's Hospital, 1 cap).
Debut v Scotland, 6 March 1876.
Born: 22 October 1855; Died: 7 April 1941.
Educated: Uppingham School.
Clubs: St George's Hospital, Middlesex.

He was the brother of Edward Beadon and served as a major-general during World War One. He was awarded the CB in 1917 and the KBE (Military) in 1919.

TURNER
Martin Frederick

Wing. 1948 (Blackheath, 2 caps).
Debut v Scotland, 20 March 1948.
Born: 1 August 1921.
Educated: Whitgift School, Cambridge University.
Clubs: Cambridge University (Blue 1946), Old Whitgiftians (two spells), Blackheath, London Counties, Surrey, Barbarians.

Martin Turner was a formidable player in full flight, a tremendous tackler and one of the biggest men to play on the wing. During World War Two he served in the Fleet Air Arm, joining them in 1940. He was captain of his school XV and had two spells with the Old Whitgiftians club, latterly being president. He was the Surrey CB representative, an RFU selector in 1972 and chairman of the Surrey selectors. He was also a referee for over 16 years, a Surrey County panel referee, team secretary and secretary of Surrey, and team secretary of London Counties in 1972.

TURQUAND-YOUNG
David ('Turkey')

Number 8/Lock. 1928-1929 (Richmond, 5 caps).
Debut v Australia, 7 January 1928.
Clubs: Richmond, Army, Hampshire Barbarians.

David Turquand-Young

He played five times for the Army, against the Royal Navy, RAF and French Army, and also represented the Army in the modern pentathlon. A fast and tireless player, he was known as a real 'goer'. He lived mainly in South Africa.

TWYNHAM
Henry Thomas

Half-back. 1879-1884 (Richmond, 8 caps).
Debut v Ireland, 24 March 1878.
Born: 1852; Died: 19 May 1899, Kensington.
Educated: Sherborne School, Richmond.
Club: Richmond.

A solicitor, he scored a try on his international debut.

UNDERWOOD
Adrian Martin

Wing/Centre. 1962-1964 (Exeter, 5 caps).
Debut v Wales, 20 January 1962.
Born: 19 July 1940.
Educated: King Charles 1 Grammar School (Kidderminster), St Luke's College (Exeter).
Clubs: Northampton, Exeter, East Midlands, Devon.

Underwood played as a centre for Northampton and as a wing for England. A PE lecturer at Northampton Grammar School.

Rory Underwood

UNDERWOOD
Rory, MBE

Wing. 1984-1992 (Leicester, RAF, 55 caps).
Debut v Ireland, 18 February 1984.
Born: 19 June 1963, Middlesbrough.
Educated: Barnard Castle School (Durham).
Clubs: RAF, Middlesbrough, Leicester, Yorkshire (20 appearances), Barbarians.

Rory Underwood, an RAF flight-lieutenant, was the first man to play 50 times for England when he appeared against Scotland in October 1991, during the World Cup. Against Fiji in November 1989, he scored five tries to equal an England record set in 1907, and he is England's most capped wing three-quarter and their leading try-scorer in internationals. And, of course, he was in the 1991 and 1992 Grand Slam teams.

Born of a Malaysian mother, part of his childhood was spent in Malaysia before the family returned to England and he went to school in Durham.

Underwood was capped for England Students, England Colts, England Under-23s and England 'B' and went on the England tours to Italy in 1982 and to Australia and Fiji in 1991. He was unable to tour with England to New Zealand in 1985 and to South Africa in 1984 because of his RAF duties. He has played against France in nine consecutive seasons and represented the Five Nations XV v Overseas XV in 1986, and played for the North and for the Barbarians against New Zealand in 1989.

He went on the British Lions tour to Australia in 1989, playing in three Tests, Altogether he made eight appearances on the tour, scoring four tries. He is equally comfortable at left or right-wing positions. He helped the RAF win the Inter-Services Championship in 1990-1991.

Underwood, who has now retired from international rugby, played cricket and swam for Bernard Castle School. His brother Tony, a Cambridge Blue, plays for Leicester and has been capped by England 'B'. MBE in June 1992.

UNWIN
Ernest James

Wing. 1937-1938 (Rosslyn Park, Army, 4 caps).
Debut v Scotland, 20 March 1937.
Born: 18 September 1912, Birdbrook.
Educated: Haileybury and Imperial Service College, Royal Military Academy (Sandhurst).
Clubs: Rosslyn Park, Army, Eastern Counties (25 appearances), Barbarians.

Unwin went on the British Lions tour to Argentina in 1936 and to South Africa in 1938, when he was runner-up to Elvet Jones in the try-scoring table as he made 15 appearances including two in Tests. The first player to be capped from Rosslyn Park, he was a strong player, always using his height and weight to good advantage. He had a powerful hand-off which often saw opponents being left grounded.

He served in the Middlesex Regiment and played ten times for the Army between 1934 and 1939, against the Royal Navy and the RAF. Commissioned in February 1933, he served during World War Two and retired in October 1949 with the rank of major (honorary lieutenant-colonel). He played cricket for Suffolk and Essex and is still living in his place of birth.

UNWIN
Geoffrey Thomas

Fly half. 1898 (Blackheath, 1 cap).
Debut v Scotland, 12 March 1898.
Born: 1 June 1874; Died: 12 February 1948.
Educated: Marlborough College, Oxford University.

Clubs: Oxford University (Blues 1894-6), Moseley, Blackheath, Cheltenham, Middlesex, Barbarians.
He was a civil engineer.

UREN
Richard

Full-back. 1948-1950 (Waterloo, 4 caps).
Debut v Ireland, 14 February 1948.
Born: 26 February 1926.
Clubs: Waterloo, Cheshire, Barbarians.

Uren converted two tries by R.H. Guest on his international debut. He was a member of the Cheshire side that won the County Championship for the first time in 1950. He took part in the international Olympic yachting trials and represented Cheshire at golf.

UTTLEY
Roger Miles, OBE

Flanker/Number 8. 1973-1980 (Gosforth, 23 caps).
Debut v Ireland, 10 February 1973.

Roger Uttley

Born: 11 September 1949, Blackpool.

Educated: Montgomery Secondary School, Blackpool Grammar School, Northumberland College.

Clubs: Gosforth, Wasps, Barbarians.

Roger Uttley, a school teacher at Harrow, was voted the game's top coach in 1990-91. Uttley was plagued by injury during 1975-6, but came back as England captain in 1977 and went on to lead his country five times. He went on the British Lions tour of South Africa in 1974, playing in 16 games, and played in England's Grand Slam season of 1980.

On the 1989 Lions tour to Australia he was the coach. His autobiography *Pride in England* (with David Norrie) was published in 1981. He retired as England coach after the 1991 World Cup, his replacement being Dick Best. He was perhaps not given the full credit he deserved on the coaching side and he is the only man to have both played in and then coached England Grand Slam sides.

In February 1992, Uttley took part in the World Indoor ERGO Rowing Championships in Boston, USA, in which he competed with another former England rugby international, Andrew Ripley. Uttley is Britain's Over-40's ERGO champion, ERGO being a form of exercise using the rowing machine. He was awarded the OBE in 1991 and is now Richmond's coach.

VALENTINE
James

Back. 1890-1896 (Swinton, 4 caps).
Debut v Wales, 15 February 1890.
Born: 29 July 1866; Died: 25 July 1904.

Educated: Brindley Heath.

Clubs: Swinton, Lancashire (60 appearances).

Valentine was 'capped' in the England side of 1888 that did not play. During the 1889-90 season he notched 61 tries, with five drop-goals, and kicked 35 goals. He was banned by the Rugby Union after Swinton joined the Northern Union in 1896. A licensee, he was killed by lightning.

VANDERSPAR
Charles Henry Richard

Back. 1873 (Richmond, 1 cap).
Debut v Scotland, 3 March 1873.
Born: 1852; Died: 9 April 1877, Ceylon.

Educated: Wellington College.

Club: Richmond.

Vanderspar worked mainly in business in Ceylon and Australia.

VAN RYNEVELD
Clive Berrange

Centre. 1949 (Oxford University, 4 caps).
Debut v Wales, 15 January 1949.
Born: 19 March 1928, South Africa.

Educated: Dicocesan College (Cape

James Valentine

Town), Cape Town University, Oxford University.

Clubs: Oxford University (Blues 1947-9), Barbarians.

Van Ryneveld, who went on to become a South African Test cricketer, played for England in all four internationals of the 1948-9 season. A nephew of J.M.Blankenburg, he won cricket Blues at Oxford and was captain in 1950. He made 19 appearances for South Africa from 1951 to 1958, captaining his country on several occasions, and also played for Western Province from 1946-7, captaining them in 1952-3 and 1957-8. A solicitor who was admitted to the Cape Bar, he retired from cricket to enter politics and was a member of the South African House of Assembly.

VARLEY
Harry

Scrum half. 1892 (Liversedge, 1 cap)
Debut v Scotland, 5 March 1892.
Born: 25 November 1868, Cleckheaton, Yorkshire; Died: 21 November 1915, Oldham.
Clubs: Liversedge, Yorkshire (7 appearances), Lancashire, Oldham RL.

Employed as a licensee, he turned to Rugby League when Liversedge helped form the Northern Union in 1895, and joined Oldham in 1895-6, going on to captain that club.

VASSALL
Harry

Forward. 1881-1883 (Blackheath, 5 caps).
Debut v Wales, 19 February 1881.
Born: 22 October 1860; Died: 5 January 1926.
Educated: Marlborough College, Oxford University.
Clubs: Yeovil, Oxford University (Blues 1879-82, captain 1881-2), Marlborough Nomads, Blackheath, Somerset (captain).

Uncle of H.H. ('Jumbo') Vassall, he scored three tries on his international debut and captained the England XV twice. Indeed, he was one of the greatest players of the Victorian era, drilling his unbeaten Oxford side into developing a passing game which revolutionised rugby, whilst his ideas dominated the international game. In the 'golden era' of Oxford rugger, he steered his university through 70 matches without defeat in his three years as captain.

A great forward in his own right, he influenced club as well as country and conceived the idea of the forwards playing in unison with the backs. His theories were revolutionary and, put to the test, proved devastating. It was during the Vassall era and just after it that Oxford registered their four successive wins over Cambridge, between 1882 and 1885. He had enormous calves and was able to shove in the scrum

because of them. He was the RFU treasurer from 1884 to 1894 and the author of *Rugby Football*

VASSALL
Henry Holland ('Jumbo')

Centre. 1908 (Blackheath, 1 cap).
Debut v Ireland, 8 February 1908.
Born: 23 March 1887, Devon; Died: 8 October 1949.
Educated: Bedford Grammar School, Oxford University.
Clubs: Oxford University (Blues 1906-08), Yeovil, East Midlands, Somerset, Barbarians.

He worked in the Colonial Service and was the nephew of Harry Vassall. Henry went on the British Lions tour of Australia and New Zealand in 1908 and played a major part in Oxford's second 'golden era', that of 1907 to 1912, a span which saw them defeat Cambridge four times and draw the fifth. A magnificent centre three-quarter, he was considered by many to be the greatest ever.

VAUGHAN
Douglas Brian

Number 8. 1948-1950 (Headingley, 8 caps).
Debut v Australia, 3 January 1948.
Born: 15 July 1925, Wrexham; Died: 19 April 1977, Isle of Man.
Educated: Luton School, Cambridge University.
Clubs: Cambridge University (no Blue), Royal Navy, Headingley, Harlequins, Devonport Services, United Services (Portsmouth), Yorkshire (16 appearances, captain 1949-50), Hampshire (9 appearances), Devon, Barbarians.

He was an England selector from 1959 to 1962 and from 1965 to 1966. He played cricket for Devon and the Royal Navy but was invalided out of the RN in 1964.

VAUGHAN-JONES
Arthur

Flanker. 1932-1933 (Army, 3 caps).
Debut v Ireland, 13 February 1932.
Born: 25 September 1909.
Clubs: United Services (Portsmouth), Army.

He served in the Royal Artillery and represented the Army once, against the Royal Navy in 1932.

VERELST
Courtenay Lee

Forward. 1875-1878 (Liverpool, 2 caps).
Debut v Ireland, 13 December 1875.
Born: 16 November 1855; Died: 9 January 1890, Ceylon.
Educated: Charterhouse School.
Clubs: Liverpool, Lancashire.

VERNON
George Frederick

Forward. 1878-1881 (Blackheath, 5 caps).
Debut v Scotland, 4 March 1878.
Born: 20 June 1856, London; Died: 10 August 1902, West Africa.
Educated: Rugby School.
Clubs: Blackheath, Middlesex.

Vernon played for England in the first Calcutta Cup match against Scotland and was one of the first line-out specialists. He played cricket for Middlesex from 1878 to 1897 and appeared in one Test in Australia in 1882. He also took his own cricket teams to Australia in 1887 and to India in 1889-90. A barrister, he was called to the Bar in 1880.

VICKERY
George

Forward. 1905 (Aberavon, 1905, 1 cap).
Debut v Ireland, 11 February 1905.
Born: 29 May 1879, Chard; Died: July 1970.
Clubs: Chard, Aberavon, Bath, Somerset.

George Vickery was a policeman and the father of Walter Vickery, the Aberavon player who gained four Welsh caps in 1938-9.

VIVYAN
Elliott John

Wing. 1901-1904 (Devonport Albion, 4 caps).
Debut v Wales, 5 January 1901.
Born: 6 January 1879, Devonport; Died: 3 December 1935.
Educated: Stoke School (Devonport).
Clubs: Devonport Albion, Devon.

Vivyan was the first player to score ten points in a match for England, against Ireland in 1904. He worked as a draughtsman at Devonport Dockyard and was known as something of an eccentric genius who could have been one of the greatest threequarters in English rugby.

VOYCE
Anthony Thomas, OBE

Flanker. 1920-1926 (Gloucester, 27 caps).
Debut v Ireland, 14 February 1920.
Born: 18 May 1897; Died: 22 January 1980, Gloucester.
Clubs: Gloucester, Cheltenham, Richmond, Blackheath, Army, Gloucestershire, Barbarians.

Voyce, a slim, sinewy player, possessed pace and a safe pair of hands and his sense of positioning made him an essential member of any team. Indeed, he is still regarded as one of the greatest back-row specialists the game has ever produced and was a member of three Grand Slam teams — 1921, 1923 and 1924. And with his wavy ginger hair,

Anthony Voyce

he was one of the most easily recognised players of his era.

He began his career at school as a fly-half and played for England Under-15s against Wales in 1911. On the British Isles tour of South Africa in 1924, he was leading points scorer and played in the flanker, wing and full-back positions when injuries crippled the squad.

Voyce, who was RFU president in 1960-61, served the Gloucester club as a player, administrator and president (1920 to 1980) and was also president of Gloucestershire and represented the county on the RFU from 1931 to 1970. He was awarded the OBE in 1962.

During World War One he served with the Gloucestershire Regiment and he was wounded in an eye. In World War Two he was a major in the RASC.

WACKETT
John Arthur Sibley

Hooker. 1959 (Rosslyn Park, 2 caps).
Debut v Wales, 17 January 1959.
Born: 27 September 1930, Hertfordshire.
Clubs: Welwyn, Rosslyn Park, Hertfordshire.

WADE
Charles Gregory, QC KCMG

Back. 1883-1886 (Richmond, 8 caps).
Debut v Wales, 16 December 1883.
Born: 26 January 1863, Australia; Died: 26 September 1922.
Educated: All Saints' College, Bathurst (NSW), King's School (Parramatta), Oxford University.
Clubs: Oxford University (Blues 1882-4), Richmond, Middlesex, New South Wales.

Wade, who was once described as the best threequarter back that England ever had, was the first overseas player to appear for England and scored three tries on his international debut and a try in each of his first four appearances. He also scored three tries in the 1883 Varsity match. A barrister, he was called to the Bar in 1886 and became a QC in 1891. He returned to his native Australia and joined New South Wales, playing for them against the British Isles in 1888. He went into politics and was New South Wales' Attorney-General, then Minister of Justice in 1904 and Prime Minister in 1907. He was awarded the KCMG in 1920.

WADE
Michael Richard

Centre. 1962 (Cambridge University, 3 caps).
Debut v Wales, 20 January 1962.
Born: 1938.
Educated: Wyggeston School (Leicester), Cambridge University.
Clubs: Cambridge University (Blues 1958-61), RAF, Leicester, Barbarians.

WAKEFIELD
William Wavell (Lord)

Flanker/Number 8. 1920-1927 (Harlequins, 31 caps).
Debut v Wales, 17 January 1920.
Born: 10 March 1898, Beckenham; Died: 12 August 1983, Kendal.
Educated: Craig Prep School, Sedburgh School, Cambridge University.
Clubs: Cambridge University (Blues 1921-2), RAF, Leicester, Harlequins, Middlesex.

William Wavell Wakefield is one of the greatest figures in the history of the Rugby Union game. He captained each club for whom he played, being the first skipper of the RAF XV in 1920 and leading the Harlequins in 1920-21, despite being handicapped by a wound suffered during World War One. He captained England on 13 occasions and led the side that won the Grand Slam in 1924. He also played in 29 consecutive internationals between 1920 and 1926, an England record until J.V.Pullin beat it.

It was Wakefield who allotted each forward a specific function, both in the scrummage and out of it, and he is therefore known as the man responsible for the development of forward play into the specialised form we know it today. He was deemed the fastest British forward in the inter-war years and a great dribbler. He represented the RAF on the RFU from 1922 to 1924, was an International Board member from 1954 to 1961 and president of the RFU in 1950-51. In 1922 he played for Harlequins Past against Harlequins Present in aid of King Edward VII's Hospital Fund.

He distinguished himself in many other sports, including athletics, cricket and skiing, and was chairman of the British Ski Racing Committee, president of the British Water Ski Federation and

William Wakefield

William Wakefield

president of the British Sub Aqua club.

During World War One he served with the Royal Naval Air Service (later the Fleet Air Arm) before transferring to the Royal Flying Corps. He was mentioned in despatches and was the first pilot to land an aeroplane on a ship (HMS Vindictive). He retired from the RAF in 1923 but rejoined it in 1939 and was appointed director of the Air Training Corps, a government organisation for selecting schoolboys for training for various aircrew positions.

He later had a distinguished Army career and in 1940 was serving in the Middle East, at 47 years old. At 51 he was invalided out of the service after being disabled. He resigned his Regular Army commission but maintained his connection through a Territorial commission in the Royal Engineers.

Wakefield served as Conservative MP for Swindon from 1935 before transferring to Marylebone, which constituency he represented from 1945 to 1963, when he became the 1st Baron Wakefield of Kendal

He did radio broadcasts for the BBC on rugby, cricket, soccer and tennis, giving the first running commentary broadcast in Great Britain, on the England-Wales game in 1927. In 1938 he gave the first TV commentary on a cricket Test match, the England v Australia game at Lord's. He is the author of *Twickenham Calling, And the Whistle's Gone,* and *Harlequin Story.*

WALKER
George Augustus ('Gus'), (Sir), GCB CBE DSO DFC AFC

Fly half. 1939. (Blackheath, 2 caps).
Debut v Wales, 21 January 1939.
Born: 24 August 1912, Garforth; Died: 11 December 1986.
Educated: St Bees School, Cambridge University.
Clubs: Cambridge University (no Blue), RAF, Blackheath, Eastern Counties, Yorkshire (4 appearances), Barbarians.

As an air chief marshall, Gus Walker is the highest-ranked England international. He represented the RAF on the RFU from 1946 to 1948 and from 1950 to 1965, and he was president of the RFU in 1965-6. He became a first-class referee during the post-war years.

Walker joined the RAF in 1924 and during World War Two served in Bomber Command, being awarded the DFC and DSO in 1941 and the CBE in 1945. His DFC was awarded in December 1941 when, as a wing-commander, he extricated his 'plane from an enemy balloon barrage and bombed his objective, all the time evading heavy flak. He lost an arm when a bomber crashed on the airfield he was commanding and exploded whilst he was helping to rescue the crew. He was awarded the AFC in 1956, the CB in 1959 and was knighted in 1962.

WALKER
Harry W.

Prop. 1947-1948 (Coventry, 9 caps).
Debut v Wales, 18 January 1947.
Born: 11 December 1915.
Clubs: Coventry, Warwickshire, Barbarians.

Harry Walker was a licensee.

WALKER
Roger

Forward. 1874-1880 (Manchester, 5 caps).
Debut v Scotland, 23 February 1874.
Born: 18 September 1846, Bury; Died: 11 November 1919, Reading.
Educated: Rossall School.
Clubs: Manchester, Berkshire Wanderers, Lancashire.

Roger Walker, who was a touch-judge in the Scotland-England game of 1896, was an International Board member from 1895 to 1899 and president of the RFU from 1894 to 1896. He managed the British Isles tour of South Africa in 1896.

Walker was also a good cricketer, a member of MCC who played for Lancashire in 1874 and 1875. It was said that he was a good average batsman and usually fielded at long-leg, cover point or as wicketkeeper. He was a member of Bury CC and a friend of A.N.Hornby,

Roger Walker

a fellow Lancashire cricketer and England rugby international. He became a member of the Lancashire CCC committee in 1880.

WALLENS
J.N.S.

Full-back. 1927 (Waterloo, 1 cap).
Debut v France, 2 April 1927.
Clubs: Waterloo, Lancashire (12 appearances).

WALTON
Ernest John

Scrum half. 1901-1902 (Castleford, 4 caps).
Debut v Wales, 5 January 1901.

Born: November 1879; Died: 8 April 1947.
Educated: St Peter's School (York), Oxford University.
Clubs: Old Dewsburians, Oxford University (Blues 1900-01), Castleford, Yorkshire (5 appearances, captain 1900-01), Barbarians.

WALTON
William

Forward. 1894 (Castleford, 1 cap).
Debut v Scotland, 17 March 1894.
Born: 23 September 1874; Died: 1 June 1940.
Clubs: Castleford, Yorkshire (14 appearances), Wakefield Trinity RL.

A licensee by trade, he joined Wakefield Trinity in 1895 and scored their first try under Northern Union rules, on 21 September 1895 in a 15-9 win over Wigan at Belle Vue.

WARD
George

Number 8. 1913-1914 (Leicester, 6 caps).
Debut v Wales, 18 January 1913.
Born: 19 March 1885; Died: 1963.
Clubs: Belgrave, Leicester, Leicestershire, Midland Counties.

WARD
Herbert

Full-back. 1895 (Bradford, 1 cap).
Debut v Wales, 5 January 1895.
Born: 1873, Bradford; Died: 18 February 1955, Bradford.
Clubs: Bradford, Shipley, Yorkshire (23 appearances), Bradford RL.
Bert Ward joined Bradford RL in 1899 and was a member of their team that won the Championship in 1900, 1901 and 1904. He played for them until 1905.

WARD
James Ibbotson

Forward. 1881-1882 (Richmond, 2 caps).
Debut v Ireland, 5 February 1881.
Born: 24 April 1858; Died: 28 September 1924.
Educated: Tonbridge School.
Clubs: Gipsies, Richmond, Middlesex.
He was HM Lieutenant of the City of London and a member of the Stock Exchange.

WARD
John Willie

Forward. 1896 (Castleford, 3 caps).
Debut v Wales, 4 January 1896.
Born: 29 January 1873, Castleford; Died: 30 April 1939.
Clubs: Castleford, Yorkshire (16 appearances), Castleford RL.
Ward played for Castleford RL in 1896-7.

WARDLOW
Christopher Story

Full-back. 1969-1971 (Northampton, 6 caps).
Debut v South Africa, 20 December 1969.
Born: 12 July 1942, Carlisle.
Educated: Creighton School (Carlisle).
Clubs: Carlisle, Northampton, Northampton Crusaders, Coventry, North West Counties, Cumberland & Westmorland, Barbarians.
Wardlow, who joined the Carlisle club as a 16-year-old, moved to Coventry in the 1972 close season and played in their RFU Club KO Cup-winning side of 1972-3. He made his international debut as a replacement when Bob Hiller was injured, but missed the British Lions

Chris Wardlow

tour of New Zealand in 1971 due to an injury which resulted in a cartilage operation. He has worked as a salesman and as a transport manager.

WARFIELD
Peter John

Centre. 1973-1975 (Rosslyn Park, Durham University, 6 caps).
Debut v New Zealand, 6 January 1973).
Born: Waddington, Lincolnshire.
Educated: Haileybury, Durham University, Cambridge University.
Clubs: Durham University, Cambridge University (Blue 1974), Rosslyn Park, Durham County, Barbarians.
Peter Warfield played in the Haileybury Under-15 XV and upon leaving school spent some time at a University in America. After travelling in Europe and South Africa, he went to Durham University and played in the Durham County side for several games, which

brought him to the attention of the England selectors.
Warfield appeared in a regional trial at Broughton Park in December 1972 and the following week played against the New Zealanders for the North-East Counties. The following month he won his first cap. He played for England Under-23s against Japan in 1973 and against Tonga, when he suffered a broken nose. His Barbarians appearances include a game against New Zealand and the annual fixture against Leicester, in 1974. He also appeared in the UAU side and for British Universities.

WARR
Anthony Lawley

Wing. 1934 (Oxford University, 2 caps).
Debut v Wales, 20 January 1934.
Born: 15 May 1913, Birmingham.
Educated: Bromsgrove School, Oxford University.
Clubs: Oxford University (Blues 1933-4),

Weston-super-Mare, Moseley, Harlequins, Old Leodiensians, Wakefield, Gloucester, Richmond, Middlesex, Yorkshire (7 appearances), Barbarians.

John Watkins made his England debut in place of I.A.Booth, who was taken ill on the morning of the match. Watkins also played four games for Oxford University CC in 1933 and 1934. He was a school teacher.

WATKINS
John Arthur

Flanker. 1972-1975 (Gloucester, 7 caps).
Debut v South Africa, 3 June 1972.
Born: 28 November 1946, Gloucester.
Educated: Linden Secondary Modern School (Gloucester).
Clubs: Gordon League (local Gloucester club), Gloucester, Gloucestershire. Barbarians.

He was a member of Gloucestershire's 1972-3 County Championship runners-up team and went on the England tour to South Africa in 1972. A keen cricketer, he was vice-captain of Gloucester club, Arcadians CC.

WATKINS
John Kingdon, CBE OBE

Forward. 1939 (United Service (Portsmouth), Royal Navy, 3 caps).

Debut v Wales, 21 January 1939.
Born: 24 February 1913; Died: 13 May 1970.
Educated: Epsom College.
Clubs: Devonport Services, United Services (Portsmouth), Royal Navy, Combined Services, Somerset (25 appearances), Barbarians.
A rear admiral, he was awarded the OBE in 1945 and the CBE in 1967.

WATSON
Fischer Burges, CBE DSO

Forward. 1908-1909 (United Services Portsmouth, Royal Navy, 2 caps).
Debut v Scotland, 21 March 1908.
Born: September 1884; Died: 14 August 1960.
Educated: Ashdown House (Forest Row), HMS Britannia.
Clubs: United Services (Portsmouth), Royal Navy, Surrey, Barbarians.

He was awarded the DSO in 1917 and the CBE and bar to DSO in 1943. A rear admiral, he is also the son of a rear admiral. He served in both World War One and World War Two.

WATSON
James Henry Digby ('Bungy')

Centre. 1914 (Blackheath, 3 caps).
Debut v Wales, 17 January 1914.
Born: 31 August 1890; Died: 15 October 1914 (killed in action).
Educated: Kings School (Canterbury), Edinburgh Academy.
Clubs: Blackheath, London Hospital, Barbarians.

Picked as a reserve for Scotland in 1912-13, he gained his full cap as an England player. The son of J.D.Watson, a New Zealand player, he was the Edinburgh University middleweight boxing champion and also represented Scotland in the long jump in 1912. He served in World War One as a Royal Navy surgeon and was drowned when HMS Hawke was sunk by a German submarine.

WATT
David Edward James

Lock. 1967 (Bristol, 4 caps).
Debut v Ireland, 11 February 1967.
Born: 5 July 1938.
Educated: Kingsdown Secondary School, Bristol Cathedral School.
Clubs: St Mary's Old Boys, Harlequins, Bristol, Gloucestershire, Barbarians.

Watt played soccer until he was 19 before taking up rugby. He made over 500 appearances for Bath and was in their 1972-3 RFU Club KO Cup Final team. He also captained Gloucestershire and was in the side which won the County Championship in 1971-2. He retired from first-class rugger in 1975 when a leg injury suffered at Newbridge ended his career. At 17st he was one of the heaviest men to have played for England. Employed as a sales executive.

WEBB
Charles Samuel Henry

Lock. 1932-1936 (Devonport Services, Royal Navy, 12 caps).
Debut v South Africa, 2 January 1932.
Born: 1902; Died: 28 October 1961.
Clubs: Devonport Services, Royal Navy, Devon, Cornwall (23 appearances), Auckland (New Zealand).

He served with the Royal Marines before emigrating to New Zealand in 1938, when he signed for the Auckland club.

WEBB
Jonathan Mark

Full-back. 1987-1992 (Bristol, Bath, 27 caps).
Debut v Australia, 23 May 1987.
Born: 24 August 1963, London.
Educated: Royal Grammar School (Newcastle upon Tyne), Bristol University, Royal College of Surgeons.
Clubs: Northern, Bristol, Bath, Barbarians.

A doctor of medicine, Jonathan Webb began his career at Northern, signing for Bristol when his medical studies forced a move to the West Country. He represented England 'B' before making his full England debut as a replacement for the concussed Marcus Rose in the 1987 World Cup, and in his four games went on to became England's leading points scorer in the competition with 43.

Webb returned to Australia on the 1988 England tour and after winning 16 caps he lost his full-back position in the England side to Simon Hodgkinson in May 1989. He joined Bath late in the 1989-90 season, went on the England tour to Australia and Fiji 1991, when he regained his place, and played in the 1991 World Cup Final, scoring 56 points including an English record of 24 points in the match against Italy.

During the 1992 Grand Slam season, Webb passed Dusty Hare's record of 25 appearances as an England full-back. He is the only Englishmen to have reached the 200-points mark in international rugby and his 22 against Ireland at Twickenham in February 1992 equalled the Five Nations record for a single match, set by Don Lambert in 1911. A member of the Bristol team which finished runners-up in the 1988 JPS Cup Final, he was in the Bath team which won the Pilkington Cup and Courage League double in 1992.

He comes from a medical family: his father is a professor of paediatrics and he has four brothers, all of whom are doctors. Webb himself is a surgeon.

WEBB
J.W.G.

Number 8. 1926-1929 (Northampton, 3 caps).
Debut v France, 27 February 1926.
Club: Northampton.
He worked for a local shoe-makers.

Jonathan Webb

WEBB
Rodney Edward

Left-wing. 1967-1972 (Coventry, 12 caps).
Debut v Scotland, 18 March 1967.
Born: 18 August 1943, Newbold-on-Avon (Warwickshire).
Educated: Newbold Granger High School.
Clubs: Newbold-on-Avon, Coventry, Midlands, Warwickshire, Barbarians.

He scored a try on his international debut and went on the England tour of Canada in 1967. His brother, Richard, toured with Australia to the British Isles and France in 1966 and Rodney's debut came just as he had bid farewell to Richard, who was leaving for Australia. Rodney was also the Warwickshire javelin champion. He owned a sports goods shop and was then a planning engineer.

WEBB
St Lawrence Hugh

Prop. 1959 (Bedford, 4 caps).
Debut v Wales, 17 January 1959.
Born: 7 March 1931, Australia; Died: 30 May 1978.
Educated: St George's School (Harpenden), Willesden Technical College.
Clubs: Bedford, Aldershot Services, Blackheath, Hertfordshire, Royal Engineers, Barbarians.
Webb began his rugby career as a wing forward. He disappeared when a private aeroplane, in which he was flying, went missing over the English Channel and he was declared dead. He had been in business with fellow England international, John Wackett.

WEBSTER
Jan Godfrey

Scrum half. 1972-1975 (Moseley, 11 caps).
Debut v Wales, 15 January 1972.
Born: 24 August 1946, Southport.
Educated: Queen Mary's Grammar School (Walsall), City of Birmingham College of Commerce.
Clubs: Walsall, Moseley, Staffordshire, Midland Counties, Barbarians.

Jan Webster

He captained England against Wales and Ireland in 1971-2 and went on the tours to South Africa in 1972 and Japan and the Far East in 1971. A promising schoolboy player, he had three full England trials in 1967. A sports outfitter, he played for the Midland Counties against South Africa in the 1969-70 season. Despite being only 5ft 5in tall, he was a particularly brave player in the tackle.

WEDGE
Thomas George

Scrum-half. 1907-1909 (St Ives, 2 caps).
Debut v France, 5 January 1907.
Clubs: St Ives, Cornwall (29 appearances).
A fisherman, he played for Cornwall when they won an Olympic silver medal for Great Britain in 1908.

WEIGHILL
Robert Harold George, DFC

Number 8. 1947-1948 (RAF, Harlequins, 4 caps).
Debut v Scotland, 15 March 1947.

Born: 9 September 1920.
Educated: Wirral Grammar School.
Club: Birkenhead Park, Waterloo, RAF, Harlequins, Leicester, Cheshire, Barbarians.
Weighill was serving as a young fighter pilot and playing as a wing forward in 1944 when he first made his mark in rugby. He captained England in Paris in March 1948. He was the RAF representative on the RFU from 1959 to 1970 and an England selector from 1959 to 1964. He served in World War Two with Fighter Command and was awarded the DFC in 1944. In 1968 was ADC to HM the Queen. He served as secretary of the RFU from 1971 to 1986.

WELLS
Cyril Mowbray

Half-back. 1893-1897 (Cambridge University, Harlequins, 6 caps).
Debut v Scotland, 4 March 1893.
Born: 21 March 1871, London; Died: 22 August 1963, London.
Educated: Dulwich College, Cambridge University.
Clubs: Cambridge University (Blues 1891-2), Harlequins, Surrey, Middlesex, Barbarians.
At Cambridge he played in every position, at one time or another, behind the scrummage. He was at full-back when he won his first Blue in 1891 and later moved to half-back, his true position. He was proclaimed as one of the most brilliant individual players to have played for Harlequins and England. He also won cricket Blues (1891-3) and played for Surrey, Middlesex and for the Gentleman v Players. He taught at Eton College.

WEST
Bryan Ronald

Flanker. 1968-1970 (Loughborough Colleges, Northampton, 8 caps).
Debut v Wales, 20 January 1968.
Born: 7 June 1948.
Educated: Northampton Grammar School, Loughborough Colleges.
Clubs: Loughborough Colleges, Northampton, East Midlands, Barbarians, Wakefield Trinity RL.
West, who also won three England Schoolboy caps, went on the British Lions tour of South Africa in 1968. He has played in all the positions in the back row. A second-row forward for Wakefield Trinity, he made 30 appearances for them, scoring one try and three points. He joined the Rugby League club in 1970-71 and remained with them for only one season. He is a PE teacher.

WESTON
Henry Thomas Franklin

Forward. 1901 (Northampton, 1 cap).
Debut v Scotland, 9 March 1901.
Born: 9 July 1869; Died: 5 April 1955.
Clubs: Northampton, East Midlands.
He became an international player at the age of 31, the first from the Northampton club. His son, William Henry Weston, was also an England international. A farmer by occupation.

WESTON
Lionel Edward

Scrum-half. 1972 (West of Scotland, 2 caps).
Debut v France, 26 February 1972.
Born: 22 February 1947, Shropshire.
Educated: Bedford Modern School, Loughborough Colleges.
Clubs: Bedford, West of Scotland, East Midlands, Rosslyn Park, Leicestershire, Glasgow District.

Cyril Wells

A school master, he went on the England tour of South Africa in 1972.

WESTON
Michael Philip, JP

Centre/Fly half. 1960-1968 (Richmond, Durham City, 28 caps).
Debut v Wales, 16 January 1960.
Born: 21 August 1938, Durham.
Educated: Durham School.
Clubs: Richmond, Durham City, Durham County, Barbarians.

Micheal Weston

Weston was once England's most capped three-quarters and gained 12 consecutive caps before being dropped for the match against Scotland in 1962. An all-round sportsman, he was a very strong player who had great speed. Originally a fly-half, he was converted to the centre position after being noticed by the England selectors in a trial match at Birkenhead in 1958.

He went on the British Lions tour to South Africa 1962, when he was the only three-quarter to play in all Tests and made 15 appearances altogether. He also made the Lions tour of Australia and New Zealand in 1966, scored 24 points, and captained the England tour of Australia and New Zealand in 1963.

He finished his career after captaining England in 1968. His 29th cap, then a record for an England back, was won against Scotland at Murrayfield on 16 March 1968. He was on the 1989 British Lions selection committee and was chairman of the England selectors in 1985-6. He coached the Durham University side in the early 1970s and played cricket for Durham CCC. An actioneer and estate agent, he was appointed a JP in 1969.

WESTON
William Henry

Flanker. 1933-1938 (Northampton, 16 caps).
Debut v Ireland, 11 February 1933.
Born: 21 December 1905; Died: 8 January 1987.
Educated: Oakham School.
Clubs: Northampton, East Midlands, Barbarians.

The son of Henry Thomas Weston, also an England international, he went on the British Lions tour of Argentina in 1937. He played for the East-Midlands against South Africa in 1931. He was a farmer.

WHEATLEY
Arthur A.

Lock. 1937-1938 (Coventry, 5 caps).
Debut v Wales, 16 January 1937.
Born: 9 December 1908.
Educated: South Street School (Hillfields).
Clubs: Coventry, Warwickshire, Midland Counties.

Brother Harold, also an England international, they played together three times for their country. A member of the 1937 Triple Crown team. He served with the Home Guard during World War Two.

WHEATLEY
Harold F.

Prop. 1936-1939 (Coventry, 7 caps).
Debut v Ireland, 8 Feburary 1936.
Born: 25 December 1912, Coventry.
Clubs: Coventry, Warwickshire.

His brother Arthur was also an England international and they played in the same England side on three occasions.

WHEELER
Peter John

Hooker. 1975-1984 (Leicester, 41 caps).
Debut v France, 1 February 1975.
Born: 26 November 1948, London.

Peter Wheeler

Educated: Brockley Comprehensive School (South London).

Clubs: Old Brockleians, Leicester, Barbarians, Kent, Leicestershire.

Upon his retirement from international rugby, Peter Wheeler was the third-most-capped player in England's history. A technically sound player, he possessed skills which made him an all-round performer and proved a tireless worker in the loose. He played in England's Grand Slam win in 1980, their first for 27 years, and went on the England tours to the Far East (in 1971 and 1979) and to Canada and the USA in 1981. He also went on the British Lions tours to New Zealand in 1977 (when he played 13 games) and to South Africa in 1980 (11 appearances).

His other representative honours include: Home Counties XV v RFU President's XV in 1972; captain of Midland Counties (East) v New Zealand in 1973, Australia 1975, New Zealand 1978, New Zealand 1979; for the Midland Counties against Australia 1981; French President's XV v France in 1977 (scoring a try); England-Wales v Scotland-Ireland in 1980; WRU President's XV v Wales in 1981; Five Nations v Western Province and v South African President's XV in 1983; and an England XV v Argentina in 1978 and v Fiji in 1982.

Wheeler also captained Leicester in their record three successive JPS Cup victories in 1979, 1980 and 1981. He is an insurance broker.

WHITE
Colin

Prop. 1983-1984 (Gosforth, 4 caps).
Debut v New Zealand, 19 November 1983.
Born: 3 March 1948, Newcastle upon Tyne.
Clubs: Gosforth, North, North-East Counties.

Colin White first played for England 'B' v Romania in 1978 and was 34 when he won his first full cap. Originally employed as a PE teacher at Walbottle Grammar School, Newcastle upon Tyne, he was working in the forestry industry when he lost three fingers in an accident in 1978.

WHITE
Donald Frederick

Flanker. 1947-1953 (Northampton, 14 caps).
Debut v Wales, 18 January 1947.
Born: 16 January 1926, Northamptonshire.
Educated: Wellingborough Grammar School.
Clubs: Wellingborough Old Grammarians, Northampton, Army, Combined Services, East Midlands, Midland Counties, Barbarians.
Donald White played for Northampton from 1944 to 1961 and spent seven

seasons as captain. He served in the Northamptonshire Regiment from 1946 to 1948 and represented the Army eight times, against the Royal Navy, RAF and French Army. He scored a try on his international debut and was later an England selector and also coach from 1969 to 1971. He works in the family shoe business.

WHITELEY
Eric Cyprian Perry, TD

Full-back. 1931 (Old Alleynians, 2 caps).
Debut v Scotland, 21 March 1931.
Born: 18 July 1904.
Educated: Dulwich College.
Clubs: Old Alleynians, Surrey, Barbarians.

WHITELEY
W.

Forward. 1896 (Bramley, 1 cap).
Debut v Wales, 4 January 1896.
Born: 1871.
Clubs: Bramley, Yorkshire (3 appearances)
Whiteley, a Leeds policeman, made his Yorkshire debut against Lancashire and his final appearance against Durham and Northumberland.

WHITLEY
Herbert

Scrum half. 1929 (Northern, 1 cap).
Debut v Wales, 19 January 1929.
Born: 26 August 1903; Died: 1975.
Educated: Durham School.
Clubs: Northern, Northumberland.
Before gaining his full England cap, he went on the British Isles tour of South Africa in 1924 and played in ten matches, including three Tests. He appeared in the North side which played England in a trial match in 1923. A small player who had an abundance of skills and nerve, he was a fearless defender. He served in World War Two with the Royal Marines and was a brother-in-law of Alan Robson.

WIGGLESWORTH
Henry John

Back. 1884 (Thornes, 1 cap).
Debut v Ireland, 4 February 1884.
Born: 1861; Died: 3 March 1925, Leeds.
Clubs: Thornes, Yorkshire (6 appearances).
He made his Yorkshire debut against Northumberland and his last appearance against Oxford University.

WIGHTMAN
Brian John

Number 8. 1959-1963 (Moseley, Coventry, 5 caps).
Debut v Wales, 17 January 1959.
Born: 23 September 1936, Birmingham.
Educated: King Edward's School (Birmingham), Loughborough Colleges.

Clubs: Loughborough Colleges, Old Edwardians, UAU, Coventry, Mossley, Rosslyn Park, North Midlands.

Wightman joined Moseley as a schoolboy in 1952, after representing England Under-15s at Newport in 1951-52. He went on the England tour to Australia and New Zealand in 1963. A school teacher, he emigrated to Canada in 1964.

WILKINS
Dennis Thomas

Lock. 1951-1953 (United Services (Portsmouth), Royal Navy, Roundhay, 13 caps).
Debut v Wales, 20 January 1951.
Born: 26 December 1924, Leeds.
Clubs: United Services (Portsmouth), Royal Navy, Combined Services, Roundhay, Yorkshire (21 appearances, captain 1951-2).

Dennis Wilkins is Roundhay's most capped player and the first to be capped for England directly from the club. In World War Two he served as a Fleet Air Arm pilot.

WILKINSON
Edgar

Forward. 1886-1887 (Bradford, 5 caps).
Debut v Wales, 2 January 1886.
Born: 1863, Bradford; Died: 27 August 1896, Bradford.
Clubs: Bradford, Yorkshire (21 appearances).
He scored a try on his international debut.

WILKINSON
Harry

Flanker. 1929-1930 (Halifax, 4 caps).

Harry Wilkinson

Debut v Wales, 19 January 1929.
Born: 22 March 1903.

Educated: Fettenhall College.

Clubs: Halifax, Yorkshire (48 appearances, captain 1929-30).

A fast attacking wing-forward, who had excellent positional sense, he scored two tries on his international debut. He made his Yorkshire debut against New Zealand and also played for the county in their inaugural match against Ulster. His father, Harry James Wilkinson, played for England against the first Maoris' side in 1889.

WILKINSON
Harry James

Forward. 1889 (Halifax, 1 cap).
Debut v Maoris, 16 February 1889.
Born: 1864 Halifax; Died: 7 June 1942, Halifax.

Clubs: Halifax, Yorkshire (13 appearances).

He first played for Halifax in 1886, the club's first season at Thrum Hall. His last game for the club was in 1893, when he was brought out of retirement to help an injury-hit side in the later rounds of the Yorkshire Cup, which Halifax went on to win. He was a life member of the Yorkshire RFU and although Halifax helped form the Northern Union in 1895, he did not play the Northern Union code. He was a licensee and his son, Harry, was also an England international.

WILKINSON
P.

Half-back. 1872 (Law Society Club, 1 cap).
Debut v Scotland, 5 February 1872.
Clubs: Harlequins, Law Society Club.

WILKINSON
Robert Michael

Lock. 1975-1976 (Bedford, 6 caps).
Debut v Australia, 31 May 1975.
Born: 25 July 1951, Luton.

Educated: St Albans School, Cambridge University.

Clubs: Cambridge University (Blues 1971-3), Bedford, Barbarians.

Wilkinson played for the Public School Wanderers VII which reached the 1973 Middlesex Sevens Final. He was also capped for England Under-23s and went on the full England tours to Argentina in 1973, to New Zealand in 1973 and to Australia in 1975.

WILLCOCKS
T.J.

Forward. 1902 (Plymouth Albion, 1 cap).
Debut v Wales, 11 January 1902.
Clubs: Buckfastleigh, Plymouth Albion, Devon.

Willcocks was the first English international to be capped from Plymouth Albion.

John Willcox

WILLCOX
John Graham

Full-back. 1961-1964 (Oxford University, Harlequins, 16 caps).
Debut v Ireland, 11 February 1961.
Born: 16 February 1937.

Educated: Ratcliffe College (Leicester), Royal Military Academy (Sandhurst), Oxford University.

Clubs: Fylde, Army, Oxford University (Blues 1959-62, captain 1961), Harlequins, Headingley, Malton, Lancashire (33 appearances), Barbarians, Paris University.

The Press described John Willcox as

'the man who knows no fear', and on the British Lions tour of South Africa in 1962, he played in three of the four Tests and was leading scorer, kicking 11 penalties and 17 conversions in 15 matches.

Earlier he had served in the East Lancashire Regiment, mainly at Preston, and played three times for the Army in 1958 before going up to Oxford, where he also gained a boxing Blue as a heavyweight in 1960.

He also studied at the Sorbonne in France and taught at the Rueil School near Paris in 1963, when he played for Paris University. Later that year he taught languages and coached rugby at Ampleforth College. Willcox, who wore contact lenses, ceased playing rugby in 1967. His sister, Sheila, was a fine horsewoman who won the Badminton three-day event in 1956, 1957 and 1958 and a European championship in 1957 and 1959.

WILLIAM-POWLETT
Peveril Barton Reiby Wallop, KCB KCMG CBE DSO

Prop. 1922 (United Services (Portsmouth), Royal Navy, 1 cap).
Debut v Scotland, 18 March 1922.
Born: 5 March 1898, Abergavenny; Died: 10 November 1985.
Educated: Cordwalles School, Royal Naval College (Osborne), Royal Naval College (Dartmouth).
Clubs: United Services (Portsmouth), Blackheath, United Services (Devonport), Wanderers, Hampshire, Royal Navy.

He joined the Royal Navy as a 19-year-old and spent all his life attached to the Navy, eventually leaving with the rank of vice-admiral, although he worked mainly with the Colonial Service. He represented the Navy at soccer (colts) and polo as well as rugger. He served in World War One, fighting in the Dardanells and at Jutland, and in World War Two he served aboard HMS Fiji, which was sunk off Crete on 22 May 1941. He was awarded the KCB in 1953, the KCMG in 1959 and was Governor of Rhodesia from 1954 to 1959.

WILLIAMS
Christopher Gareth

Fly half. 1976 (Gloucester, RAF, 1 cap).
Debut v France, 20 March 1976.
Born: 21 December 1950.
Clubs: Gloucester, RAF.

WILLIAMS
Cyril Stoate

Full-back. 1910 (Manchester, 1 cap).
Debut v France, 3 March 1910.
Born: 17 November 1887, Stroud.
Educated: Truro College, Mill Hill School, Manchester University.

Clubs: Manchester, Lancashire (12 appearances).

Cyril Williams was a respected rugby player who went on to become one of the game's leading referees. He was also a cricket umpire.

WILLIAMS
John Edward

Scrum half. 1954-1965 (Old Millhillians, Sale, 9 caps).
Debut v France, 10 April 1954.
Born: 31 January 1932, Leeds.
Educated: Mill Hill School.
Clubs: Army, Headingley, Old Millhillians, Harlequins, Sale, London Counties, Cheshire, Middlesex, Barbarians.

He went on the British Lions tour of South Africa in 1955.

WILLIAMS
John Michael

Centre. 1951 (Penzance-Newlyn, 2 caps).
Debut v Ireland, 10 February 1951.
Born: 24 August 1927.
Educated: Rugby School, Cambridge University.
Clubs: Cambridge University (Blue 1949), Penzance-Newlyn, Richmond, Cornwall (27 appearances), Barbarians.

A solicitor by profession, he took part in England trials in 1952, played cricket for Cornwall CCC and was Cornwall's RFU's president in 1991. He was captain of Rugby School in 1944.

WILLIAMS
Peter Nicholas

Stand-off. 1987 (Orrell, 4 caps).
Debut v Scotland, 4 April 1987.
Born: 14 December 1958.
Clubs: Orrell, Lancashire (16 appearances), Salford RL.

He signed for Salford in March 1988, on a five-year contract, for a reputed fee of over £15,000, and made his debut against Leigh. He was said to be one of the more exciting players in Rugby Union until his defection to the League code.

WILLIAMS
S.G.

Forward. 1902-1907 (Devonport Albion, 7 caps).
Debut v Wales, 11 January 1902.
Clubs: Devonport Albion, Devon.

WILLIAMS
Stanley Horatio, DSO

Full-back. 1922 (Newport, 4 caps).
Debut v Wales, 21 January 1911.
Born: 2 November 1886, Gwent; Died: 30 April 1936 (lost at sea).
Educated: Newport Intermediate School.
Clubs: Newport, Monmouth.

The son of a vicar, he played soccer at school before reverting to the rugby

code, and played in an international trial for Wales before becoming an 'uncapped' British Lion. He went on the Lions tour of South Africa in 1910 and was acclaimed as the best British back, playing in 16 matches including all the Tests. He played for England in the 1922 Championship season, retiring at the end of that campaign.

Employed as a manager at the Ebbw Vale Iron Ore Mines Company, he served in World War One as a captain in the Royal Field Artilley, was gassed twice, twice mentioned in despatches and awarded the DSO in 1917. He was deemed 'lost overboard' when returning to the UK by sea from a business trip to South America in 1936.

WILLIAMSON
Rupert Henry

Scrum-half. 1908-1909 (Oxford University, 5 caps).
Debut v Wales, 18 January 1908.
Born: 22 November 1886; Died: 16 March 1946.
Educated: St Andrew's College (Grahamstown, South Africa), Oxford University.
Clubs: Oxford University (Blues 1906-08), Blackheath, Barbarians.

He scored a try on his international debut. Employed in the Transvaal as a mining manager from 1910 to 1946, he served in World War One.

WILSON
Arthur James

Forward. 1909 (Camborne School of Mines, 1 cap).
Debut v Ireland, 13 February 1909.
Born: 29 December 1886; Died: 1 July 1917, Flanders (killed in action).
Educated: Glenalmond School, Camborne School of Mines.
Clubs: Northern, Camborne, Camborne School of Mines, Camborne Students, Cornwall (17 appearances).

Arthur Wilson was in the Cornwall team which won the rugby silver medal for Great Britain at the 1908 Olympic Games. He was a mining engineer in South Africa before moving to India to become a tea planter. He served World War One and was killed in action whilst a private in the Royal Fusiliers.

WILSON
Charles Edward

Forward. 1898 (Blackheath, 1 cap).
Debut v Ireland, 5 February 1898.
Born: 2 June 1871, County Cork; Died: 17 September 1914, River Aisne, France (killed in action).
Educated: Dover College.
Clubs: Blackheath, Army, Surrey.

Charles Wilson had mainly a service career. During the Boer War he was with the Queen's Royal West Surrey Regiment and was mentioned in despatches. He saw action at the Relief of Ladysmith and later served as a captain in India before being killed in World War One. He was awarded the Legion d' Honeur.

WILSON
Charles Plumpton

Forward. 1881 (Cambridge University, Marlborough, 1 cap).
Debut v Wales, 19 February 1881.
Born: 12 May 1859, Roydon (Norfolk); Died: 9 March 1938.
Educated: Uppingham School, Marlborough College, Cambridge University.
Clubs: Marlborough Nomads, Cambridge University (Blues 1877-81, captain 1881).

When he was capped for England against Wales, he became one of only three men to have played for his country at rugby and soccer. He was also a cricket Blue (1880-81) and played for Norfolk CCC from 1881 to 1885, and a cycling Blue (1880). He was a master at Elstree School from 1881 to 1920 and joint headmaster of Sandroyd School, Surrey, from 1898 to 1920. In soccer, he played at wing-half and was capped twice in 1884, against Scotland and Wales, whilst playing for Hendon AFC. He also turned out for the Casuals and the Corinthians at the round ball game. He was the brother of G.P.Wilson, who played soccer for England at inside-left.

WILSON
Dyson Stayt ('Tug').

Flanker. 1953-1955 (Metropolitan Police, Harlequins, 8 caps).
Debut v France, 28 February 1953.
Born: 7 October 1926, South Africa.
Educated: Rydal School, King Edward VIII Grammar School (Stafford).
Clubs: Metropolitan Police, Harlequins, Middlesex (captain 1954-55), London Counties.

A policeman, serving in one of the undercover branches of the force, he had England trials in 1952. He came to the UK with his family when he was eight but returned to his native South Africa after his international career ended.

WILSON
Guy Summerfield.

Wing. 1929 (Tyldesley, 2 caps).
Debut v Wales, 19 January 1929.
Born: 30 August 1907; Died: 8 July 1979.
Clubs: Tyldesley, Manchester, Birkenhead Park, Lancashire (35 appearances), Barbarians.

Guy Wilson was a convert to rugby from soccer. A very clever, deceptively quick player who had a well-judged swerve, his only England score was when he converted one of H.Wilkinsons two tries on his international debut. He played

Guy Wilson

for Lancashire in the 1928-9 County Championship Final. He was an insurance broker.

WILSON
Kenneth James

Prop. 1963 (Gloucester, 1 cap).
Debut v France, 23 February 1963.
Born: 25 November 1938, Newark.
Educated: King's Grammar School (Grantham).
Clubs: Kesteven, Cheltenham, RAF, Gloucester, Combined Services, Gloucestershire, Oldham RL.

A former RAF heavyweight boxing champion, he joined Oldham RL in 1963 and captained their side.

WILSON
Roger Parker, CIE

Forward. 1891 (Liverpool Old Boys, 3 caps).
Debut v Wales, 3 January 1891.
Born: 13 May 1870; Died: 12 December 1943.
Educated: Liverpool College, Liverpool University.
Clubs: Liverpool Old Boys, Liverpool University, St Bartholomew's Hospital, Lancashire.

A professor of surgery, he served in the Indian Army and from 1903 worked in that country as Superintendent of Gaols.

WILSON
Walter Carandini, CBE DSO MC

Wing. 1907 (Richmond, 2 caps).

Debut v Ireland, 9 February 1907.
Born: 22 June 1885; Died: 12 April 1968.
Educated: Tonbridge School.
Clubs: United Services (Portsmouth), Army, Richmond, Barbarians.

Walter Wilson, a very good three-quarter player, first served in the Leicester Regiment (as it was then known) and played for the Army five times, against the Royal Navy, between 1907 and 1911. He helped his regiment win the Army Cup in 1908, on their first appearance in the competition and reach the 1909-10 Final, when the Leicesters and Gloucesters had the honour of being the first two army sides to play at Twickenham. In 1908 he was on a committee which selected a combined Army-Navy side to meet the Australians.

He served in World War One, was wounded, won the Military Cross and DSO and was mentioned in despatches three times He retired from the Army in 1932 and joined the RAF in 1939, retiring as a group captain in 1944. He worked for BOAC from 1944 to 1945 and later became administrative director of the Greyhound Racing Association.

WINN
Christopher Elliott

Wing. 1952-1954 (Rosslyn Park, 8 caps).
Debut v South Africa, 5 January 1952.
Born: 13 November 1926, Beckenham.
Educated: King's College School (Wimbledon), Oxford University.
Clubs: Oxford University (Blue 1950), Rosslyn Park, London Counties, Surrey (10 appearances), Sussex (8 appearances), Barbarians.

Winn's try on his international debut was England's only score of that game. He won cricket Blues (1948-51) and played cricket for Sussex (1948-52) and MCC (two appearances, 1959 and 1961). His wife Valerie (neé Ball) was an Olympic athlete and former world record holder for the 880 yards.

WINTERBOTTOM
Peter James

Flanker. 1982-1992 (Headingley, Harlequins, 52 caps).
Debut v Australia, 2 January 1982.
Born: 31 May 1960, Horsforth, Leeds.
Educated: Rossall School, Seale Hayne Agricultural College (Devon).
Clubs: Fleetwood, Headingley, Exeter, Napier HS Old Boys (New Zealand), Hawke's Bay (New Zealand), Durban High School Old Boys (South Africa), Merolomas (Vancouver, Canada), Harlequins, Otley, Barbarians, Yorkshire (22 appearances).

Peter Winterbottom, who was in England's 1987 World Cup squad, their 1991 World Cup Final team and the 1991 and 1992 Grand Slam sides, is England's most capped forward and only the second England player, after Rory Underwood, to reach 50 caps.

Peter Winterbottom

A former Lancashire Schools 16 and 19 group player, he was England Colts' number 8 before switching to flanker, and played for England 'B' against France 1981. In 1983 he played for an England XV v Canada, and for the North v New Zealand at Gateshead in 1983-4. He went on the British Lions tour to New Zealand in 1983, playing in 12 games out of 18, including four Tests, and on the England tours to South Africa in 1984 and to Australia and Fiji in 1991.

He is a former schools lawn tennis champion and has even appeared on Bruce Forsyth's *Generation Game*. Once a farmer, he now works in international finance. His father played for Headingley and is a past president of that club, whilst brother Michael played for Poverty Bay (New Zealand)

WINTLE
Trevor Clifford

Scrum half. 1966-1969 (Northampton, 5 caps).
Debut v Scotland, 19 March 1966.
Born: 10 January 1940.
Educated: Lydney Grammar School, Cambridge University.
Clubs: Lydney, Cambridge University (Blues 1960-61), Rosslyn Park, St Mary's Hospital, Northampton, Gloucestershire, Middlesex, East Midlands, Barbarians.
Wintle is the most-capped player to have appeared with the Lydney club. He was known for his use of the diving pass, which spread the ball more quickly to his stand-off partners.

WODEHOUSE
Norman Atherton, CB

Forward. 1910-1913 (United Services (Portsmouth), Royal Navy, 14 caps).
Debut v France, 3 March 1910.
Born: 18 May 1887; Died: 4 September 1941 (missing at sea).
Clubs: HMS Britannia, United Services (Portsmouth), Royal Navy, Hampshire, Barbarians.
Wodehouse, a famed line-out expert who captained England in 1913, served in World War One as a lieutenant and was later ADC to HM King George VI. During World War Two he was posted missing overboard, presumed drowned, whilst on Atlantic Convoy duty.

WOOD
Albert

Forward. 1884 (Halifax, 1 cap).
Debut v Ireland, 4 February 1884.
Clubs: Halifax, Yorkshire (10 appearances).
Albert Wood emigrated to Australia 1884.

WOOD
Alfred Ernest

Full-back. 1908 (Gloucester, Cheltenham, 3 caps).

Debut v France, 1 January 1908.
Born: 1882, Bristol; Died: 15 February 1963, Oldham.
Clubs: Gloucester, Cheltenham, Oldham RL.
He joined Oldham RL in 1908-09.

WOOD
George William

Scrum half. 1914 (Leicester, 1 cap).
Debut v Wales, 17 January 1914.
Born: 5 February 1886; Died: 12 June 1969.
Educated: Melbourne Road School (Leicester).
Clubs: Melbourne Road Old Boys, Leicester, Nuneaton, Leicestershire, Midland Counties.
In 1914, Wood helped the Midland Counties to their only County Championship title.

WOOD
Robert

Half-back. 1894 (Liversedge, 1 cap).
Debut v Ireland, 3 February 1894.
Born: 1873.
Clubs: Liversedge, Yorkshire (14 appearances).
Bob Wood turned to the Rugby League code when Liversedge helped form the Northern Union in 1895. He was a licensee in Liversedge.

WOOD
Robert Dudley

Forward. 1901-1903 (Liverpool Old Boys, 3 caps).
Debut v Ireland, 9 February 1901.
Born: 1873, Liverpool.
Clubs: Liverpool Old Boys, Lancashire (41 appearances), Barbarians.

WOODGATE
Edmund Elliott.

Prop. 1952 (Paignton, 1 cap).
Debut v Wales, 19 January 1952.
Born: 21 January 1922.
Educated: Dartmouth Secondary Modern School.
Clubs: Paignton, Devon, Chepstow, Barbarians.
Woodgate later served on the Chepstow club's committee.

WOODHEAD
Ernest

Forward. 1880 (Huddersfield, 1 cap).
Debut v Ireland, 30 January 1880.
Born: 22 February 1857, Huddersfield; Died: 10 June 1944.
Educated: Huddersfield College, Edinburgh University, Dublin University.
Clubs: Edinburgh University, Dublin University, Huddersfield, Yorkshire (5 appearances).
As a student in Dublin, Woodhead was called into the England team when one of the forwards suffered sea-sickness whilst crossing the Irish sea. He became

editor of the *Huddersfield Examiner* and later chairman of that newspaper which was founded by his father.

WOODRUFF
Charles Garfield

Wing. 1951 (Harlequins, 4 caps).
Debut v Wales, 20 January 1951.
Born: 30 October 1920.
Educated: Newport High School.
Clubs: Harlequins, Cheltenham, London Counties, Kent, Gloucestershire, Barbarians.
He also played for London Civil Service and worked at the Air Ministry. He served in World War Two with the RAF.

WOOD
Samuel Moses James

Forward. 1890-1895 (Cambridge University, Wellington, 13 caps).
Debut v Wales, 15 February 1890.
Born: 14 April 1868, Glenfield, NSW, Australia; Died: 30 April 1931.
Educated: Sydney Grammar School (Australia) Brighton College, Cambridge University.
Clubs: Cambridge University (Blues 1888-1890), Wellington, Blackheath, Bridgwater, Taunton, Somerset (30 appearances, captain 1893-6), Barbarians.
Samuel Wood, who skippered England at rugby, also played Test cricket for both England and Australia. He had an outstanding match in the 1890 Varsity match and gained his rugby caps as a member of the England pack. He was a founder member of the Barbarians in 1890 and was one of nine Blackheath players in the England team of 1895. He played for Australia at cricket in 1888, when an undergraduate at Cambridge, and toured South Africa with Lord Hawke's England team in 1895-6, playing in three Tests. He played for Somerset from 1894 and 1906 and was a popular captain. He was Somerset CCC's secretary for some 30 years. Against Sussex at Hove in 1895, he scored 215 out of 282 in two and a half hours. He served in World War One with the Somerset Light Infantry. His autobiography *My Reminiscences* was published in 1925.

WOODS
Thomas

Forward. 1908 (Bridgwater, 1 cap).
Debut v Scotland, 21 March 1908.
Born: 9 February 1883, Bridgwater; Died: 12 April 1955, Rochdale.
Clubs: Bridgwater Albion, Somerset (26 appearances, captain 1907-09), Rochdale Hornets RL.
A licensee, he was later groundsman at Rochdale Hornets, the club he first joined in 1909.

WOODS
Tom

Lock. 1920-1921 (United Services (Portsmouth), Royal Navy, 5 caps).
Debut v Scotland, 20 March 1920.

Clubs: Devonport Services, United Services (Portsmouth), Royal Navy, Newbridge, Pontypool, Wigan RL.

He signed for Wigan at the same time as his Pontypool teammate, Wilf Hodder, in 1921. A leading stoker in the Navy, Tom Woods made 68 appearances for Wigan, scoring eight tries and one goal, and also appeared for the Welsh RL team.

WOODWARD
Clive Ronald

Centre. 1980-1984 (Leicester, 21 caps).
Debut v Ireland, 19 January 1980.
Born: 6 January 1956, Ely, Cambs.
Educated: HMS Conway, Loughborough Colleges.
Clubs: Loughborough Colleges, Harlequins, Leicester, Oxfordshire, Eastern Counties.

Perhaps one of the most elusive of modern England centres, Clive Woodward, who was born into a services family, was chosen to play in a Welsh Schools trial but had to withdraw due to injury. Indeed, his rugby career has been hampered by injury and he has twice broken a leg, once during the England Under-23 game against Italy in 1976. He played in England's Grand Slam season of 1980, making his debut as a replacement for A.M.Bond, and toured with England to the USA and Canada in 1982.

Woodward was on the British Lions tour to South Africa in 1980, playing in the Second and Third Tests and making 11 tour appearances overall, scoring 53 points. He also went on the Lions tour of New Zealand in 1983 and played for Midland Division v New Zealand in 1980.

Woodward was involved in preparing the Oxford University side for the 1990 Varsity match and the England Under-23 team to meet Holland in 1988. A sales executive he is married to Helen, a hockey international. He lived in Australia for a time, playing club rugby for Manley in Sydney,

WOODWARD
John Edward

Wing. 1952-1956 (Wasps, 15 caps).
Debut v South Africa, 5 January 1952.
Born: 17 April 1931, Buckinghamshire.
Educated: Royal Grammar School (High Wycombe).
Clubs: Old Wycombensians, RAF, Wasps, Buckinghamshire, East Midlands, Middlesex (captain 1958-59), Barbarians.

John Woodward

The Wasps' most capped player, he is brother-in-law of Ron Syrett. A life vice-president of High Wycombe RFC and a former England Schools sprint champion, he worked as a butcher.

WOOLDRIDGE
Charles Sylvestor

Forward. 1883-1885 (Oxford University, Blackheath, 7 caps).
Debut v Wales, 16 December 1883.
Born: 31 December 1858, Winchester;
Died: 19 February 1941.

Clive Woodward

Educated: Winchester College, Oxford University.

Clubs: Oxford University (Blue 1882), Blackheath, Hampshire.

He played soccer at school before reverting to rugby. One of the first Wykehemists to gain a rugby Blue, he was a solicitor by profession.

WORDSWORTH
Alan John ('Nellie')

Fly half. 1975 (Cambridge University, 1 cap).
Debut v Australia, 24 May 1975.
Born: 9 November 1953, Thornton Heath.

Educated: Whitgift School, Cambridge University.

Clubs: Cambridge University (Blues 1973-4), Harlequins.

Wordsworth played centre in his first Varsity match before reverting to fly-half for his second. He gained his only England cap at fly-half when he replaced the injured W.N.Bennett, in the first Test at Sydney on the 1975 tour.

WORTON
James Robert Bute. ('John')

Scrum half. 1926-1927 (Harlequins, Army, 2 caps).
Debut v Wales, 16 January 1926.
Born: 31 March 1901, London; Died: 14 January 1991.

Educated: Haileybury and Imperial Services College, Royal Military Academy (Sandhurst).

Clubs: Harlequins, Army, Combined Services, Surrey, Barbarians.

A member of the Harlequins team which won the first Middlesex Sevens in 1926, James Worton was a travelling reserve for England whilst still a cadet at Sandhurst. His two caps came before his regiment was posted to Shanghai.

He joined the 1st Battalion of the Middlesex Regiment in 1921 and served in Northern Ireland, Aldershot, Mill Hill Barracks, Cologne and Shanghai. During World War Two he was posted to France with the BEF and survived the retreat at Dunkirk in 1940, getting away from the beaches on the last day of evacuation.

He completed the war in charge of battle-training school in Devon, then served in Greece and in Palestine during the 1948 troubles, then in Kenya, Germany and Tunis. He retired from the Army in 1953 with the rank of lieutenant-colonel and took a part-time post as a ring inspector at race meetings. He was a member of North Hampshire Golf Club for over 30 years and had a handicap of 11.

WRENCH
David Frederick Bryan

Prop. 1964 (Harlequins, 2 caps).
Debut v France, 22 February 1964.
Born: 27 November 1936.

Educated: Sandwich School, Leeds University, Cambridge University.

Clubs: Winnington Park, Wilmslow, Leeds University, UAU, Cambridge University (Blue 1960), Harlequins, Wolfhounds (Ireland), Cheshire, Barbarians.

A school teacher, he also played cricket for the Gentlemen of Hertfordshire.

WRIGHT
Cyril Carne Glenton

Centre. 1909 (Cambridge University, Blackheath, 2 caps).
Debut v Ireland, 13 February 1909.
Born: 7 March 1887; Died: 15 September 1960.

Educated: Tonbridge School, Cambridge University.

Clubs: Cambridge University (Blues 1907-08), Blackheath, Kent, Barbarians.

He also won cricket Blues (1907-08) and was later a school teacher. During World War One he served with the Durham Light Infantry.

WRIGHT
Frank Thurlow

Half-back. 1881 (Edinburgh Academicals, Manchester, 1 cap).
Debut v Scotland, 19 March 1881.
Born: 2 July 1862, Leigh; Died: 1934, Marseilles, France.

Educated: Edinburgh Academy, Edinburgh University.

Clubs: Edinburgh Academicals, Tyldesley, Manchester, Lancashire.

A solicitor and the son of a local MP, Caleb Wright, he was one of the best-known players in the country and, although he assisted Tyldesley on occasion, his rugby was mainly played at the Manchester club.

WRIGHT
Ian Douglas

Fly-half. 1971 (Northampton, 4 caps).

Ian Wright

Debut v Wales, 16 January 1971.
Born: 24 December 1945, Croydon.

Educated: Felixstowe Grammar School, Worthing High School, St Luke's College (Exeter).

Clubs: Rosslyn Park, Northampton, Old Azurians, Sussex, London Counties, Surrey, Devon.

A school teacher, he also represented England Under-25s against Fiji in 1970 and played cricket for Sussex.

WRIGHT
James F.

Half-back. 1890 (Bradford, 1 cap).
Debut v Wales, 15 February 1890.
Born: 1 April 1863, York; Died: 4 October 1932.

Clubs: Bowling Old Lane (Bradford), Idle, Bradford, Yorkshire (6 appearances).

A licensee, he became one of the first Englishman to win only one cap and suffer defeat against the Welsh.

WRIGHT
John Cecil

Lock. 1934 (Metropolitan Police, 1 cap).
Debut v Wales, 20 January 1934.
Born: 6 August 1910.

Educated: Sedbergh School.

Clubs: Crewe and Nantwich, Metropolitan Police, British Police, Newport, Middlesex, Monmouth.

John Wright was the first player to be capped from the Metropolitan Police. He was a policeman until the outbreak of World War Two, when he joined the 1st Battalion of the King's Shropshire Light Infantry. After the war he became a farmer in Lincolnshire. His only cap is said to be in the hands of the Newport club.

WRIGHT
Thomas Peter

Prop. 1960-1962 (Blackheath, 13 caps).
Debut v Wales, 16 January 1960.
Born: 28 February 1931.

Educated: Judd School (Tonbridge).

Clubs: Tonbridge, Blackheath, Penarth, Devizes, Kent, Barbarians.

WRIGHT
William Henry George, ISM

Prop. 1920 (Plymouth Albion, 2 caps).
Debut v Wales, 17 January 1920.
Born: 6 June 1889.

Clubs: Plymouth Albion, Devon.

He was awarded the Imperial Service Medal in 1949.

WYATT
Derek M.

Wing. 1976 (Bedford, 1 cap).
Debut v Scotland, 21 February 1976.
Born: 4 December 1949, London.

Educated: Royal Grammar School (Colchester), Oxford University.

Clubs: Oxford University (Blue 1981), Ipswich, Bedford, Bath, Eastern Counties.

In 1973-4, Wyatt's first season with the Bedford club, he scored 50 tries, 33 of them for the 1st XV; and he totalled 176 tries in less than five seasons with the club. He joined Bath in 1979 and scored 35 tries in his first season — 29 of them in Bath's colours to equal the club record established by George Hayden in the 1930s. Wyatt was in the Eastern Counties side that reached the County Championship Final. He was on the England tour of Australia in 1975. He has worked in publishing and teaching.

YARRANTON
Sir Peter George

Lock. 1954-1955 (RAF, Wasps, 5 caps).
Debut v Wales, 16 January 1954.
Born: 30 September 1924, Acton.
Educated: Willesden Technical College.
Clubs: RAF, Combined Services, Wasps, London Counties, Middlesex, Barbarians.

Peter Yarranton, who captained every team for whom he played, except England, has enjoyed a distinguished career in sports administration. He joined the Wasps as a junior player and was captain from 1960 to 1962, secretary in 1972-3 and club president from 1982 to 1985.

He was RFU president for 1991-2 and his other posts include: RFU Executive Committee member; PRO adviser to the RFU; chairman of the RFU Senior Clubs' Committee; RFU vice-president (1974 and 1990-91); Middlesex president (1985-6); Middlesex Memorial Trust Fund member; London and Middlesex chairman of selectors; Lensbury RFC president; Rugby Internationals' Golfing Society; Sports Council chairman (1989).

He is also a Freeman of Liveryman of the City of London, being admitted to the Court of The Worshipful Company of Gold and Silver Wyre Drawers in October 1987. He was also a swimming and water polo player for London and Middlesex and skippered the RAF swimming and water polo teams.

Yarranton was commissioned into the RAF as a pilot in Canada in 1942 and served in World War Two with over 3,000 operational hours, mainly in Burma and South-East Asia as a flight-lieutenant on Liberators. When he left the RAF in 1957 he joined Shell-Mex and then BP, retiring in December 1977 to become general manager of the Lensbury Club. For ten years he was a regular rugby broadcaster for BBC Radio London. Knighted in June 1992.

YIEND
William

Forward. 1889-1893 (Harlepool Rovers, Gloucester, 6 caps).
Debut v Maoris, 16 February 1889.

Born: 1861, Winchcombe, Gloucestershire; Died: 22 January 1939.
Clubs: Hartlepool Rovers, Gloucester, Leicester, Keighley, Peterborough, Durham County, Barbarians.

Yiend was employed on the railways. He captained the Hartlepool club from 1890 to 1893.

YOUNG
Arthur Tudor

Scrum-half. 1924-1929 (Cambridge University, Blackheath, Army 18 caps).
Debut v Wales, 19 January 1924.
Born: 14 October 1901, India; Died: 22 June 1933, India.
Educated: Tonbridge School, Cambridge University.
Clubs: Cambridge University (Blues 1922-4, also captain), Blackheath, Army, Kent, Barbarians.

Arthur Young

Affectionately known as England's 'little man', he was known as the most daringly original scrum-half of his era. He went on the British Isles tour of South Africa in 1924 and whilst serving in the Royal Tank Corps he played for the Army ten times between 1926 and 1929, against the Royal Navy, RAF and French Army. He was ADC to General Sir Norman MacMullen, GOC East Command, when he died from pneumonia following a bout of influenza.

YOUNG
John Robert Chester

Wing. 1958-1961 (Oxford University, Harlequins, 9 caps).
Debut v Ireland, 8 February 1958.
Born: 6 September 1937, Chester.
Educated Bishop's Vesey Grammar

School (Birmingham), Oxford University.
Clubs: Old Veseyans, Oxford University (Blues 1958-60), Moseley, Harlequins, London Counties, Warwickshire, Surrey, Barbarians.

Young, who also won an athletics Blue, went on the British Lions tour to Australia and New Zealand in 1959 and on the Oxford-Cambridge tour of East Africa in 1957. He was AAA's 100 yards champion in 1956. A barrister, he was called to the Bar in 1961.

YOUNG
Malcolm

Scrum-half. 1977-1979 (Gosforth, 10 caps).
Debut v Scotland, 15 January 1977.
Born: 4 January 1946, Mickley, Northumberland.

Malcolm Young

Educated: Queen Elizabeth's Grammar School (Hexham), Cambridge University.
Clubs: Cambridge University (no Blue), Gosforth.

He scored 423 points during the 1972-1973 season and scored a try on his international debut.

YOUNG
Peter Dalton

Lock. 1954-1955 (Dublin Wanderers, 9 caps).
Debut v Wales, 16 January 1954.
Born: 9 November 1927.
Educated: Clifton College, Cambridge University.
Clubs: Cambridge University (Blue 1949), Clifton, Rosslyn Park, Dublin Wanderers, Gloucestershire.
Peter Young captained England against France and Scotland in 1955.

YOUNGS
Nicholas Gerald

Scrum-half. 1983-1984 (Leicester, 6 caps).
Debut v Ireland, 19 March 1983.
Born: 15 December 1959, Norfolk.
Educated: Greshams School, Shuttleworth Agricultural College.
Clubs: Bedford, Leicester.

Nicky Youngs

He won nine caps for England Secondary Schools, went on the England Under-23 tour of France in 1979 and captained the Under-23s against the Netherlands in 1980. He played for an England XV v Canada in 1983 and is an England 'B' international.

International Appearances 1870-1992

Abbreviations:
World Cup matches are shown in *italics*.
After each players name the number in brackets in total number of caps won.
The numerals besides the country the player appeared against are the Test matches, (i.e. Andrew C.R. 1987 Australia (1,2) indicates that he appeared in both Test matches).

AARVOLD, C.D. (16) 1928 Australia. Wales, Ireland, France, Scotland; 1929 Wales, Ireland, France; 1931 Wales, Scotland, France; 1932 South Africa, Wales, Ireland, Scotland; 1933 Wales.

ACKFORD, P.J. (22) 1988 Australia; 1989 Scotland, Ireland, France, Wales, Romania, Fiji; 1990 Wales Ireland, France, Scotland, Argentine; 1991 Wales, Scotland, Ireland, France, Australia; *New Zealand, Italy, France, Scotland, Australia.*

ADAMS, A.A. (1) 1910 France.

ADAMS, F.R. (7) 1875 Ireland, Scotland; 1876 Scotland; 1877 Ireland; 1878 Scotland; 1879 Scotland, Ireland.

ADEY, G.J. (2) 1976 Ireland, France.

ADKINS, S.J. (7) 1950 Ireland, France, Scotland; 1953 Wales, Ireland, France, Scotland.

AGAR, A.E. (7) 1952 South Africa, Wales, Scotland, Ireland, France; 1953 Wales, Ireland.

ALCOCK, A. (1) 1906 South Africa.

ALDERSON, F.H.R. (6) 1891 Wales, Ireland, Scotland; 1892 Wales, Scotland; 1893 Wales.

ALEXANDER, H. (7) 1900 Ireland, Scotland; 1901 Wales, Ireland, Scotland; 1902 Wales, Ireland.

ALEXANDER, W (1) 1927 France.

ALLISON, D.F. (7) 1956 Wales, Ireland, Scotland, France; 1957 Wales; 1958 Wales, Scotland.

ALLPORT, A. (5) 1892 Wales; 1893 Ireland; 1894 Wales, Ireland, Scotland.

ANDERSON, S. (1) 1899 Ireland.

ANDERSON, W.F. (1) 1973 New Zealand (1st Test).

ANDERTON, C. (1) 1889 Maoris.

ANDREW, C.R. (48) 1985 Romania, France, Scotland, Wales, Ireland; 1986 Wales, Scotland, Ireland, France; 1987 Ireland, France, Wales, *Japan, USA*; 1988 Scotland, Ireland (1 & 2), Australia (1 & 2), Fiji, Australia; 1989 Scotland, Ireland, France, Wales, Romania, Fiji; 1990 Ireland, France, Wales, Scotland, Argentina; 1991 Wales, Scotland, Ireland, France, Australia, Fiji, *New Zealand, Italy, USA, France, Scotland, Australia;* 1992 Scotland, Ireland, France, Wales.

ARCHER, H (3) 1909 Wales, France, Ireland.

ARMSTRONG, R. (1) 1925 Wales.

ARTHUR, T.G. (2) 1966 Wales, Ireland.

ASHBY, R.C. (3) 1966 Ireland, France; 1967 Australia.

ASHCROFT, A. (16) 1956 Wales, Ireland, Scotland, France; 1957 Wales, Ireland, France, Scotland; 1958 Wales, Australia, Ireland, France, Scotland; 1959 Ireland, France, Scotland.

ASHCROFT, A.H. (1) 1909 Australia.

ASHFORD, W. (4) 1897 Wales, Ireland; 1898 Scotland Wales.

ASHWORTH, A. (1) 1892 Ireland.

ASKEW, J.G. (3) 1930 Wales, Ireland, France.

ASLETT, A.R. (6) 1926 Wales, Ireland, France, Scotland; 1929 Scotland, France.

ASSINDER, E.W. (2) 1909 Australia, Wales.

ASTON, R.L. (2) 1890 Scotland, Ireland.

AUTY, J.R. (1) 1935 Scotland.

BAILEY, M.D. (7) 1984 South Africa (1 & 2); 1987 *USA*; 1989 Fiji; 1990 Ireland, France, Scotland (R).

BAINBRIDGE, S. (17) 1982 France, Wales; 1983 France, Wales, Scotland, Ireland, New Zealand; 1984 Scotland, Ireland, France, Wales; 1985 New Zealand (1 & 2); 1987 France, Wales, Scotland, *Japan, USA.*

BAKER, D.G.S. (4) 1955 Wales, Ireland, France, Scotland.

BAKER, E.M. (7) 1895 Wales, Ireland, Scotland; 1896 Wales, Ireland, Scotland; 1897 Wales.

BAKER, H.C. (1) 1887 Wales.

BANCE, J.F. (1) 1954 Scotland.

BARLEY, B. (7) 1984 Ireland, France, Wales, Australia; 1988 Australia (1 & 2), Fiji.

BARNES, S. (8) 1984 Australia; 1985 Romania (R), New Zealand (1 & 2); 1986 Scotland (R), France (R); 1987 Ireland (R); 1988 Fiji.

BARR, R.J. (3) 1932 South Africa, Wales, Ireland.

BARRETT, E.I.M. (1) 1903 Scotland.

BARRINGTON, T.J.M. (2) 1931 Wales, Ireland.

BARRINGTON-WARD, L.E. (4) 1910 Wales, Ireland, France, Scotland.

BARRON, J.H. (3) 1896 Scotland; 1897 Wales, Ireland.

BARTLETT, J.T. (1) 1951 Wales.

BARTLETT, R.M. (7) 1957 Wales, Ireland, France, Scotland; 1958 Ireland, France, Scotland.

BARTON, J. (4) 1967 Ireland, France, Wales; 1972 France.

BATCHELOR, T.B. (1) 1907 France.

BATES, S.M. (1) 1989 Romania.

BATESON, A.H. (4) 1930 Ireland, France, Scotland.

BATESON, H.D. (1) 1879 Ireland.

BATSON, T. (3) 1872 Scotland; 1874 Scotland; 1875 Ireland.

BATTEN, J.M. (1) 1874 Scotland.

BAUME, J.L. (1) 1950 Scotland.

BAXTER, J. (3) 1900 Wales, Ireland, Scotland.

BAYFIELD, M. (6) 1991 Fiji, Australia; 1992 Scotland, Ireland, Frances, Wales.

BAZLEY, R.C. (10) 1952 Ireland, France; 1953 Wales, Ireland, France, Scotland; 1955 Wales, Ireland, France, Scotland.

BEAUMONT, W.B. (34) 1975 Ireland, Australia (1 (R) & 2); 1976 Australia, Wales, Scotland, Ireland, France; 1977 Scotland, Ireland, France, Wales; 1978 France, Wales, Scotland, Ireland, New Zealand; 1979 Scotland, Ireland, France, Wales, New Zealand; 1980 Ireland, France, Wales, Scotland; 1981 Wales, Scotland, Ireland, France, Argentina (1 & 2); 1982 Australia, Scotland.

BEDFORD, H. (3) 1889 Maoris; 1890 Scotland, Ireland.

BEDFORD, L.L. (2) 1931 Wales, Ireland.

BEER, I.D.S. (2) 1955 France, Scotland.

BEESE, M.C. (3) 1972 Wales, Ireland, France.

BELL, F.J. (1) 1900 Wales.

BELL, H. (1) 1884 Ireland.

BELL, J.L. (1) 1878 Ireland.

BELL, P.J. (4) 1968 Wales, Ireland, France, Scotland.

BELL, R.W. (3) 1900 Wales, Ireland, Scotland.

BENDON, G.J. (4) 1959 Wales, Ireland, France, Scotland.

BENNETT, N.O. (7) 1947 Wales, Scotland, France; 1948 Australia, Wales, Ireland, Scotland.

BENNETT, W.N. (7) 1975 Scotland, Australia (1); 1976 Scotland (R); 1979 Scotland, Ireland, France, Wales.

BENNETTS, B.B. (2) 1909 Australia, Wales.

BENTLEY, J. (2) 1988 Ireland (2), Australia (1).

BENTLEY, J.E. (2) 1871 Scotland; 1872 Scotland.

BERRIDGE, M.J. (2) 1949 Wales, Ireland.

BERRY, H. (4) 1910 Wales, Ireland, France, Scotland.

BERRY, J. (3) 1891 Wales, Ireland, Scotland.

BERRY, J.T.W. (3) 1939 Wales, Ireland, Scotland.

BESWICK, E. (2) 1882 Ireland, Scotland.

BIGGS, J.M. (2) 1878 Scotland; 1879 Ireland.

BIRKETT, J.G.G. (21) 1906 Scotland, France, South Africa; 1907 France, Wales, Scotland; 1908 France, Wales, Ireland, Scotland; 1910 Wales, Ireland, Scotland; 1911 Wales, France, Ireland, Scotland; 1912 Wales, Ireland, Scotland, France.

BIRKETT, L. (3) 1875 Scotland; 1877 Ireland, Scotland.

BIRKETT, R.H. (4) 1871 Scotland; 1875 Scotland; 1876 Scotland; 1877 Ireland.

BISHOP, C.C. (1) 1827 France.

BLACK, B.H. (10)) 1930 Wales, Ireland, France, Scotland; 1931 Wales, Ireland, Scotland, France; 1932 Scotland; 1933 Wales.

BLACKLOCK, J.H. (2) 1898 Ireland; 1899 Ireland.

BLAKEWAY, P.J. (19) 1980 Ireland, France, Wales, Scotland; 1981 Wales, Scotland, Ireland, France; 1982 Ireland, France, Wales; 1984 Ireland, France, Wales, South Africa (1); 1985 Romania, France, Scotland, Ireland.

BLAKISTON, A.F. (17) 1920 Scotland; 1921 Wales, Ireland, Scotland, France; 1922 Wales; 1923 Scotland, France; 1924 Wales, Ireland, France, Scotland; 1925 New Zealand, Wales, Ireland, Scotland, France.

BLATHERWICK, T. (1) 1878 Ireland.

BODY, J.A. 1872 Scotland; 1873 Scotland.

BOLTON, C.A. (1) 1909 France.

BOLTON, R. (5) 1933 Wales; 1936 Scotland; 1937 Scotland; 1938 Wales, Ireland.

BOLTON, W.N. (11) 1882 Ireland, Scotland; 1883 Wales, Ireland, Scotland; 1884 Wales, Ireland, Scotland; 1885 Ireland; 1887 Ireland, Scotland.

BONAVENTURA, M.S. (1) 1931 Wales.

BOND, A.M. (6) 1978 New Zealand; 1979 Scotland, Ireland, New Zealand; 1980 Ireland; 1982 Ireland.

BONHAM-CARTER, E. (1) 1891 Scotland.

BONSOR, F. (6) 1886 Wales, Ireland, Scotland; 1887 Wales, Scotland; 1889 Maoris.

BOOBBYER, B. (9) 1950 Wales, Ireland, France, Scotland; 1951 Wales, France; 1952 Scotland, Ireland, France.

BOOTH, L.A. (7) 1933 Wales, Ireland, Scotland; 1934 Scotland; 1935 Wales, Ireland, Scotland.

BOTTING, I.J. (2) 1950 Wales, Ireland.

BOUGHTON, H.J. (3) 1935 Wales, Ireland, Scotland.

BOYLE, C.W. (1) 1873 Scotland.

BOYLE, S.B. (3) 1983 Wales, Scotland, Ireland.

BOYLEN, F. (4) 1908 France, Wales, Ireland, Scotland.

BRADBY, M.S. (2) 1922 Ireland, France.

BRADLEY, R. (1) 1908 Wales.

BRADSHAW, H. (7) 1892 Scotland; 1893 Wales, Scotland, Ireland; 1894 Wales, Ireland, Scotland.

BRAIN, S.E. (13) 1984 South Africa (2), Australia (R); 1985 Romania, France, Scotland, Ireland, Wales, New Zealand (1 & 2); 1986 Wales, Scotland, Ireland, France.

BRAITHWAITE, J. (1) 1905 New Zealand.

BRAITHWAITE-EXLEY, B. (1) 1949 Wales.

BRETTARGH, A.T. (8) 1900 Wales; 1903 Ireland, Scotland; 1904 Wales, Ireland, Scotland; 1905 Ireland, Scotland.

BREWER, J. (1) 1876 Ireland.

BRIGGS, A. (3) 1892 Wales, Ireland, Scotland.

BRINN, A. (3) Wales, Ireland, Scotland.

BROADLEY, T. (6) 1893 Wales, Scotland; 1894 Wales, Ireland, Scotland; 1896 Scotland.

BROMET, W.E. (12) 1891 Wales, Ireland; 1892 Wales, Ireland, Scotland; 1893 Wales, Ireland, Scotland; 1895 Wales, Ireland, Scotland; 1896 Ireland.

BROOK, P.W.P. (3) 1930 Scotland; 1931 France; 1936 Scotland.

BROOKE, T.J. (2) 1968 France, Scotland.

BROOKS, F.G. (1) 1906 South Africa.

BROOKS, M.J. (1) 1874 Scotland.

BROPHY, T.J. (8) 1964 Ireland, France, Scotland; 1965 Wales, Ireland; 1966 Wales, Ireland, France.

BROUGH, J.W. (2) 1925 New Zealand, Wales.

BROUGHAM, H. (4) 1912 Wales, Ireland, Scotland, France.

BROWN, A.A. (1) 1938 Scotland.

BROWN, L.G. (18) 1911 Wales, France, Ireland, Scotland; 1913 South Africa, Wales, France, Ireland, Scotland; 1914 Wales, Ireland, Scotland, France; 1921 Wales, Ireland, Scotland, France; 1922 Wales.

BROWN, T.W. (9) 1928 Scotland; 1929 Wales, Ireland, Scotland, France; 1932 Scotland 1933 Wales, Ireland, Scotland.

BRUNTON, J. (3) 1914 Wales, Ireland, Scotland.

BRUTTON, E.B. (1) 1886 Scotland.

BRYDEN, C.C. (2) 1876 Ireland; 1877 Scotland.

BRYDEN, H.A. (1) 1874 Scotland.

BUCKINGHAM, R.A. (1) 1927 France.

BUCKNALL, A.L. (10) 1968 South Africa; 1970 Ireland, Wales, Scotland, France. 1971 Wales, Ireland, France, Scotland (2, 1 Centenary).

BUCKTON, J.R.D. (1) 1988 Argentina (R).

BUDD, A. (5) 1878 Ireland; 1879 Scotland, Ireland; 1881 Wales, Scotland.

BUDWORTH, R.T.D. (3) 1890 Wales; 1891 Wales, Scotland.

BULL, A.G. (1) 1914 Wales.

BULLOUGH, E. (3) 1892 Wales, Ireland, Scotland.

BULPITT, M.P. (1) 1970 Scotland.

BULTEEL, A.J. (1) 1876 Ireland.

BUNTING, W.L. (9) 1897 Ireland, Scotland; 1898 Ireland, Scotland, Wales; 1899 Scotland; 1900 Scotland; 1901 Ireland, Scotland.

BURLAND, D.W. (8) 1931 Wales, Ireland, France; 1932 Ireland, Scotland; 1933 Wales, Ireland, Scotland.

BURNS, B.H. (1) 1871 Scotland.

BURTON, G.W. (6) 1879 Scotland, Ireland; 1880 Scotland; 1881 Ireland, Wales, Scotland.

BURTON, H.C. (1) 1926 Wales.

BURTON, M.A. (17) 1972 Wales, Ireland, France, Scotland, South Africa; 1974 France, Wales; 1975 Scotland, Australia (1 & 2); 1976 Australia, Wales, Scotland, Ireland, France; 1978 France, Wales.

BUSH, J.A. (5) 1872 Scotland; 1873 Scotland; 1875 Scotland; 1876 Ireland, Scotland.

BUTCHER, C.J.S. (3) 1984 South Africa (1 & 2), Australia.

BUTCHER, W.V. (7) 1903 Scotland; 1904 Wales, Ireland, Scotland; 1905 Wales, Ireland, Scotland.

BUTLER, A.G. (2) 1937 Wales, Ireland.

BUTLER, P.E. (2) 1975 Australia (1); 1976 France.

BUTTERFIELD, J. (28) 1953 France, Scotland; 1954 Wales, New Zealand, Ireland, Scotland, France; 1955 Wales, Ireland, Scotland, France; 1956 Wales, Ireland, Scotland, France.

BUTTERFIELD, J. 1957 Wales, Ireland, France, Scotland; 1958 Wales, Australia, France, Scotland; 1959 Wales, Ireland, France, Scotland.

BYRNE, F.A. (1) 1897 Wales.

BYRNE, J.F. (13) 1894 Wales, Ireland, Scotland; 1895 Ireland, Scotland; 1896 Ireland; 1897 Wales, Ieland, Scotland; 1898 Ireland, Scotland, Wales; 1899 Ireland.

CAIN, J.J. (1) 1950 Wales.

CAMPBELL, D.A. (2) 1937 Wales, Ireland.

CANDLER, P.L. (10) 1935 Wales; 1936 New Zealand, Wales, Ireland, Scotland; 1937 Wales, Ireland, Scotland; 1938 Wales, Scotland.

CANNELL, L.B. (19) 1948 France; 1949 Wales, Ireland, France, Scotland; 1950 Wales, Ireland, France, Scotland; 1952 South Africa, Wales; 1953 Wales, Ireland, France; 1956 Ireland, Scotland, France; 1957 Wales, Ireland.

CAPLAN, D.W.N. (2) 1978 Scotland, Ireland.

CARDUS, R.M. (2) 1979 France, Wales.

CAREY, G.M. (5) 1895 Wales, Ireland, Scotland; 1896 Wales, Ireland.

CARLETON, J. (26) 1979 New Zealand; 1980 Ireland, France, Wales, Scotland; 1981 Wales, Scotland, Ireland, France, Argentina (1 & 2); 1982 Australia, Scotland, Ireland, France, Wales; 1983 France, Wales, Scotland, Ireland, New Zealand; 1984 Scotland, Ireland, France, Wales, Australia.

CARLING, W.D.C. (36) 1988 France, Wales, Scotland, Ireland (1 & 2), Australia (2), Fiji, Australia; 1989 Scotland, Ireland, France, Wales, Fiji; 1990 Ireland, France, Wales, Scotland, Artentina (1 & 2), Argentina; 1991 Scotland, Ireland, France, Fiji, Australia, *New Zealand, Italy, USA, France, Scotland, Australia*; 1992 Scotland, Ireland, France, Wales.

CARPENTER, A.D. (1) 1932 South Africa.

CARR, R.S.L. (3) 1939 Wales, Ireland, Scotland.

CARTWRIGHT, V.H. (14) 1903 Wales, Ireland, Scotland; 1904 Wales, Scotland; 1905 Wales, Ireland, Scotland, New Zealand; 1906 Wales, Ireland, Scotland, France, South Africa.

CATCHESIDE, H.C. (8) 1924 Wales, Ireland, France, Scotland; 1926 Wales, Ireland; 1927 Ireland, Scotland.

CATTELL, R.H.B. (7) 1895 Wales, Ireland, Scotland; 1896 Wales, Ireland, Scotland; 1900 Wales.

CAVE, J.W. (1) 1889 Maoris.

CAVE, W.T.C. (1) 1905 Wales.

CHALLIS, R. (3) 1957 Ireland, France, Scotland.

CHAMBERS, E.L. (3) 1908 France; 1910 Wales, Ireland.

CHANTRILL, B.S. (4) Wales, Ireland, France, Scotland.

CHAPMAN, C.E. (1) 1884 Wales.

CHAPMAN, F.E. (7) 1910 Wales, Ireland, France, Scotland; 1912 Wales; 1914 Wales, Ireland.

CHEESMAN, W.I. (4) 1913 South Africa, Wales, France, Ireland.

CHESTON, E.C. (5) 1873 Scotland; 1874 Scotland; 1875 Ireland, Scotland; 1876 Scotland.

CHILCOTT, G.J. (14) 1984 Australia; 1986 Ireland, France; 1987 France (R), Wales *Japan, USA, Wales (R)*; 1988 Ireland (2R), Fiji; 1989 Ireland (R), France, Wales, Romania (R).

CHRISTOPHERSON, P. (2) 1891 Wales, Scotland.

CLARK, C.W.H. (1) 1876 Ireland.

CLARKE, A.J. (6) 1935 Wales, Ireland, Scotland; 1936 New Zealand, Wales, Ireland.

CLARKE, S.J.S. (13) 1963 Wales, Ireland, France, Scotland, New Zealand (1 & 2), Australia; 1964 New Zealand, Wales, Ireland; 1965 Ireland, France, Scotland.

CLAYTON, J.H. (1) 1871 Scotland.

CLEMENTS, J.W. (3) 1959 Ireland, France, Scotland.

CLEVELAND, C.R. (2) 1887 Wales, Scotland.

CLIBBORN, W.G. (6) 1886 Wales, Ireland, Scotland; 1887 Wales, Ireland, Scotland.

CLOUGH, F.J. (4) 1986 Ireland, France; 1987 *Japan (R)*, USA.

COATES, C.H. (3) 1880 Scotland; 1881 Scotland; 1882 Scotland.

COATES, V.H.M. (5) 1913 South Africa, Wales, France, Ireland, Scotland.

COBBY, W. (1) 1900 Wales.

COCKERHAM, A. (1) 1900 Wales.

COLCLOUGH, M.J. (25) 1978 Scotland, Ireland; 1979 New Zealand; 1980 France, Wales, Scotland; 1981 Wales, Scotland, Ireland, France; 1982 Australia, Scotland, Ireland, France, Wales; 1983 France, New Zealand; 1984 Scotland, Ireland, France, Wales; 1986 Wales, Scotland, Ireland, France.

COLEY, E. (2) 1929 France; 1932 Wales.

COLLINS, P.J. (3) 1952 Scotland, Ireland, France.

COLLINS, W.E. (5) 1874 Scotland; 1875 Ireland, Scotland; 1876 Ireland, Scotland.

CONSIDINE, S.G.U. (1) 1925 France.

CONWAY, G.S. (18) 1920 France, Ireland, Scotland; 1921 France; 1922 Wales, Ireland, France, Scotland; 1923 Wales, Ireland, Scotland, France; 1924 Wales, Ireland, France, Scotland; 1925 New Zealand; 1927 Wales.

COOK, J.G (1) 1937 Scotland.

COOK, P.W. (2) 1965 Ireland, France.

COOK, D.A. (4) 1976 Wales, Scotland, Ireland, France.

COOKE, D.H. (12) 1981 Wales, Scotland, Ireland, France; 1984 Ireland; 1985 Romania, France, Scotland, Ireland, Wales, New Zealand (1 & 2).

COOKE, P. (2) 1939 Wales, Ireland.

COOP, T. (1) 1892 Scotland.

COOPER, J.G. (2) 1909 Australia, Wales.

COOPER, M.J. (11) 1973 France, Scotland, New Zealand (2R); 1975 France, Wales; 1976 Australia, Wales; 1977 Scotland, Ireland, France, Wales.

COOPPER, S.F. (7) 1900 Wales; 1902 Wales, Ireland; 1905 Wales, Ireland, Scotland; 1907 Wales.

CORBETT, L.F. (16) 1921 France; 1923 Wales, Ireland; 1924 Wales, Ireland, France, Scotland; 1925 New Zealand, Wales, Ireland, Scotland, Fance; 1927 Wales, Ireland, Scotland, France.

CORLESS, B.J. (9) 1976 Australia (R); 1977 Scotland, Ireland, France, Wales; 1978 France, Wales, Scotland, Ireland.

COTTON, F.E. (30) 1971 Scotland (2, 1 Centenary), President's Overseas XV, RFU's Centenary; 1973 Wales, Ireland, France, Scotland, New Zealand (2), Australia; 1974

Scotland, Ireland; 1975 Ireland, France, Wales; 1976 Australia, Wales, Scotland, Ireland, France; 1977 Scotland, Ireland, Wales; 1978 Scotland, Ireland; 1979 New Zealand; 1980 Ireland, France, Wales, Scotland; 1981 Wales.

COULMAN, M.J. (9) 1967 Australia, Ireland, France, Scotland, Wales; 1968 Wales, Ireland, France, Scotland.

COULSON, T.J. (3) 1927 Wales; 1928 Australia, Wales.

COURT, E.D. (1) 1885 Wales.

COVERDALE, H. (4) 1910 France; 1912 Ireland, France; 1920 Wales.

COVE-SMITH, R. (29) 1921 Scotland, France; 1922 Ireland, France, Scotland; 1923 Wales, Ireland, Scotland, France; 1924 Wales, Ireland, Scotland, France; 1925 New Zealand, Wales, Ireland, Scotland, France; 1927 Wales, Ireland, Scotland, France; 1928 Australia, Wales, Ireland, France, Scotland; 1929 Wales, Ireland.

COWLING, R.J. (8) 1977 Scotland, Ireland, France, Wales; 1978 France, New Zealand; 1979 Scotland, Ireland.

COWMAN, A.R. (4) 1971 Scotland (2, 1 Centenary), President's Overseas XV, RFU Centenary); 1973 Wales, Ireland.

COX, N.S. (1) 1901 Scotland.

CRANMERE, P. (16) 1934 Wales, Ireland, Scotland; 1935 Wales, Ireland, Scotland; 1936 New Zealand, Wales, Ireland, Scotland; 1937 Wales, Ireland, Scotland; 1938 Wales, Ireland, Scotland.

CREED, R.N. (1) 1971 President's Overseas XV., RFU Centenary.

CRIDLAN, A.G. (3) 1935 Wales, Ireland, Scotland.

CROMPTON, C.A. (1) 1871 Scotland.

CROSSE, C.W. (2) 1874 Scotland; 1875 Ireland.

CUMBERLEGE, B.S. (8) 1920 Wales, Ireland, Scotland; 1921 Wales, Ireland, Scotland, France; 1922 Wales.

CUMMING, D.C. (2) 1925 Scotland, France.

CUNLIFFE, F.L. (1) 1874 Scotland.

CURREY, F.I. (1) 1872 Scotland.

CURRIE, J.D. (25) 1956 Wales, Ireland, Scotland, France; 1957 Wales, Ireland, France, Scotland; 1958 Wales, Australia, Ireland, France, Scotland; 1959 Wales, Ireland, France, Scotland; 1960 Wales, Ireland, France, Scotland; 1961 South Africa; 1962 Wales, Ireland, France.

CUSANI, D.A. (1) 1987 Ireland.

CUSWORTH L. (12) 1979 New Zealand; 1982 France, Wales; 1983 France, Wales, New Zealand; 1984 Scotland, Ireland, France, Wales; 1988 France, Wales.

D'AGUILAR, F.B.G. (1) 1872 Scotland.

DALTON, T.J. (1) 1969 Scotland (R).

DANBY, T. (1) 1949 Wales.

DANIELL, J. (7) 1899 Wales; 1900 Ireland, Scotland; 1902 Ireland, Scotland; 1904 Ireland, Scotland.

DARBY, A.J.L. (1) 1899 Ireland.

DAVENPORT, A. (1) 1871 Scotland.

DAVEY, J. (2) 1908 Scotland; 1909 Wales.

DAVEY, R.F. (1) 1931 Wales.

DAVIDSON, Jason (5) 1897 Scotland; 1898 Scotland, Wales; 1899 Ireland, Scotland.

DAVIDSON, Jos (2) 1899 Wales, Scotland.

DAVIES, G.H. (20) 1981 Scotland, Ireland, France, Argentina (1 & 2); 1982 Australia, Scotland, Ireland; 1983 France, Wales, Scotland; 1984 Scotland, South Africa (1 & 2); 1985 Romania (R), New Zealand (1 & 2); 1986 Wales, Scotland, Ireland, France.

DAVIES, P.H. (1) 1927 Ireland.

DAVIES, V.G. (2) 1922 Wales; 1925 New Zealand.

DAVIES, W.J.A. (22) 1913 South Africa, Wales, France, Ireland, Scotland; 1914 Ireland, Scotland, France; 1920 France, Ireland, Scotland; 1921 Wales, Ireland, Scotland, France; 1922 Ireland, France, Scotland; 1923 Wales, Ireland, Scotland, France.

DAVIES, W.P.C. (11) 1953 Scotland; 1954 New Zealand, Ireland; 1955 Wales, Ireland, France, Scotland; 1956 Wales; 1957 France, Scotland; 1958 Wales.

DAVIS, A.M. (16) 1963 Wales, Ireland, Scotland, New Zealand (1 & 2); 1964 New Zealand, Wales, Ireland, France, Scotland; 1966 Wales; 1967 Australia; 1969 South Africa; 1970 Ireland, Wales, Scotland.

DAWE, R.G.R. (4) 1987 Ireland, France, Wales, *USA*.

DAWSON, E.F. (1) 1878 Ireland.

DAY, H.L.V. (4) 1920 Wales; 1922 Wales, France; 1926 Scotland.

DEAN, G.J. (1) 1931 Ireland.

DEE, J.M. (2) 1962 Scotland; 1963 New Zealand (1).

DEVITT, T.G. (4) 1926 Ireland, France; 1928 Australia, Wales.

DEWHURST, J.H. (4) 1887 Wales, Ireland, Scotland; 1890 Wales.

De WINTON, R.F.C. (1) 1893 Wales.

DIBBLE, R. (19) 1906 Scotland, France, South Africa; 1908 France, Wales, Ireland, Scotland; 1909 Australia, Wales, France, Ireland, Scotland; 1910 Scotland; 1911 Wales, France, Scotland; 1912 Wales, Ireland, Scotland.

DICKS, J. (8) 1934 Wales, Ireland, Scotland; 1935 Wales, Ireland, Scotland; 1936 Scotland; 1937 Ireland.

DILLON, E.W. (4) 1904 Wales, Ireland, Scotland; 1905 Wales.

DINGLE, A.J. (3) 1913 Ireland; 1914 Scotland, France.

DIXON, P.J. (22) 1971 President's Overseas XV, RFU Centenary; 1972 Wales, Ireland, France, Scotland; 1973 Ireland, France, Scotland; 1974 Scotland, Ireland, France, Wales; 1975 Ireland; 1976 France; 1977 Scotland, Ireland, France, Wales; 1978 France, Scotland, Ireland, New Zealand.

DOBB, G.E.B. (2) 1906 Wales, Ireland.

DOBLE, S.A. (3) 1972 South Africa; 1973 New Zealand (1), Wales.

DOBSON, D.D (6) 1902 Wales, Ireland, Scotland; 1903 Wales, Ireland, Scotland.

DOBSON, T.H. (1) 1895 Scotland.

DODGE, P.W. (32) 1978 Wales, Scotland, Ireland, New Zealand; 1979 Scotland, Ireland, France, Wales; 1980 Wales, Scotland; 1981 Wales, Scotland, Ireland, France, Argnetina (1 & 2); 1982 Australia, Scotland, France, Wales; 1983 France, Wales, Scotland, Ireland, New Zealand; 1985 Romania France, Scotland, Ireland, Wales, New Zealand (1 & 2).

DONNELLY, M.P. (1) 1947 Ireland.

DOOLEY, W.A. (50) 1985 Romania, France, Scotland, Ireland, Wales, New Zealand 2 (R); 1986 Wales, Scotland, Ireland, France; 1987 France, Wales, *Australia, USA,*

Wales; 1988 France, Wales, Scotland, Ireland (1 & 2), Australia (1 & 2), Fiji, Australia; 1989 Scotland, Ireland, France, Wales, Romania, Fiji; 1990 Ireland, France, Wales, Scotland, Argentina (1 & 2), Argentina; 1991 Wales, Scotland, Ireland, France, *New Zealand, USA, France, Scotland, Australia;* 1992 Scotland, Ireland, France, Wales.

DOVEY, B.A. (2) 1963 Wales, Ireland.

DOWN, P.J. (1) 1909 Australia.

DOWSON, A.O. (1) 1899 Scotland.

DRAKE-LEE, N.J. (8) 1963 Wales, Ireland, France, Scotland; 1964 New Zealand, Wales, Ireland; 1965 Wales.

DUCKETT, H. (2) 1893 Ireland, Scotland.

DUCKHAM, D.J. (36) 1969 Ireland, France, Scotland, Wales, South Africa; 1970 Ireland, Wales, Scotland, France; 1971 Wales, Ireland, France, Scotland (2, 1 Centenary), Presidents Oversea's XV, RFU Centenary); 1972 Wales, Ireland, France, Scotland; 1973 New Zealand (1), Wales, Ireland, France, Scotland, New Zealand (2), Australia; 1974 Scotland, Ireland, France, Wales; 1975 Ireland, France, Wales; 1976 Australia, Wales, Scotland.

DUDGEON, H.W. (7) 1897 Scotland; 1898 Ireland, Scotland, Wales; 1899 Wales, Ireland, Scotland.

DUGDALE, J.M. (1) 1871 Scotland.

DUN, A.F. (1) 1984 Wales.

DUNCAN, R.F.H. (3) 1922 Ireland, France, Scotland.

DUNKLEY, P.E. (6) 1931 Ireland, Scotland; 1936 New Zealand, Wales, Ireland, Scotland.

DUTHIE, J. (1) 1903 Wales.

DYSON, J.W. (4) 1890 Scotland; 1892 Scotland; 1893 Ireland, Scotland.

EBDON, P.J. (2) 1897 Wales, Ireland.

EDDISON, J.H. (4) 1912 Wales, Ireland, Scotland, France.

EDGAR, C.S. (1) 1901 Scotland.

EDWARDS, R. (11) 1921 Wales, Ireland, Scotland, France; 1922 Wales, France; 1923 Wales; 1924 Wales, France, Scotland; 1925 New Zealand.

EGERTON, D.W. (6) 1988 Ireland (2), Australia (1), Fiji (R), Australia; 1990 Ireland.

ELLIOT, C.H. (1) 1886 Wales.

ELLIOT, E.W. (4) 1901 Wales, Ireland, Scotland; 1904 Wales.

ELLIOT, W. (7) 1932 Ireland, Scotland; 1933 Wales, Ireland, Scotland; 1934 Wales, Ireland.

ELLIOTT, A.E. (1) 1894 Scotland.

ELLIS, J. (1) 1939 Scotland.

ELLIS, S.S. (1) 1880 Ireland.

EMMOTT, C. (1) 1892 Wales.

ENTHOVEN, H.J. (1) 1878 Ireland.

ESTCOURT, N.S.D. (1) 1955 Scotland.

EVANS, B.J. (2) 1988 Australia (2), Fiji.

EVANS, E. (30) 1948 Australia; 1950 Wales; 1951 Ireland, France, Scotland; 1952 South Africa, Wales, Scotland, Ireland, France; 1953 Ireland, France, Scotland; 1954 Wales, New Zealand, Ireland, France; 1956 Wales, Ireland, Scotland, France; 1957 Wales, Ireland, France, Scotland; 1958 Wales, Australia, Ireland, France, Scotland.

EVANS, G.W. (9) 1972 Scotland; 1973 Wales (R), France, Scotland, New Zealand (2); 1974 Scotland, Ireland, France, Wales.

EVANS, N.L. (5) 1932 Wales, Ireland, Scotland; 1933 Wales, Ireland.

EVANSON, A.M. (4) 1883 Wales, Ireland, Scotland, 1884 Scotland.

EVANSON, W.A.D. (5) 1875 Scotland; 1877 Scotland; 1878 Scotland; 1879 Scotland, Ireland.

EVERSHED, F. (10) 1889 Maoris; 1890 Wales, Scotland, Ireland; 1892 Wales, Ireland, Scotland; 1893 Wales, Ireland, Scotland.

EYRES, W.C.T. (1) 1927 Ireland.

FAGAN, A.R. St.L. (1) 1887 Ireland.

FAIRBROTHER, K.E. (12) 1969 Ireland, France, Scotland, Wales, South Africa; 1970 Ireland Wales, Scotland, France; 1971 Wales, Ireland, France.

FAITHFUL, C.K.T. (3) 1924 Ireland; 1926 France, Scotland.

FALLAS, H. (1) 1884 Ireland.

FEGAN, J.H.C. (3) 1895 Wales, Ireland, Scotland.

FERNANDES, C.W.L. (3) 1881 Ireland, Wales, Scotland.

FIDLER, J.H. (4) 1981 Argentina (1 & 2); 1984 South Africa (1 & 2).

FIELD, E. (2) 1893 Wales, Ireland.

FIELDING, K.J. (10) 1969 Ireland, France, Scotland, South Africa; 1970 Ireland, France; 1972 Wales, Ireland, France, Scotland.

FINCH, R.T. (1) 1880 Scotland.

FINLAN, J.F. (13) 1967 Ireland, France, Scotland, Wales, New Zealand; 1968 Wales, Ireland; 1969 Ireland, France, Scotland, Wales; 1970 France; 1973 New Zealand (1).

FINLINSON, H.W. (3) 1895 Wales, Ireland, Scotland.

FINNEY, S. (2) 1872 Scotland; 1873 Scotland.

FIRTH, F. (3) 1894 Wales, Ireland, Scotland.

FLETCHER, N.C. (4) 1901 Wales, Ireland, Scotland; 1903 Scotland.

FLETCHER, T. (1) 1897 Wales.

FLETCHER, W.R.B. (2) 1873 Scotland; 1875 Scotland.

FOOKES, E.F. (10) 1896 Wales, Ireland, Scotland; 1897 Wales, Ireland, Scotland; 1898 Ireland, Wales; 1899 Ireland, Scotland.

FORD, P.J. (4) 1964 Wales, Ireland, France, Scotland.

FORREST, J.W. (10) 1930 Wales, Ireland, France, Scotland; 1931 Wales, Ireland, Scotland, France; 1934 Ireland, Scotland.

FORREST, R. (6) 1899 Wales; 1900 Scotland; 1902 Ireland, Scotland; 1908 Ireland, Scotland.

FOULDS, R.T. (2) 1929 Wales, Ireland.

FOWLER, F.D. (2) 1878 Scotland; 1879 Scotland.

FOWLER, H. (3) 1878 Scotland; 1881 Wales, Scotland.

FOWLER, R.H. (1) 1877 Ireland.

FOX, F.H. (2) 1890 Wales, Scotland.

FRANCIS, T.E.S. (4) 1926 Wales, Ireland, France, Scotland.

FRANKCOM, G.P. (4) 1965 Wales, Ireland, France, Scotland.

FRASER, E.C. (1) 1875 Ireland.

FRASER, G. (5) 1902 Wales, Ireland, Scotland; 1903 Wales, Ireland.

FREAKES, H.D. (3) 1938 Wales; 1939 Wales, Ireland.

FREEMAN, H. (3) 1872 Scotland; 1873 Scotland; 1874 Scotland.

FRENCH, J.R. (4) 1961 Wales, Ireland, France, Scotland.

FRY, H.A. (3) 1934 Wales, Ireland, Scotland.

FRY, T.W. (3) 1880 Ireland, Scotland; 1881 Wales.

FULLER, H.G. (6) 1882 Ireland, Scotland; 1883 Wales, Ireland, Scotland; 1884 Wales.

GADNEY, B.C. (14) 1932 Ireland, Scotland; 1933 Ireland, Scotland; 1934 Wales, Ireland, Scotland; 1935 Scotland; 1936 New Zealand, Wales, Ireland, Scotland; 1937 Scotland; 1938 Wales.

GAMLIN, H.T. (15) 1899 Wales, Scotland; 1900 Wales, Ireland, Scotland; 1901 Scotland; 1902 Wales, Ireland, Scotland; 1903 Wales, Ireland, Scotland; 1904 Wales, Ireland, Scotland.

GARDNER, E.R. (10) 1921 Wales, Ireland, Scotland; 1922 Wales, Ireland, France; 1923 Wales, Ireland, Scotland, France.

GARDNER, H.P. (1) 1878 Ireland.

GARNETT, H.W.T. (1) 1877 Scotland.

GAVINS, M.N. (1) 1961 Wales.

GAY D.J. (4) 1968 Wales, Ireland, France, Scotland.

GENT, D.R. (5) 1905 New Zealand; 1906 Wales, Ireland; 1910 Wales, Ireland.

GENTH, J.S.M. (2) 1874 Scotland; 1875 Scotland.

GEORGE, J.T. (3) 1947 Scotland, France; 1949 Ireland.

GERRARD, R.A. (14) 1932 South Africa, Wales, Ireland, Scotland; 1933 Wales, Ireland, Scotland; 1934 Wales, Ireland, Scotland; 1936 New Zealand, Wales, Ireland, Scotland.

GIBBS, G.A. (2) 1947 France; 1948 Ireland.

GIBBS, J.C. (7) 1925 New Zealand, Wales; 1926 France; 1927 Wales, Ireland, Scotland, France.

GIBBS, N. (2) 1954 Scotland, France.

GIBLIN, L.F. (3) 1896 Wales, Ireland; 1897 Scotland.

GIBSON, A.S. (1) 1871 Scotland.

GIBSON, C.O.P. (1) 1901 Wales.

GIBSON, G.R. (2) 1899 Wales; 1901 Scotland.

GIBSON, T.A. (2) 1905 Wales, Scotland.

GILBERT, F.G. (2) 1923 Wales, Ireland.

GILBERT, R. (3) 1908 Wales, Ireland, Scotland.

GILES, J.L. (6) 1935 Wales, Ireland; 1937 Wales, Ireland; 1938 Ireland, Scotland.

GITTINGS, W.J. (1) 1967 New Zealand.

GLOVER, P.B. (3) 1967 Australia; 1971 France, President's Overseas XV, RFU Centenary).

GODFRAY R.E. (1) 1905 New Zealand.

GODWIN, H.O. (11) 1959 France, Scotland; 1963 Scotland, New Zealand (1 & 2), Australia; 1964 New Zealand, Ireland, France, Scotland; 1967 New Zealand.

GORDON-SMITH, G.W. (3) 1900 Wales, Ireland, Scotland.

GOTLEY, A.L.H. (6) 1910 France, Scotland; 1911 Wales, France, Ireland, Scotland.

GRAHAM, D. (1) 1901 Wales.

GRAHAM H.J. (4) 1875 Ireland, Scotland; 1876 Ireland, Scotland.

GRAHAM, J.D.G. (1) 1876 Ireland.

GRAY, A. (3) 1947 Wales, Ireland, Scotland.

GREEN, J. (8) 1905 Ireland; 1906 Scotland, France, South Africa; 1907 France, Wales, Ireland, Scotland.

GREEN, J.F. (1) 1871 Scotland.

GREENWELL, J.H. (2) 1893 Wales, Ireland.

GREENWOOD, J.E. (13) 1912 France; 1913 South Africa, Wales, France, Ireland, Scotland; 1914 Wales, Scotland, France; 1920 Wales, France, Ireland, Scotland.

GREENWOOD, J.R.H. (5) 1966 Ireland, France, Scotland; 1967 Australia; 1969 Ireland.

GREG, W. (2) 1876 Ireland, Scotland.

GREGORY, G.G. (13) 1931 Ireland, Scotland, France; 1932 South Africa, Wales, Ireland, Scotland; 1933 Wales, Ireland, Scotland; 1934 Wales, Ireland, Scotland.

GREGORY, J.A. (1) 1949 Wales.

GRYLLS, W.M. (1) 1905 Ireland.

GUEST, R.H. (13) 1939 Wales, Ireland, Scotland; 1947 Wales, Ireland, Scotland, France; 1948 Australia, Wales, Scotland; 1949 France, Scotland.

GUILLEMARD, A.G. (2) 1871 Scotland; 1872 Scotland.

GUMMER, C.H.A. (1) 1929 France.

GUNNER, C.R. (1) 1876 Ireland.

GURDON, C. (14) 1880 Ireland; Scotland; 1881 Ireland, Wales, Scotland; 1882 Ireland, Scotland; 1883 Scotland; 1884 Wales, Scotland; 1885 Ireland; 1886 Wales, Ireland, Scotland.

GURDON, E.T. (16) 1878 Scotland; 1879 Ireland; 1880 Scotland; 1881 Ireland, Wales, Scotland; 1882 Scotland; 1883 Wales, Ireland, Scotland; 1884 Wales, Ireland, Scotland; 1885 Wales, Ireland; 1886 Scotland.

GUSCOTT, J.C. (22) 1989 Romania, Fiji; 1990 Ireland, France, Wales, Scotland, Argentina; 1991 Wales, Scotland, Ireland; France, Fiji, Australia, *New Zealand, Italy, France, Scotland, Australia*; 1992 Scotland, Ireland, France, Wales.

HAIGH, L. (7) 1910 Wales, Ireland, Scotland; 1911 France, Wales, Ireland, Scotland.

HALE, P.M. (3) 1969 South Africa; 1970 Ireland, Wales.

HALL, C. (2) 1901 Ireland, Scotland.

HALL, J. (3) 1894 Wales, Ireland, Scotland.

HALL, J.P. (19) 1984 Scotland (R), Ireland, France, South Africa (1 & 2), Australia; 1985 Romania, France, Scotland, Ireland, Wales, New Zealand (1 & 2); 1986 Wales, Scotland; 1987 Ireland, France, Wales, Scotland.

HALL, N.M. (17) 1947 Wales, Ireland, Scotland, France; 1949 Wales, Ireland; 1952 South Africa, Wales, Scotland, Ireland, France; 1953 Wales, Ireland, France, Scotland; 1955 Wales, Ireland.

HALLIDAY, S.J. (23) 1986 Wales, Scotland; 1987 Scotland; 1988 Scotland, Ireland (1 & 2), Australia (1), Australia; 1989 Scotland, Ireland, France, Wales, Romania, Fiji (R); 1990 Wales, Scotland; 1991 *USA, Scotland, Australia*; 1992 Scotland, Ireland, France, Wales.

HAMERSLEY, A.St.G. (4) 1871 Scotland; 1872 Scotland; 1873 Scotland; 1874 Scotland.

HAMILTON-HILL, E.A. (3) 1936 New Zealand, Wales, Ireland.

HAMILTON-WICKES, R.H. (10) 1924 Ireland; 1925 New Zealand, Wales, Ireland, Scotland, France; 1926 Wales, Ireland, Scotland; 1927 Wales.

HAMMETT, E.D.G. (8) 1920 Wales, France, Scotland; 1921 Wales, Ireland, Scotland, France; 1922 Wales.

HAMMOND, C.E.L. (8) 1905 Scotland, New Zealand; 1906 Wales, Ireland, Scotland, France; 1908 Wales, Ireland.

HANCOCK, A.W. (3) 1965 France, Scotland; 1966 France.

HANCOCK, G.E. (3) 1939 Wales, Ireland, Scotland.

HANCOCK, J.H. (2) 1955 Wales, Ireland.

HANCOCK, P.F. (3) 1886 Wales, Ireland; 1890 Wales.

HANCOCK, P.S. (3) 1904 Wales, Ireland, Scotland.

HANDFORD, F.G. (4) 1909 Wales, France, Ireland, Scotland.

HANDS, R.H.M. (2) 1910 France, Scotland.

HANLEY, J. (7) 1927 Wales, Scotland, France; 1928 Wales, Ireland, Scotland, France.

HANNAFORD, R.C. (3) 1971 Wales, Ireland, France.

HANVEY, R.J. (4) 1926 Wales, Ireland, France, Scotland.

HARDING, E.H. (1) 1931 Ireland.

HARDING, R.M. (12) 1985 Romania, France, Scotland; 1987 Scotland, *Australia, Japan, Wales*; 1988 Ireland (1 R & 2), Australia (1 & 2), Fiji.

HARDING, V.S.L. (6) 1961 France, Scotland; 1962 Wales, Ireland, France, Scotland.

HARDWICK, P.F. (8) 1902 Ireland, Scotland; 1903 Wales, Ireland, Scotland; 1904 Wales, Ireland, Scotland.

HARDY, E.M.P. (3) 1951 Ireland, France, Scotland.

HARE, W.H. (25) 1974 Wales; 1978 France, New Zealand; 1979 New Zealand; 1980 Ireland, France, Wales, Scotland; 1981 Wales, Scotland, Argentina (1 & 2); 1982 France, Wales; 1983 France, Wales, Scotland, Ireland, New Zealand; 1984 Scotland, Ireland, France, Wales, South Africa (1 & 2).

HARPER, C.H. (1) 1899 Wales.

HARRIMAN, A.T. (1) 1988 Australia.

HARRIS, S.W. (2) 1920 Ireland, Scotland.

HARRIS, T.W. (2) 1929 Scotland; 1932 Ireland.

HARRISON, A.C. (2) 1931 Ireland, Scotland.

HARRISON, A.L. (2) 1914 Ireland, France.

HARRISON, G. (7) 1877 Ireland, Scotland; 1897 Scotland, Ireland; 1880 Scotland; 1885 Wales, Ireland.

HARRISON, H.C. (4) 1909 Scotland; 1914 Ireland, Scotland, France.

HARRISON, M.E. (15) 1985 New Zealand (1 & 2); 1986 Scotland, Ireland, France; 1987 Ireland, France, Wales, Scotland, *Australia, Japan, USA, Wales*; 1988 France, Wales.

HARTLEY, B.C. (2) 1901 Scotland; 1902 Scotland.

HASLETT, L.W. (2) 1926 Ireland, France.

HASTINGS, G.W.D. (13) 1955 Wales, Ireland, France, Scotland; 1957 Wales, Ireland, France, Scotland; 1958 Wales, Ireland, Australia, France, Scotland.

HAVELOCK, H. (3) 1908 France, Wales, Ireland.

HAWCRIDGE, J.J. (2) 1885 Wales, Ireland.

HAYWARD, L.W. (1) 1910 Ireland.

HAZELL, D.St.G. (4) 1955 Wales, Ireland, France, Scotland.

HEARN, R.D. (6) 1966 France, Scotland; 1967 Ireland, France, Scotland, Wales.

HEATH, A.H. (1) 1876 Scotland.

HEATON, J. (9) 1935 Wales, Ireland, Scotland; 1939 Wales, Ireland, Scotland; 1947 Ireland, Scotland, France.

HENDERSON, A.P. (9) 1947 Wales, Ireland, Scotland, France; 1948 Ireland, Scotland, France; 1949 Wales, Ireland.

HENDERSON, R.S.F. (5) 1883 Wales, Scotland; 1884 Wales, Scotland; 1885 Wales.

HEPPELL, W.G. (1) 1903 Ireland.

HERBERT, A.J. (6) 1958 France, Scotland; 1959 Wales, Ireland, France, Scotland.

HESFORD, R.J. (10) 1981 Scotland (R); 1982 Australia, Scotland, France (R); 1983 France (R); 1985 Romania, France, Scotland, Ireland, Wales.

HESLOP, N.J. (10) 1990 Argentina (1 & 2), Argentina; 1991 Wales, Scotland, Ireland, France, *USA, France*; 1992 Wales (R).

HETHERINGTON, J.G.G. (6) 1958 Australia, Ireland; 1959 Wales, Ireland, France, Scotland.

HEWITT, E.N. (3) 1951 Wales, Ireland, France.

HEWITT, W.W. (4) 1881 Ireland, Wales, Scotland; 1882 Ireland.

HICKSON, J.L. (6) 1887 Wales, Ireland, Scotland; 1890 Wales, Scotland, Ireland.

HIGGINS, R. (13) 1954 Wales, New Zealand, Ireland, Scotland; 1955 Wales, Ireland, France, Scotland; 1957 Wales, Ireland, France, Scotland; 1959 Wales.

HIGNELL, A.J. (14) 1975 Australia (2); 1976 Australia, Wales, Scotland, Ireland; 1977 Scotland, Ireland, France, Wales; 1978 Wales; 1979 Scotland, Ireland, France, Wales.

HILL, B.A. (9) 1903 Ireland, Scotland; 1904 Wales, Ireland; 1905 Wales, New Zealand; 1906 South Africa; 1907 France, Wales.

HILL, R.J. (28) 1984 South Africa (1 & 2); 1985 Ireland (R), New Zealand (2R); 1986 France (R); 1987 Ireland, France, Wales, USA; 1989 Fiji; 1990 Ireland, France, Wales, Scotland, Argentina (1 & 2), Argentina; 1991 Wales, Scotland, Ireland, Fiji, Australia, *New Zealand, Italy, USA, France, Scotland, Australia*.

HILLARD, R.J. (1) 1925 New Zealand.

HILLER, R. (18) 1968 Wales, Ireland, France, Scotland; 1969 Ireland, France, Scotland, Wales, South Africa; 1970 Ireland, Wales, Scotland; 1971 Ireland, France, Scotland (2, 1 Centenary), President's Overseas XV (RFU Centenary); 1972 Wales, Ireland.

HIND, A.E. (2) 1905 New Zealand; 1906 Wales.

HIND, G.R. (2) 1910 Scotland; 1911 Ireland.

HOBBS, R.F.A. (2) 1899 Scotland; 1903 Wales.

HOBBS, R.G.S. (4) 1932 South Africa, Wales, Ireland, Scotland.

HODGES, H.A. (2) 1906, Wales, Ireland.

HODGKINSON, S.D. (14) 1989 Romania, Fiji; 1990 Ireland, France, Wales, Scotland, Argentina, Argentina (1 & 2); 1991 Wales, Scotland, Ireland, France, *USA*.

HODGSON, J.McD (7) 1932 South Africa, Wales, Ireland, Scotland; 1934 Wales, Ireland; 1936 Ireland.

HODGSON, S.A.M. (11) 1960 Wales, Ireland, France, Scotland; 1961 South Africa, Wales; 1962 Wales, Ireland, France, Scotland; 1964 Wales.

HOFMEYR, M.B. (3) 1950 Wales, France, Scotland.

HOGARTH, T.B. (1) 1906 France.

HOLFORD, G. (2) 1920 Wales, France.

HOLLAND, D. (3) 1912 Wales, Ireland, Scotland.

HOLLIDAY, T.E. (7) 1923 Scotland, France; 1925 Ireland, Scotland, France; 1926 France, Scotland.

HOLMES, C.B. (3) 1947 Scotland; 1948 Ireland, France.

HOLMES, E. (2) 1890 Scotland, Ireland.

HOLMES, W.A. (16) 1950 Wales, Ireland, France, Scotland; 1951 Wales, Ireland, France, Scotland; 1952 South Africa, Scotland, Ireland, France; 1953 Wales, Ireland, France, Scotland.

HOLMES, W.B. (4) 1949 Wales, Ireland, France, Scotland.

HOOK, W.G. (3) 1951 Scotland; 1952 South Africa, Wales.

HOOPER, C.A. (3) 1894 Wales, Ireland, Scotland.

HOPLEY, F.J.V. (3) 1907 France, Wales; 1908 Ireland.

HORDERN, P.C. (4) 1931 Ireland, Scotland, France; 1934 Wales.

HORLEY, C.H. (1) 1885 Ireland.

HORNBY, A.N. (9) 1877 Ireland, Scotland; 1878 Scotland, Ireland; 1880 Ireland; 1881 Ireland, Scotland; 1882 Ireland, Scotland.

HORROCKS-TAYLOR, J.P. (9) 1958 Wales, Australia; 1961 Scotland; 1962 Scotland; 1963 New Zealand (1 & 2), Australia; 1964 New Zealand, Wales.

HORSFALL, E.L. (1) 1949 Wales.

HORTON, A.L. (7) 1965 Wales, Ireland, France, Scotland; 1966 France, Scotland; 1967 New Zealand.

HORTON, J.P. (13) 1978 Wales, Scotland, Ireland, New Zealand; 1980 Ireland, France, Wales, Scotland; 1981 Wales; 1983 Scotland, Ireland; 1984 South Africa (1 & 2).

HORTON, N.E. (20) 1969 Ireland, France, Scotland, Wales; 1971 Ireland, France, Scotland; 1974 Scotland; 1975 Wales; 1977 Scotland, Ireland, France, Wales; 1978 France, Wales; 1979 Scotland, Ireland, France, Wales; 1980 Ireland.

HOSEN, R.W. (10) 1963 New Zealand (1 & 2), Australia; 1964 France, Scotland; 1967 Australia, Ireland, France, Scotland, Wales.

HOSKING, G.R.d'A (5) 1949 Wales, Ireland, France, Scotland; 1950 Wales.

HOUGHTON, S. (2) 1892 Ireland; 1896 Wales.

HOWARD, P.D. (8) 1930 Wales, Ireland, France, Scotland; 1931 Wales, Ireland, Scotland, France.

HUBBARD, G.C. (2) 1892 Wales, Ireland.

HUBBARD, J.C. (1) 1930 Scotland.

HUDSON, A. (8) 1906 Wales, Ireland, France; 1908 France, Wales, Ireland, scotland; 1910 France.

HUGHES, G.E. (1) 1896 Scotland.

HULME, F.C. (4) 1903 Wales, Ireland; 1905 Wales, Ireland.

HUNT, J.T. (3) 1882 Ireland, Scotland; 1884 Wales.

HUNT, R. (4) 1880 Ireland; 1881 Wales, Scotland; 1882 Ireland.

HUNT, W.H. (4) 1876 Scotland; 1877 Ireland, Scotland; 1878 Ireland.

HUNTSMAN, R.P. (2) 1985 New Zealand (1 & 2).

HURST, A.C.B. (1) (1962) Scotland.

HUSKISSON, T.F. (8) 1937 Wales, Ireland, Scotland; 1938 Wales, Ireland, Scotland; 1939 Wales, Ireland, Scotland.

HUTCHINSON, F. (3) 1909 France, Ireland, Scotland.

HUTCHINSON, J.E. (1) 1906 Ireland.

HUTCHINSON, W.C. (2) 1876 Scotland; 1877 Ireland.

HUTCHINSON, W.H.H. (2) 1875 Ireland; 1876 Ireland.

HUTCH, H. (1) 1879 Scotland.

HYDE, J.P. (2) 1950 France, Scotland.

HYNES, W.B. (1) 1912 France.

IBBITSON, E.D. (4) 1909 Wales, France, Ireland, Scotland.

IMRIE, H.M. (2) 1906 New Zealand; 1907 Ireland.

INGLIS, R.E. (3) 1886 Wales, Ireland, Scotland.

IRVIN, S.H. (1) 1905 Wales.

ISHERWOOD, F.W. (1) 1872 Scotland.

JACKETT, E.J. (13) 1905 New Zealand; 1906 Wales, Ireland, Scotland, France, South Africa; 1907 Wales, Ireland, Scotland; 1909 Wales, France, Ireland, Scotland.

JACKSON, A.H. (2) 1878 Ireland; 1880 Ireland.

JACKSON, B.S. (2) 1970 Scotland (R), France.

JACKSON, P.B. (20) 1956 Wales, Ireland, France; 1957 Wales, Ireland, France, Scotland; 1958 Wales, Australia, France, Scotland; 1959 Wales, Ireland, France, Scotland; 1961 Scotland; 1963 Wales, Ireland, France, Scotland.

JACKSON, W.J. (1) 1894 Scotland.

JACOB, F. (8) 1897 Wales, Ireland, Scotland; 1898 Ireland, Scotland, Wales; 1899 Wales, Ireland.

JACOB, H.P. (5) 1924 Wales, Ireland, France, Scotland; 1930 France.

JACOB, P.G. (1) 1898 Ireland.

JACOBS, C.R. (29) 1956 Wales, Ireland, Scotland, France; 1957 Wales, Ireland, France, Scotland; 1958 Wales, Australia, Ireland, France, Scotland; 1960 Wales, Ireland, France, Scotland; 1961 South Africa, Wales, Ireland, France, Scotland; 1963 New Zealand (1 & 2), Australia; 1964 Wales, Ireland, France, Scotland.

JAGO, R.A. (5) 1906 Wales, Ireland, South Africa; 1907 Wales, Ireland.

JANION, J.P.A.G. (12) 1971 Wales, Ireland, France, Scotland (2, 1 centenary), President's Overseas XV (RFU Centenary); 1972 Wales, Scotland, South Africa; 1973 Australia; 1975 Australia (1 & 2).

JARMAN, J.W. (1) 1900 Wales.

JEAVONS, N.C. (14) 1981 Scotland, Ireland, France, Argentina (1 & 2); 1982 Australia, Scotland, Ireland, France, Wales; 1983 France, Wales, Scotland, Ireland.

JEEPS, R.E.G. (24) 1956 Wales; 1957 Wales, Ireland, France, Scotland; 1958 Wales, Australia, Ireland, France, Scotland; 1959 Ireland; 1960 Wales, Ireland, France, Scotland; 1961 South Africa, Wales, Ireland, France, Scotland; 1962 Wales, Ireland, Scotland, France.

JEFFERY, G.L. (6) 1886 Wales, Ireland, Scotland; 1887 Wales, Ireland, Scotland.

JENNINS, C.R. (3) 1967 Australia, Ireland, France.

JEWITT, J. (1) 1902 Wales.

JOHNS, W.A. (7) 1909 Wales, France, Ireland, Scotland; 1910 Wales, Ireland, France.

JOHNSTON, W.R. (16) 1910 Wales, Ireland, Scotland; 1912 Wales, Ireland, Scotland, France; 1913 South Africa, Wales, France, Ireland, Scotland; 1914 Wales, Ireland, Scotland, France.

JONES, F.P. (1) 1893 Scotland.

JONES, H.A. (3) 1950 Wales, Ireland, France.

JORDEN, A.M. (7) 1970 France; 1973 Ireland, France, Scotland; 1974 France; 1975 Wales, Scotland.

JOWETT, D. (6) 1889 Maoris; 1890 Scotland, Ireland; 1891 Wales, Ireland, Scotland.

JUDD, P.E. (23) 1962 Wales, Ireland, France, Scotland; 1963 Scotland, New Zealand (1 & 2), Australia; 1964 New Zealand; 1965 Ireland, France, Scotland; 1966 Wales, Ireland, France, Scotland; 1967 Australia, Ireland, France, Scotland, Wales, New Zealand.

KAYLL, H.E. (1) 1878 Scotland.

KEELING, J.H. (2) 1948 Australia, Wales.

KEEN, B.W. (4) 1968 Wales, Ireland, France, Scotland.

KEETON, G.H. (3) 1904 Wales, Ireland, Scotland.

KELLY, G.A. (4) 1947 Wales, Ireland, Scotland; 1948 Wales.

KELLY, T.S. (12) 1906 Wales, Ireland, France, South Africa; 1907 France, Wales, Ireland, Scotland; 1908 France, Ireland, Scotland.

KEMBLE, A.T. (3) 1885 Wales, Ireland; 1887 Ireland.

KEMPT, D.T. (1) 1935 Wales.

KEMPT, T.A. (5) 1937 Wales, Ireland; 1939 Scotland; 1948 Australia, Wales.

KENDALL, P.D. (3) 1901 Scotland; 1902 Wales; 1903 Scotland.

KENDALL-CARPENTER, J.MacG.K. (23) 1949 Ireland, France, Scotland; 1950 Wales, Ireland, France, Scotland; 1951 Ireland, France, Scotland; 1952 South Africa, Wales, Scotland, Ireland, France; 1953 Wales, Ireland, France, Scotland; 1954 Wales, New Zealand, Ireland, France.

KENDREW, D.A. (10) 1930 Wales, Ireland; 1933 Ireland, Scotland; 1934 Scotland; 1935 Wales, Ireland; 1936 New Zealand, Wales, Ireland.

KENNEDY, R.D. (3) 1949 Ireland, France, Scotland.

KENT, C.P. (5) 1977 Scotland, Ireland, France, Wales; 1978 France (R).

KENT, T. (6) 1891 Wales, Ireland, Scotland; 1892 Wales, Ireland, Scotland.

KERSHAW, C.A. (16) 1920 Wales, France, Ireland, Scotland; 1921 Wales, Ireland, Scotland, France; 1922 Wales, Ireland, France, Scotland; 1923 Wales, Ireland, Scotland, France.

KEWLEY, E. (7) 1874 Scotland; 1875 Scotland; 1876 Ireland, Scotland; 1877 Ireland, Scotland; 1878 Scotland.

KEWNEY, A.L. (16) 1906 Wales, Ireland, Scotland, France; 1909 Australia, Wales, France, Ireland, Scotland; 1911 Wales, France, Ireland, Scotland; 1912 Ireland, Scotland; 1913 South Africa.

KEY, A (2) 1930 Ireland; 1933 Wales.

KEYWORTH, M. (4) 1976 Australia, Wales, Scotland, Ireland.

KILNER, B. (1) 1880 Ireland.

KINDERSLEY, R.S. (3) 1883 Wales; 1884 Scotland; 1885 Wales.

KING, I. (3) 1954 Wales, New Zealand, Ireland.

KING, J.A. (12) 1911 Wales, France, Ireland, Scotland; 1912 Wales, Ireland, Scotland; 1913 South Africa, Wales, France, Ireland, Scotland.

KING, Q.E.M.A. (1) 1921 Scotland.

KINGSTON, P. (5) 1975 Australia (1 & 2); 1979 Ireland, France, Wales.

KITCHING, A.E. (1) 1913 Ireland.

KITTERMASTER, H.J. (7) 1925 New Zealand, Wales, Ireland; 1926 Wales, Ireland, France, Scotland.

KNIGHT, F. (1) 1909 Australia.

KNIGHT, P.M. (3) 1972 France, Scotland, South Africa.

KNOWLES, E. (2) 1896 Scotland; 1897 Scotland.

KNOWLES, T.C. (1) 1931 Scotland.

KRIGE, J.A. (1) 1920 Wales.

LABUSCHAGNE, N.A. (5) 1953 Wales; 1955 Wales, Ireland, France, Scotland.

LAGDEN, R.O. (1) 1911 Scotland.

LAIRD, H.C.C. (10) 1927 Wales, Ireland, Scotland; 1928 Australia, Wales, Ireland, Scotland, France; 1929 Wales, Ireland.

LAMBERT, D. (7) 1907 France; 1908 France, Wales, Scotland; 1911 Wales, France, Ireland.

LAMPKOWSKI, M.S. (4) 1976 Australia, Wales, Scotland, Ireland.

LAPAGE, W.N. (4) 1908 France, Wales, Ireland, Scotland.

LARTER, P.J. (24) 1967 Australia, New Zealand; 1968 Wales, Ireland, France, Scotland; 1969 Ireland, France, Scotland, Wales, South Africa; 1970 Ireland, Wales, France, Scotland; 1971 Wales, Ireland, France, Scotland (2, 1 Centenary), President's Overseas XV (RFU Centenary); 1972 South Africa; 1973 New Zealand (1), Wales.

LAW, A.F. (1) 1977 Scotland.

LAW, D.E. (1) 1927 Ireland.

LAWRENCE, H.A. (4) 1873 Scotland; 1874 Scotland; 1875 Ireland, Scotland.

LAWRIE, P.W. (2) 1910 Scotland; 1911 Scotland.

LAWSON, R.G. (1) 1925 Ireland.

LAWSON, T.M. (2) 1928 Australia, Wales.

LEADBETTER, M.M. (1) 1970 France.

LEADBETTER, V.H. (2) 1954 Scotland, France.

LEAKE, W.R.M. (3) 1891 Wales, Ireland, Scotland.

LEATHER, G. (1) 1907 Ireland.

LEE, F.H. (2) 1876 Scotland; 1877 Ireland.

LEE, H. (1) 1907 France.

Le FLEMING, J. (1) 1887 Wales.

LEONARD, J. (19) 1990 Argentina (1 & 2), Argentina; 1991 Wales, Scotland, Ireland, France, Fiji, Australia, *New Zealand, Italy, USA, France, Scotland, Australia*; 1992 Scotland, Ireland, France, Wales.

LESLIE-JONES, F.A. (2) 1895 Wales, Ireland.

LEWIS, A.O. (10) 1952 South Africa, Wales, Scotland, Ireland, France; 1953 Wales, Ireland, France, Scotland; 1954 France.

LEYLAND, R. (3) 1935 Wales, Ireland, Scotland.

LINNETT, M.S. (1) 1989 Fiji.

LIVESAY, R.O'H. (2) 1898 Wales; 1899 Wales.

LLOYD, R.H. (5) 1967 New Zealand; 1968 Wales, Ireland, France, Scotland.

LOCKE, H.M. (12) 1923 Scotland, France; 1924 Wales, France, Scotland 1925 Wales, Ireland, Scotland, France; 1927 Wales, Ireland, Scotland.

LOCKWOOD, R.E. (14) 1887 Wales, Ireland, Scotland; 1889 Maoris; 1891 Wales, Ireland, Scotland; 1892 Wales, Ireland, Scotland; 1893 Wales, Ireland; 1894 Wales, Ireland.

LOGIN, S.H.M. (1) 1876 Ireland.

LOHDEN, F.C. (1) 1893 Wales.

LONGLAND, R.J. (19) 1932 Scotland; 1933 Wales, Scotland; 1934 Wales, Ireland, Scotland; 1935 Wales, Ireland, Scotland; 1936 New Zealand, Wales, Ireland, Scotland; 1937 Wales, Ireland, Scotland; 1938; Wales, Ireland, Scotland.

LOWE, C.N. (25) 1913 South Africa, Wales, France, Ireland, Scotland; 1914 Wales, Ireland, Scotland, France; 1920 Wales, France, Ireland, Scotland; 1921 Wales, Ireland, Scotland, France; 1922 Wales, Ireland, France, Scotland; 1923 Wales, Ireland, Scotland, France.

LOWRIE, F. (2) 1889 Maoris; 1890 Wales.

LOWRY, W.M. (1) 1920 France.

LOZOWWSKI, R.A.P. (1) 1984 Australia.

LUDDINGTON, W.G.E. (13) 1923 Wales, Ireland, Scotland, France; 1924 Wales, Ireland, France, Scotland; 1925 Wales, Ireland, Scotland, France; 1926 Wales.

LUSCOMBE, F. (6) 1872 Scotland; 1873 Scotland; 1875 Ireland Scotland; 1876 Ireland, Scotland.

LUSCOMBE, J.H. (1) 1871 Scotland.

LUXMOORE, A.F.C.C. (2) 1900 Scotland; 1901 Wales.

LUYA, H.F. (5) 1948 Wales, Ireland, Scotland, France; 1949 Wales.

LYON, A. (1) 1871 Scotland.

LYON, G.H.D'O. (2) 1908 Scotland; 1909 Australia.

McCARLIS, M.A. (2) 1931 Wales, Ireland.

McFADYEAN, C.W. (11) 1966 Ireland, France, Scotland; 1967 Australia, Ireland, France, Scotland, Wales, New Zealand; 1968 Wales, Ireland.

MacILWAINE, A.H. (5) 1912 Wales, Ireland, Scotland, France; 1920 Ireland.

MACKIE, O.G. (2) 1897 Scotland; 1898 Ireland.

MacKINLAY, J.E.H. (3) 1872 Scotland; 1873 Scotland; 1875 Ireland.

MacLAREN, W. (1) 1871 Scotland.

MacLENNAN, R.R.F. (3) 1925 Ireland, Scotland, France.

McLEOD, N.F. (2) 1879 Scotland, Ireland.

MADGE, R.J.P. (4) 1948 Australia, Wales, Ireland, Scotland.

MALIR, F.W.S. (3) 1930 Wales, Ireland, Scotland.

MANGLES, R.H. (2) 1897 Wales, Ireland.

MANLEY, D.C. (4) 1963 Wales, Ireland, France, Scotland.

MANN, W.E. (3) 1911 Wales, France, Ireland.

MANTELL, N.D. (2) 1975 Australia, Ireland.

MARKENDALE, E.T. (1) 1880 Ireland.

MARQUES, R.W.D. (23) 1956 Wales, Ireland, Scotland, France; 1957 Wales, Ireland, France, Scotland; 1958 Wales, Australia, Ireland, France, Scotland; 1959 Wales, Ireland, France, Scotland; 1960 Wales, Ireland, France, Scotland; 1961 South Africa, Wales.

MARQUIS, J.C. (2) 1900 Ireland, Scotland.

MARRIOTT, C.J.B. (7) 1884 Wales, Ireland, Scotland; 1886 Wales, Ireland, Scotland; 1887 Ireland.

MARRIOTT, E.E. (1) 1876 Ireland.

MARRIOTT, V.R. (4) 1963 New Zealand (1 & 2), Australia; 1964 New Zealand.

MARSDEN, G.H. (3) 1900 Wales, Ireland, Scotland.

MARSH, H. (1) 1873 Scotland.

MARSH, J. (1) 1892 Ireland.

MARSHALL, H (1) 1893 Wales.

MARSHALL, M.W. (10) 1873 Scotland; 1874 Scotland; 1875 Ireland, Scotland; 1876 Ireland, Scotland; 1877 Ireland, Scotland; 1878 Scotland, Ireland.

MARSHALL, R.M. (5) 1938 Ireland, Scotland; 1939 Wales, Ireland, Scotland.

MARTIN, C.R. (4) 1985 France, Scotland, Ireland, Wales.

MARTIN, N.O. (1) 1972 France (R).

MARTINDALE, S.A. (1) 1929 France.

MASSEY, E.J. (3) 1925 Wales, Ireland, Scotland.

MATHIAS, J.L. (4) 1905 Wales, Ireland, Scotland, New Zealand.

MATTERS, J.C. (1) 1899 Scotland.

MATTHEWS, J.R.C. (10) 1949 France, Scotland; 1950 Ireland, France, Scotland; 1952 South Africa, Wales, Scotland, Ireland, France.

MAUD, P. (2) 1893 Wales, Ireland.

MAXWELL, A.W. (7) 1975 Australia (1); 1976 Australia, Wales, Scotland, Ireland, France; 1978 France.

MAXWELL-HYSLOP, J.E. (3) 1922 Ireland, France, Scotland.

MAYNARD, A.F. (3) 1914 Wales, Ireland, Scotland.

MEIKLE, G.W.C. (3) 1934 Wales, Ireland, Scotland.

MEIKLE, S.S.C. (1) 1929 Scotland.

MELLISH, F.W. (6) 1920 Wales, France, Ireland, Scotland; 1921 Wales, Ireland.

MELVILLE, N.D. (13) 1984 Australia; 1985 Ireland, Wales, New Zealand (1 & 2); 1986 Wales, Scotland, Ireland, France; 1988 France, Wales, Scotland, Ireland (1).

MERRIAM, L.P.B. (2) 1920 Wales, France.

MICHELL, A.T. (3) 1875 Ireland, Scotland; 1876 Ireland.

MIDDLETON, B.B. (2) 1882 Ireland; 1883 Ireland.

MIDDLETON, J.A. (1) 1922 Scotland.

MILES, J.H. (1) 1903 Wales.

MILLETT, H. (1) 1920 France.

MILLS, F.W. (2) 1872 Scotland; 1873 Scotland.

MILLS, S.G.F. (5) 1981 Argentina (1 & 2); 1983 Wales; 1984 South Africa (1), Australia.

MILLS, W.A. (11) 1906 Wales, Ireland, Scotland, France, South Africa; 1907 France, Wales, Ireland, Scotland; 1908 France, Wales.

MILMAN, D.L.K. (4) 1937 Wales; 1939 Wales, Ireland, Scotland.

MILTON, C.H. (1) 1906 Ireland.

MILTON, J.G. (5) 1904 Wales, Ireland, Scotland; 1905: Scotland; 1907 Ireland.

MILTON, W.H. (2) 1874 Scotland; 1875 Ireland.

MITCHELL, F. (6) 1895 Wales, Ireland, Scotland; 1896; Wales, Ireland, Scotland.

MITCHELL, W.G. (7) 1890 Wales, Scotland, Ireland; 1891 Wales, Ireland, Scotland; 1893 Scotland.

MOBB, E.R. (7) 1909 Australia, Wales, France, Ireland, Scotland; 1910 Ireland, France.

MOBERLY, W.O. (1) 1872 Scotland.

MOORE, B.C. (40) 1987 Scotland, *Australia, Japan, Wales*; 1988 France, Wales, Scotland (1 & 2), Australia (1 & 2), Fiji, Australia; 1989 Scotland, Ireland, France, Wales, Romania, Fiji; 1990 Ireland, France, Wales, Scotland, Argentina (1 & 2); 1991 Wales, Scotland, Ireland, France, Fiji, Australia, *New Zealand, Italy, France, Scotland, Australia;* 1992 Scotland, Ireland, France, Wales.

MOORE, E.J. (2) 1883 Ireland, Scotland.

MOORE, N.J.N.H. (3) 1904 Wales, Ireland, Scotland.

MOORE, P.B.C. (1) 1951 Wales.

MOORE, W.K.T. (7) 1947 Wales, Ireland; 1949 France, Scotland; 1950 Ireland, France, Scotland.

MORDELL, R.J. (1) 1978 Wales.

MORFITT, S. (6) 1894 Wales, Ireland, Scotland; 1896 Wales, Ireland, Scotland.

MORGAN, J.R. (1) 1920 Wales.

MORGAN, W.G.D. (9) 1960 Wales, Ireland, France, Scotland; 1961 South Africa, Wales, Ireland, France, Scotland.

MORLEY, A.J. (7) 1972 South Africa; 1973 New Zealand (1), Wales, Ireland; 1975 Scotland, Australia (1 & 2).

MORRIS, A.D.W. (3) 1909 Australia, Wales, France.

MORRIS, C.D. (9) 1988 Australia; 1989 Scotland, Ireland, France, Wales; 1992 Scotland, Ireland, France, Wales.

MORRISON, P.H. (4) 1890 Wales, Scotland, Ireland; 1891 Ireland.

MORSE, S. (3) 1873 Scotland; 1874 Scotland; 1875 Scotland.

MORTIMER, W. (1) 1899 Wales.

MORTON, H.J.S. (4) 1909 Ireland, Scotland; 1910 Wales, Ireland.

MOSS, F. (3) 1885 Wales, Ireland; 1886 Wales.

MULLINS, A.R. (1) 1989 Fiji.

MYCOCK, J. (5) 1947 Wales, Ireland, Scotland, France; 1948 Australia.

MYERS, E. (18) 1920 Ireland, Scotland; 1921 Wales, Ireland; 1922 Wales, Ireland, France, Scotland; 1923 Wales, Ireland, Scotland, France; 1924 Wales, Ireland, France, Scotland; 1925 Scotland, France.

MYERS, H. (1) 1898 Ireland.

NANSON, W.M.B. (2) 1907 France, Wales.

NASH, E.H. (1) 1875 Ireland.

NEALE, B.A. (3) 1951 Ireland, France, Scotland.

NEALE, M.E. (1) 1912 France.

NEAME, S. (4) 1879 Scotland, Ireland; 1880 Ireland, Scotland.

NEARY, A. (43) 1971 Wales, Ireland, France, Scotland (2, 1 Centenary), Presidents Overseas XV (RFU Centenary); 1972 Wales, Ireland, France, Scotland, South Africa; 1973 New Zealand (1), Wales, Ireland, France, Scotland, New Zealand (2), Australia; 1974 Scotland, Ireland, France, Wales; 1975 Ireland, France, Wales, Scotland, Australia (1); 1976 Wales, Australia, Scotland, Ireland, France; 1977 Ireland; 1978 France (R); 1979 Scotland, Ireland, France, Wales, New Zealand; 1980 Ireland, France, Wales, Scotland.

NELMES, B.G. (6) 1975 Australia (1 & 2); 1978 Wales, Scotland, Ireland, New Zealand.

NEWBOLD, C.J. (6) 1904 Wales, Ireland, Scotland; 1905 Wales, Ireland, Scotland.

NEWMAN, S.C. (3) 1947 France; 1948 Australia, Wales.

NEWTON, A.W. (1) 1907 Scotland.

NEWTON, P.A. (1) 1882 Scotland.

NEWTON-THOMPSON, J.O. (2) 1947 Scotland, France.

NICHOL, W. (2) 1892 Wales, Scotland.

NICHOLAS, P.L. (1) 1902 Wales.

NICHOLSON, B.E. (2) 1938 Wales, Ireland.

NICHOLSON, E.S. (5) 1935 Wales, Ireland, Scotland; 1936 New Zealand, Wales.

NICHOLSON, E.T. (2) 1900 Wales, Ireland

NICHOLSON, T. (1) 1893 Ireland.

NINNES, B.F. (1) 1971 Wales.

NORMAN, D.J. (2) 1932 South Africa, Wales.

NORTH, E.H.G. (3) 1891 Wales, Ireland, Scotland

NORTHMORE, S. (1) 1897 Ireland.

NOVAK, M.J. (3) 1970 Wales, Scotland, France.

NOVIS, A.L. (7) 1929 Scotland, France; 1930 Wales, Ireland, France; 1933 Ireland, Scotland.

OAKELEY, F.E. (4) 1913 Scotland; 1914 Ireland, Scotland, France.

OAKES, R.F. (8) 1897 Wales, Ireland, Scotland; 1898 Ireland, Scotland, Wales; 1899 Wales, Scotland.

OAKLEY, L.F.L. (1) 1951 Wales.

OBOLENSKY, A. (4) 1936 New Zealand, Wales, Ireland, Scotland.

OLD, A.G.B. (16) 1972 Wales, Ireland, France, Scotland, South Africa; 1973 New Zealand (2), Australia; 1974 Scotland, Ireland, France, Wales; 1975 Ireland, Australia (2); 1976 Scotland, Ireland; 1978 France.

OLDHAM, W.L. (2) 1908 Scotland; 1909 Australia.

OLVER, C.J. (2) 1990 Argentina, USA.

O'NEILL, A (3) 1901 Wales, Ireland, Scotland.

OPENSHAW, W.E. (1) 1879 Ireland.

ORWIN, J. (14) 1985 Romania, France, Scotland, Ireland, Wales, New Zealand (1 & 2); 1988 France, Wales, Scotland, Ireland (1 & 2), Australia (1 & 2).

OSBORNE, R.R. (1) 1871 Scotland.

OSBORNE, S.H. (1) 1905 Scotland.

OTI, C. (11) 1988 Scotland, Ireland (1); 1989 Scotland, Ireland, France, Wales, Romania; 1991 Fiji, Australia, *New Zealand, Italy.*

OUGHTRED, B. (6) 1901 Scotland; 1902 Wales, Ireland, Scotland; 1903 Wales, Ireland.

OWEN, J.E. (14) 1963 Wales, Ireland, France, Scotland, Australia; 1964 New Zealand; 1965 Wales, Ireland, France, Scotland; 1966 Ireland, France, Scotland; 1967 New Zealand.

OWEN-SMITH, H.G.O. (10) 1934 Wales, Ireland, Scotland; 1936 New Zealand, Wales, Ireland, Scotland; 1937 Wales, Ireland, Scotland.

PAGE, J.J. (5) 1971 Wales, Ireland, France, Scotland; 1975 Scotland.

PALLANT, J.N. (3) 1967 Ireland, France, Scotland.

PLAMER, A.C. (2) 1909 Ireland, Scotland.

PALMER, F.H. (1) 1905 Wales.

PALMER, G.V. (3) 1928 Ireland, France, Scotland.

PALMER, J.A. (3) 1984 South Africa (1 & 2); 1986 Ireland (R).

PARGETTER, T.A. (3) 1962 Scotland; 1963 France, New Zealand (1).

PARKER, G.W. (2) 1938 Ireland, Scotland.

PARKER, Hon.S. (2) 1874 Scotland; 1875 Scotland.

PARSONS, E.I. (1) 1939 Scotland.

PARSONS, M.J. (4) 1968 Wales, Ireland, France, Scotland.

PATTERSON, W.M. (2) 1961 South Africa, Scotland.

PATTISON, R.M. (2) 1883 Ireland, Scotland.

PAUL, J.E. (1) 1875 Scotland.

PAYNE, A.T. (2) 1935 Ireland, Scotland.

PAYNE, C.M. (10) 1964 Ireland, France, Scotland; 1965 Ireland, France, Scotland; 1966 Wales, Ireland, France, Scotland.

PAYNE, J.H. (7) 1882 Scotland; 1883 Wales, Ireland, Scotland; 1884 Ireland; 1885 Wales, Ireland.

PEARCE, G.S. (36) 1979 Scotland, Ireland, France, Wales; 1981 Argentina (1 & 2); 1982 Australia, Scotland; 1983 France, Wales, Scotland, Ireland, New Zealand; 1984 Scotland, South Africa (2), Australia; 1985 Romania, France, Scotland, Ireland, Wales, New Zealand (1 & 2); 1986 Wales, Scotland, Ireland, France; 1987 Ireland, France, Wales, Scotland, *Australia, USA, Wales;* 1988 Fiji, USA.

PEARSONS, A.W. (7) 1875 Ireland, Scotland; 1876 Ireland, Scotland; 1877 Scotland; 1878 Scotland, Ireland.

PEART, T.G.A.H. (2) 1964 France, Scotland.

PEASE, F.E. (1) 1887 Ireland.

PENNY, S.H. (1) 1909 Australia.

PENNY, W.J. (3) 1878 Ireland; 1879 Scotland, Ireland.

PERCIVAL, L.J. (3) 1891 Ireland; 1892 Ireland; 1893 Scotland.

PERITON, H.G. (21) 1925 Wales; 1926 Wales, Ireland, France, Scotland; 1927 Wales, Ireland, Scotland, France; 1928 Australia, Ireland, France, Scotland; 1929 Wales, Ireland, Scotland, France; 1930 Wales, Ireland, France, Scotland.

PERROTT, E.S. (1) 1875 Ireland.

PERRY, D.G. (15) 1963 France, Scotland, New Zealand (1 & 2), Australia; 1964 New Zealand, Wales, Ireland; 1965 Wales, Ireland, France, Scotland; 1966 Wales, Ireland, France.

PERRY, S.V. (7) 1947 Wales, Ireland; 1948 Australia, Wales, Ireland, Scotland, France.

PETERS, J. (5) 1906 Scotland, France; 1907 Ireland, Scotland; 1908 Wales.

PHILLIPS, C. (3) 1880 Scotland; 1881 Ireland Scotland.

PHILLIPS, M.S. (25) 1958 Australia, Ireland, France, Scotland; 1959 Wales, Ireland, France, Scotland; 1960 Wales, Ireland, France, Scotland; 1961 Wales; 1963 Wales, Ireland, France, Scotland, new Zealand (1 & 2), Australia; 1964 New Zealand, Wales, Ireland, France, Scotland.

PICKERING, A.S. (1) 1907 Ireland.

PICKERING, R.D.A. (6) 1967 Ireland, France, Scotland, Wales; 1968 France, Scotland.

PICKLES, R.C.W. (2) 1922 Ireland, France.

PIERCE, R. (2) 1898 Ireland; 1903 Scotland.

PILKINGTON, W.N. (1) 1898 Scotland.

PILLMAN, C.H. (18) 1910 Wales, Ireland, France, Scotland; 1911 Wales, France, Ireland, Scotland; 1912 Wales, France; 1913 South Africa, Wales, France, Ireland, Scotland; 1914 Wales, Ireland, Scotland.

PILLMAN, R.L. (1) 1914 France.

PINCH, J (3) 1896 Wales, Ireland; 1897 Scotland.

PINCHING, W.W. (1) 1872 Scotland.

PITMAN, I.J. (1) 1922 Scotland.

PLUMMER, K.C. (4) 1969 Wales; 1976 Scotland, Ireland, France.

POOLE, F.O. (3) 1895 Wales, Ireland, Scotland.

POOLE, R.W. (1) 1896 Scotland.

POPE, E.B. (3) 1931 Wales, Scotland, France.

PORTUS, G.V. (2) 1908 France, Ireland.

POULTON, R.W. (17) 1909 France, Ireland, Scotland; 1910 Wales; 1911 Scotland; 1912 Wales, Ireland, Scotland; 1913 South Africa, Wales, France, Ireland, Scotland; 1914 Wales, Ireland, Scotland, France.

POWELL, D.L. (11) 1966 Wales, Ireland; 1969 Ireland, France, Scotland, Wales; 1971 Wales, Ireland, France, Scotland (2, 1 centenary).

PRATTEN, W.E. (2) 1927 Scotland, France.

PREECE, I. (12) 1948 Ireland, Scotland, France; 1949 France, Scotland; 1950 Wales, Ireland, France, Scotland; 1951 Wales, Ireland, France.

PREECE, P.S. (12) 1972 South Africa; 1973 New Zealand (1), Wales, Ireland, France, Scotland, New Zealand (2); 1975 Ireland, France, Wales, Australia (2); 1976 Wales (R).

PREEDY, M. (1) 1984 South Africa (1).

PRENTICE, F.D. (3) 1928 Ireland, France, Scotland.

PRESCOTT, R.E. (6) 1937 Wales, Ireland; 1938 Ireland; 1939 Wales, Ireland, Scotland.

PRESTON, N.J. (3) 1979 New Zealand; 1980 Ireland, France.

PRICE, H.L. (4) 1922 Ireland, Scotland; 1923 Wales, Ireland.

PRICE, J. (1) 1961 Ireland.

PRICE, P.L.A. (3) 1877 Ireland, Scotland; 1878 Scotland.

PRICE, T.W. (6) 1948 Scotland, France; 1949 Wales, Ireland, France, Scotland.

PROBYN, J.A. (33) 1988 France, Wales, Scotland, Ireland (1 & 2), Australia; 1989

Scotland, Ireland, Romania (R); 1990 Ireland, France, Wales, Scotland, Argentina (1 & 2), Argentina; 1991 Wales, Scotland, Ireland, France, Fiji, Australia, *New Zealand, Italy, France, Scotland, Australia*; 1992 Scotland, Ireland, France, Wales.

PROUT, D.H. (2) 1968 Wales, Ireland.

PULLIN, J.V. (41) 1966 Wales; 1968 Wales, Ireland, France, Scotland; 1969 Ireland, France, Scotland, Wales, South Africa; 1970 Ireland, Wales, Scotland, France; 1971 Wales, Ireland, France, Scotland (2, 1 centenary), Presidents Overseas XV (RFU Centenary); 1972 Wales, Ireland, France, Scotland, South Africa; 1973 New Zealand (1), Wales, Ireland, France, Scotland, New Zealand (2), Australia; 1974 Scotland, Ireland, France, Wales; 1975 Ireland, Wales (R), Scotland, Australia (1 & 2); 1976 France.

PURDY, S.J. (1) 1962 Scotland.

PYKE, J. (1) 1892 Wales.

PYM, J.A. (4) 1912 Wales, Ireland, Scotland, France.

QUINN, J.P. (5) 1954 Wales, New Zealand, Ireland, Scotland, France.

RAFTER, M. (17) 1977 Scotland, France, Wales; 1978 France, Wales, Scotland, Ireland, New Zealand; 1979 Scotland, Ireland, France, Wales, New Zealand; 1980 Wales (R); 1981 Wales, Argentina (1 & 2).

RALSTON, C.W. (22) 1971 Scotland (Centenary), Presidents Overseas XV (RFU Centenary); 1972 Wales, Ireland, France, Scotland, South Africa; 1973 New Zealand (1), Wales, Ireland, France, Scotland, New Zealand (2), Australia; 1974 Scotland, Ireland, France, Wales; 1975 Ireland, France, Wales, Scotland.

RAMSDEN, H.E. (2) 1898 Wales, Scotland.

RANSOM, J.M. (7) 1963 New Zealand (1 & 2), Australia; 1964 Wales, Ireland, France, Scotland.

RAPHAEL, J.E. (9) 1902 Wales, Ireland, Scotland; 1905 Wales, Scotland, New Zealand; 1906 Wales, Scotland, France.

RAVENSCROFT, J. (1) 1881 Ireland.

RAWLINSON, W.C.W. (1) 1876 Scotland.

REDFERN, S (1) 1984 Ireland (R).

REDMAN, N.C. (11) 1984 Australia; 1986 Scotland (R); 1987 Ireland, Scotland, *Australia, Japan, Wales;* 1988 Fiji; 1991 Fiji.*Italy, USA.*

REDMOND, G.F. (1) 1970 France.

REDWOOD, B.W. (2) 1968 Wales, Ireland.

REES, G.W. (21) 1984 South Africa (2) (R), Australia; 1986 Ireland, France; 1987 France, Wales, Scotland, *Australia, Japan, USA, Wales;* 1988 Scotland (R), Ireland (1 & 2), Australia (1 & 2), Fiji, 1989 Wales (R), Romania (R), Fiji (R); 1991 Fiji, *USA.*

REEVE, J.S.R. (8) 1929 France; 1930 Wales, Ireland, France, Scotland; 1931 Wales, Ireland, Scotland.

REGAN, M. (12) 1953 Wales, Ireland, France, Scotland; 1954 Wales, New Zealand, Ireland, Scotland, France; 1956 Ireland, Scotland, France.

RENDALL, P.A.G. (28) 1984 Wales, South Africa (2); 1986 Wales, Scotland; 1987 Ireland, France, Scotland, *Australia, Japan, Wales;* 1988 France, Wales, Scotland, Ireland (1 & 2), Australia (1 & 2), Australia; 1989 Scotland, Ireland, France, Wales, Romania; 1990 Ireland, France, Wales, Scotland 1991 *Italy (R).*

REW, H. (10) 1929 Scotland, France; 1930 France, Scotland; 1931 Wales, Scotland, France; 1934 Wales, Ireland, Scotland.

REYNOLDS, F.J. (3) 1937 Scotland; 1938 Ireland, Scotland.

REYNOLDS, S. (4) 1900 Wales, Ireland, Scotland; 1901 Ireland.

RHODES, J. (3) 1896 Wales, Ireland, Scotland.

RICHARDS, D. (31) 1986 Ireland, France; 1987 Scotland, *Australia, Japan, USA, Wales;* 1988 France, Wales, Scotland, Ireland (1), Australia (1 & 2), Fiji, Australia; 1989 Scotland, Ireland, France, Wales, Romania; 1990 Argentina; 1991 Wales, Scotland, Ireland, Australia, *New Zealand, Italy, USA;* 1992 Scotland (R), France, Wales.

RICHARDS, E.E. (2) 1929 Scotland, France.

RICHARDS, J. (3) 1891 Wales, Ireland, Scotland.

RICHARDS, S.B. (9) 1965 Wales, France, Scotland; 1967 Australia, Ireland, France, Scotland, Wales.

RICHARDSON, J.V. (5) 1928 Australia, Wales, Ireland, France, Scotland.

RICHARDSON, W.R. (1) 1881 Ireland.

RICKARDS, C.H. (1) 1873 Scotland.

RIMMER, G. (12) 1949 Wales, Ireland; 1950 Wales; 1951 Wales, Ireland, France; 1952 South Africa, Wales; 1954 Wales, New Zealand, Ireland, Scotland.

RIMMER, L.I. (5) 1961 South Africa, Wales, Ireland, France, Scotland.

RIPLEY, A.G. (24) 1972 Wales, Ireland, France, Scotland, South Africa; 1973 New Zealand (1), Wales, Ireland, France, Scotland, New Zealand (2), Australia; 1974 Scotland, Ireland, France, Wales; 1975 Ireland, France, Scotland, Australia (1 & 2); 1976 Australia, Wales, Scotland.

RISMAN, A.B.W. (8) 1959 Wales, Ireland, France, Scotland; 1961 South Africa, Wales, Ireland, France.

RITSON, J.A.S. (8) 1910 France; Scotland; 1912 France; 1913 South Africa, Wales, France, Ireland, Scotland.

RITTSON-THOMAS, G.C. (3) 1951 Wales, Ireland, France.

ROBBINS, G.L. (2) 1986 Wales, Scotland.

ROBBINS, P.G.D. (19) 1956 Wales, Ireland, Scotland, France; 1957 Wales, Ieland, France, Scotland; 1958 Wales, Australia, Ireland, Scotland; 1960 Wales, Ireland, France, Scotland; 1961 South Africa, Wales; 1962 Scotland.

ROBERTS, A.D. (8) 1911 Wales, France, Ireland, Scotland; 1912 Ireland, Scotland, France; 1914 Ireland.

ROBERTS, E.W. (6) 1901 Wales, Ireland; 1905 New Zealand; 1906 Wales, Ireland; 1907 Scotland.

ROBERTS, G.D. (3) 1907 Scotland; 1908 France, Wales.

ROBERTS, J. (18) 1960 Wales, Ireland, France, Scotland; 1961 South Africa, Wales, Ireland, France, Scotland; 1962 Wales, Ireland, France, Scotland; 1963 Wales, Ireland, France, Scotland; 1964 New Zealand.

ROBERTS, R.S. (1) 1932 Ireland.

ROBERTS, S (2) 1887 Wales, Ireland.

ROBERTS, V.G. (16) 1947 France; 1949 Wales, Ireland, France, Scotland; 1950 Ireland, France, Scotland; 1951 Wales, Ireland, France, Scotland; 1956 Wales, Ireland, Scotland, France.

ROBERTSHAW, A.R. (5) 1886 Wales, Ireland, Scotland; 1887 Wales, Scotland.

ROBINSON, A. (4) 1889 Maoris; 1890 Wales, Scotland, Ireland.

ROBINSON, E.F. (4) 1954 Scotland; 1961 Ireland, France, Scotland.

ROBINSON, G.C. (8) 1897 Ireland, Scotland; 1898 Ireland; 1899 Wales; 1900 Ireland, Scotland; 1901 Ireland, Scotland.

ROBINSON, J.J. (4) 1893 Scotland; 1902 Wales, Ireland, Scotland.

ROBINSON, R.A. (7) 1988 Australia (2), Fiji, Australia; 1989 Scotland, Ireland, France, Wales.

ROBSON, A. (5) 1924 Wales, Ireland, France, Scotland; 1926 Wales.

ROBSON, M. (4) 1930 Wales, Ireland, France, Scotland.

RODBER, T.A. (2) 1992 Scotland, Ireland.

ROGERS, D.P. (34) 1961 Ireland, France, Scotland; 1962 Wales, Ireland, France; 1963 Wales, Ireland, France, Scotland, New Zealand (1 & 2), Australia; 1964 New Zealand, Wales, Ireland, France, Scotland; 1965 Wales, Ireland, France, Scotland; 1966 Wales, Ireland, France, Scotland; 1967 Austrlia, Scotland, Wales, New Zealand; 1969 Ireland, France, Scotland, Wales.

ROGERS, J.H. (4) 1890 Wales, Scotland, Ireland; 1891 Scotland.

ROGERS, W.L.Y. (2) 1905 Wales, Ireland.

ROLLITT, D.M. (7) 1967 Ireland, France, Scotland, Wales; 1975 Scotland, Australia (1 & 2).

RONCORONI, A.D.S. (3) 1933 Wales, Ireland, Scotland.

ROSE, W.M.H. (10) 1981 Ireland, France; 1982 Australia, Scotland, Ireland; 1987 Ireland, France, Wales, Scotland, *Australia*.

ROSSBOROUGH, P.A. (7) 1971 Wales; 1973 New Zealand (2), Australia; 1974 Scotland, Ireland; 1975 Ireland, France.

ROSSER, D.W.A. (5) 1965 Wales, Ireland, France, Scotland; 1966 Wales.

ROTHERHAM, Alan (12) 1883 Wales, Scotland; 1884 Wales, Scotland; 1885 Wales, Ireland; 1886 Wales, Ireland, Scotland; 1887 Wales, Ireland, Scotland.

ROTHERHAM, Arthur (5) 1898 Scotland, Wales; 1899 Wales, Ireland, Scotland.

ROUGHLEY, D. (3) 1973 Australia; 1974 Scotland, Ireland.

ROWELL, R.E. (2) 1964 Wales; 1965 Wales.

ROWLEY, A.J. (1) 1932 South Africa.

ROWLEY, H.C. (9) 1879 Scotland; Ireland; 1880 Ireland, Scotland; 1881 Ireland, Wales, Scotland; 1882 Ireland, Scotland.

ROYDS, P.M.R. (3) 1898 Scotland, Wales; 1899 Wales.

ROYLE, A.V. (1) 1889 Maoris.

RUDD, E.L. (6) 1965 Wales, Ireland, Scotland; 1966 Wales, Ireland, Scotland.

RUSSELL, R.F. (1) 1905 New Zealand.

RUTHERFORD, D. (14) 1960 Wales, Ireland, France, Scotland; 1961 South Africa; 1965 Wales, Ireland, France, Scotland. 1966 Wales, Ireland, France, Scotland; 1967 New Zealand.

RYALLS, H.J. (2) 1885 Wales, Ireland.

RYAN, D. (2) 1990 Argentina (1 & 2).

RYAN, P.H. (2) 1955 Wales, Ireland.

SADLER, E.H. (2) Ireland, Scotland, 1933.

SAGAR, J.W. (2) 1901 Wales, Ireland.

SALMON, J.L.B. (12) 1985 New Zealand (1 & 2); 1986 Wales, Scotland; 1987 Ireland, France, Wales, Scotland, *Australia, Japan, USA, Wales*.

SAMPLE, C.H. (3) 1884 Ireland; 1885 Ireland; 1886 Scotland.

SANDERS, D.L. (9) 1954, Wales, New Zealand, Ireland, Scotland, France; 1956 Wales, Ireland, Scotland, France.

SANDERS, F.W. (3) 1923 Ireland, Scotland, France.

SANDFORD, J.R.P. (1) 1906 Ireland.

SANGWIN, R.D. (2) 1964 New Zealand, Wales.

SARGENT, G.A.F. (1) 1981 Ireland (R).

SAVAGE, K.F. (13) 1966 Wales, Ireland, France, Scotland; 1967 Australia, Ireland, France, Scotland, Wales, New Zealand; 1968 Wales, France, Scotland.

SAWYER, C.M. (2) 1880 Scotland; 1881 Ireland.

SAXBY, L.E. (2) 1932 South Africa, Wales.

SCHOFIELD, J.W. (1) 1880 Ireland.

SCHOLFIELD, J.A. (1) 1911 Wales.

SCHWARZ, R.O. (3) 1899 Scotland; 1901 Wales, Ireland.

SCORFIELD, E.S. (1) 1910 France.

SCOTT, C.T. (4) 1900 Wales, Ireland; 1901 Ireland, Wales.

SCOTT, E.K. (5) 1947 Wales; 1948 Australia, Wales, Ireland, Scotland.

SCOTT, F.S. (1) 1907 Wales.

SCOTT, H. (1) 1955 France.

SCOTT, J.P. (30) 1978 France, Wales, Scotland, Ireland, New Zealand; 1979 Scotland (R), Ireland, France, Wales, New Zealand; 1980 Ireland, France, Wales, Scotland, Argentina (1, 2); 1982 Ireland, France, Wales; 1983 France, Wales, Scotland, Ireland, New Zealand; 1984 Scotland, Ireland, France, Wales, South Africa (1, 2).

SCOTT, J.S.M. (1) 1958 France.

SCOTT, M.T. (3) 1887 Ireland; 1890 Scotland, Ireland.

SCOTT, W.M. (1) 1889 Maoris.

SEDDON, R.L. (3) 1887 Wales, Ireland, Scotland.

SELLAR, K.A. (7) 1927 Wales, Ireland, Scotland; 1928 Australia, Wales, Ireland, France.

SEVER, H.S. (10) 1936 New Zealand, Wales, Ireland, Scotland; 1937 Wales, Ireland, Scotland; 1938 Wales, Ireland, Scotland.

SHACKLETON, I.R. (4) 1969 South AFrica; 1970 Ireland, Wales, Scotland.

SHARP, R.A.W. (14) 1960 Wales, Ireland, France, Scotland; 1961 Ireland, France; 1962 Wales, Ireland, France; 1963 Wales, Ireland, France, Scotland; 1967 Australia.

SHAW, C.H. (6) 1906 Scotland, South Africa; 1907 France, Wales, Ireland, Scotland.

SHAW, F. (1) 1898 Ireland.

SHAW, J.F. (2) 1898 Scotland, Wales.

SHEPPARD, A. (2) 1981 Wales (R); 1985 Wales.

SHERRARD, C.W. (2) 1871 Scotland; 1872 Scotland.

SHERRIFF, G.A. (3) 1966 Scotland; 1967 Australia, New Zealand.

SHEWRING, H.E. (10) 1905 Ireland, New Zealand; 1906 Wales, Scotland, France, South Africa; 1907 France, Wales, Ireland, Scotland.

SHOOTER, J.H. (4) 1899 Ireland, Scotland; 1900 Ireland Scotland.

SHUTTLEWORTH, D.W. (2) 1951 Scotland; 1953 Scotland.

SIBREE, H.J.H. (3) 1908 France; 1909 Ireland, Scotland.

SILK, N. (4) 1965 Wales, Ireland, France, Scotland.

SIMMS, K.G. (15) 1985 Romania, France, Scotland, Ireland, Wales; 1986 Ireland, France; 1987 Ireland, France, Wales, *Australia, Japan, Wales*; 1988 France, Wales.

SIMPSON, C.P. 1965 Wales.

SIMPSON, P.D. (3) 1983 New Zealand; 1984 Scotland; 1987 Ireland.

SIMPSON, T. (11) 1902 Scotland; 1903 Wales, Ireland, Scotland; 1904 Ireland, Scotland; 1905 Ireland, Scotland; 1906 Scotland, South Africa; 1909 France.

SKINNER, M.G. (21) 1988 France, Wales, Scotland, Ireland (1, 2); 1989 Fiji; 1990 Ireland, France, Wales, Scotland, Argentina (1, 2); 1991 Fiji (R), *USA, France, Scotland, Australia*; 1992 Scotland, Ireland, France, Wales.

SLADEN, G.M. (3) 1929 Wales, Ireland, Scotland.

SLEMEN, M.A.C. (31) 1976 Ireland, France; 1977 Scotland, Ireland, France, Wales; 1978 France, Wales, Scotland, Ireland, New Zealand; 1979 Scotland, Ireland, France, Wales, New Zealand; 1980 Ireland, France, Wales, Scotland; 1981 Wales, Scotland, Ireland, France; 1982 Australia, Scotland, Ireland, France, Wales; 1983 New Zealand; 1984 Scotland.

SLOCOCK, L.A.N. (8) 1907 France, Wales, Ireland, Scotland; 1908 France, Wales, Ireland, Scotland.

SLOW, C.F. (1) 1934 Scotland.

SMALL, H.D. (4) 1950 Wales, Ireland, France, Scotland.

SMALLWOOD, A.M. (14) 1920 France, Ireland; 1921 Wales, Ireland, Scotland, France; 1922 Ireland, Scotland; 1923 Wales, Ireland, Scotland, France; 1925 Ireland, Scotland.

SMART, C.E. (17) 1979 France, Wales, New Zealand; 1981 Scotland, Ireland, France, Argentina (1, 2); 1982 Australia, Scotland, Ireland, France, Wales; 1983 France, Wales, Scotland, Ireland.

SMART, S.E.J. (12) 1913 South Africa, Wales, France, Ireland, Scotland; 1914 Wales, Ireland, Scotland, France; 1920 Wales, Ireland, Scotland.

SMEDDLE, R.W. (4) 1929 Wales, Ireland, Scotland; 1931 France.

SMITH, C.C. (1) 1901 Wales.

SMITH, D.F. (2) 1910 Wales, Ireland.

SMITH, J.V. (4) 1950 Wales, Ireland, France, Scotland.

SMITH, K. (4) 1974 France, Wales; 1975 Wales, Scotland.

SMITH, M.J.K. (1) 1956 Wales.

SMITH, S.J. (28) 1973 Ireland, France, Scotland, Australia; 1974 Ireland, France; 1975 Wales (R); 1976 France; 1977 France (R); 1979 New Zealand; 1980 Ireland, France, Wales, Scotland; 1981 Wales, Scotland, Ireland, France, Argentina (1, 2); 1982 Australia, Scotland, Ireland, France, Wales; 1983 France, Wales, Scotland.

SMITH, S.R. (5) 1959 Wales, France, Scotland; 1964 France, Scotland.

SMITH, S.T. (9) 1095 Romania, France, Scotland, Ireland, Wales, New Zealand (1, 2); 1986 Wales, Scotland.

SMITH, T.A. (1) 1951 Wales.

SOBEY, W.H. (5) 1930 Wales, France, Scotland; 1932 South Africa, Wales.

SOANE, F. (4) 1893 Scotland; 1894 Wales, Ireland, Scotland.

SOLOMON, B. (1) 1910 Wales.

SPARKS, R.H.W. (9) 1928 Ireland, France, Scotland; 1929 Wales, Ireland, Scotland; 1931 Ireland, Scotland, France.

SPEED, H. (4) 1894 Wales, Ireland, Scotland; 1896 Scotland.

SPENCE, F.W. (1) 1890 Ireland.

SPENCER, J. (1) 1966 Wales.

SPENCER, J.S. (15) 1969 Ireland, France, Scotland, Wales, South Africa; 1970 Ireland, Wales, Scotland, France; 1971 Wales, Ireland, Scotland (2, 1 centenary), President's Overseas XV (RFU Centenary).

SPONG, R.S. (8) 1929 France; 1930 Wales, Ireland, France, Scotland; 1931 France; 1932 South Africa, Wales.

SPOONER, R.H. (1) 1903 Wales.

SPRINGMAN, H.H. (2) 1879 Scotland; 1887 Scotland.

SPURLING, A. (1) 1882 Ireland.

SPURLING, N. (3) 1886 Ireland, Scotland; 1887 Wales.

SQUIRES, P.J. (29) 1973 France, Scotland, New Zealand (2), Australia; 1974 Scotland, Ireland, France, Wales; 1975 Ireland, France, Wales, Scotland, Australia (1, 2); 1976 Australia, Wales; 1977 Scotland, Ireland, France, Wales; 1978 France, Wales, Scotland, Ireland, New Zealand; 1979 Scotland, Ireland, France, Wales.

STAFFORD, R.C. (4) 1912 Wales, Ireland, Scotland, France.

STAFFORD, W.F.H. (1) 1874 Scotland.

STANBURY, E. (16) 1926 Wales, Ireland, Scotland; 1927 Wales, Ireland, Scotland, France; 1928 Australia, Wales, Ireland, Scotland, France; 1929 Wales, Ireland, Scotland, France.

STANDING, G. (2) 1883 Wales, Ireland.

STANGER-LEATHES, C.F. (1) 1905 Ireland.

STARK, K.J. (9) 1927 Wales, Ireland, Scotland, France; 1928 Australia, Wales, Ireland, Scotland, France.

STARKS, A. (2) 1896 Wales, Ireland.

STARMER-SMITH, N.C. (7) 1969 South Africa; 1970 Ireland, Wales, Scotland, France; 1971 Scotland (Centenary), President's Overseason XV (RFU Centenary).

START, S.P. (1) 1907 Scotland.

STEEDS, J.H. (5) 1949 France, Scotland; 1950 Ireland, France, Scotland.

STEELE-BODGER, M.R. (9) 1947 Wales, Ireland, Scotland, France; 1948 Australia, Wales, Ireland, Scotland, France.

STEINTHAL, F.E. (2) 1913 Wales, France.

STEVENS, C.B. (25) 1969 South Africa; 1970 Ireland, Wales, Scotland; 1971 President's Overseas XV (RFU Centenary season); 1972 Wales, Ireland, France, Scotland, South Africa; 1973 New Zealand (1), Wales, Ireland, France, Scotland, New Zealand (2), Australia; 1974 Scotland, Ireland, France, Wales; 1975 Ireland, France, Wales, Scotland.

STILL, E.R. (1) 1873 Scotland.

STIRLING, R.V. (18) 1951 Wales, Ireland, France, Scotland; 1952 South Africa, Wales, Scotland, Ireland, France; 1953 Wales, Ireland, France, Scotland; 1954 Wales, New Zealand, Ireland, Scotland, France.

STODDART, A.E. (10) 1885 Wales, Ireland, 1886 Wales, Ireland, Scotland; 1889 Maoris; 1890 Wales, Ireland; 1893 Wales, Scotland.

STODDART, W.B. (3) 1897 Wales, Ireland, Scotland.

STOKES, F. (3) 1871 Scotland; 1872 Scotland; 1873 Scotland.

STOKE, L. (12) 1875 Ireland; 1876 Scotland; 1977 Ireland, Scotland; 1878 Scotland; 1879 Scotland, Ireland; 1880 Scotland, Ireland, Scotland 1881 Ireland, Wales, Scotland.

STONE, F.Le.S. (1) 1914 France.

STOOP, A.D. (15) 1905 Scotland; 1906 Scotland, France, South Africa; 1907 France, Wales; 1910 Wales, Ireland, Scotland; 1911 Wales, France, Ireland, Scotland; 1912 Wales, Scotland.

STOOP, F.M. (4) 1910 Scotland; 1911 France, Ireland; 1913 South Africa.

STOUT, F.M. (14) 1897 Wales, Ireland; 1898 Ireland, Scotland, Wales; 1899 Ireland, Scotland; 1903 Scotland; 1904 Wales, Ireland, Scotland; 1905 Wales, Ireland, Scotland.

STOUT, P.W. (5) 1898 Scotland, Wales; 1899 Wales, Ireland, Scotland.

STRINGER, N.C. (5) 1982 Australia (R); 1983 New Zealand (R); 1984 South Africa (1R), Australia; 1985 Romania.

STRONG, E.L. (3) 1884 Wales, Ireland, Scotland.

SUMMERSCALES, G.E. (1) 1906 New Zealand.

SUTCLIFFE, J.W. (1) 1889 Maoris.

SWARBRICK, D.W. (6) 1947 Wales, Ireland, France; 1948 Australia, Wales; 1949 Ireland.

SWAYNE, D.H. (1) 1931 Wales.

SWAYNE, J.W.R. (1) 1929 Wales.

SWIFT, A.H. (6) 1981 Argentina (1, 2); 1983 France, Wales, Scotland; 1984 South Africa (2).

SYDDALL, J.P. (2) 1982 Ireland; 1984 Australia.

SYKES, A.R.V. (1) 1914 France.

SYKES, F.D. (4) 1955 France, Scotland; 1963 New Zealand (2), Australia.

SYKES, P.W. (7) 1948 France; 1952 Scotland, Ireland, France; 1953 Wales, Ireland, France.

SYRETT, R.E. (11) 1958 Wales, Australia, Ireland, France; 1960 Wales, Ireland, France, Scotland; 1962 Wales, Ireland, France.

TALLENT, J.A. (5) 1931 Scotland, France; 1932 South Africa, Wales; 1935 Ireland.

TANNER, C.C. (5) 1930 Scotland; 1932 South Africa, Wales, Ireland, Scotland.

TARR, F.N. (4) 1909 Australia, Wales, France; 1913 Scotland.

TATHAM, W.M. (7) 1882 Scotland; 1883 Wales, Ireland, Scotland; 1884 Wales, Ireland, Scotland.

TAYLOR, A.S. (4) 1883 Wales, Ireland; 1886 Wales, Ireland.

TAYLOR, E.W. (14) 1892 Ireland; 1893 Ireland; 1894 Wales, Ireland, Scotland; 1895 Wales, Ireland, Scotland; 1896 Wales, Ireland; 1897 Wales, Ireland, Scotland; 1899 Ireland.

TAYLOR, F. (2) 1920 France, Ireland.

TAYLOR, F.M. (1) 1914 Wales.

TAYLOR, H.H. (5) 1879 Scotland; 1880 Scotland; 1881 Wales, Ireland; 1882 Scotland.

TAYLOR, J.T. (11) 1897 Ireland; 1899 Ireland; 1900 Ireland; 1901 Wales, Ireland; 1902 Wales, Ireland, Scotland; 1903 Wales, Ireland; 1905 Scotland.

TAYLOR, P.J. (6) 1955 Wales, Ireland; 1962 Wales, Ireland, France, Scotland.

TAYLOR, R.B. (16) 1966 Wales; 1967 Ireland, France, Scotland, Wales, New Zealand; 1969 France, Scotland, Wales, South Africa; 1970 Ireland, Wales, Scotland, France; 1971 Scotland (2, 1 Cent).

TAYLOR, W.J. (5) 1928 Australia, Wales, Ireland, France, Scotland.

TEAGUE, M.C. (21) 1985 France (R), New Zealand (1, 2); 1989 Scotland, Ireland, France, Wales, Romania; 1990 France, Wales, Scotland; 1991 Wales, Ireland, Scotland, Ireland, Australia, Fiji, *New Zealand, Italy, France, Scotland, Australia*.

TEDEN, D.E. (3) 1939 Wales, Ireland, Scotland.

TEGGIN, A. (6) 1884 Ireland; 1885 Wales; 1886 Ireland, Scotland; 1887 Ireland, Scotland.

TETLEY, T.S. (1) 1876 Scotland.

THOMAS, C. (4) 1895 Wales, Ireland, Scotland; 1899 Ireland.

THOMPSON, P.H. (17) 1956 Wales, Ireland, Scotland, France; 1957 Wales, Ireland, France, Scotland; 1958 Wales, Australia, Ireland, France, Scotland; 1959 Wales, Ireland, France, Scotland.

THOMSON, G.T. (9) 1878 Scotland; 1882 Ireland, Scotland; 1883 Wales, Ireland, Scotland; 1884 Ireland, Scotland; 1885 Ireland.

THOMSON, W.B. (4) 1892 Wales; 1895 Wales, Ireland, Scotland.

THORNE, J.D. (3) 1963 Wales, Ireland, France.

TINDALL, V.R. (4) 1951 Wales, Ireland, France, Scotland.

TOBIN, F. (1) 1871 Scotland.

TODD, A.F. (2) 1900 Ireland, Scotland.

TODD, R. (1) 1877 Scotland.

TOFT, H.B. (10) 1936 Scotland; 1937 Wales, Ireland, Scotland; 1938 Wales, Ireland, Scotland; 1939 Wales, Ireland, Scotland.

TOOTHILL, J.T. (12) 1890 Scotland, Ireland; 1891 Wales, Ireland; 1892 Wales, Ireland, Scotland; 1893 Wales, Ireland, Scotland; 1894 Wales, Ireland.

TOSSWILL, L.R. (3) 1902 Wales, Ireland, Scotland.

TOUZEL, C.J.C. (2) 1877 Ireland, Scotland.

TOWELL, A.C. (2) 1948 France; 1951 Scotland.

TRAVERS, B.H. (6) 1947 Wales, Ireland; 1948 Australia, Wales; 1949 France, Scotland.

TREADWELL, W.T. (3) 1966 Ireland, France, Scotland.

TRICK, D.M. (2) 1983 Ireland; 1984 South Africa (1).

TRISTRAM, H.B. (5) 1883 Scotland; 1884 Wales, Scotland; 1885 Wales; 1887 Scotland.

TROOP, C.L. (2) 1933 Ireland, Scotland.

TUCKER, J.S. (27) 1922 Wales; 1925 New Zealand, Wales, Ireland, Scotland, France; 1926 Wales, Ireland, France, Scotland; 1927 Wales, Ireland, Scotland, France; 1928 Australia, Wales, Ireland, France, Scotland; 1929 Wales, Ireland, France; 1930 Wales, Ireland, France, Scotland; 1931 Wales.

TUCKER, W.E. (5) 1894 Wales, Ireland; 1895 Wales, Ireland, Scotland.

TUCKER, W.E. (3) 1926 Ireland, 1930 Wales, Ireland.

TURNER, D.P. (6) 1871 Scotland; 1872 Scotland; 1873 Scotland; 1874 Scotland; 1875 Ireland, Scotland.

TURNER, E.B. (3) 1876 Ireland; 1877 Ireland; 1878 Ireland.

TURNER, G.R. (1) 1876 Scotland.

TURNER, H.J.C. (1) 1871 Scotland.

TURNER, M.F. (2) 1948 Scotland, France.

TURQUAND-YOUNG, D. (5) 1928 Australia, Wales; 1929 Ireland, Scotland, France.

TWYNAM, H.T. (8) 1879 Ireland; 1880 Ireland; 1881 Wales; 1882 Ireland; 1883 Ireland; 1884 Wales, Ireland, Scotland.

UNDERWOOD, A.M. (5) 1962 Wales, Ireland, France, Scotland; 1964 Ireland.

UNDERWOOD, R. (55) 1984 Ireland, France, Wales, Australia; 1985 Romania, France, Scotland, Ireland, Wales; 1986 Wales, Ireland, France; 1987 Ireland, France, Wales, Scotland, *Australia, Japan Wales;* 1988 France, Wales, Scotland, Ireland (1, 2), Fiji, Australia (1, 2), Austalia; 1989 Scotland, Ireland, France, Wales, Romania, Fiji; 1990 Ireland, France, Wales, Scotland, Argentina; 1991 Wales, Scotland, Ireland, France, Fiji, Australia, *New Zealand, Italy, USA, France, Scotland, Australia;* 1992 Scotland, Ireland, France, Wales.

UNWIN, E.J. (4) **1937 Scotland; 1938 Wales, Ireland, Scotland.**

UNWIN, G.T. (1) 1898 Scotland.

UREN, R. (4) 1948 Ireland, Scotland, France; 1950 Ireland.

UTTLEY, R.M. (23) 1973 Ireland, France, Scotland, New Zealand (2), Australia; 1974 Ireland, France, Wales; 1975 France, Wales, Scotland, Australia (1, 2); 1977 Scotland, Ireland, France, Wales; 1978 New Zealand; 1979 Scotland; 1980 Ireland, France, Wales, Scotland.

VALENTINE, J. (4) 1890 Wales; 1896 Wales, Ireland, Scotland.

VANDERSPAR, C.H.R. (1) 1873 Scotland.

Van RYNEVELD, C.B. (4) 1949 Wales, Ireland, France, Scotland.

VARLEY, H. (1) 1892 Scotland.

VASSALL, H. (5) 1881 Wales, Scotland; 1882 Ireland, Scotland; 1883 Wales.

VASSALL, H.H. (1) 1908 Ireland.

VAUGHAN, D.B. (8) 1948 Australia, Wales, Ireland, Scotland; 1949 Ireland, France, Scotland; 1950 Wales.

VAUGHAN-JONES, A. (3) 1932 Ireland, Scotland; 1933 Wales.

VERESLST, C.L. (2) 1876 Ireland; 1878 Ireland.

VERNON, G.F. (5) 1878 Scotland, Ireland; 1880 Ireland, Scotland; 1881 Ireland.

VICKERY, G. (1) 1905 Ireland.

VIVYAN, E.J. (4) 1901 Wales; 1904 Wales, Ireland, Scotland.

VOYCE, A.T. (27) 1920 Ireland, Scotland; 1921 Wales, Ireland, Scotland, France; 1922 Wales, Ireland, France, Scotland; 1923 Wales, Ireland, Scotland, France; 1924 Wales, Ireland, France, Scotland; 1925 New Zealand, Wales, Ireland, Scotland, France; 1926 Wales, Ireland, France, Scotland.

WACKETT, J.A.S. (2) 1959 Wales, Ireland.

WADE, C.G. (8) 1883 Wales, Ireland, Scotland; 1884 Wales, Scotland; 1885 Wales; 1886 Wales, Ireland.

WADE, M.R. (3) 1962 Wales, Ireland, France.

WAKEFIELD, W.W. (31) 1920 Wales, France, Ireland, Scotland; 1921 Wales, Ireland, Scotland, France; 1922 Wales, Ireland, France, Scotland; 1923 Wales, Ireland, Scotland, France; 1924 Wales, Ireland, France, Scotland; 1925 New Zealand, Wales, Ireland, Scotland, France; 1926 Wales, Ireland, France, Scotland.

WALKER, G.A. (2) 1939 Wales, Ireland.

WALKER, H.W. (9) 1947 Wales, Ireland, Scotland, France; 1948 Australia, Wales, Ireland, Scotland, France.

WALKER, R. (5) 1874 Scotland; 1875 Ireland; 1876 Scotland; 1879 Scotland; 1880 Scotland.

WALLENS, J.N.S. (1) 1927 France.

WALTON, E.J. (4) 1901 Wales, Ireland; 1902 Ireland, Scotland.

WALTON, W. (1) 1894 Scotland.

WARD, G. (6) 1913 Wales, France, Scotland; 1914 Wales, Ireland, Scotland.

WARD, H. (1) 1895 Wales.

WARD, J.I. (2) 1881 Ireland; 1882 Ireland.

WARD, J.W. (3) 1896 Wales, Ireland, Scotland.

WARDLOW, C.S. (6) 1969 South Africa (R); 1971 Wales, Ireland, France, Scotland (2, 1 centenary).

WARFIELD, P.J. (6) 1973 New Zealand (1), Wales, Ireland; 1975 Ireland, France, Scotland.

WARR, A.L. (2) 1934 Wales, Ireland.

WATKINS, J.A. (7) 1972 South Africa; 1973 New Zealand (1), Wales, New Zealand (2), Australia; 1975 France, Wales.

WATKINS, J.K. (3) 1939 Wales, Ireland, Scotland.

WATSON, F.B. (2) 1908 Scotland; 1909 Scotland.

WATSON, J.H.D. (3) 1914 Wales, Scotland, France.

WATT, D.E.J. (4) 1967 Ireland, France, Scotland, Wales.

WEBB, C.S.H. (12) 1932 South Africa, Wales, Ireland, Scotland; 1933 Wales, Ireland, Scotland; 1935 Scotland; 1936 New Zealand, Wales, Ireland, Scotland.

WEBB, J.M. (27) 1987 *Australia (R), Japan, USA, Wales;* 1988 France, Wales, Scotland, Ireland (1, 2); Australia (1, 2), Australia; 1989 Scotland, Ireland, France, Wales; 1991 Fiji, Australia, *New Zealand, Italy, France, Scotland, Australia;* 1992 Scotland, Ireland, France, Wales.

WEBB, J.W.G. (3) 1926 France, Scotland; 1929 Scotland.

WEBB, R.E. (12) 1967 Scotland, Wales, New Zealand; 1968 Ireland, France, Scotland; 1969 Ireland, France, Scotland, Wales; 1972 Ireland, France.

WEBB, St.L.H. (4) 1959 Wales, Ireland, France, Scotland.

WEBSTER, J.G. (11) 1972 Wales, Ireland, South Africa; 1972 New Zealand (1), Wales, New Zealand (2); 1974 Scotland, Wales; 1975 Ireland, France, Wales.

WEDGE, T.G. (2) 1907 France; 1909 Wales.

WEIGHILL, R.H.G. (4) 1947 Scotland, France; 1948 Scotland, France.

WELLS, C.M. (6) 1893 Scotland; 1894 Wales, Scotland; 1896 Scotland; 1897 Wales, Scotland.

WEST, B.R. (8) 1968 Wales, Ireland, France, Scotland; 1969 South Africa; 1970 Ireland, Wales, Scotland.

WESTON, H.T.F. (1) 1901 Scotland.

WESTON, L.E. (2) 1972 France, Scotland.

WESTON, M.P. (28) 1960 Wales, Ireland, France, Scotland; 1961 South Africa, Wales,

Ireland, France, Scotland; 1962 Wales, Ireland, France; 1963 Wales, Ireland, France, Scotland, New Zealand (2), Australia; 1964 New Zealand (1, 2), Australia, Wales, Ireland, France, Scotland; 1965 France, Scotland; 1966 Scotland, 1968 France, Scotland.

WESTON, W.H. (16) 1933 Ireland, Scotland; 1934 Wales, Ireland, Scotland; 1935 Wales, Ireland, Scotland; 1936 New Zealand, Wales, Ireland, Scotland; 1937 Wales, Ireland, Scotland; 1938 Wales, Ireland, Scotland.

WHEATLEY, A.A. (5) 1937 Wales, Ireland, Scotland; 1938 Wales, Scotland.

WHEATLEY, H.F. (7) 1936 Ireland; 1937 Scotland; 1938 Wales, Scotland; 1939 Wales, Ireland, Scotland.

WHEELER, P.J. (41) 1975 France, Wales; 1976 Australia, Wales, Scotland, Ireland; 1977 Scotland, Ireland, France, Wales; 1978 France, Wales, Scotland, Ireland, New Zealand; 1979 Scotland, Ireland, France, Wales, New Zealand; 1980 Ireland, France, Wales, Scotland; 1981 Wales, Scotland, Ireland, France; 1982 Australia, Scotland, Ireland, France, Wales; 1983 France, Scotland, Ireland, New Zealand; 1984 Scotland, Ireland, France, Wales.

WHITE, C. (4) 1983 New Zealand; 1984 Scotland, Ireland, France.

WHITE, D.F. (14) 1947 Wales, Ireland, Scotland; 1948 Ireland, France; 1951 Scotland; 1952 South Africa, Wales, Scotland, Ireland, France; 1953 Wales, Ireland, Scotland.

WHITELEY, E.C.P. (2) 1931 Scotland, France.

WHITELEY, W. (1) 1896 Wales.

WHITLEY, H. (1) 1929 Wales.

WIGHTMAN, B.J. (5) 1959 Wales; 1963 Wales, Ireland, New Zealand (2), Australia.

WIGGLESWORTH, H.J. (1) 1884 Ireland.

WILKINS, D.T. (13) 1951 Wales, Ireland, France, Scotland; 1952 South Africa, Wales, Scotland, Ireland, France; 1953 Wales, Ireland, France, Scotland.

WILKINSON, E. (5) 1886 Wales, Ireland, Scotland; 1887 Wales, Scotland.

WILKINSON, H. (4) 1929 Wales, Ireland, Scotland; 1930 France.

WILKINSON, H.J. (1) 1889 Maoris.

WILKINSON, P. (1) 1872 Scotland.

WILKINSON, R.M. (6) 1975 Australia (2); 1976 Australia, Wales, Scotland, Ireland, France.

WILLCOCKS, T.S. (1) 1902 Wales.

WILLCOX, J.G. (16) 1961 Ireland, France, Scotland; 1962 Wales, Ireland, France, Scotland; 1963 Wales, Ireland, France, Scotland; 1964 New Zealand, Wales, Ireland, France, Scotland.

WILLIAM-POWLETT, P.B.R.W. (1) 1922 Scotland.

WILLIAMS, C.G. (1) 1976 France.

WILLIAMS, C.S. (1) 1910 France.

WILLIAMS, J.E. (9) 1954 France; 1955 Wales, Ireland, France, Scotland; 1956 Ireland, Scotland, France; 1965 Wales.

WILLIAMS, J.M. (2) 1951 Ireland, Scotland.

WILLIAMS, P.N. (4) 1987 Scotland, *Australia, Japan, Wales.*

WILLIAMS, S.G. (7) 1902 Wales, Ireland, Scotland; 1903 Ireland, Scotland.

WILLIAMS, S.H. (4) 1911 Wales, France, Ireland, Scotland.

WILLIAMSON, R.H. (5) 1908 Wales, Ireland, Scotland; 1909 Australia, France.

WILSON, A.J. (1) 1909 Ireland.

WILSON, C.E. (1) 1898 Ireland.

WILSON, C.P. (1) 1881 Wales.

WILSON, D.S. (8) 1953 France; 1954 Wales, New Zealand, Ireland, Scotland, France; 1955 France, Scotland.

WILSON, G.S. (2) 1929 Wales, Ireland.

WILSON, K.J. (1) 1963 France.

WILSON, R.P. (3) 1891 Wales, Ireland, Scotland.

WILSON, W.C. (2) 1907 Ireland, Scotland.

WINN, C.E. (8) 1952 South Africa, Wales, Scotland, Ireland, France; 1954 Wales, Scotland, France.

WINTERBOTTOM, P.J. (52) 1982 Australia, Scotland, Ireland, France, Wales; 1983 France, Wales, Scotland, Ireland, New Zealand; 1984 Scotland, France, Wales, South Africa (1, 2); 1986 Wales, Scotland, Ireland, France; 1987 Ireland, France, Wales, *Australia, Japan, USA, Wales*; 1988 France, Wales, Scotland; 1989 France, Romania, Japan; 1990 Ireland, France, Wales, Scotland, Argentina (1, 2); 1991 Wales, Scotland, Ireland, France, Australia, *New Zealand, Italy, France, Scotland, Australia*; 1992 Scotland, Ireland, France, Wales.

WINTLE, T.C. (5) 1966 Scotland; 1969 Ireland, France, Scotland, Wales.

WODEHOUSE, N.A. (14) 1910 France; 1911 Wales, France, Ireland, Scotland; 1912 Wales, Ireland, Scotland, France; 1913 South Africa, Wales, France, Ireland, Scotland.

WOOD, A. (1) 1884 Ireland.

WOOD, A.E. (3) 1908 France, Wales, Ireland.

WOOD, G.W. (1) 1914 Wales.

WOOD, R. (1) 1894 Ireland.

WOOD, R.D. (3) 1901 Ireland; 1903 Wales, Ireland.

WOODGATE, E.E. (1) 1952 Wales.

WOODHEAD, E. (1) 1880 Ireland.

WOODRUFF, C.G. (4) 1951 Wales, Ireland, France, Scotland.

WOODS, S.M.J. (13) 1890 Wales, Scotland, Ireland; 1891 Wales, Ireland, Scotland; 1892 Ireland, Scotland; 1893 Wales, Ireland; 1895 Wales, Ireland, Scotland.

WOODS, T. (1) 1908 Scotland.

WOODS, T. (5) 1920 Scotland; 1921 Wales, Ireland, Scotland, France.

WOODWARD, C.R. (21) 1980 Ireland (R), France, Wales, Scotland; 1981 Wales, Scotland, Ireland, France, Argentina (1, 2); 1982 Australia, Scotland, Ireland, France, Wales; 1983 Ireland, New Zealand; 1984 Scotland, Ireland, France, Wales.

WOODWARD, J.E. (15) 1952 South Africa, Wales, Scotland; 1953 Wales, Ireland, France, Scotland; 1954 Wales, New Zealand, Ireland, Scotland, France; 1955 Wales, Ireland; 1956 Scotland.

WOOLDRIDGE, C.S. (7) 1883 Wales, Ireland, Scotland; 1884 Wales, Ireland, Scotland; 1885 Ireland.

WORDSWORTH, A.J. (1) 1975 Australia (1R).

WORTON, J.R.B. (2) 1926 Wales; 1927 Wales.

WRENCH, D.F.B. (2) 1964 France, Scotland.

WRIGHT, C.C.G. (2) 1909 Ireland, Scotland.

WRIGHT, I.D. (4) 1971 Wales, Ireland, France, Scotland (R).

WRIGHT, J.C. (1) 1934 Wales.

WRIGHT, J.F. (1) 1890 Wales.

WRIGHT, T.P. (13) 1960 Wales, Ireland, France, Scotland; 1961 South Africa, Wales, Ireland, France, Scotland; 1962 Wales, Ireland, France, Scotland.

WRIGHT, W.H.G. (2) 1920 Wales, France.

WYATT, D.M. (1) 1976 Scotland (R).

YARRANTON, P.G. (5) 1954 Wales, New Zealand, Ireland; 1955 France, Scotland.

YIEND, W. (6) 1889 Maoris; 1892 Wales, Ireland, Scotland; 1893 Ireland, Scotland.

YOUNG, A.T. (18) 1924 Wales, Ireland, France, Scotland; 1925 New Zealand, France; 1926 Ireland, France, Scotland; 1927 Ireland, Scotland, France; 1928 Australia, Wales, Ireland, France, Scotland; 1929 Ireland.

YOUNG, J.R.C. (9) 1958 Ireland; 1960 Wales, Ireland, France, Scotland; 1961 South Africa, Wales, Ireland, France.

YOUNG, M. (10) 1977 Scotland, Ireland, France, Wales; 1978 France, Wales, Scotland, Ireland, New Zealand; 1979 Scotland.

YOUNG, P.D. (9) 1954 Wales, New Zealand, Ireland, Scotland, France; 1955 Wales, Ireland, France, Scotland.

YOUNGS, N.G. (6) 1983 Ireland, New Zealand; 1984 Scotland, Ireland, France, Wales.

Bibliography

The Phoenix Book of International Rugby Records John Griffiths.

The Book of England International Rugby John Griffiths.

Rothman's Rugby Yearbooks.

RFU Handbooks.

England Rugby Barry Bowker.

History of the Rugby Football Union O.L.Owen.

History of Army Rugby John Mclaren.

Various issues of *Guy's Hospital Gazette.*

Various issues of *Rugby World Magazine; Rugby World & Post.*

Encyclopaedia of Rugby Football J.R.Jones.

Numerous club history books, county Rugby Union history books, biographies and autobiographies.

Handbooks from The Football Association, English Golf Union, Lawn Tennis Association.

Various editions of *Wisden Cricketers' Almanack, The Cricketer, Lancashire Cricket Annual* and other county cricket year books.